GENDER INEQUALITY

Feminist Theories and Politics

Fourth Edition

Judith Lorber

Graduate Center and Brooklyn College
City University of New York

New York   Oxford
OXFORD UNIVERSITY PRESS
2010

Oxford University Press, Inc., publishes works that further
Oxford University's objective of excellence
in research, scholarship, and education.

Oxford New York
Auckland Cape Town Dar es Salaam Hong Kong Karachi
Kuala Lumpur Madrid Melbourne Mexico City Nairobi
New Delhi Shanghai Taipei Toronto

With offices in
Argentina Austria Brazil Chile Czech Republic France Greece
Guatemala Hungary Italy Japan Poland Portugal Singapore
South Korea Switzerland Thailand Turkey Ukraine Vietnam

Published by Oxford University Press, Inc.
198 Madison Avenue, New York, New York 10016
http://www.oup.com

Library of Congress Cataloging-in-Publication Data
Lorber, Judith.
    Gender inequality : feminist theories and politics / Judith Lorber.—4th ed.
        p. cm.
    Includes bibliographical references and index.
    ISBN 978-0-19-537522-0 (alk. paper)
  1. Sex discrimination against women. 2. Sex role. 3. Women—Social
conditions. 4. Equality. 5. Feminist theory. I. Title.
    HQ1237.L67 2010
    305.4201—dc22
                                                          2008053886

Printing number: 9 8 7 6 5 4 3 2 1

Printed in the United States of America
on acid-free paper

In Memory of Zina Segre
May 8, 1933–April 27, 1997

"Her wounds came from the same source as her power."
—Adrienne Rich

CONTENTS

PREFACE

Do we still need feminism? What has it done and what is there still to do? Feminism has transformed the social and cultural landscape in many countries in the past 40 years, but gender inequality still exists.

Gender Inequality: Feminist Theories and Politics presents the variety of feminist theories developed to explain the sources of gender inequality, and how the various theories have diverged and converged in the second wave of feminism as a political movement. My intent is to describe feminism's significant contributions to redressing gender inequality in order to document its enormous accomplishments in the last 40 years, to describe ongoing political activism, and to indicate the work still to be done.

The Fourth Edition continues the main perspectives of the first three editions—laying out the sources of gender inequality as seen by a variety of feminisms, and the politics to redress gender inequality. All of the chapters have been updated, and some have been expanded, rewritten, or reorganized. There are 17 new readings and new sections on feminism in China, India, South Korea, and Japan. In addition, the bulleted lists introducing each type of feminism include the critique as well as the feminism's theories of the sources of gender inequality, its politics, and its contributions. Many new suggested sources for research have been added. The Internet sources have been omitted, as these change and proliferate too rapidly to be kept up-to-date, and also can be accessed more easily using key words directly from Internet search engines. As in the Third Edition, the book ends with a consideration of whether we need a new conceptualization of gender inequality, and discusses new guidelines for feminist research and politics.

Some sections of this text have been adapted from my books *Paradoxes of Gender* (New Haven, CT: Yale University Press, 1994) and *Breaking the Bowls: Degendering and Feminist Change* (New York: W. W. Norton, 2005), and from my chapter, "Constructing Gender: The Dancer and the Dance" in *Handbook of Constructionist Research*, edited by James A. Holstein and Jaber F. Gubrium (New York, Guilford Publications, 2008).

The Redstockings Manifesto was issued in New York City on July 7, 1969. It first appeared as a mimeographed flier, designed for distribution at women's liberation events. This and other documents from the 1960s rebirth years of feminism are available through the Redstockings Women's Liberation Archives for Action Distribution Project, P.O. Box 2625, Gainesville, FL 32602 or http://www.redstockings.org.

Note that the full title of *Signs* is *Signs: Journal of Women in Culture and Society.*

Throughout the various editions, I have benefited from discussions on feminism and current politics with students and colleagues, and in particular, from the insights and critiques of Maren Carden, Carolle Charles, Susan Farrell, Eileen Moran, and Barbara Katz Rothman—my multi-feminist writing group. I particularly thank Susan Farrell for her information on women ethicists and feminist religions. The comments of the reviewers of the last edition have guided the changes in this edition. I also thank Claude Teweles for getting me started on this book, and Sherith Pankratz and Whitney Laemmli for working closely with me on this edition.

Judith Lorber
New York City

FEMINISMS AND THEIR CONTRIBUTIONS TO GENDER EQUALITY

Feminism is a social movement whose basic goal is equality between women and men. In many times and places in the past, people have insisted that women and men have similar capabilities and have tried to better the social position of all women, as well as the status of disadvantaged men. As an organized movement, modern feminism rose in the nineteenth century in Europe, America, and Japan in response to the great inequalities between the legal statuses of women and men citizens.

MODERN FEMINISM'S FIRST WAVE

The *first-wave* feminists of the nineteenth and early twentieth centuries fought for rights we take for granted today. It is hard to believe these rights were among those once denied to women of every social class, racial category, ethnicity, and religion—the right to vote (suffrage), to own property and capital, to borrow money, to inherit, to keep money earned, to initiate a divorce, to retain custody of children, to go to college, to become a professionally certified physician, to argue cases in court, and to serve on a jury.

The theory of equality that feminists of the nineteenth century used in their fight for women's rights came out of liberal political philosophy, which said that all men should be equal under the law, that no one should have special privileges or rights. Of course, when the U.S. Constitution was written, that concept of equality excluded enslaved men and indentured menservants, because they were not free citizens, as well as all women, no matter what their social status, because they were not really free either. The legal status of supposedly free women was the same as that of children— economically dependent and deriving their social status from their father or husband. In Ibsen's famous nineteenth-century play *A Doll's House*, Nora forges her dead father's signature because she cannot legally sign her own name to the loan she needs to save her sick husband's life, and she works at home in secret to pay it back. When her husband finds out, he does not thank her but rather condemns her as immoral and dishonest and not a fit mother for their children. He eventually forgives her, but Nora refuses to continue to live as a doll-wife, and she leaves him, slamming the door of the doll's house behind her.

First-wave feminism's goal was to get equal legal rights for women, especially the vote, or suffrage. (Feminists were often called *suffragists*.) In the United States, women did not get the right to vote nationally until 1920.[1] Many European countries also gave women the right to vote after World War I, in repayment for their war efforts. French women, however, did not get suffrage until after World War II, when a grateful Charles de Gaulle enfranchised them for their work in the underground fight against the Nazis and the collaborationist government of Nazi-occupied France. Japanese women were also granted the right to vote after World War II in the constitution written under the American occupation of Japan.

The Russian revolution of the early twentieth century gave women equal rights, even though the Bolsheviks criticized the individualism of "bourgeois feminism." Their emphasis was on work in the collective economy, with prenatal care and child care provided by the state so women could be both workers and mothers. Chinese women had legal equal rights after the Chinese communist revolution of 1948, but patriarchal families, especially in rural areas, restricted their actual liberty.

Suffrage was the main goal of women's liberation in the first wave of feminism in Western countries, but rights concerning property, earnings, and higher education—many of which were granted by the end of the nineteenth century—gave women a chance for economic independence. These rights were vital for raising married women's status from childlike dependence on a husband and for giving widows and single women some way of living on their own instead of as a poor relation in their father's or brother's or son's household. Liberated women in the first part of the twentieth century included independent factory girls who worked all day and went dancing at night, and middle- and upper-class educated women who had "Boston marriages" (were housemates for life).

Another branch of nineteenth-century feminism did not focus on equal rights but on a woman's right to "own" her body and to plan her pregnancies. A twentieth-century feminist struggle that was as hard fought in Western countries as that for suffrage was the fight for legal means of contraception that could be controlled by the woman. Women could not be free to be good mothers and wives, especially if they were poor, if they had one child after another. But doctors were forbidden to fit women with diaphragms or cervical caps (the precursors of the coil and the pill). In the United States, even mailing information across state lines was illegal. The widespread use of contraception by married women was feared by traditionalists, who saw the downfall of the family. Feminists feared that men would sexually exploit unmarried women who were protected against pregnancy. For women themselves, the positive outcome of this long battle for legalized woman-controlled contraception has been both greater sexual freedom before marriage and planned parenthood after marriage.

As is evident from this brief overview, the first-wave feminist movement had many of the theoretical and political differences of the feminist movement that succeeded it. The question of differences between women and men, and whether they should be treated *equally* because they are essentially the same or *equitably* because they are essentially different, is still under debate. The question of where feminist politics should put the most effort—the public sphere (work and government) or the private sphere (family and sexuality)—is also still with us.

FEMINISM'S SECOND AND THIRD WAVES

The *second wave* of the modern feminist movement[2] began with the publication in France in 1949 of Simone de Beauvoir's *The Second Sex*. This sweeping account of the historical and current status of women in the Western world argues that men set the standards and values, and women are the Other who lack the qualities the dominants exhibit. Men are the actors, women the reactors. Men thus are the first sex, women always the second sex. Men's dominance and women's subordination is not a biological phenomenon, de Beauvoir insisted, but a social creation: "One is not born, but rather becomes, a woman...; it is civilization as a whole that produces this creature...which is described as feminine" (1953, 267).

Although *The Second Sex* was widely read, the second wave of feminism did not take shape as an organized political movement until the late 1960s, when young people were publicly criticizing many aspects of Western society. In the years since, the feminist movement has made many contributions to social change by focusing attention on the continued ways women are more socially disadvantaged than men, by analyzing the sexual oppressions women suffer, and by proposing interpersonal as well as political and legal solutions. However, the feminist view of what makes women and men unequal is less unified today than in first-wave feminism, and there is a myriad of feminist solutions to gender inequality. If feminist voices seem to be much more fragmented than they were in the nineteenth century, it is the result of a deeper understanding of the sources of gender inequality. It is also the contradictory effect of uneven success. Feminists who are now members of corporations, academia, or government, or who are lawyers or doctors or respected artists and writers, are well aware of the limitations of their positions, given glass ceilings and sexual harassment. But their viewpoint is different from that of the more radical antiestablishment feminist critics, who decry institutionalized sexual oppression and pervasive devaluation of women.

In the 1970s and 1980s. many feminists concentrated on increasing women's legal rights, political representation, and entry into occupations and professions dominated by men. Other feminists worked to eliminate sexual violence, prostitution, and pornography; sexist depictions of women in the media and cultural productions; and sexual harassment of women workers and students. Still others focused on changing language, knowledge, and history to reflect women's previously invisible experiences and contributions.

The feminisms that emerged in the 1990s—multiracial/multiethnic feminism, feminist studies of men, constructionist, postmodern, and queer theories, challenge "what everyone knows" about sex, sexuality, and gender. Not content with reforming or resisting the patriarchy and misogyny of the gendered social order, these feminisms challenge the duality and oppositeness of female and male, homosexual and heterosexual, women and men. They argue that there are many sexes, sexualities, and genders, and many ways to express masculinity and femininity. By rebelling against conventional deep-seated assumptions and value judgments, they force us to look at how we "do gender" and how in the process we have built and maintain an unequal social order.

Third-wave feminism, which also emerged in the 1990s, is a movement of younger feminists who grew up with feminism. Inheritors of women's studies curricula in school and a much less gender-segregated social, economic, and political world, they reject the idea that women are oppressed by men. Rather, they include men as feminist activists. They assume that gender equality is the norm, and that women's agency and female sexuality are forms of power.

GENDER INEQUALITY

The goal of feminism as a political movement is to make women and men more equal legally, socially, and culturally. *Gender inequality* takes many different forms, depending on the economic structure and social organization of a particular society and on the culture of any particular group within that society. Although we speak of *gender* inequality, it is usually women who are disadvantaged relative to similarly situated men.

Women often receive lower pay for the same or comparable work, and they are frequently blocked in their chances for advancement, especially to top positions. There is usually an imbalance in the amount of housework and child care a wife does compared to her husband, even when both spend the same amount of time in paid work outside the home. When women professionals are matched with men of comparable productiveness, men still get greater recognition for their work and move up career ladders faster. On an overall basis, gender inequality means that work most often done by women, such as teaching small children and nursing, is paid less than work most often done by men, such as construction and mining.

Gender inequality can also take the form of girls getting less education than boys of the same social class. Nearly two-thirds of the world's illiterates are women, but in Western societies, the gender gap in education is closing at all levels of schooling, and among some groups, women surpass men in higher education degrees. In many countries, men get priority over women in the distribution of health care services. Contraceptive use has risen in industrial countries, but in developing countries, complications in childbirth are still a leading cause of death for young women. AIDS takes an even more terrible toll on women than men globally, since women's risk of becoming infected with HIV during unprotected sex is two to four times higher than in men. The World Health Organization's 2007 AIDS Epidemic Update reported that about 33 million people are living with HIV/AIDS, and that half were women.[3] Sexual politics influence the transmission of HIV/AIDS. Many women with HIV/AIDS have been infected through early sexual exploitation or by husbands who have multiple sexual partners but who refuse to use condoms.

Sexual exploitation and violence against women are part of gender inequality in many other ways. In wars and national uprisings, women of one racial ethnic group are often raped by the men of the opposing racial ethnic group as a deliberate weapon of shaming and humiliation. Domestically, women are vulnerable to beatings, rape, and murder—often by their husbands or boyfriends, and especially when they try to leave an abusive relationship. The bodies of girls and women are used in sex work—pornography and prostitution. They are on display in movies, television, and advertising in Western cultures. In some African and Middle Eastern cultures, their genitals are ritually cut and their bodies are covered from head to toe in the name of chastity. They may be forced to bear children they do not want or to have abortions or be sterilized against their will. In some countries with overpopulation, infant girls are much more often abandoned in orphanages than infant boys. In other countries, if the sex of the fetus can be determined, it is girls who are aborted.

Gender inequality can also disadvantage men. In many countries, only men serve in the armed forces, and in most countries, only men are sent into direct combat. It is mostly men who do the more dangerous work, such as firefighting and policing. Although women have fought in wars and are entering police forces and fire departments, the gender arrangements of most societies assume that women will do the work of bearing and caring for children while men will do the work of protecting and supporting them economically.

This gendered division of labor is rooted in the survival of small groups living at subsistence level, where babies are breast-fed and food is obtained for older children and adults by foraging and hunting. The child-care providers (mostly women) gather fruits and vegetables and hunt small animals, while babies are carried in slings and older children are helpers. Those not caring for children (mostly men, but also unmarried women) can travel farther in tracking large animals—more dangerous work. Hunters who come back with meat and hides may be highly praised, but if the hunt was unsuccessful, they still have something to eat when they return to the home camp, thanks to the child-minders' more reliable foraging.

Most women in industrial and postindustrial societies do not spend their lives having and caring for babies, but most women throughout the world do paid and unpaid work to supply their families with food, clothing, and shelter, even while they are taking care of children. The modern forms of gender inequality are not a complementary exchange of responsibilities but an elaborate system within which, it was estimated by a United Nations report in 1980, women do two-thirds of the world's work, receive 10 percent of the world's income, and own 1 percent of the world's property. The gender gap in paid work is narrowing, but women still do most of the domestic work and child care, and at the same time do agricultural labor, run small businesses, and do a great deal of home-based paid work, all of which is low-waged labor.

The major social and cultural institutions support this system of gender inequality. Religions legitimate the social arrangements that produce inequality, justifying them as right and proper. Laws support the status quo and also often make it impossible to redress the outcomes—to prosecute husbands for beating their wives, or men for raping vulnerable young girls. In the arts, women's productions have been ignored so often that they have been virtually invisible, leading Virginia Woolf to conclude that Anonymous must have been a woman. Sciences have been accused of asking biased questions and ignoring findings that do not support conventional beliefs about sex differences.

Except for the Scandinavian countries, which have the most gender-equal laws and state policies, most governments are run by socially dominant men, and their policies reflect their interests. In every period of change, including those of revolutionary upheaval, men's interests, not women's, have prevailed, and many men, but few women, have benefited from progressive social policies. Equality and justice for all usually means for men only. Women have never had their revolution because the structure of gender as a social institution has never been seriously challenged. Therefore, all men benefit from *patriarchal privileges*—women's unpaid work maintaining homes and bringing up children; women's low-paid work servicing hospitals, schools, and myriad other workplaces; and women's emotional nurturing and caretaking.

The main point recent feminisms have stressed about gender inequality is that it is not an individual matter, but is deeply ingrained in the structure of societies. Gender inequality is built into the organization of marriage and families, work and the economy, politics, religions, the arts and other cultural productions, and the very language we speak. Making women and men equal, therefore, necessitates social and not individual solutions. These solutions have been framed as feminist politics that emerge from feminist theories about what produces gender inequaltiy.

FEMINIST THEORIES

The foregoing portrait of a gender-unequal world is a summation of the work of generations of feminist researchers and scholars. Feminist theories were developed to explain the reasons for this pervasive gender inequality. Feminists are not satisfied with the explanation that it is natural, God-given, or necessary because women get pregnant and give birth and men do not. Each of the feminisms described in this book has theories of gender inequality, some similar and overlapping, and some quite different.

The theories of the feminisms I have termed *reformist* focus on the unequal gendered division of labor in the home and in the workplace, the devaluation of women's work, and the uneven presence of women in the main institutions of society, especially politics and the law.

Resistant feminist theories of inequality coalesce around the concept of patriarchy, a system of interlocked oppressions and exploitations of women's bodies, sexuality, labor, and emotions.

Feminisms I have termed *rebellious* see gender inequality as embedded in the social construction and maintenance of the gendered social order through doing gender as individuals, in interaction, and as part of families, work organizations, and throughout cultural and knowledge productions.

Many feminists have incorporated into their theories of gender inequality the ways that women's and men's social statuses, personal identities, and life chances are intricately tied up with their racial, ethnic, and religious groups, their social class and family background, and their place of residence. Nonetheless, these widely differing groups of people have to fit into two and only two socially recognized and legal genders in Western societies— "men" and "women." The members of these two major status categories are supposed to be different from each other, and the members of the same category are supposed to have essential similarities. Work and family roles, as well as practically all other aspects of social life, are built on these two major divisions of people. This gendering produces the *gendered social order*. Gender inequality is built into the structure of the gendered social order because the two statuses—women and men—are treated differently and have significantly different life chances. How and why these social processes have come about and continue to operate is the subject of feminist theories. What to do about them is the aim of feminist politics.

FEMINIST POLITICS

While much of the feminist movement of the twentieth century has happened in the United States, Canada, England, Australia, and Europe, there have also been vital and important struggles for resources and empowerment for girls and women in Asian, African, and South and Central American countries. As these countries broke free of colonial control after World War II and set up independent governments, they, too, gave their women citizens the right to vote. Thanks to strong women's movements, many of the new states wrote equal rights for women into their constitutions, and some even mandated guaranteed political representation. In 2008, in the new democracy of Rwanda, 56 percent of its parliament were women, thanks to its 2003 constitution requiring that at least 30 percent of all parliamentary and cabinet seats go to women.[4] In contrast, after the 2008 election, 17 percent of the United States Senate were women, and 14 percent of the House of Representatives.

Many countries throughout the world have had elected women heads of state in the past 50 years, but the United States has yet to elect a woman president.[5] The presence of a woman head of state does not necessarily represent a triumph of feminism, as most women politicians do not present themselves as champions of women but as leaders of everyone. Feminist political and legal changes are much more likely to come from grassroots political movements and single-issue or general feminist organizations.

At the other end of the political scale, in some Muslim countries, women still cannot vote, leave the country without their husband's permission, or get licenses to drive cars. In the Middle East, women and men have struggled to reconcile the rights of women with the traditional precepts of Islam and Judaism. In Asia, the problems of poverty and overpopulation, even though they more often adversely affect women and girls, need remedies that affect everyone. Women's political movements in these countries may not be called "feminist," but they are gender-based battles nevertheless.

Feminist politics does not refer only to the arena of government or the law; it can be confrontational protests, such as Take Back the Night marches, or work through organizations with a broad base, such as the National Organization of Women (NOW) and the National Organization for Men Against Sexism (NOMAS). It can take place in service centers, such as battered women's shelters, and informational activities, such as gender-sensitivity and anti-rape sessions for college men.

Neighborhood or grassroots feminist activism tends to be woman-focused and concerned with local problems, while transnational nongovernmental organizations (NGOs) and national and international governing bodies and agencies are loci for diversity-based political action. Some feminists have despaired as women's movements break up over racial ethnic, religious, and national identity politics. The *borderlands* view offers the possibility of perspectives and politics based on panethnic and cross-racial affiliations and coalitions.

Changing language and media presentations to remove sexist put-downs that denigrate women is also feminist politics. Other remedies for redressing gender inequality, such as creating culture, knowledge, ethics, and theology from a woman's point of view, may not look political, but to feminists, they are deeply political because their intent is to change the way people think about the world.

FEMINISM AND THE GENDERED SOCIAL ORDER

Second-wave feminism's major theoretical accomplishment has been to make visible the structure, practices, and inequities of the gendered social order. It took gender beyond individual attributes and identities and showed that gender, like social class and racial categories, is imposed on, rather than developed from, individuals. Gendering divides the social world into two complementary but unequal sets of people—"women" and "men." This binary division confers a legal, social, and personal status that overrides individual differences and intertwines with other major social statuses— racial categorization, ethnic grouping, economic class, age, religion, and sexual orientation. We act out gender norms and expectations constantly in our interactions with others, building and maintaining the gendered social order. Gender organizes the processes and practices of a society's major sectors—work, family, politics, law, education, medicine, the military, religions, and culture. Gender is a system of power in that it privileges some groups of people and disadvantages others in conjunction with other systems of power (racial categories, ethnicity, social class, and sexual orientation).

Gender operates at one and the same time to give individuals status and identities and to shape their everyday behavior, and also as a significant factor in face-to-face relationships and organizational practices. Each level supports and maintains the others, but—and this is the crucial aspect of gender—the effects of gender work from the top down. The gendered social order constrains the behavior of gender deviants through stigmatization, punishment, and legal ostracism. Gendered norms and expectations pattern the practices of people in workplaces, in families, groups, and intimate relationships, and in creating individual identities and self-assessments. Peoples' gender conformity supports the gendered social order; peoples' gender diversity and deviance challenge it, but there is no recognized gender status outside of the binaries—boy/girl, man/woman.

The gendered social order is very resistant to individual challenge. Its power is such that people act in gendered ways based on their position within the gender structure without reflection or question. We "do gender" and participate in its construction once we have learned to take our place as a member of a gendered social order. Our gendered practices construct and maintain the gendered social order. As the social order changes, and as we participate in different social institutions and organizations throughout our lives, our gendered behavior changes. Politically, the major types of feminism have confronted the gendered social order in three different ways: *reform, resistance,* and *rebellion.*

TYPES OF FEMINISMS

In this book, current feminisms are categorized according to their *theory* or *theories of gender inequality*—what they consider the main reasons for women having a lesser social status and fewer advantages than men of similar education, class background, religion, racial category, and ethnic group. From these theories follow the feminism's proposed solutions or remedies—its *politics.*

Gender reform feminisms (liberal, Marxist, socialist, postcolonial, and Asian), were the theorists and activists that predominated in the 1970s.[6] They locate gender inequality in the structure of the gendered social order. Politically, their goal is to achieve a gender balance, so that women and men are positioned in equal numbers throughout the society, and have equal power, prestige, and economic resources. A reformed gendered social order would thus eradicate gender inequality.

Gender reform feminisms have made visible the pervasiveness of discriminatory practices, both formal and informal, in the work world and in the distribution of economic resources and family responsibilities. The 1970s brought dissatisfaction with conventional ideas about women and men, their bodies, sexualities, psyches, and behavior. The beliefs prevalent at that time about women and men tended to stress differences between them and to denigrate women in comparison with men, who were seen as stronger, smarter, and generally more capable than women—except when it came to taking care of children. Mothering was seen as women's strength and responsibility, so women were seen as mothers before, during, and after they were anything else. The extent of the work women did—in the family, in kinship networks, as volunteers and as "off-the-books" workers, and in family enterprises— was virtually invisible and uncounted in national economic statistics.

Gender reform feminisms argue that the sources of gender inequality are structural and not the outcome of personal attributes, individual choices, or unequal interpersonal relationships. The structural sources are women's relegation to low-paid work and a devaluation of the work women do, overwhelming responsibilities for child care and housework, and unequal access to education, health care, and political power. These inequalities are built into national and international social structures, and so have to be redressed structurally.

An overall strategy for political action to reform the unequal gendered social structure is *gender balance*. The goal of gender balance is to attain equality or parity in numbers of women and men throughout society, in their domestic responsibilities, and in their access to work and business opportunities, positions of authority, political power, education, and health care. Affirmative action in workplaces and universities and mandated quotas to increase the number of women in government are common gender-balancing policies.

Gender reform feminisms want women to be valued as much as men and to be free to live their lives according to their *human* potential. People should be able to work, parent, produce culture and science, govern, and otherwise engage in social life as they choose, whether they are women or men. Gender *mainstreaming* helps to achieve the goal of equal participation of women and men in all walks of life and equal recognition and reward for the work they do.

In sum, gender reform feminisms want to purge the gendered social order of practices that discriminate against women. These feminisms accept the existing gender structure (two classes of people) and work toward erasing the inequalities between the two classes, women and men, by policies to advance women in the workplace and positions of power, in education and other important venues, and by minimizing the differences between them. Their goal is to reform the social order so that although it is still gendered, it is more equal.

Gender resistance feminisms (radical, lesbian, psychoanalytic, standpoint), emergent in the 1980s, claim that the gender order cannot be made equal through gender balance because men's dominance is overwhelming. Gender equality, they argue, ends up with women becoming like men. By examining the gender order from the perspective of women, they make visible the hidden relationships among organizations, institutions, and daily practices that allow men to control women's lives. They call it *patriarchy,* a concept referring to men's family domination introduced by Marxist feminism and expanded by radical feminism to encompass the entire gender order. To gender resistance feminism, patriarchy is what makes men dominant and women subordinate. Politically, gender resistance feminisms argue that it is not enough to achieve gender balance or gender mainstreaming; a new perspective is needed—a perspective based on women's experiences. This perspective resists male-dominated values and their legitimation in a male-dominated gendered social order.

Gender resistance feminisms developed an important theoretical insight—the power of *gender ideology,* the values and beliefs that justify the gendered social order. Gender resistance feminisms argue that gender inequality has been legitimated by major religions that say men's dominance is a reflection of God's will, by sciences that claim that dominance is a result of genetic or hormonal differences, by legal systems that deny women full citizenship status, and by religions that worship a supreme being that is male. The mass media, sports, and pornography encourage the excesses of men's power— violence, rape, and sexual exploitation.

Gender resistance feminisms identify the most oppressive sources of gender inequality in the exploitation of women's bodies, sexuality, and emotions. They argue that this exploitation and women's intellectual and cultural productions are repressed by a *phallocentric,* or male-centered, Western culture. Women's voices—their perspectives, their knowledge, and their view of the world around them—are unheard.

Gender resistance feminisms want women's voices and perspectives to reshape the gendered social order. These feminisms confront the existing gender structure by turning it upside down. They value women and womanly attributes over men and manly attributes—emotional sensitivity over objectivity, nurturance over aggression, parenting over the marketplace, and so on. Radical feminism in particular is critical of men's sexuality and sexual violence—in fact, violence in general.

In their politics, gender resistance feminisms tend to be confrontational in challenging the confines of the male-dominated gendered social order. They resist by putting women first; their goal is a social order that values women and women's contributions to social life and that is protective of women's bodies and sexualities. They argue that women should create their own public spheres in politics, religion, education, the arts, and popular culture. While the systemic violence against women and exploitation of women's sexuality demands continued political engagement with the larger society, woman-only spaces are needed for refuge, recreation, religious worship, and cultural production.

Gender resistance feminisms stress the importance of countering the negative evaluations of women by valorizing their nurturance, emotional supportiveness, and mothering capacities, by encouraging pride in women's bodies, and by teaching women how to protect themselves against sexual violence. Their focus on *standpoint*—the view of the world from where you are located physically, mentally, emotionally, and socially—is a major theoretical contribution and springboard for action. Although women's voices were the original source of standpoint theory, the concept has been successfully used by women and men of diverse classes, racial ethnic groups, nations, and cultures to make their values and accomplishments visible to the dominant society.

Gender rebellion feminisms (multiracial/multiethnic, feminist studies of men, social construction, postmodern, third wave), are feminisms of the 1990s, looking forward to and now part of the twenty-first century. They show how gender is socially constructed and maintained through *doing gender*, and how it could be undercut by not doing gender. These feminisms continue to focus on multiple sources of inequality—race, ethnicity, and social class in particular—which are also reproduced through individual actions and social interactions, but the target is the binary gendered social order. The constraints of gender categories and gendered norms and expectations diminish women and give the men of their social group continued patriarchal privileges. The goal of gender rebellion feminisms is to dismantle gender categories. That would overturn the gendered social order and ultimately create a non-gendered social order.

Multiracial/multiethnic feminisms trace the intersections of gender, racial category, and ethnicity to show how people become advantaged or disadvantaged in a *matrix of domination*. The gendered social order, they argue, sets men against men as well as men against women. Men and women of the same racial ethnic group or in the same economic stratum have much in common with each other, more than men may have with men or women with women in other groups. Politically, then, women and men in the same racial ethnic group band together to rebel against inequalities, but sometimes women link to other disadvantaged women to create *womanist* culture, ethics, and theology, a woman-oriented rebellion against the male domination within their racial ethnic groups.

Feminist studies of men bring a critical men's perspective to feminism. Women feminists have written about men and masculinity, both in relationship to women and separately; studies of men by feminist men adds an additional dimension. These studies follow in the footsteps of working-class social research and politics, and expand their political arena to include gay men. Feminist men have gone directly to men in college workshops, seminars, and conferences to make them aware of how their sexually oppressive behavior can be so harmful to women. Their condemnation of the price paid for the rewards of professional sports and the physical and sexual violence they foster is another part of feminist men's political agenda. Feminist men's rebellion encompasses giving up their patriarchal privileges, sharing domestic work and child care, and joining feminist women in their fight for equal pay and positions of authority.

Postmodern feminism and queer theory attack the gender order directly by multiplying gender categories and undermining the boundaries between women and men, female and male, heterosexual and homosexual. Feminist *deconstruction* of the discourses that create the content of gendered and sexual norms shows how their taken-for-grantedness maintains the heterosexual gender order. By questioning the dualities—male and female, heterosexual and homosexual, masculine and feminine, man and woman—postmodern feminism and queer theory undermine the legitimacy of favoring one group over its opposite. According to postmodern feminism, personal identities and the identity politics of groups are constantly shifting, making room for individual and social change, for new kinds of relationships, and for multiple sexualities. "Queering" gender by ignoring categorical restrictions and blurring boundaries is gender rebellion pushed to its ultimate.

Third-wave feminism is a theoretical perspective that is both a continuation of and a break with second-wave feminisms. It builds on multiracial/multiethnic feminism, feminist studies of men, and postmodern feminism. It is inclusive of multiple cultures and feminist men, and plays with sex, sexuality, and gender. It rejects the sense of women as oppressed victims and heterosexual sex as dangerous. It is gender rebellion with a twist—*girl power* flaunts the strengths of girls and feminine women. It valorizes women's agency and female sexuality as forms of power. Politically, third-wave feminism is more concerned with gender-inclusive causes, such as peace, the environment, gay, lesbian, and transgender rights, than advancing the status of women. To this generation of feminists, women have achieved equality; it is time to rebel socially by using their power.

CONTINUITIES, CONVERGENCES, AND CHANGES

Gender reform feminisms provided the theoretical groundwork for second-wave feminism by making visible the structural underpinnings of the gendered social order. Their politics of gender balance and gender mainstreaming are practical and perhaps the best way to redress gender inequality at the present time. The fight for equal legal status and political representation for women and men, and for autonomy for women in making procreative, sexual, and marital choices, still has not been won in most countries of the world. Gender segregation in the workplace and lower pay for women's work is pervasive in all kinds of economies. The global economy exploits poor women as cheap labor, and economic restructuring in industrializing and postindustrial economies has reduced social-service benefits to mothers and children. These economic problems are still an arena for feminist gender politics.

Although the politics of gender reform feminisms spill over into the politics for every disadvantaged person, the battles of gender resistance feminisms are for women alone. Fighting to protect women's bodies against unwanted pregnancies and sterilizations, abortions of female fetuses, genital mutilation, rape, beatings, and murder has been an enormous and never-ending struggle. The sexual integrity of women and girls needs protection from forced prostitution, exploitative sex work in pornographic productions and strip clubs, and unwanted arranged marriages. Lesbian, gay, and transgendered people need to be able to live free of discrimination and violent attacks, but many lesbian women also want their own physical space and cultural communities, where they can be safe from sexual harassment and men's domination, nourish their loves and friendships, and produce books, music, art, and drama that reflect their different ways of thinking and feeling. Standpoint feminists argue that women's experiences and distinctive outlooks on life have to be included in the production of knowledge, especially in science and social science research. It is not enough to just add women subjects to research designs; questions have to be asked from a critical feminist perspective, data have to include women's voices, and analysis has to reflect the points of view of those who have been marginalized and silenced.

Picking up on the importance of social position and distinctive standpoints, gender rebellion feminisms exploded the categories of women and men into all sorts of multiples. Multiracial/multiethnic feminisms are part of a powerful political movement to redress past and present legal and social discrimination of disadvantaged women in many societies, and to produce woman-centered culture, theology, and ethics. Feminist studies of men have analyzed the racial ethnic and social class aspects of masculinity and the interplay of power and privilege, powerlessness and violence. They have described the hierarchies of men in a society and the ways that less advantaged men retain patriarchal control over women in their status group.

Social construction, postmodern, and third-wave feminisms have just begun to translate their destabilization of the gender order into politics or praxis. Degendering needs to be translated into everyday interaction, which could be revolutionary enough. But to fulfill their political potential, the gender rebellion feminisms need to spell out what precisely has to be done in all the institutions and organizations of a society—family, workplace, government, the arts, religion, law, and so on—to ensure equal participation and opportunity for every person in every group. Gender rebellion feminists have said that there are multiple voices in this world; now they have to figure out how to ensure that every voice can be heard in the production of knowledge and culture and in the power systems of their societies. That means a dismantling of the matrix of domination embedded in the major social statuses of the social order—gender, social class, racial ethnic, and sexual identity.

VOCABULARY AND DEFINITIONS

Although there is considerable overlap among them, it is useful to separate the concepts of gender, sex, and sexuality in order to illustrate how gendering modifies bodies and sexual behavior. This book uses the following vocabulary and definitions.

GENDER: A social status, a legal designation, and a personal identity. Through the social processes of gendering, gender divisions and their accompanying norms and role expectations are built into the major social institutions of society, such as the economy, the family, the state, culture, religion, and the law—the gendered social order. *Woman* and *man, girl* and *boy* are used when referring to gender.

SEX: A complex interplay of genes, hormones, environment, and behavior, with loop-back effects between bodies and society. *Male, female,* and *intersex* are used when referring to sex.

SEXUALITY: Lustful desire, emotional involvement, and fantasy, as enacted in a variety of long- and short-term intimate relationships. *Homosexuality, heterosexuality,* and *bisexuality* are used when referring to sexuality.

TRANSGENDER: Chosen gender that is different from the one assigned at birth, with or without surgical and hormonal transformation of bodies. *Transwomen, transmen, male-to-female (MTF),* and *female-to-male (FTM)* are used when referring to transgender.

Recent feminist theories have analyzed the complex interplay of sex, sexuality, and gender. These theories speak of genders, sexes, and sexualities. The two "opposites" in each case—women and men, female and male, homosexual and heterosexual—have become multiple. Since recent research has shown that female and male physiology is produced and maintained by both female and male hormones, the new theories argue that sex is more of a continuum than a sharp dichotomy. Similarly, studies of sexual orientation have shown that neither homosexuality nor heterosexuality is always fixed for life, and that bisexuality, in feelings and in sexual relationships, is widespread.

The phenomenon of *transgendering* further complicates the interplay of sex, sexuality, and gender. The goal of many transgendered people is to "pass" as a "normal" gendered person, but many are now open about their transitioning and new gender status. Transgendered people usually take hormones to change their body shapes and secondary sex characteristics, such as facial hair, but they do not always have surgery to modify genitalia.

Transgendered people may be heterosexual, homosexual, or bisexual. Thus, transgendering is not always a clear-cut exchange of one gender and sex for another, but is often a blurring of sex, sexuality, and gender boundaries.

Radical gender-benders, who sometimes call themselves "gender queers," do not claim identity with men or women, heterosexuals or homosexuals. Gender queers openly subvert binary gender and sexual categories through their deliberate mixtures of clothing, makeup, jewelry, hair styles, behavior, relationships, and use of language. By not constructing gender and sexuality in expected ways, they make visible, in Judith Butler's term, the *performativity* on which the whole gender order depends. They parody and play with gender, transgressing gender norms, expectations, and behavior.

ORGANIZATION OF THE BOOK

The focus of this book is the continuities, discontinuities, and convergences in recent feminist theories and politics. I will be combining ideas from different feminist writers, and usually I will not be talking about any specific writers, except for the excerpted authors. A list of suggested readings can be found at the end of each chapter.

Because I am not examining the ideas of particular feminists but speaking of ideas that have emerged from many theorists, I will usually talk of feminisms rather than feminists. Any feminist may incorporate ideas and politics from several feminisms, and many feminists have shifted their views over the years. I myself was originally a liberal feminist, then a socialist feminist, and now consider myself to be primarily a social constructionist gender rebellion feminist.

What I am looking at first are *feminist theories* about why women and men are unequal, and second, *feminist politics*, the activities and strategies for remedying gender inequality. Feminist theories and feminist politics are the result of personal experiences shared among friends and in consciousness-raising groups. They are developed in classes and conferences on all kinds of topics. They are refined in journals and books. And they are translated into political action through large and small feminist organizations, in marches and voting booths, in the marble halls of the United Nations, and in grassroots efforts in urban racial ethnic ghettos and developing countries of Africa, South and Central America, and Asia.

In Parts I through III, the theories and politics of *gender reform, gender resistance,* and *gender rebellion feminisms* are first described in a general way, followed by more detailed descriptions of the feminisms within the larger grouping. Each discussion of a particular feminism begins with an outline of its attribution of the main causes of gender inequality, its politics, its shortcomings, and its contributions to social change. The discussion of each type of feminism includes two excerpts from feminist theorists who use that viewpoint, one more theoretical, the other more focused on current politics. Each chapter ends with a discussion of the feminism's theoretical and political limitations.

In the final section, "Do We Have a New Feminism?" I present my own ideas about fruitful theoretical and political directions for feminism today.

NOTES

1. The Nineteenth Amendment, called the Susan B. Anthony Amendment, was ratified by Tennessee on August 18, 1920, and became law on August 26, 1920.
2. There is some question about the dating of the second and third waves. In this book, I consider the second wave to last from 1970 to 2000 and to encompass post-modern feminism and queer theory. I reserve the third wave for a feminism that began in the 1990s.
3. http://data.unaids.org/pub/EPISlides/2007/2007_epiupdate_en.pdf
4. Stephanie McCrummen, "Women Run the Show in a Recovering Rwanda," *Washington Post*, October 27, 2008, A01.
5. By coming in second in the 2008 Democratic primaries for president, Hillary Rodham Clinton said there were 18 million more cracks in the glass ceiling (her popular vote). Sarah Palin (Republican) was the second woman vice-presidential nominee in a general election; the first was Geraldine Ferraro (Democrat), who ran with Walter Mondale in 1984.
6. The decade time line is a depiction of when different feminist theories and politics emerged as predominant. Although many theories were correctives and expansions of earlier theories, all of the feminisms are still thriving.

SUGGESTED READINGS—OVERVIEWS AND HISTORY

Aikau, Hokulani K., Karla A. Erickson, and Jennifer L. Pierce, eds. 2007. *Feminist Waves, Feminist Generations: Life Stories from the Academy*. Minneapolis: University of Minnesota Press.

Andersen, Margaret. 2005. "Thinking about Women: A Quarter Century's View." *Gender & Society* 19:437–455. Also see Symposium on Andersen, *Gender & Society* 22:83–125, 2008.

Bem, Sandra Lipsitz. 1993. *The Lenses of Gender: Transforming the Debate on Sexual Inequality*. New Haven, CT: Yale University Press.

Bernard, Jessie. 1981. *The Female World*. New York: Free Press.

Breines, Wini. 2006. *The Trouble Between Us: An Uneasy History of White and Black Women in the Feminist Movement*. New York: Oxford University Press.

Bronfen, Elisabeth, and Misha Kavka, eds. 2001. *Feminist Consequences: Theory for the New Century*. New York: Columbia University Press.

Butler, Judith. 1990. *Gender Trouble: Feminism and the Subversion of Identity*, 10th Anniversary edition, 1999. New York: Routledge.

Chafetz, Janet Saltzman. 1990. *Gender Equity: An Integrated Theory of Stability and Change*. Thousand Oaks, CA: Sage.

Chafetz, Janet Saltzman, and Anthony Gary Dworkin. 1986. *Female Revolt: Women's Movements in World and Historical Perspective*. Totowa, NJ: Rowman & Allanheld.

Clough, Patricia Ticineto. 1994. *Feminist Thought: Desire, Power, and Academic Discourse.* Cambridge, MA: Blackwell.

Collins, Patricia Hill. 1990. *Black Feminist Thought: Knowledge, Consciousness, and the Politics of Empowerment.* Boston: Unwin Hyman. 2nd ed., 2000. New York: Routledge.

Connell, R. W. 1987. *Gender and Power.* Stanford, CA: Stanford University Press.

———. 1995. *Masculinities.* Berkeley: University of California Press.

Cott, Nancy F. 1987. *The Grounding of Modern Feminism.* New Haven, CT: Yale University Press.

de Beauvoir, Simone. [1949] 1953. *The Second Sex.* Trans. H. M. Parshley. New York: Knopf.

De Lauretis, Teresa. 1987. *Technologies of Gender.* Bloomington: Indiana University Press.

Epstein, Cynthia Fuchs. 1988. *Deceptive Distinctions: Sex, Gender and the Social Order.* New Haven, CT: Yale University Press.

Evans, Judith. 1995. *Feminist Theory Today: An Introduction to Second-Wave Feminism.* Thousand Oaks, CA: Sage.

Evans, Sara M. 2002. "Re-viewing the Second Wave." *Feminist Studies* 28:259–267.

Fausto-Sterling, Anne. 2000. *Sexing the Body: Gender Politics and the Construction of Sexuality.* New York: Basic Books.

Ferree, Myra Marx, Judith Lorber, and Beth B. Hess, eds. 1999. *Revisioning Gender.* Thousand Oaks, CA: Sage.

Ginzberg, Lori D. 2002. "Re-viewing the First Wave." *Feminist Studies* 28:419–434.

Gordon, Linda. 1990. *Woman's Body, Woman's Right: Birth Control in America.* Rev. ed. Baltimore, MD: Penguin.

Harrison, Wendy Cealey, and John Hood-Williams. 2002. *Beyond Sex and Gender.* Thousand Oaks, CA: Sage.

Heywood, Leslie, ed. 2006a. *The Women's Movement Today: An Encyclopedia of Third-Wave Feminism, vol. 1, A-Z.* Westport, CT: Greenwood.

———. 2006b. *The Women's Movement Today: An Encyclopedia of Third-Wave Feminism, vol. 2, Primary Documents.* Westport, CT: Greenwood.

hooks, bell. [1984] 2000. *Feminist Theory: From Margin to Center.* Boston: South End Press.

Hull, Gloria T., Patricia Bell Scott, and Barbara Smith, eds. 1982. *All the Women Are White, All the Blacks Are Men, But Some of Us Are Brave: Black Women's Studies.* New York: Feminist Press.

Jackson, Robert Max. 1998. *Destined for Equality: The Inevitable Rise of Women's Status.* Cambridge, MA: Harvard University Press.

Jaggar, Alison M. 1983. *Feminist Politics and Human Nature.* Totowa, NJ: Rowman & Allanheld.

Joseph, Gloria I., and Jill Lewis, eds. 1981. *Common Differences: Conflicts in Black and White Feminist Perspectives.* Garden City, NY: Doubleday Anchor.

Kessler, Suzanne J., and Wendy McKenna. 1978. *Gender: An Ethnomethodological Approach.* Chicago: University of Chicago Press.

Kraditor, Aileen S. 1981. *The Ideas of the Woman Suffrage Movement/1890–1920.* New York: W. W. Norton.

Lerner, Gerda. 1986. *The Creation of Patriarchy.* New York: Oxford University Press.

Lorber, Judith. 1994. *Paradoxes of Gender.* New Haven, CT: Yale University Press.

———. 2005. *Breaking the Bowls: Degendering and Feminist Change.* New York: W. W. Norton.

Mackie, Vera. 2003. *Feminism in Modern Japan*. Cambridge, UK: Cambridge University Press.

Marks, Elaine, and Isabelle de Courtivron, eds. 1981. *New French Feminisms*. New York: Schocken.

Martin, Patricia Yancey. 2004. "Gender as Social Institution." *Social Forces* 82: 1249–73.

McCann, Carole R., and Seung-Kyung Kim, eds. 2002. *Feminist Theory Reader: Local and Global Perspectives*. New York: Routledge.

Mernissi, Fatima. 1987. *Beyond the Veil: Male-Female Dynamics in Modern Muslim Society*. Bloomington: Indiana University Press.

Millett, Kate. 1970. *Sexual Politics*. Garden City, NY: Doubleday.

Moi, Toril. 1985. *Sexual/Textual Politics: Feminist Literary Theory*. New York: Methuen.

Oakley, Ann. 2002. *Gender on Planet Earth*. New York: The New Press.

Rasmusson, Sarah L. 2003. "Third Wave Feminism: History of a Social Movement." In Immanuel Ness, ed., *Encyclopedia of American Social Movements*. Armonk, NY: M.E. Sharpe.

Richards, Amy, and Jennifer Baumgardner. 2000. *Manifesta: Young Women, Feminism, and the Future*. New York: Farrar, Straus, and Giroux.

Riley, Denise. 1988. *Am I That Name? Feminism and the Category of Women in History*. Minneapolis: University of Minnesota Press.

Rosenberg, Karen Esther, and Judith A. Howard. 2008. "Finding Feminist Sociology: A Review Essay." *Signs* 33:675–696.

Rossi, Alice S., ed. 1973. *The Feminist Papers: From Adams to de Beauvoir*. New York: Columbia University Press.

Roth, Benita. 2004. *Separate Roads to Feminism: Black, Chicana, and White Feminist Movements in America's Second Wave*. New York: Cambridge University Press.

Rowbotham, Sheila. 1973. *Women's Consciousness, Man's World*. New York: Penguin.

———. 1974. *Women, Resistance and Revolution: A History of Women and Revolution in the Modern World*. New York: Vintage.

———. 1976. *Hidden from History: Rediscovering Women in History from the 17th Century to the Present*. New York: Vintage.

———. 1989. *The Past Is Before Us: Feminism in Action Since the 1960s*. Boston: Beacon Press.

Sanday, Peggy Reeves. 1981. *Female Power and Male Dominance: On the Origins of Sexual Inequality*. Cambridge, UK: Cambridge University Press.

Scott, Joan Wallach. 1988. *Gender and the Politics of History*. New York: Columbia University Press.

Showalter, Elaine, ed. 1985. *The New Feminist Criticism: Essays on Women, Literature, and Theory*. New York: Pantheon.

Smith, Barbara, ed. [1983] 2000. *Home Girls: A Black Feminist Anthology*. New Brunswick, NJ: Rutgers University Press.

Snitow, Ann, Christine Stansell, and Sharon Thompson, eds. 1983. *Powers of Desire: The Politics of Sexuality*. New York: Monthly Review Press.

Snyder, R. Claire, 2008. "What Is Third-Wave Feminism? A New Directions Essay." *Signs* 34: 175–196.

Stites, Richard. [1978] 1990. *The Women's Liberation Movement in Russia: Feminism, Nihilism, and Bolshevism, 1860–1930*. Princeton, NJ: Princeton University Press.

Thompson, Becky. 2002. "Multiracial Feminism: Recasting the Chronology of Second Wave Feminism." *Feminist Studies* 28:337–355.

Tong, Rosemarie. 1989. *Feminist Thought: A Comprehensive Introduction*. Boulder, CO: Westview Press.

Warhol, Robyn R., and Diane Price Herndl, eds. 1991. *Feminisms: An Anthology of Literary Theory and Criticism*. New Brunswick, NJ: Rutgers University Press.

Wing, Adrien Katherine, ed. 2000. *Global Critical Race Feminism: An International Reader*. New York: New York University Press.

Woolf, Virginia. 1929 [1957]. *A Room of One's Own*. New York: Harcourt, Brace & World.

PART I

GENDER REFORM FEMINISMS

The feminisms of the 1960s and 1970s were the beginning of the *second wave* of feminism. Like the first wave of feminism, which sought equal rights as citizens for women in Western societies, liberal feminism's roots are in eighteenth and nineteenth century political philosophies that developed the idea of individual rights. *Liberal feminism* asks why women's rights are not part of these individual human rights. Marxist feminism's base is Marx's nineteenth-century analysis of capitalism and the division of labor. *Marxist feminism* argues that women's place in the capitalist division of labor is invisible because housework is not recognized as work. *Socialist feminism* inserts gender into current debates over class and racial ethnic relations and the complex inequalities that result from their multiple effects. *Postcolonial and Asian feminisms* use ideas of national development and economic globalization and examine their effects on women in developing countries and in Asia. The countries are diverse, but there is a thread of unity that is both generally feminist and distinctively national in experiences, empirical data, and politics.

From the beginning of the second wave, the goal of gender reform feminisms has been *gender equality*—legally treating women and men alike, even while granting that they are biologically different. Gender reform feminisms argue that society creates or exaggerates sex differences, especially in the socialization of children. Their main argument about socialization is that it constructs personality and attitude differences in boys and girls to prepare them to live different lives—men as power brokers, bosses, laborers, soldiers, assertive husbands, and authoritative fathers; women as helpers, clerical workers, teachers, nurses, dedicated mothers, and compliant wives.

Gender reform feminisms are critical of the exploitation of women's labor and emotions in the service of marriage and motherhood. They argue that the gendered division of labor makes women dependent on a waged husband or the state. Their main solution has been the encouragement of women's entry into the labor force or, in developing countries, support for women's land ownership and small businesses. These solutions give women economic independence, but do not address the problem of the "second shift," a woman's continued responsibility for the maintenance of the household and the needs of her husband and children, even when she has a full-time job. Given the unequal distribution of domestic work, mothers who work outside the home constantly juggle work and family. With their time binds and relegation to lower-paying jobs, gender equality is an elusive goal. Racial ethnic inequalities further undermine the goal of equality for women of disadvantaged groups.

Gender reform feminisms see men as advantaged in the sphere of paid work, in that their jobs usually pay more, and they are more often in positions of authority. However, there are social class differences. Theoretically, men's work should allow them to support a wife and children, but throughout the world and throughout history, women have taken care of children and also produced food, clothing, and other material necessities as part of their work for their family. When the industrial revolution moved the production of commodities outside of the home into the factory, not only men, but women and children, went to work for wages. The men who could support their families completely were the factory owners and those who had inherited wealth, and their wives were expected to be hostesses and supervisors of the household servants. By the middle of the twentieth century, working-class women were still juggling family work and paid work to supplement the family income, and middle-class, college-educated women were languishing in the suburbs, feeling useless once their children were in school.

In the last 25 years, middle-class women have stayed in or re-entered the labor force, often in high-pressured professional and managerial occupations. The workplace, however, has not altered to meet the needs of "working families"—households where parents are economic providers and child caregivers at the same time. It is this historically intertwined structure of work and family and women's roles within it that gender reform feminisms tackle.

From an international perspective, the goals of gender equality are to achieve education of girls, maternal and child health care, and economic resources for women who contribute heavily to the support of their families. However, feminist gender politics of equality may run into opposition from traditional cultural values and practices that give men power over their daughters and wives. The women's own solution to this dilemma is community organizing around their family roles, another form of feminism.

Gender reform feminisms' politics are based in concepts of equality, domestic and economic exploitation of women's labor, and the global economy. These feminisms do not challenge the gendered division of the social order; their focus is the devaluation of women's paid work and in particular, work for the family, and the continuing gender discrimination in many areas of society that keeps women subordinate to men. The feminist goal of gender equality and the feminist policies to achieve it are current in national and international political activities that are not necessarily called feminism but do have the goal of advancing the status of women, placing their needs into policy agendas, and recognizing that, as Hillary Rodham Clinton said in 1995 at the UN Fourth World Conference on Women in Beijing, "Human rights are women's rights and women's rights are human rights."[1]

NOTE

1. http://www.americanrhetoric.com/speeches/hillaryclintonbeijingspeech.htm

1

Liberal Feminism

SOURCES OF GENDER INEQUALITY

- Gendered socialization of children
- Women's primary responsibility for child care and household maintenance
- Division of paid work into women's jobs and men's jobs
- Devaluation and low pay for women's jobs
- Restricted entry into top positions (glass ceiling)
- Limitations on procreative choice

POLITICS

- Gender-neutral child-rearing and education
- Bringing women into occupations and professions dominated by men and breaking through the glass ceiling to positions of authority (*affirmative action*)
- Bringing more women into politics through equal-representation rules and financial support
- Promoting *gender mainstreaming* in laws and policies ensuring attention to women's needs
- Sharing parenting and subsidizing child care
- Legal, accessible, and affordable procreative services

CRITIQUE

- Too much emphasis on the similarities of women and men, hiding the positive qualities of women, such as empathy and nurturance
- Too much attention to paid work and careers for women as the most meaningful life style
- Too little recognition of the divisions among women, especially racial, ethnic, and social class status that confer additional disadvantages
- Too little attention to sexual violence and rape

CONTRIBUTIONS

- Making language, children's books, and education more gender neutral
- Making formal and informal gender discrimination visible and countering its effects by mentoring and networking in women's professional and occupational associations
- Working with civil rights organizations to frame affirmative action guidelines and to bring lawsuits for women and disadvantaged men
- Getting more women elected and appointed to government positions
- Encouraging employers and governments to provide workplace child care and paid parental leave
- Getting abortion legalized and procreative rights recognized as human rights

In the 1960s and 1970s, the feminist focus in the United States was on women as individuals and the narrowness of their lives. Liberal feminism's complaint that women were confined to a main "job" of wife-mother, with anything else they did having to take a backseat to child care and housework, was the theme of Betty Friedan's best-selling book *The Feminine Mystique*. Women who wanted careers or who were ambitious to make a mark in the arts or in politics were suspect unless they were also "good" wives and mothers (especially mothers). Another problem that kept women down was men's devaluation of them as not too bright, clothes-conscious, and overly emotional. Of course, these impressions were exactly what a woman was taught to convey to a man if she wanted to get a husband.

Liberal feminism claims that gender differences are not based in biology and therefore that women and men are not all that different. Their common humanity supersedes their procreative differences. If women and men are not so different, then they should not be treated differently under the law. Women should have the same legal rights as men and the same educational and work opportunities. Liberal feminism accepts and works within the gendered social order, with the goal of purging it of its discriminatory effects on women. Today this goal is termed *undoing gender*—reversing and counteracting the effects of gender discrimination. A parallel current goal is *gender mainstreaming*—ensuring that government laws and organizational policies do not adversely affect women and do address women's needs.

The early appeals of liberal feminism were open and straightforward—stop calling a wife "the little woman," use Ms. instead of Mrs. or Miss, recognize women's past achievements and current capabilities in many fields, let women do the kind of work they want to do outside the home, get husbands to share some of the housework and child care, legalize abortion. It does not sound very earth-shaking today because so many of these goals have been achieved, including the routine use of "he and she" in public discourse. Women have entered every field, from mining to space travel. Women in the police force and the military are no longer an oddity, and women in high positions, including leaders of countries, are no longer a rarity.

Other liberal feminist goals are still being debated. One is the question of whether men can be as good at parenting as women. Liberal feminism argues that gendered characteristics, such as women's parenting abilities, may seem biological but are really social products. Their proof that mothering skills are learned and not inborn, for example, is that men learn them, too, when they end up with the responsibility for raising children alone. But when there is a woman around, the assumption is that she is better at child care than any man, and so women end up doing most of the physically and emotionally intensive work of bringing up children. Mothers' primary responsibility for child care undermines the goal of gender equality in paid jobs, since employers assume that mothers cannot be as committed to their work as fathers or childless women.

A second continuing problem is that families, teachers, picture books, school books, and the mass media still encourage boys to be "masculine" and girls to be "feminine," even when they show adult women and men acting in more gender-neutral ways. Gender inequality is built into this socialization because supposedly masculine characteristics, such as assertiveness, are more highly valued than supposedly feminine characteristics, such as emotional supportiveness. Liberal feminism promotes nonsexist socialization and education of children as well as media presentations of men and women in nontraditional roles, especially men as caring and competent fathers. These areas still need constant monitoring—computer software programs for girls feature sexy Barbie dolls and kissing skills, while boys' computer games feature violent adventure fantasies.

The Persistence of Gender Inequality

In her 2006 presidential address to the American Sociological Association, Cynthia Fuchs Epstein asked why the global subordination of women and girls persists despite changes in societies. She argues that the processes that allow men to retain power over women start with the creation of and belief in sex differences.

A Theory of Female Subordination

Cynthia Fuchs Epstein

Graduate Center, City University of New York

I propose an even more basic explanation for the persistence of inequality, and often a reversion to inequality, when equality seems to be possible or near attainment. In *Deceptive Distinctions* (1988) I proposed the

Reprinted from "Great Divides: the Cultural, Cognitive, and Social Bases of the Global Subordination of Women," *American Sociological Review* 2007, 72:15–17. Copyright © 2007 by the American Sociological Association. Reprinted by permission.

theory that the division of labor in society assigns women the most important survival tasks—reproduction and gathering and preparation of food. All over the world, women do much of the reproductive work, ensuring the continuity of society. They do this both in physical terms and in symbolic terms. Physically, they do so through childbirth and child care. They do much of the daily work any social group needs for survival. For example, half of the world's food, and up to 80 percent in developing countries, is produced by women (Food and Agriculture Organization of the United Nations n.d.; Women's World Summit Foundation 2006). They also prepare the food at home, work in the supermarkets, behind the counters, and on the conveyor belts that package it. In their homes and in schools, they produce most preschool and primary school education. They take care of the elderly and infirm. They socialize their children in the social skills that make interpersonal communication possible. They are the support staffs for men. This is a good deal—no, a great deal—for the men.

Controlling women's labor and behavior is a mechanism for male governance and territoriality. Men's authority is held jealously. Men legitimate their behavior through ideological and theological constructs that justify their domination. Further, social institutions reinforce this.[a]

I shall review the mechanisms:

We know about the use and threat of force (Goode 1972).[b] We know as well about the role of law and justice systems that do not accord women the same rights to protection, property, wealth, or even education enjoyed by men. We know that men control and own guns and the means of transport, and they often lock women out of membership and leadership of trade unions, political parties, religious institutions, and other powerful organizations. We know too that huge numbers of men feel justified in threatening and punishing females who deviate from male-mandated rules in public and private spaces. That's the strong-arm stuff.

But everywhere, in the West as well as in the rest of the world, women's segregation and subjugation is also done culturally and through cognitive mechanisms that reinforce existing divisions of rights and labor and award men authority over women. Internalized cultural schemas reinforce men's views that their behavior is legitimate and persuade women that their lot is just. The media highlight the idea that women and men think differently and naturally gravitate to their social roles.[c] This is more than just "pluralistic ignorance" (Merton [1948] 1963). Bourdieu ([1979] 1984) reminds us that dominated groups often contribute to their own subordination because of perceptions shaped by the conditions of their existence—the dominant system made of binary oppositions. Using Eviatar Zerubavel's (1997) term, "mindscapes" set the stage for household authorities and heads of clans, tribes, and communities to separate and segregate women in the belief that the practice is inevitable and right. Such mindscapes also persuade the females in their midst to accept the legitimacy and inevitability of their subjection, and even to defend it, as we have seen lately in some academic discourses.

The mindscapes that legitimate women's segregation are the cognitive translations of ideologies that range the spectrum from radical fundamentalism to difference feminism; all are grounded in cultural–religious or pseudoscientific views that women have different emotions, brains, aptitudes, ways of thinking, conversing, and imagining. Such mindsets are legitimated every day in conventional understandings expressed from the media, pulpits, boardrooms, and in departments of universities. Psychologists call them schemas (Brewer and Nakamura 1984)—culturally set definitions that people internalize. Gender operates as a cultural "superschema" (Roos and Gatta 2006) that shapes interaction and cues stereotypes (Ridgeway 1997). Schemas that define femaleness and maleness are basic to all societies. Schemas also define insiders and outsiders and provide definitions of justice and equality.

In popular speech, philosophical musings, cultural expressions, and the banter of everyday conversation, people tend to accept the notion of difference. They accept its inevitability and are persuaded of the legitimacy of segregation, actual or symbolic. Thus, acceptance of difference perspectives—the idea that women often have little to offer to the group, may result in rules that forbid women from speaking in the company of men (in a society governed by the Taliban) or may result in senior academics' selective deafness to the contributions of a female colleague in a university committee room.

In conclusion I want to reiterate certain observations:

Intrinsic qualities are attributed to women that have little or nothing to do with their actual characteristics or behavior. Because those attributions are linked to assigned roles their legitimation is an ongoing project. Changing these ideas would create possibilities for changing the status quo and threaten the social institutions in which men have the greatest stake and in which some women believe they benefit.

Is women's situation different from that of men who, by fortune, color of skin, or accident of birth also suffer from exploitation by the powerful? I am claiming yes, because they carry not only the hardships—sometimes relative hardships—but the ideological and cognitive overlay that defines their subordination as legitimate and normal. Sex and gender are the organizing markers in all societies. In no country, political group, or community are men defined as lesser human beings than their female counterparts. But almost everywhere women are so defined.

Why is this acceptable? And why does it persist?

So many resources are directed to legitimating females' lower place in society. So few men inside the power structure are interested in inviting them in. And so many women and girls accept the Orwellian notion that restriction is freedom, that suffering is pleasure, that silence is power.[d]

Of course this is not a static condition, nor, I hope, an inevitable one. Women in the Western world, and in various sectors of the rest of the world, have certainly moved upward in the continuum toward equality. Thirty-five years ago I noted how women in the legal profession in the United States were excluded from the informal networks that made inclusion and mobility possible. Now, noticeable numbers have ventured over the barriers. Similarly, there has been a large increase in the numbers of women who have entered the sciences,[e] business, medicine, and veterinary medicine (Cox and Alm 2005). This has changed relatively swiftly. Women didn't develop larger brains—nor did their reasoning jump from left brain to right brain or the reverse. Nor did they leave Venus for Mars. Rather, they learned that they could not be barred from higher education and they could get appropriate jobs when they graduated. The problem is no longer one of qualifications or entry but of promotion and inclusion into the informal networks leading to the top. But the obstacles are great.

In his review of cognitive sociological dynamics, DiMaggio (1997) reminds us of Merton's notion of "pluralistic ignorance," which is at work when people act with reference to shared collective opinions that are empirically incorrect. There would not be a firm basis for the subordinate condition of females were there not a widespread belief, rooted in folk culture, in their essential difference from males in ability and emotion. This has been proven time and time again in research in the "real" world of work and family institutions (e.g., Epstein et al. 1995) and laboratory observations (Berger, Cohen, and Zelditch 1966; Frodi et al. 1977; Ridgeway and Smith-Lovin 1999).

We know full well that there are stories and master social narratives accepted by untold millions of people that have no basis in what social scientists would regard as evidence. The best examples are the basic texts of the world's great religions. But there are also societywide beliefs of other kinds. Belief systems are powerful. And beliefs that are unprovable or proven untrue often capture the greatest number of believers. Sometimes, they are simply the best stories.

We in the social sciences have opened the gates to a better understanding of the processes by which subordinated groups suffer because the use of categories such as race and ethnicity rank human beings so as to subordinate, exclude, and exploit them (Tilly 1998). However, relatively few extend this insight to the category of gender or sex. The sexual divide so defines social life, and so many people in the world have a stake in upholding it, that it is the most resistant of all categories to change. Today, Hall and Lamont (2009; Lamont 2005) are proposing that the most productive societies are those with porous boundaries between categories of people. Perhaps there is an important incentive in a wider understanding of this idea. Small groups of men may prosper by stifling women's potential, but prosperous nations benefit from women's full participation and productivity in societies. Societies might achieve still more if the gates were truly open.

Notes

a. Where religious laws govern such areas of civic life as family relations, inheritance, and punishment for crimes, for example, they invariably institutionalize women's subordinate status.

b. As one of many possible examples: when hundreds of women gathered in downtown Tehran on July 31, 2006 to protest institutionalized sex discrimination in Iran (in areas such as divorce, child custody, employment rights, age of adulthood, and court proceedings where a woman's testimony is viewed as half of a man's), 100 male and female police beat them. Reports also noted a tightening of the dress code and segregation on buses and in some public areas such as parks, sidewalks, and elevators. Another demonstration on March 8, 2006 was dispersed as police dumped garbage on the heads of participants (Stevens 2006).

c. The recent book by Louann Brizendine (2006), which asserts that the female and male brains are completely different, offering such breezy accounts as "woman is weather, constantly changing and hard to predict" and "man is mountain," has been on the top 10 on the Amazon.com book list and led to her prominent placement on ABC's 20/20 and morning talk shows. Thanks to Troy Duster for passing this on.

d. For example, a recent poll cited in the New York Times (June 8, 2006) indicates that a majority of women in Muslim countries do not regard themselves as unequal (Andrews 2006). Of course, this attitude is widespread throughout the world, including Western societies.

e. Comparing percentages of women attaining doctorates in the sciences from 1970–71 to 2001–2002 the increases were: Engineering 2–17.3; Physics 2.9–15.5; Computer Science 2.3–22.8; Mathematics 7.6–29.

References

Andrews, Helena. 2006. "Muslim Women Don't See Themselves as Oppressed, Survey Finds." *New York Times*. June 7, A9.

Berger, Joseph, Bernard P. Cohen, and Morris Zelditch Jr. 1966. "Status Characteristics and Expectation States." In Joseph Berger, Morris Zelditch Jr., and Bo Anderson, ed., *Sociological Theories in Progress*, vol. I. Boston, MA: Houghton Mifflin.

Bourdieu, Pierre. [1979] 1984. *Distinctions: A Social Critique of the Judgment of Taste*. Cambridge, MA: Harvard University Press.

Brewer, William F. and Glenn Nakamura. 1984. "The Nature and Functions of Schemas." In R. S. Wyer and T. K. Srull. Hillsdale, ed., *Handbook of Social Cognition*, vol. 1. NJ: Erlbaum.

Brizendine, Louann. 2006. *The Female Brain*. New York: Morgan Road Books.

Cox, W. Michael and Richard Alm. 2005. "Scientists are Made, Not Born." *New York Times*, February 25, A25.

DiMaggio, Paul. 1997. "Culture and Cognition." *Annual Review of Sociology* 23:263–87.

Epstein, Cynthia Fuchs. 1988. *Deceptive Distinctions*. New Haven, CT: Yale University Press and New York: Russell Sage Foundation.

Epstein, Cynthia Fuchs, Robert Sauté, Bonnie Oglensky, and Martha Gever. 1995. "Glass Ceilings and Open Doors: The Mobility of Women in Large Corporate Law Firms." *Fordham Law Review* LXIV:291–449.

Food and Agriculture Organization of the United Nations. N.d. "Gender and Food Security: Agriculture." Retrieved August 5, 2006 (http://www.fao. org/gender/en/agri-e.htm).

Frodi, Ann, Jacqueline Macaulay, and Pauline Robert Thome. 1977. "Are Women Always Less Aggressive than Men? A Review of the Experimental Literature." *Psychological Bulletin* 84:634–60.

Goode, William J. 1972. "The Place of Force in Human Society." *American Sociological Review* 37:507–19.

Hall Peter A. and Michele Lamont eds. 2009. *Successful Societies: How Institutions and Culture Affect Health*. New York: Cambridge University Press.

Lamont, Michele. 2005. "Bridging Boundaries: Inclusion as a Condition for Successful Societies." Presented at the Successful Societies Program of the Canadian Institute for Advanced Research, October, Montebello, Quebec, Canada.

Merton, Robert K. [1949] 1963. *Social Theory and Social Structure*. Glencoe, IL: The Free Press.

Ridgeway, Cecelia L. 1997. "Interaction and the Conservation of Gender Inequality: Considering Employment." *American Sociological Review* 62:218–35.

Ridgeway, Cecelia L. and Lynn Smith-Lovin. 1999. "The Gender System and Interaction." *Annual Review of Sociology* 25:19–216.

Roos, Patricia and Mary L. Gatta. 2006. "Gender Inquiry in the Academy." Presented at the Annual Meeting of the American Sociological Association, August 14, Montreal, Canada.

Stevens, Alison. 2006. "Iranian Women Protest in Shadow of Nuclear Face-off." *Women's eNews*, June 16. Retrieved September 28, 2006 (http://www.wom-ensenews.org/article.cfm/dyn/aid/2780).

Tilly, Charles. 1998. *Durable Inequality*. Berkeley, CA: University of California Press.

Zerubavel, Eviatar. 1997. *Social Mindscapes: An Invitation to Cognitive Sociology*. Cambridge, MA: Harvard University Press.

Successes and Failures in the Workplace

The gates that men guard, so that "entry to the unauthorized is forbidden,"[1] have been breached in the last 25 years through liberal feminist politics of affirmative action to ensure gender balance and lawsuits charging discrimination against women in hiring, promotion, and salaries. These efforts have let women into the echelons of higher education, the professions of law and medicine, the sciences, and all sorts of workplaces, from large-scale corporations to coal mines.

While the workplace is an arena where liberal feminism has made significant contributions, women are a long way from gender equality. Sexist patterns of hiring and promotion still produce workplaces where men and women work at different jobs and where most of the top positions are held by men. Liberal feminism has developed theories to explain the persistence of the *gender segregation* of jobs (men work with men and women work with women) and the *gender stratification* of organizational hierarchies (the top of the pyramid is invariably almost all men).

The entry of more women in a workplace was supposed to have a psychological effect on both men and women. Earlier theories had argued that women were not aggressive about competing with men on the job or at school because they feared that success would make them so disliked that they would never have a social life. Rosabeth Moss Kanter, a sociologist and management researcher, said in *Men and Women of the Corporation* (1977) that it was token status as the lone woman among men, visible and vulnerable, that created women's fears. The *Kanter hypothesis* predicted that as workplaces became more gender-balanced, men would become more accepting of women colleagues, and women would have other women to bond with instead of having to go it alone as the single token woman.

The recognition that a token or two did not make for a truly diversified workplace provided the impetus for *affirmative action*. The strategy of *affirmative action* was developed to redress the gender, racial, and ethnic imbalance in workplaces, schools, and job-training programs. Employers are legally mandated to hire enough workers of different racial and ethnic categories and genders to achieve a reasonable balance in their workforce. The law also requires employers to pay the workers the same and to give them an equal chance to advance in their careers. Affirmative action programs develop a gender-diversified pool of qualified people by encouraging men to train for such jobs as nurse, elementary school teacher, and secretary, and women to go into fields like engineering, construction, and police work.

The goal is not perfect balance but a workplace where different kinds of people are fully integrated and respected colleagues. The Kanter hypothesis predicted a positive attitude change when a formerly imbalanced workplace becomes more gender-balanced. However, later research found that as more women enter an organization, there is often a backlash in the form of increasing sexual harassment and denigration of women's capabilities— a defense against what is felt to be the encroachment of women on men's territory. Men's stonewalling is particularly likely when women are competing with them for jobs on the fast track up the career ladder.

Another contradiction to the Kanter hypothesis is that men who are tokens in women-dominated occupations, such as social work, tend to be pushed into administrative jobs. This phenomenon became known as the *glass escalator,* a contrast to the *glass ceiling* that keeps women from the top jobs in occupations dominated by men. Where there are few administrative positions, men in "women's work" tend to gravitate to specialties that seem more masculine. For example, in nursing, men choose emergency, trauma, coronary, and intensive care and anesthesia, areas that are fast-paced, technological, autonomous, and physical (Snyder and Green 2008).

Gatekeeping and the Glass Ceiling

The concept of *gatekeeping* explains how most women are kept from getting to the top in occupations and professions dominated by men. Gatekeeping used to keep women out of those fields entirely. Now gatekeeping keeps women out of the line for promotion to top positions. The ways that most people move up in their careers are through *networking* (making professional contacts and using them for job and promotion opportunities) and *mentoring* (being coached by a protective senior about the informal norms of the workplace). Becoming part of a network and getting a mentor are made much easier if you become a *protégée* of a senior colleague.

In professions and in managerial positions, where jobs pay the best, have the most prestige, and command the most authority, few senior men take on women as their *protégées*. As a result, there has been a *glass ceiling* on the advancement of women in every field they have entered in the last 25 years. The concept of the glass ceiling assumes that women have the motivation, ambition, and capacity for positions of power and prestige, but hidden barriers keep them from reaching the top. They can see their way to their goal, but they bump their heads on a ceiling that is both invisible and impenetrable. Similar processes of informal discrimination hinder the careers of men of disadvantaged groups as well; women of color have had to face both racism and sexism.

The theory of *gendered job queues* argues that the best jobs are kept for men of the dominant racial ethnic group. When a job no longer pays well or has deteriorating working conditions, dominant men leave for other work, and men of disadvantaged racial ethnic groups and all women can move into them. Occupations stay segregated, but who does the job changes. Some jobs have shifted from men's work to women's work within a decade. A typical case is a bank teller in the United States. Disadvantaged groups of workers continue to get lower pay and have poorer working conditions than the dominant group because the new crop of "best jobs" again goes to the most advantaged group of workers. Thus, in the United States, White men monopolize the most lucrative financial and banking jobs.

Despite the glass ceiling, the efforts of liberal feminism to make women equal to men in the workplace in Western societies have succeeded. Women now receive the higher education and professional training needed to enter medicine and law, and have entered these fields in large numbers. Women have formed professional associations and unions by occupation, and also by racial ethnic groups, to enhance the networking and mentoring so useful in getting jobs and then getting promoted. Although men in work and other organizations still bypass women for promotion (and the organizations are getting successfully sued for such behavior), the liberal feminist goal of workplace gender equality is a major accomplishment. But this accomplishment is foundering for mothers.

Work-Family Balance

Liberal feminism has always claimed that women and motherhood are not synonymous. Its proponents argue that the assumption that mothers have prime responsibility for child care and cannot therefore be responsible workers builds gender discrimination into the workplace. Childless women can be treated as men workers are. For them and for fathers, employers demand that work comes before family. For high-powered professions and politics, so-called "greedy occupations," the pressure to put the job first is even more intense. Mothers are bounced between two powerful cultural commitments—their children and their work.

When workplaces do not accommodate to family needs and fathers do not share child care, mothers pay a price in lowered wages, reduced lifetime earnings, and minimal pensions because of part-time and interrupted work. When they want to return to full-time work or get off the "mommy track," they are discriminated against in hiring and promotions. Thus, mothers bear most of the economic and occupational cost of parenting, even though everyone in a society benefits from good child care.

Many European countries and Israel have policies of maternal leave and subsidized child care that encourage women with small children to stay in the paid workforce, but because they have the organizational and emotional responsibility for their families, they are discouraged from competing with men for high-level, better-paid, full-time positions. Some countries subsidize mothers and children but do not provide child care; that policy encourages women to stay out of the paid workforce. Countries like the United States, which subsidize neither mothers nor child care, make the "juggling act" between parenting and earning a living the responsibility of individual families.

The other part of the balance, the workplace, has felt less governmental and social pressure to adjust to 25 years of married mothers' staying on the job. In much of the literature on dual-career and two-job families, liberal feminism has suggested that an obvious way to accommodate workers' family responsibilities is to expand the use of *flextime*. Flextime offers employees a choice of what hours and what days of the week to work. But it has to guarantee equal benefits, such as health insurance, advancement opportunities, and seniority tracks. Family-friendly workplaces have for a long time provided flextime, parental leaves, on-site child care, and referral services for care of children and the elderly. But they have not offered them without penalties in advancement or the stigmatization of part-time work. Formal policies and informal practices need to reflect awareness of the whole lives of every worker if the transformation in families is to be met with transformation in the workplace.

The following excerpt from *The Time Divide* by Jerry Jacobs and Kathleen Gerson, two sociologists who have separately contributed excellent research to gender, work and family issues, lays out the crucial issues in balancing work and family and how the problems might be remedied.

Integrating Family and Work in the 21st Century

Jerry A. Jacobs

Professor of Sociology, University of Pennsylvania

Kathleen Gerson

Professor of Sociology, New York University

Efforts to achieve gender equality, like policies that call for government regulation or spending, continue to evoke deep ambivalence and considerable opposition. Several decades ago, when women's movement into paid work began to elicit popular notice, criticism often focused on the costs women bore as they moved away from domestically centered lives. Some even argued, in Sylvia Ann Hewlett's words, that these changes meant a "lesser life" for women.[a] Several decades later, this argument appears far less tenable. As women have established themselves across an array of jobs and occupations, most have welcomed their increased economic and social autonomy. Women continue to face obstacles at work and in the home, but the solutions to these problems can be found in creating more equal opportunities, not in confining women to domesticity.

The more common focus of contemporary critiques of women's equality has moved from adults to children. According to this argument, women's workplace commitments may appeal to adults, but they pose dangers for the young. The concern over "neglected" or "latchkey" children has insidious overtones, implying maternal indifference and fueling a moral panic over the transformation in women's lives. While it is appropriate and important to focus on the ways our society is not meeting the needs of children, it is equally important to disentangle these concerns from parental, and especially maternal, blame. The dangers to children rest not with their mothers' work commitments, but rather with the paucity of supports—at the workplace and in our communities—for employed parents and their children.

Rather than causing harm, the paid employment of mothers tends to enhance children's well-being in a number of ways. Most obviously, women's employment provides economic resources to their families; whether they live in a two-income or a single-parent home, children depend on their mothers' earnings. Equal economic opportunity for women thus protects children from poverty and improves their life chances.

Children tend to recognize the benefits of having an employed mother, as well as the challenges posed by long hours and inflexible work settings. Most children support their working parents and believe employed mothers are making crucial contributions to their welfare (Galinsky 1999; Gerson 2001). They report emotional and social benefits as well. Both daughters and sons tend to see employed mothers as uplifting models for women and dual-income partnerships as attractive models for marriage (Barnett and Rivers 1996; Gerson 2002). And when the focus is on direct, "quality" time devoted to children, employed mothers appear to spend almost as much time with their children as do nonemployed mothers (Bianchi 2000).

While children appreciate the resources their parents' jobs provide, they also recognize the toll that long days and unsatisfying work can take on mothers and fathers alike. What children need, then, are flexible, family-friendly workplaces for their parents as well as family-supportive communities for children and adolescents (Glass 2000). Rather than focusing on maternal employment as a social problem, we need to attend to the ways that workplaces and communities can better accommodate this fundamental transformation in family life.

Concerns over replacing full-time maternal care with other forms of child rearing are also based on the dubious, but persisting, belief that biological mothers are uniformly and universally superior to all other caretakers. It is hard to imagine any other form of work for which such a claim could be made or taken seriously. Mothers are an enormously large and varied group, with differing interests, desires, and talents. It makes little sense to assume that they are all equally and uniquely prepared to be their child's only or best caretaker. Instead, children benefit from having a range of committed, concerned caretakers—including fathers, other relatives, and paid professionals. They also benefit from having parents who are satisfied with their choices, whether that means working or staying home.[b]

The expansion of opportunities for professional women in the United States and other countries has fueled a demand for paid caretakers, especially in the absence of widely available, high-quality, publicly sponsored child care. Conservatives, uneasy with women's march into the workplace, have consistently raised concerns about the propriety of relying on paid caretakers to help rear children. Recently, however, some feminists have joined the chorus of critics who worry about this strategy, especially when these caretakers are drawn from the ranks of immigrants from poorer countries. Some worry that the expanded market for paid caretaking encourages working parents—especially full-time employed mothers—to participate in a new form of international colonialism. From this perspective, affluent families in rich countries are extracting caregiving and even love from poorer immigrants, who may leave their own children behind (Ehrenreich and Hochschild 2002).

In a society that fails to accord appropriate social or economic value to the care of children, all child-care workers (like all involved parents) face disadvantage and discrimination. Immigrants and other women who work as caretakers in private households may, indeed, be even more vulnerable than others who care for children in public settings, especially if they do not speak English and can count on few friends or relatives for support. Like their American-born counterparts, immigrant domestic workers may not be paid fairly or regularly and may be physically or emotionally abused; unlike their American peers, they may be threatened with deportation if they complain. And the problems facing private domestic workers, whether or not they are immigrants, are especially prone to invisibility because the isolation of these workers limits their options for organizing as a group or informing others of their plight.

The deficiencies and dangers of an inadequate child-care system should not, however, be laid at the feet of employed mothers, who confront equally perplexing obstacles. Such an approach pits women against each other, making it seem that the economic independence of middle-class women comes at the expense of poor, immigrant women and their children. By framing paid caretaking as the "commodification" of care, this perspective adds to the critique facing all women who hold paid jobs, whether in public workplaces or private homes. As important, the focus on private child care obscures the more widespread trend toward greater reliance on child-care centers, where the conditions of work and the rights of workers are more visible....

The policies we suggest represent only a few of the myriad of possible approaches to address the dilemmas created by work and family change. Effective policies, whatever their form, can only emerge from a national debate that extends beyond cultural critiques and a framework of parental blame to reconsider workplace organization, community support, and the structure of opportunities confronting workers and their families.

The time balance people are able to strike in their lives matters, but the picture is not a simple one of overwork. For the "overworked Americans," job flexibility and genuine formal and informal support for family life matter as much as, and possibly more than, actual hours. For the underworked, who are concentrated in the less rewarded jobs, security and opportunity are paramount for their own welfare and that of their children.

One facet of change, however, spans occupation and class: the emergence of women as a large and committed group of workers. They need and have a right to expect the same opportunities afforded men, and their families depend on their ability to gain these opportunities. There are significant points of convergence between women and men in their commitment to work and their desire for family supports. However, women workers, especially those putting in long days at the workplace, do not enjoy the same level of support as do their male counterparts.

Principles of justice as well as the new realities of families suggest that gender equity needs to be integral to any policy initiatives aimed at easing the conflicts between family and work.

At the broadest level, our discovery of multiple and intertwined time divides suggests that reform efforts should uphold two important principles: equality of opportunity for women and men, and generous support for all involved parents regardless of gender or class position. We cannot afford to build work-family policies on old, outdated stereotypes, in which women are seen as less committed to work than men. Yet we can also not afford to build our policies on new stereotypes, in which working mothers and, to a lesser extent, fathers are depicted as avoiding their families and neglecting their children.

These images place all too many workers in a difficult bind, in which work commitment is defined as family neglect and family involvement is defined as a lack of work commitment. These are inaccurate images that result in untenable choices. If our findings are a guide, what workers need most is flexible, satisfying, and economically rewarding work in a supportive setting that offers them a way to integrate work and family life. With these supports, contemporary workers and the generations to follow will be able to bridge the time divides they face.

Notes

a. See Hewlett 1986. Sylvia Hewlett's recent book, *Creating a Life* (2002), focuses on the relatively high rates of childlessness among highly accomplished professional women, using this development as a cautionary tale about the costs of success for women. The real story here, however, is not women's ticking biological clock, but rather the lack of change in the time demands and "career clocks" of highly rewarded jobs to accommodate the needs of working women.

b. Recent research shows that the absolute amount of time spent with children is less important than the amount of support and sensitivity parents provide. A. C. Crouter and colleagues (1999), for example, report that children's willingness to share information with their parents matters more than parental monitoring of their time. These researchers also find that when mothers work, fathers become more knowledgeable about, and involved in, their children's care.

References

Barnett, Rosalind C., and Caryl Rivers. 1996. *She Works/He Works: How Two-Income Families Are Happier, Healthier, and Better-Off.* San Francisco, CA: HarperCollins.

Bianchi, Suzanne M. 2000. "Maternal Employment and Time With Children: Dramatic Change or Surprising Continuity?" *Demography* 37:401–414.

Ehrenreich, Barbara, and Arlie R. Hochschild, eds. 2002. *Global Woman: Nannies, Maids, and Sex Workers in the New Economy.* New York: Metropolitan Books.

Galinsky, Ellen, Stacy S. Kim, and James T. Bond. 2001. *Feeling Overworked: When Work Becomes Too Much*. New York: Families and Work Institute.

Gerson, Kathleen. 2001. "Children of the Gender Revolution: Some Theoretical Questions and Findings from the Field." In Victor W. Marshall, Walter R. Heinz, Helga Krueger, and Anil Verma, eds., *Restructuring Work and the Life Course*. Toronto: University of Toronto Press.

———. 2002. "Moral Dilemmas, Moral Strategies, and the Transformation of Gender: Lessons from Two Generations of Work and Family Change." *Gender & Society* 16:8–28.

Glass, Jennifer. 2000. "Toward a Kinder, Gentler Workplace: Envisioning the Integration of Family and Work." *Contemporary Sociology* 29:129–143.

Hewlett, Sylvia A. 1986. *A Lesser Life: The Myth of Women's Liberation in America*. New York. Morrow.

———. 2002. *Creating a Life: Professional Women and the Quest for Children*. New York: Miramax.

As long as work-family balance is the burden of individual families or mothers alone, there will continue to be gender inequality in the family and in the workplace. Few men feel they can afford, economically and psychologically, to jeopardize their financial support of their families. Similarly, few mothers feel they can live with the burden of guilt over splitting their time between their job and their children in the light of the continuing moral imperative to be a good (i.e., intensive) mother.

Critique

There is an internal theoretical contradiction in liberal feminism that centers on the question of whether women and men have to be the same to be equal. The campaign to bring up children in a gender-neutral way has meant encouraging a mixture of existing masculine and feminine characteristics and traits, so that boys and girls will be similar in personalities and behavior. The corollary campaign to integrate women into all parts of public life, especially the workplace, and for men to share parenting and other family roles, means that women and men can be more interchangeable.

The logical outcome of liberal feminism is a society that is not based on dividing people into two and only two separate and distinct sex-gender categories. But because of men's social domination, the actual thrust of both gender neutrality and gender integration is often the continued predominance of masculine traits and values, such as devotion to a career, with the consequence that women are expected to act like men. For this reason, liberal feminism has been accused of denigrating *womanliness* (nurturance, empathy, care) and pregnancy and childbirth in their fight to advance the social status of women.

The goal of liberal feminism in the United States was embodied in the Equal Rights Amendment to the U.S. Constitution, which was never ratified. It said, "Equality of rights under the law shall not be denied or abridged by the United States or any state on account of sex." The negative response of the American public to the Equal Rights Amendment may have been a gut reaction to the revolutionary possibilities of an absolutely even-handed legal status for women and men. When laws speak of "pregnant persons," as did a Supreme Court decision equating pregnancy with disability or illness, many people, including some feminists, feel that gender neutrality has gone too far. The feminists who fought for the legalization of abortion and still fight for women to control their procreative lives pushed liberal feminism to recognize that the battle for gender equality could not be confined to advancing women in the workplace.

Summary

The main contribution of liberal feminism has been to show how much modern society discriminates against women by treating women and men differently. Liberal feminist theory says that biological differences are not the reason for gender differences, but women's domestic responsibility for children and the family and their consequent handicaps in the workplace. Liberal feminism insists that women and men should be treated in a gender-neutral manner, especially under the law. One of liberal feminism's main accomplishments has been to get gender equality at work and in education written into civil rights laws.

Liberal feminism has been successful in breaking down many barriers to women's entry into jobs and professions formerly dominated by men, in helping to equalize wage scales, and in legalizing abortion. But liberal feminism has not been able to overcome the prevailing belief that women and men are intrinsically different. Although gender differences can coexist with equitable or even-handed treatment, the way women are treated in modern society, especially in the workplace, still produces large gaps in salaries, job opportunities, and advancement. Liberal feminism recognized early on that the gendered structure of organizations and the uneven distribution of domestic work were the intertwined sources of workplace inequality.

Politically, liberal feminism's focus has been on visible sources of gender discrimination, such as gendered job markets and inequitable wage scales, and with getting women into positions of authority in the professions, government, and cultural institutions. Liberal feminist politics takes important weapons of the civil rights movement—antidiscrimination legislation and affirmative action programs—and uses them to fight gender inequality, especially in the job market. Liberal feminism has been less successful in fighting the informal processes of discrimination and exclusion that have produced the glass ceiling that so many women face in their career advancement.

The great strides that women of the last generation have made have led many young people to think that feminism is passé. But the gender equality in the workplace and the home that liberal feminism achieved depends on good jobs, steady incomes, two-parent households, and family-friendly employers and colleagues. The Scandinavian countries have achieved gender equality through welfare-state benefits to all parents and children. They also have many more women in government and in policy-making positions than the rest of the Western world, and so are able to promote gender sensitivity in many public arenas. Most of the world's women, however, have very little economic security. Their social problems produce a level of gender inequality that needs quite different feminist theories and politics.

In sum, liberal feminism is best applicable to postindustrial societies and to issues of gender discrimination in the workplace, professions, education, and politics, and also to the inequitable division of domestic work in heterosexual families. Although its theoretical emphasis on the similar capabilities of women and men implies their interchangeability, politically, liberal feminism did not attempt to challenge the structure of gendered social order but rather to redress some of its inequities.

NOTE

1. Translation of a typical German "keep out" sign, *zutritt für Unbefugte verboten*. It was used as the translation of "guarding the gates" in the German edition of *Paradoxes of Gender*.

SUGGESTED READINGS IN LIBERAL FEMINISM

Family

Bem, Sandra Lipsitz. 1998. *An Unconventional Family*. New Haven, CT: Yale University Press.

Coltrane, Scott. 1996. *Family Man: Fatherhood, Housework, and Gender Equity*. New York: Oxford University Press.

———. 1998. *Gender and Families*. Thousand Oaks, CA: Pine Forge Press.

Crittenden, Ann. 2001. *The Price of Motherhood: Why the Most Important Job in the World Is Still the Least Valued*. New York: Metropolitan Books.

Deutsch, Francine M. 1999. *Halving It All: How Equally Shared Parenting Works*. Cambridge, MA: Harvard University Press.

Dienhart, Anna. 1998. *Reshaping Fatherhood: The Social Construction of Shared Parenting*. Thousand Oaks, CA: Sage.

Ehrensaft, Diane. 1987. *Parenting Together: Men and Women Sharing the Care of Their Children*. Urbana, IL: University of Illinois Press.

Fineman, Martha Albertson. 1995. *The Neutered Mother, the Sexual Family and Other Twentieth Century Tragedies*. New York: Routledge.

Friedan, Betty. 1963. *The Feminine Mystique*. New York: W. W. Norton.

Greif, Geoffrey L. 1985. *Single Fathers*. Lexington, MA: Lexington Books.

Hobson, Barbara, ed. 2002. *Making Men into Fathers: Men, Masculinities and the Social Politics of Fatherhood*. Cambridge, UK: Cambridge University Press.

Lamb, Michael E., ed. 1987. *The Father's Role: Cross-cultural Perspectives*. Hillsdale, NJ: Lawrence Erlbaum.

Okin, Susan Moller. 1989. *Justice, Gender and the Family.* New York: Basic Books.

Risman, Barbara J. 1998. *Gender Vertigo: American Families in Transition.* New Haven, CT: Yale University Press.

Stacey, Judith. 1991. *Brave New Families: Stories of Domestic Upheaval in Late Twentieth-Century America.* New York: Basic Books.

———. 1996. *In the Name of the Family: Rethinking Family Values in the Postmodern Age.* Boston: Beacon Press.

Weitzman, Lenore J. 1985. *The Divorce Revolution: The Unexpected Social and Economic Consequences for Women and Children in America.* New York: Free Press.

Politics and Law

Bartlett, Katharine T., and Rosanne Kennedy, eds. 1991. *Feminist Legal Theory: Readings in Law and Gender.* Boulder, CO: Westview Press.

Eisenstein, Zillah. 1981. *The Radical Future of Liberal Feminism.* New York: Longman.

———. 1984. *Feminism and Sexual Equality: Crisis in Liberal America.* New York: Monthly Review Press.

———. 1988. *The Female Body and the Law.* Berkeley: University of California Press.

Mathews, Donald G., and Jane Sherron De Hart. 1990. *Sex, Gender, and the Politics of ERA: A State and the Nation.* New York: Oxford University Press.

Weisberg, D. Kelly, ed. 1993. *Feminist Legal Theory: Foundations.* Philadelphia, PA: Temple University Press.

Work

Boulis, Ann K., and Jerry A. Jacobs. 2008. *The Changing Face of Medicine: Women Doctors and Evolution of Health Care in America.* Ithaca, NY: Cornell University Press.

Budig, Michelle J. 2002. "Male Advantage and the Gender Composition of Jobs: Who Rides the Glass Escalator?" *Social Problems* 49:258–277.

Cockburn, Cynthia. 1991. *In the Way of Women: Men's Resistance to Sex Equality in Organizations.* Ithaca, NY: ILR Press.

Collinson, David L., David Knights, and Margaret Collinson. 1990. *Managing to Discriminate.* New York: Routledge.

Daniels, Arlene Kaplan. 1988. *Invisible Careers: Women Civic Leaders from the Volunteer World.* Chicago: University of Chicago Press.

Epstein, Cynthia Fuchs. 1971. *Women's Place: Options and Limits in Professional Careers.* Berkeley: University of California Press.

———. 1981. *Women in Law.* New York: Basic Books.

Epstein, Cynthia Fuchs, and Arne L. Kalleberg, eds. 2004. *Fighting for time: Shifting boundaries of work and social life.* New York: Russell Sage Foundation.

Gherardi, Silvia. 1995. *Gender, Symbolism and Organizational Cultures.* Thousand Oaks, CA: Sage.

Jacobs, Jerry A. 1989. *Revolving Doors: Sex Segregation and Women's Careers.* Stanford, CA: Stanford University Press.

Kanter, Rosabeth Moss. 1977. *Men and Women of the Corporation.* New York: Basic Books.

Lorber, Judith. 1984. *Women Physicians: Careers, Status, and Power.* London: Tavistock.

Martin, Patricia Yancey. 2001. "'Mobilizing Masculinities': Women's Experiences of Men at Work." *Organization* 8:587–618.

———. 2003. "'Said and Done' versus 'Saying and Doing': Gendering Practices, Practicing Gender at Work." *Gender & Society* 17:342–366.

Reskin, Barbara F., and Patricia A. Roos. 1990. *Job Queues, Gender Queues: Explaining Women's Inroads into Male Occupations.* Philadelphia: Temple University Press.

Ridgeway, Celia. 1997. "Interaction and the Conservation of Gender Inequality: Considering Employment." *American Sociological Review* 62:218–235.

Riska, Elianne. *Medical Careers and Feminist Agendas: American, Scandinavian, and Russian Women Physicians.* New York: Aldine de Gruyter.

Snyder, Karrie Ann, and Adam Isaiah Green. 2008. "Revisiting the Glass Escalator: The Case of Gender Segregation in a Female Dominated Occupation." *Social Problems* 55:271–299.

Valian, Virginia. 1998. *Why So Slow? The Advancement of Women.* Cambridge, MA: MIT Press.

Wajcman, Judy. 1998. *Managing Like a Man: Women and Men in Corporate Management.* University Park: Pennsylvania State University Press.

Williams, Christine L. 1992. "The Glass Escalator: Hidden Advantages for Men in the 'Female' Professions." *Social Problems* 39:253–267.

Work and Family

Appelbaum, Eileen, Thomas Bailey, Peter Berg, and Arne L. Kalleberg. 2002. *Shared Work, Valued Care: New Norms for Organizing Market Work and Unpaid Care Work.* Washington, DC: Economic Policy Institute.

Blair-Loy, Mary. 2003. *Competing Devotions: Career and Family Among Women Executives.* Cambridge, MA: Harvard University Press.

Epstein, Cynthia Fuchs, Carroll Seron, Bonnie Oglensky, and Robert Sauté. 1999. *The Part-Time Paradox: Time Norms, Professional Lives, Family, and Gender.* New York: Routledge.

Garey, Anita. 1999. *Weaving Work and Motherhood.* Philadelphia: Temple University Press.

Gerson, Kathleen. 1993. *No Man's Land: Men's Changing Commitments to Family and Work.* New York: Basic Books.

Hertz, Rosanna, and Nancy L. Marshall, eds. 2001. *Working Families: The Transformation of the American Home.* Berkeley: University of California Press.

Hochschild, Arlie Russell. 1989. With Anne Machung. *The Second Shift: Working Parents and the Revolution at Home.* New York: Viking.

———. 1997. *The Time Bind: When Work Becomes Home and Home Becomes Work.* New York: Metropolitan Books.

Jacobs, Jerry A., and Kathleen Gerson. 2004. *The Time Divide: Work, Family, and Gender Inequality.* Cambridge, MA: Harvard University Press.

Jacobs, Jerry A. and Janice Fanning Madden, eds. 2004. "Mommies and Daddies on the Fast Track: Success of Parents in Demanding Professions." Special Issue: *Annals of the American Academy of Political and Social Science* 596 (November).

Landry, Bart. 2000. *Black Working Wives: Pioneers of the American Family Revolution.* Berkeley: University of California Press.

Lewis, Suzan, Dafna N. Izraeli, and Helen Hootsmans, eds. 1992. *Dual-Earner Families: International Perspectives.* Thousand Oaks, CA: Sage.

Moen, Phyllis, ed. 2003. *It's About Time: Couples and Careers.* Ithaca, NY: ILR Press.

Pitt-Catsouphes, Marcie, and Bradley K. Googins, eds. 1999. "The Evolving World of Work and Family: New Stakeholders, New Voices." Special Issue: *Annals of the American Academy of Political and Social Science* 562 (March).

Potuchek, Jean L. 1997. *Who Supports the Family? Gender and Breadwinning in Dual-Earner Marriages.* Stanford, CA: Stanford University Press.

Williams, Joan. 2000. *Unbending Gender: Why Family and Work Conflict and What to Do About It.* New York: Oxford University Press.

2

Marxist Feminism

SOURCES OF GENDER INEQUALITY

- Exploitation of women in unwaged work for the family
- Use of women workers as a reserve army of labor—hired when the economy needs workers, fired when it does not
- Low pay for women's jobs

POLITICS

- Permanent waged work for women
- Government-subsidized maternal and child health care, child-care services, financial allowances for children
- Union organizing of women workers

CRITIQUE

- Early theorists neglected to integrate racial ethnic exploitation into gendered class analyses
- Permanent full-time jobs do not relieve wives and mothers of home-based responsibilities
- Reliance on welfare-state benefits locks women into child care as their prime role

CONTRIBUTIONS

- Recognition that women are subordinated as second-class citizens
- Gender analysis of the exploitation of women as paid and unpaid workers in capitalist, communist, and socialist economies
- Making visible the necessity and worth of women's unpaid work in the home to the functioning of the economy and to the social reproduction of future workers
- Concept of gender conciousness

During the 1970s, Marxist feminism argued that the economic structure and the material aspects of life were the main source of gender inequality. Marxist historical materialism says that every major change in production—from hunting and gathering to farming to the industrial revolution—changes the social organization of work and family. In preindustrial societies, women's domestic labor not only maintained the home and cared for the children but also entailed getting or growing food, making cloth and sewing clothing, and other work that allowed the family to subsist. This work was done side by side with the men and children of the family. The industrial revolution of the nineteenth century brought a major change: the removal of production work from the home to factories, and the change from household goods being made at home to their becoming mass-produced commodities that had to be purchased. The means of production, then, were no longer owned by the worker but by capitalists, who hired workers at wages low enough to make a profit.

Marx's analysis of the social structure of capitalism was supposed to apply to people of any social characteristics. If you owned the means of production, you were a member of the capitalist class; if you sold your labor for a wage, you were a member of the proletariat. That should be true of women as well, except that until the end of the nineteenth century, married women in capitalist countries were not allowed to own property in their own name; any wages they earned and their profits from any businesses they ran belonged legally to their husband.

Although Marx and other nineteenth-century economic theorists recognized the exploitation of wives' domestic labor, it was Marxist feminism that put wives and mothers at the forefront of its analysis of the gendered structure of capitalism. Wives and mothers are vital to capitalism, because their unpaid work in the home maintains bosses and workers and reproduces the next generation of bosses and workers (and their wives). Furthermore, if a bourgeois husband falls on hard times, his wife can do work in the home, such as dressmaking, to earn extra money, or can take a temporary or part-time job. And when a worker's wages fall below the level needed to feed his family, as it often does, his wife can go out to work for wages in a factory or shop or another person's home, or she can turn the home into a "cottage industry" and put everyone, sometimes including the children, to work. A gendered perspective thus blurs Marx's division of capitalists and workers and adds patriarchy to capitalism in analyzing the social position of women.

Work in the marketplace and work in the home are inextricably intertwined in a dual system of capitalism and patriarchy. Because of women's low value in the workplace, few can support themselves and their children in capitalist economies, so marriage or a man's financial help is an economic necessity. A wife earns her husband's economic support by doing housework and taking care of their children. Her work in the home is not only necessary to the physical and emotional well-being of her husband and children, it is also vital to capitalist economies. Women's housework and child care make it possible for men to go to work and children to go to school, where they learn to take their future place in society—as workers, bosses, or the wives of workers or bosses. Mothers reproduce the social values of their class by passing them on to their children, teaching future bosses to be independent and take initiative and future workers and wives to be docile and obey orders. *Social reproduction,* teaching children how to be members of society, and the domestic work of maintaining a husband and children are significant, but invisible, parts of the economic process. Because a woman does it for love, not money, she is economically dependent on a husband or on government-provided welfare. Since her prime responsibility is to her family, she can be paid lower wages if she takes a job outside the home. Wives are the main part of a *reserve army of labor,* encouraged to work when the economy needs more workers, fired when unemployment rises. Marxist feminism argues that this exploitation of women's work, both in the home and in the marketplace, is the prime source of gender inequality.

Marxist feminist politics argued for two solutions to women's exploitation in capitalism: wages for housework and government subsidization of wives and children. Each of these solutions neglected to take racial ethnic differences into consideration. Before discussing the details of these remedies to capitalist exploitation of women, it is important to understand social class as part of a system of racial as well as gender inequality.

Theorizing Class as Racialized and Gendered

In Western countries, feminist critics have pointed out that early Marxist feminist theory failed to integrate racial inequalities into their analysis of gendered class inequalities. Joan Acker, a sociologist who has been writing on these issues for 30 years, formulated a theory of social class as gendered and racialized in her 2006 book, *Class Questions: Feminist Answers.* An excerpt from this book summarizes her theory.

Theorizing Racial and Gendered Class

Joan Acker

University of Oregon

The idea of racialized and gendered class practices is an alternative to conceptualizing race, class, and gender as intersecting or interlocking systems or structures. To say that class is racialized and gendered means that gender and racial/ethnic divisions, subordinations, and meanings are created as part of the material and ideological creation and recreation of class practices and relations. Class processes are

Reprinted from *Class Questions: Feminist Answers,* 50–53, 68–72. © 2006 Rowman and Littlefield Publishers, Inc. Reprinted by permission.

shaped by gendered and/or racialized practices and privileges, justified and explained within discourses that define gender and sexuality
in racial terms (Higginbotham 1992).

I distinguish between 1) class practices, 2) gendering and racializing
processes, and 3) effects of gendered and racialized class practices. Class
practices are all those activies that organize and control production and
distribution....Gendering and racializing processes shape class practices....The effects of gendered and racialized class practices are diverse
forms of inequality: gender and racial/ethnic segregation in employment, both hierarchical and horizontal, unequal distributions of power,
types of work, and monetary rewards. For example, employers in certain
restaurants and resorts hire only young, white, attractive women as wait-
resses or hostesses (Adkins 1995). These hiring practices are gendered
and racialized and result in a gender-, race-, and age-segregated work
force. Effects and their severity change over time, and vary within and
between localities and nations. People often see gender and race effects
as natural, just the way things are. The naturalization of inequalities then
influences subsequent gendering and racializing processes, as assumptions about what is natural shape perceptions and actions. That is, there
are reciprocal, or feedback, influences between effects and practices.
For example, secretaries in the nineteenth century were usually white
men. As businesses became more complex and larger, record keeping
tasks expanded and changed, particularly with the development of the
typewriter. Employers turned to relatively well-educated young white
women for a labor force that was less expensive and more available than
a male labor force. As the occupation expanded and became a segregated
white female job, the image of the secretary changed (Kessler-Harris
1982). That image and the division of labor it represented then became
part of selection and choice practices, essentially regendering and racializing those practices, and helping to maintain "secretary" as a highly
segregated and relatively low-wage occupation.

A focus on economic class inequalities constituted as gendered and
racialized does not explore all facets of race and gender. The historically and discursively established categories of class, race, and gender
stand for different avenues of entry into complex ongoing practices.
Each entryway directs us to particular facets of social relations, to particular practices. Class provides the entry point into complex webs of
relations in which capital is accumulated, inequalities are generated,
work is accomplished, and gendered and racialized people put together
ways of surviving. Class involves the production and distribution of
material and nonmaterial things, in which gender and race processes
shape class practices and their outcomes.

Analysis could also begin from the entry point of gender relations.
From such a beginning, attention would focus on practices involved
in, for example, human reproduction, sexuality, and family, as these
are implicated in and affected by divisions of labor, exclusions, and

inequalities of race and class. "Race relations" as an entry point directs the view to exclusions, inequalities, and separateness in many areas of social life based on racial/ethnic divides and difference within both class and gender. Such an elaboration would make explicit, but with different points of departure, the processes of mutual creation of race, class, gender, and perhaps also sexuality....Description and analysis of an actually existing issue, for example, abortion rights, welfare "reform," or corporate scandals, might begin from a particular starting point and then expand to look at how the issue is constituted and dealt with, using mutually constituting gender, class, and racial processes to comprehend the practices of oppression and power.

Although the concept of gendered and racialized class relations depicts class, gender, and race as inherently interconnected, these concepts also represent differences that may be lost to view in the effort to approach them as mutually constituted. One problem is that both gender and race stand for extremely diverse realities. "Gender" represents historically varying differences across class and racial/ethnic divides, as many have pointed out. Simplifying this complexity by talking about "gender" as a general term may mean that a white, middle-class woman is still the hidden referent. Race is similarly complicated. Different racial/ethnic groups have different histories and present conditions. Differences within groups also cut across class and gender lines. For many in the United States, "race" had been historically defined as black. African Americans are in different situations than other racial/ethnic groups in this white-dominated society. As Andrew Hacker (2003, 22) has said, "none of the presumptions of inferiority associated with Africa and slavery are imposed on these other ethnicities." Studies of whiteness (e.g., Frankenberg 1993) have begun to raise the consciousness of whites about their own race privileges. Yet, as with "gender," simplifying the complexity by talking about "race" may obscure the complexity behind the category.

An important difference between gender, race, and class as processes of inequality and exploitation is the degree to which they are defined as legitimate and enforced both formally and informally. In the contemporary United States, class relations are legitimate and regulated by laws, governing practices, regulations and rules, supervisory procedures, and union-management agreements that specify, support, and sometimes limit the power of employers to control workers and the organization of production. Class-based inequalities in monetary reward and in control over resources, power, and authority, and the actions and routine practices that continually recreate them, are accepted as natural and necessary for the ongoing functioning of the socioeconomic system.

In contrast, inequality and exploitation based on gender or race are not legitimated and regulated by law, although gender and race discrimination and inequality are, of course, institutionalized in other ways and widely practiced. At one time in the not too distant past, race- and gender-based exclusion and subordination were legitimate and were written into laws in the United States. A civil war, many years of struggle by African Americans culminating in the civil rights movement, and two mass women's movements extending over a century were necessary to remove these bases for discrimination and subordination from the laws of the land and to lay the basis for a decline in their legitimacy. Thus, at the beginning of the twenty-first century in the United States, class exploitation and inequity have far more legitimacy than gender- and race-based exploitation and inequity, which are illegal and defined as discrimination, although white privilege and male privilege are ubiquitous. The legitimacy of class is, at the present time, so self-evident that no one with any political or economic power, at least in the United States, discusses eliminating wage labor and mandating a communal and cooperative organization of production, although many at least claim to be in favor of eliminating gender and race inequality, discrimination, and segregation....

Theorizing Gendered and Racialized Class: A Preliminary Sketch

1. "Class" stands for practices and relations that provide differential access to and control over the means of provisioning and survival. This is a relational, rather than a categorical, view of class. For example, class practices take place in the ongoing relations between employers and employees, or in the ongoing relations between citizens/workers and the state. These relations include: 1) paid and unpaid production/reproduction practices; 2) distribution practices through wages, personal relations, the state, and financial institutions; and 3) practices in the workplace and the home that link and coordinate these sites.

2. These relations are gendered and racialized through a number of processes:
   - *Pursuing material interests.* Corporate leaders and their political allies, acting on their interests, make decisions that shape the availability and character of gendered and racialized jobs and distribution systems. Employers acting on their perceived economic interests often hire people from particular racial/gender groups: Seeking low wage costs they may hire white women, blacks, or Hispanics, or relocate jobs to other countries with low-wage women workers. Seeking stability in a white male workforce, they may hire only, or primarily, white males. Employers may change the gender of their workforce. The gender of the new workers then becomes identified with the job (Reskin and Roos 1990). Once particular jobs are gendered, racialized, and segregated, employers may have economic interests in maintaining segregation. Pursuing material

interests and making political compromises to protect those interests, as in the design of Social Security and unemployment insurance..., may gender and racialize state distribution relations. Managerial economic decisions that are apparently gender and race neutral can have gendering and racializing effects. Workers, too, pursuing their perceived economic interests may contribute to creating, maintaining, or changing gendered and racialized class practices. For example, in local places, some male workers resisted pay equity policies because they feared their own wages would be lowered to achieve equality with women's wages (Acker 1989).

- *Organizing work, constructing rules and unwritten expectations, on the implicitly male model of the worker* who is unencumbered with caring responsibilities and ready to devote his life to the job. This worker is also usually implicitly white. This model of the workplace and the worker, institutionalized as the way (gender-neutral) things just are, places women on the periphery, a bit out of place, even when they have no caring responsibilities. Of course, some men, particularly minority men, can also be out of place. This model also implicitly casts caring work as less important than paid work. Women must comply with the expectations of this model. If they are managers, they must "manage like a man" (Wacjman 1998)....

- *Constructing and using images, stereotypes, and ideologies about race and gender.* These constructions guide, justify, and legitimate gendered and racialized decisions, ways of organizing, and divisions of labor. Images of masculinity and femininity may be crucial in developing new occupations and even whole industries. For example, Karen Ashcraft and Dennis Mumby (2004) show that in the emerging airline industry, class, gender, and race were consciously used to create images of the professional (white male) pilot and the reliable company that customers could trust with their lives. The stewardess, as caring and attentive white female, was created in the same process. Class inequalities are often justified through gendered and racial images....

  For example, assumptions about bodily differences between women and men, or assumptions about differences in reliability and intelligence between whites and people not defined as white may underlie decisions. The assumption that men "naturally" have a talent with tools, or that women are "naturally" good with human relationships, caring relations in particular, often underlies the gender stereotyping of jobs and the assignment of women and men to different jobs.

- *Interacting in and outside paid workplaces on the basis of conscious or nonconscious gendered and racialized assumptions.* Gendered and racialized assumptions and interests influence and shape the ways in which people relate to each other and carry out the ordinary work of daily life. Men often prefer to interact with other men: Homosocial patterns of informal interaction may exclude women and consolidate images of the masculine as the normal worker or manager (Kanter 1977). Bodies are always present in face-to-face interactions; the gender and race of bodies influences the class-related outcomes of interaction. For example, having a black male body reduces the possibility of getting hired for certain jobs (Royster 2003; Hossfeld 1994)....

- *Constructing and adjusting identities as gendered and racialized.* Identity, as the sense of who one is and is not, where one fits, how one should function in social life, what is appropriate behavior, can be seen as a socially produced aspect of individual consciousness. Identities may be contradictory, fluid, changing with situation and experience. Particular employers, or the culture of particular work places, may require particular identities (Gottfried 2003). Identities are important in maintaining and/or changing patterns of domination and inequality. For example, seeing the self as the head of the household and the breadwinner provided a positive identity for many white working-class men, while helping them to adjust to their powerlessness as workers (Sennett and Cobb 1972). Such male identities also assumed the relative subordination of wives and their unpaid labor in the home. Changing identities may be embedded in social movements aimed at changing gendered and racialized class inequalities. For example, participation in the feminist movement changed the identities of many women from diverse racial/ethnic groups and these altered identities contributed to the strength of the movement that, in turn, had a significant impact on the situation of middle-class women in the gendered and racialized class processes in the United States....

3. The effects of gendered and racialized class practices are inequalities of power and money, segregation of jobs and occupations, and inequalities in access to education, housing, health care, and safe community environments. The effects of class practices support or sometimes undermine the gendered and racialized images and ideologies, feeding back into these processes. For example, high proportions of women in particular jobs tend to confirm the image that these jobs are gendered as female, particularly appropriate for women.

4. Gendered and racialized class practices and inequalities are historically produced in the development of capitalism, a process dominated and defined by white masculinity. These patterns have a gendered understructure in the ways in which production is organized and in the goals of production, aimed at profit and not at provisioning ordinary people. One manifestation of this way of organizing is that organizations claim nonresponsibility for human

and environmental reproduction. The vast power of capitalist organizations in a highly monetized society, along with their nonresponsibility, contributes to the devaluation of caring work and women
who do most of this work....

5. Organizations are a primary location of the ongoing creation of gendered and racialized class relations, locally, nationally, and globally.
Large organizations, in particular, can be conceptualized as inequality regimes, or ongoing practices and processes in which racialized
and gendered class relations are reproduced....

6. Class relations are not only at the point of production, in the wage
relation or the relations of unpaid work, in personal and welfare state
distributions, but are embedded in the extended global relations
that link the low-paid worker in a nursing home in the United States
to another low-paid worker manufacturing her uniform in southeast Asia, as both are linked to U.S. and Asian corporations.... In
summary, class practices and relations are gendered and racialized
historically and in contemporary social life in processes of inclusion,
exclusion, sorting, and segregation based on economic and cultural
interests, justified through beliefs and images of racial/ethnic masculinity and femininity, reproduced in interaction patterns and
through identity constructions.

References

Acker, Joan. 1989. *Doing Comparable Worth: Gender, Class and Pay Equity.*
Philadelphia: Temple University Press.

Adkins, Lisa. 1995. *Gendered Work.* Buckingham, U.K.: Open University Press.

Ashcraft, Karen Lee, and Dennis K. Mumby. 2004. *Reworking Gender: A Feminist
Communicology of Organization.* Thousand Oaks, CA: Sage.

Frankenberg, Ruth. 1993. *White Women, Race Matters: The Social Construction of
Whiteness.* Minneapolis: University of Minnesota Press.

Gottfried, Heidi. 2003. "Temp(t)ing Bodies: Shaping Gender at Work in Japan."
Sociology 37: 257–276.

Hacker, Andrew. 2003. *Two Nations: Black and White, Separate, Hostile, Unequal.* New
York: Scribner.

Higginbotham, Evelyn Brooks. 1992. "African-American Women's History and
the Metalanguage of Race." *Signs* 17: 251–274.

Hossfeld, Karen J. 1994. "Hiring Immigrant Women: Silicon Valley's 'Simple
Formula'." In Maxine Baca Zinn and Bonnie Thornton Dill, eds., *Women of
Color in U.S. Society.* Philadelphia: Temple University Press.

Kanter, Rosabeth Moss. 1977. *Men and Women of the Corporation.* New York:
Basic Books.

Kessler-Harris, Alice. 1982. *Out to Work: A History of Wage-Earning Women in the
United States.* New York: Oxford University Press.

Reskin, Barbara F. and Patricia A. Roos. 1990. *Job Queues, Gender Queues:
Explaining Women's Inroads into Male Occupations.* Philadelphia: Temple
University Press.

Royster, Deirdre A. 2003. *Race and the Invisible Hand: How White Networks Exclude Black Men from Blue-Collar Jobs.* Berkeley: University of California Press.

Sennett, Richard, and Jonathan Cobb. 1972. *Hidden Injuries of Class.* New York: Knopf.

Wajcman, Judy. 1998. *Managing Like a Man.* University Park: Pennsylvania State University Press.

Wages for Housework and Government Subsidization

Marxist feminism proposed at one time that all women should get paid for housework and child care; they should not do it for love alone. If wives were waged workers, they would be part of the gross national product and could get raises and vacations and sick leave. But there is a sense in which wives *are* paid for their work for the family; husbands supposedly are paid enough to maintain their families as well as themselves—they are supposed to get what is called a *family wage.* The problem is that when a husband "pays" his wife for work in the home, either directly or indirectly, she is an economic dependent with few financial resources. If her husband dies, she needs to rely on insurance and social security; in a divorce or separation, she needs a good lawyer to make sure she gets adequate financial support for herself and the children—a dangerous situation should her husband become a "dead beat dad." In more affluent families, husbands pay disadvantaged women to do the housework and child care. A wife can then take on the "job" of enhancing her husband's social status by engaging in charity and community work, entertaining, and appearing in public with him as a well-dressed and socially adept companion.

In a thriving economy, working-class women can get jobs to supplement the family income once the children are in school, but what about people living in areas where neither women nor men can get jobs? Since the men in their communities are equally poor, women do not have an economic advantage in marrying. They have to rely on government support—what we call "welfare." In the United States, government welfare benefits go only to poor women (after a means test), and so these benefits—and the women who receive them—are singled out as deviant and stigmatized. In many industrialized countries, there is government financial support for all mothers, and benefits are much more extensive than in the United States. The benefits include prenatal care, paid maternity leave, maternal and child health services, cash allowances each month for each child, free education through college (including books), and child care services. Every mother in Great Britain, Scandinavia, and other European countries, and Israel receives some or most of these benefits. These *welfare states* recognize that producing children is work and that mothers therefore deserve state support. Their governments do not distinguish among poor and middle-class or wealthy women, or among full-time employees, part-time workers, and full-time homemakers. These services make it possible for all women to be both mothers and economically independent people.

Such state benefits were the norm in the former communist countries, but feminists there soon recognized that this solution to gender inequality only substitutes economic dependence on the state for dependence on a husband. Women are even more responsible for child care, since the benefits are usually for the mother and rarely for the father. (Even when it is offered to them, few fathers take advantage of paid child-care leave.) Furthermore, when women take paid jobs, either they or other women still do the child care, as mothers in a "second shift," paid workers in the home or in a child-care facility, or helping out as unpaid "other mothers." The women who do paid domestic labor in people's homes are usually from disadvantaged social groups; under capitalism, their wages tend to be minimal, and they rarely get any sick leave or health insurance, but in socialist countries, they get what any other worker receives.

Caring for Pay

Jobs that call for nurturance and empathy, such as nursing and social work—emotion work—are typically women's jobs because these attributes are supposedly natural. Women do nursing and other caretaking as part of family work, but they also do it for pay. Even if they are trained professionals, this work pays less, because it is "doing what comes naturally" to women. In the following excerpt from "The Social Construction and Institutionalization of Gender and Race: An Integrative Framework," sociologist Evelyn Nakano Glenn, 2010 president of the American Sociological Association, describes the complexities of gender, class, and racial ethnic status among women doing reproductive labor in the home and in the public sphere and the consequences for citizenship.

Gender, Race, and Citizenship

Evelyn Nakano Glenn
Professor of Women's Studies, University of California, Berkeley

The Race and Gender Division of Private Reproductive Labor. From the late nineteenth century to the mid-twentieth century, poor and working-class women not only did reproductive labor in their own homes, they also performed it for middle-class families. The division between White women and women of color grew in the latter half of the nineteenth century, when the demand for household help and the number of women employed as servants expanded rapidly (Chaplin 1978). Rising standards of cleanliness, larger and more ornately furnished homes, the sentimentalization of the home as a "haven in a heartless world," and the new emphasis on childhood and mother's role in nurturing children all served to enlarge middle-class women's responsibilities for reproduction at a time when technology had done little to reduce the sheer physical drudgery of housework (Cowan 1983; Degler 1980; Strasser 1982).

By all accounts, middle-class women did not challenge the gender-based division of labor or the enlargement of their reproductive responsibilities. To the contrary, as readers and writers of literature, and as members and leaders of clubs, charitable organizations, associations, reform movements, religious revivals, and the cause of abolition, they helped to elaborate and refine the domestic code (Epstein 1981; Ryan 1981). Instead of questioning the inequitable gender division of labor, they sought to slough off the burdensome tasks onto more oppressed groups of women (see Kaplan 1987).

In the United States, the particular groups hired for private reproductive work varied by region. In the Northeast, European immigrant women, especially Irish, were the primary servant class. In regions with a substantial racial minority population, the servant caste consisted almost exclusively of women of color. In the early years of the twentieth century, 90 percent of non-agriculturally employed Black women in the South were servants or laundresses, constituting more than 80 percent of female servants (Katzman 1978:55). In cities of the Southwest, such as El Paso and Denver, where the main division was between Anglos and Mexicans, approximately half of all employed Mexican women were domestic or laundry workers (Deutsch 1987; Garcia 1981). In the San Francisco Bay Area and in Honolulu, where there were substantial numbers of Asian immigrants, a quarter to half of all employed Japanese women were private household workers (Glenn 1986; Lind 1951, table 1:74).

Women of color shouldered not only the burdens of household maintenance, but also those of family nurturing for White middle-class women. They did both the dirty, heavy manual labor of cleaning and laundering and the emotional work of caring for children. By performing the dirty work and time-consuming tasks, they freed their mistresses for supervisory tasks, for leisure and cultural activities, or, more rarely during this period, for careers. Ironically, then, many White women were able to fulfill White society's expectation of feminine domesticity only through the domestic labor of women of color.

For the domestic worker, the other side of doing reproductive labor for White families was not being able to perform reproductive labor for their own families. Unlike European immigrant domestics, who were mainly single young women, racial ethnic servants were usually wives and mothers (Stigler 1946; Watson 1937). Yet the code that sanctified

White women's domesticity did not extend to them. In many cases, servants had to leave their own children in the care of relatives in order to "mother" their employers' children. A 6½-day workweek was typical. A Black children's nurse reported in 1912 that she worked 14 to 16 hours a day caring for her mistress' four children. Describing her existence as a "treadmill life," she said she was allowed to go home

only once in every two weeks, every other Sunday afternoon–even then I'm not permitted to stay all night. I see my own children only when they happen to see me on the streets when I am out with the children [of her mistress], or when my children come to the "yard" to see me, which isn't often, because my white folks don't like to see their servants' children hanging around their premises. (quoted in Katzman 1982:179)

The dominant group ideology naturalized the mistress-servant relationship by portraying women of color as particularly suited for service. These racialized gender constructions ranged from the view of African American and Mexican American women as incapable of governing their own lives and requiring White supervision to the view of Asian women as naturally subservient and accustomed to a low standard of living. Although racial stereotypes undoubtedly preceded their entry into domestic work, household workers were also induced to enact the role of race-gender inferiors in daily interactions with employers. Domestic workers interviewed by Rollins (1985) and Romero (1992) described a variety of rituals that affirmed their subordination and dependence; for example, employers addressed the household workers by their first names and required them to enter by the back door, eat in the kitchen, wear uniforms, and accept with gratitude "gifts" of discarded clothing and leftover food.

The lack of respect for racial ethnic women's family roles stood in marked contrast to the situation of White middle-class women in the late nineteenth and early twentieth centuries, when the cult of domesticity defined White womanhood primarily in terms of wifehood and motherhood. While the domestic code constrained White women, it placed racial ethnic women in an untenable position. Forced to work outside the home, they were considered deviant according to the dominant gender ideology. On the one hand, they were denied the buffer of a protected private sphere; on the other, they were judged deficient as wives and mothers compared with White middle-class women who could devote themselves to domesticity full-time (Pascoe 1990). Women of color had to construct their own definitions of self-worth and womanhood outside the standards of the dominant culture. Their efforts to maintain kin ties, organize family celebrations, cook traditional foods, and keep households together were crucial to the survival of ethnic communities.

The Race and Gender Construction of Public Reproductive Labor. Due to the expansion of capital into new areas for profit making, the fragmentation of families and breakdown of extended kin and community ties, and the squeeze on women's time as they moved into the labor market, the post–World War II era saw the expansion of commodified services to replace the reproductive labor formerly performed in the home (Braverman 1974:276). Among the fastest-growing occupations in the economy in the 1980s and 1990s were lower-level service jobs in health care, food service, and personal services (U.S. Department of Labor 1993). Women constitute the main labor force in these occupations. Within this new realm of "public reproductive labor," we find a clear race-gender division of labor. Women of color are disproportionately assigned to do the dirty work, as nurse's aides in hospitals, kitchen workers in restaurants and cafeterias, maids in hotels, and cleaners in office buildings. In these same institutional settings, White women are disproportionately employed as supervisors, professionals, and administrative support staff. This division parallels the earlier division between the domestic servant and the housewife. And just as in the household, dirty work is considered menial and unskilled, and the women who do it are too; moreover, White women benefit by being able to do higher-level work.

With the shift of reproductive labor from the household to market, face-to-face race and gender hierarchies have been replaced by structural hierarchies. In institutional settings, race and gender stratification is built into organizational structures, including lines of authority, job descriptions, rules, and spatial and temporal segregation. Distance between higher and lower orders is ensured by structural segregation. Much routine service work is organized to be out of sight. It takes place behind institutional walls, where outsiders rarely penetrate (nursing homes, chronic care facilities), in back rooms (restaurant kitchens), or at night or other times when occupants are gone (office buildings and hotels). Although workers may appreciate this time and space segregation, which allows them some autonomy and freedom from demeaning interactions, it also makes them and their work invisible. In this situation, more privileged women do not have to acknowledge the workers or confront any contradiction between shared womanhood and inequality by race and class.

Implications. Both historically and in the contemporary United States, the racial construction of gendered labor has created divisions between White and racial ethnic women that go beyond differences in experience and standpoint. Their situations have been interdependent: The higher status and living standards of White women have depended on the subordination and lower standards of living of women of color. Moreover, White women have been able to meet more closely the hegemonic standards of womanhood because of the devaluation of the womanhood of racial ethnic women. This analysis suggests that if these special forms of exploitation were to cease, White women as well as men would give up certain privileges and benefits. Thus, social policies to improve the lot of racial ethnic women may entail loss of privilege or status for White women and may therefore engender resistance from them as well as from men.

The Race and Gender Construction of Citizenship

The second institutional domain that often has been looked at as either gendered or raced, but rarely as both, is the state. Because the topic of the state is vast, I will focus this discussion on one aspect, namely, the construction of who is a citizen and what rights and responsibilities go with that status.

Gender and Citizenship. The denial of first-class citizenship has been a central issue for feminist political theorists. Pateman (1988, 1989), Young (1989), and Okin (1979) have analyzed the conception of citizenship in Hobbes, Locke, Rousseau, and other canonical writings and have found that the "universal citizen" defined in these writings is male. Pateman (1988, 1989), for example, traces women's exclusion to the construction of a public/private binary and other oppositions in liberal political thought. The "public" and the "private" are constructed in opposition; the public is the realm of citizenship, rights, and generality, whereas sexuality, feeling, and specificity—and women—are relegated to the private. Citizenship thus is defined in opposition to womanhood.

Recently there has been a growing interest in social citizenship, a key concept in analyses of the modern welfare state (Marshall 1950). Some feminist critics have characterized the state as patriarchal in its provision of welfare, in that it both supports the male-headed household and exerts authority over women by regulating their conduct (e.g., Abramovitz 1996; Sapiro 1986). Other critics have pointed out that from the 1890s on, the United States institutionalized a two-tiered system of social rights (e.g., Gordon 1994; Michel 1996; Nelson 1990). The upper level, consisting of entitlements such as unemployment benefits, old-age insurance, and disability payments, disproportionately goes to men by virtue of their record of regular employment; the lower level, consisting of various forms of stigmatized "welfare," such as AFDC, is what women disproportionately are forced to turn to because of need.

Race and Citizenship. Historians and sociologists looking at race and citizenship have generally been animated by Myrdal's *An American Dilemma* (1944), the disjunction between a professed belief in equal rights existing alongside the denial of fundamental civil and political rights to major segments of the population. In his monumental study, *We the People and Others,* Ringer (1983) argues that this exclusion was not a "flaw," but an inherent feature of the American political system from its very inception. According to Ringer, the United States established a dual legal political system based on colonialist principles. The "people's domain," made up of those considered full members of the national community, "among whom principles of equality and democracy might prevail despite unequal distribution of wealth, power and privilege," exists alongside a second level of those excluded from the national community, "who become the objects of control and exploitation and who are subject to the repressive powers of the state without the basic protection of citizenship" (Ringer and Lawless 1989:86).

Horsman (1981) notes that republican discourse tied the idea of Whiteness to notions of independence and self-control necessary for self-governance. This conception emerged in concert with European and Anglo-American conquest and colonization of non-Western societies. Understanding non-European others as dependent and lacking the capacity for self-governance rationalized the extermination and forced removal of Native Americans, the enslavement of Blacks, and the takeover of land from Mexicans in the Southwest. Smith (1988) notes, "From the revolution era on, many American leaders deliberately promoted the popular notion that Americans had a distinctive character, born of their freedom-loving Anglo-Saxon ancestors and heightened by the favorable conditions of the new world," that "set them above Blacks and truly Native Americans, and later Mexicans, Chinese, Filipinos, and others who were labeled unfit for self-government" (233).

Citizenship as Raced and Gendered. The problem with looking at citizenship as only gendered or only raced is the familiar one: Women of color fall through the cracks. According to existing accounts, White women were not accorded full adult citizenship by dint of having their identities subsumed by their husbands and fathers. White women were "virtual citizens" because men were assumed to represent their wives' and children's interests along with their own. Men of color were deemed noncitizens by virtue of their being "unfree labor," lacking the cultural traits of "freedom," and being "servile." The question remains: Where do women of color fit? In what follows, I attempt to synthesize the largely separate literatures on gendered citizenship and raced citizenship to trace the racialized gender construction of American citizenship. Although necessarily sketchy, this account may suggest some directions for future analyses.

At its most general level, *citizenship* refers to the status of being a full member of the community in which one lives (Hall and Held 1989). Citizenship in Western societies always has had a dual aspect as a system of equality and as a major axis of inequality. On the one hand, citizenship is defined as a universal status in which all who are included have identical rights and responsibilities, irrespective of their individual characteristics. This conception emerged out of the political and intellectual revolutions of the seventeenth and eighteenth centuries, as the older concept of society organized as a hierarchy of status, expressed by differential rights, gave way to the notion of a political order established through social contract. The concept of social contract implied free and equal status among those party to it. On the other hand, the process of defining membership and rights of citizenship entailed drawing boundaries that created "noncitizens." Rhetorically, the citizen was defined and gained meaning through its contrast with the "noncitizen" as one who lacked the essential qualities of a citizen. Materially, the autonomy and freedom of the citizen were made possible by the often involuntary labor of noncitizen wives, slaves, children, servants, and employees....

References

Abramovitz, Mimi. 1996. *Regulating the Lives of Women*. Rev ed. Boston: South End.

Braverman, Harry L. 1974. *Labor and Monopoly Capital*. New York: Monthly Review Press.

Chaplin, David. 1978. "Domestic Service and Industrialization." *Comparative Studies in Sociology* 1:97–127.

Cowan, Ruth Schwartz. 1983. *More Work for Mother*. New York: Basic Books.

Degler, Carl. 1980. *At Odds: Woman and the American Family from the Revolution to the Present*. New York: Oxford University Press.

Deutsch, Sarah. 1987. *No Separate Refuge: Culture, Class and Gender on an Anglo-Hispanic Frontier in the American Southwest, 1880–1920*. New York: Oxford University Press.

Epstein, Barbara. 1981. *The Politics of Domesticity: Women, Evangelism and Temperance in Nineteenth-Century America*. Middletown, CT: Wesleyan University Press.

Garcia, Mario. 1981. *Desert Immigrants: The Mexicans of El Paso, 1880–1920*. New Haven, CT: Yale University Press.

Glenn, Evelyn Nakano. 1986. *Issei, Nisei, Warbride: Three Generations of Japanese American Women in Domestic Service*. Philadelphia: Temple University Press.

Gordon, Linda. 1994. *Pitied but Not Entitled: Single Mothers and the History of Welfare 1890–1935*. New York: Free Press.

Hall, Stuart, and David Held. 1989. "Citizens and Citizenship." In Stuart Hall and Jacques Martin, eds., *New Times*. London: Lawrence & Wishart.

Horsman, Reginald. 1981. *Race and Manifest Destiny*. Cambridge, MA: Harvard University Press.

Kaplan, Elaine Bell. 1987. "'I Don't Do No Windows': Competition between the Domestic Worker and the Housewife." In Valerie Minor and Helen E. Longino, eds., *Competition: A Feminist Taboo?*. New York: Feminist Press.

Katzman, David. 1978. *Seven Days a Week: Women and Domestic Service in Industrializing America*. New York: Oxford University Press.

Lind, Andrew W. 1951. "The Changing Position of Domestic Service in Hawaii." *Social Process in Hawaii* 15:71–87.

Marshall, T. H. 1950. *Citizenship and Social Class and Other Essays*. Cambridge: Cambridge University Press.

Michel, Sonya. 1996. "A Tale of Two States." Presented at the Women's Studies Colloquium, University of California, Berkeley.

Myrdal, Gunnar. 1944. *An American Dilemma: The Negro Problem and Modern Democracy*. With R. Sterner and A. Rose. New York: Harper & Row.

Nelson, Barbara. 1990. "The Origins of the Two-Channel Welfare State: Workman's Compensation and Mothers' Aid." In Linda Gordon, ed., *Women, the State and Welfare.* Madison: University of Wisconsin Press.

Okin, Susan. 1979. *Women in Western Political Thought.* Princeton, NJ: Princeton University Press.

Pascoe, Peggy. 1990. *Relations of Rescue.* New York: Oxford University Press.

Pateman, Carole. 1988. *The Sexual Contract.* Cambridge: Polity.

————. 1989. *The Disorder of Women.* Stanford, CA: Stanford University Press.

Ringer, Benjamin B. 1983. *We the People and Others: Duality and America's Treatment of Its Racial Minorities.* New York: Tavistock.

Ringer, Benjamin B. and Elinor Lawless. 1989. *Race, Ethnicity and Society.* New York: Routledge.

Rollins, Judith. 1985. *Between Women: Domestics and Their Employers.* Philadelphia: Temple University Press.

Romero, Mary. 1992. *Maid in the U.S.A.* New York: Routledge.

Ryan, Mary P. 1981. *Cradle of the Middle Class: The Family in Oneida County, New York, 1790–1865.* Cambridge: Cambridge University Press.

Sapiro, Virginia. 1986. "The Gender Basis of American Social Policy." *Political Science Quarterly* 101:221–238.

Smith, Rogers M. 1988. "'One United People': Second-Class Female Citizenship and the American Quest for Community." *Yale Journal of Law and the Humanities* 1:229–293.

Stigler, George J. 1946. "Domestic Servants in the United States, 1900–1940." Occasional Paper 24, National Bureau of Economic Research, New York.

Strasser, Susan 1982. *Never Done: A History of American Housework.* New York: Pantheon.

U.S. Department of Labor, Bureau of Labor Statistics. 1993. *Occupational Outlook Quarterly* (Fall).

Watson, Amey. 1937. "Domestic Service." In *Encyclopedia of the Social Sciences.* New York: Macmillan.

Young, Iris Marion. 1989. "Polity and Group Difference: A Critique of the Ideal of Universal Citizenship." *Ethics* 99:250–274.

Gender Consciousness

The Marxist feminist critique of the family as the source of women's oppression argues that women's work as wives and mothers constructs their view of the world. Building on Marx's concept of *class consciousness,* which says that capitalists and members of the proletariat have conflicting interests and therefore an entirely different outlook on life, Marxist feminism explores the ways that a wife's work in the home shapes her consciousness to be different from that of her husband. His work is future-oriented, geared to making a product or a profit; hers is present-oriented, getting dinner on the table and the children dressed for school every day. His work is abstract, dealing with money or ideas or an object; her work is hands-on, directly involved with living people who have bodily and emotional needs. He is supposed to be cool and impersonal and rational on the job; her job as wife and mother demands sensitivity to interpersonal cues and an outpouring of affection. He works as an individual, even when he brings home his paycheck; she is first and foremost a family member.

In their ways of thinking and feeling, men and women are different, not because their brains are wired differently but because their life experiences give them diverse consciousnesses. The Marxist feminist insight into women's *class consciousness* was the basis of feminist standpoint theory and radical feminism's *consciousness raising*, a strategy for sharing personal experiences of oppression.

Women in China

China is an excellent case history in the application of Marxist feminist theory and politics to women's status. Marxist feminist theory holds that women's oppression is rooted in capitalism and private ownership; therefore, a state-owned economy should bring gender equality. In postrevolutionary Communist China, the struggle for women's emancipation from a subordinated class position has been supported by the government and government-sponsored organizations, such as the All China Women's Federation. In 1949, the constitution granted women equal rights in employment, education, social participation, and family life, and the government urged wives to "step out of the home" and take full-time jobs (Zhang 2005). Government policies ensured gender equality in education and in employment, although women and men worked in different occupations.

Unfortunately, the revolution did not bring women equality in the patriarchal family, especially in rural areas (Croll 1978; Johnson 1983; Stacey 1983). Women's roles changed, but gender expectations did not, and women continued to shoulder most of the responsibility for domestic labor, child care, and parental attention. If they challenged these expectations and the authority of their husband or mother-in-law, marital conflict ensued, as could be seen in the rising the divorce rate (Zhang 2005). The one-child policy, while freeing women from multiple pregnancies and years of child care, also had the contradictory effect of female infanticide and the abandonment of infant girls to orphanages.

In response to the growing evidence of women's continued oppression, the National Women's Federation sponsored a series of conferences to encourage women researchers and research on women in the 1980s (Wang 2005). Intense interest in women's studies (*funüxue*) led local Women's Federation cadres to form associations for research projects with outreach to universities. In 1990, the national Women's Studies Institute was formed. It publishes a journal, *Collection of Women's Studies* (*Funü yanjiu luncong*).

In the 1990s, Marxist theory became a weapon to defend the rights of women to full employment. With rising unemployment at a time of economic restructuring and increasing privatization, some economists (mostly men) argued that as a surplus reserve army of labor, women workers were expendable and should return home. The Women's Federation invoked, in studies and public debates, the Marxist contention that women must be economically independent to be equal, and they succeeded in influencing government policy (Wang 2005). A proposal to reduce women's employment levels was vetoed by the premier. On International Women's Day, March 8, 1990, the general secretary of the Communist Party gave a public speech drafted by the Women's Federation entitled "The Entire Party and the Entire Society Should Establish the Marxist Theory of Women." At the same time, Chinese feminists were getting introduced to critical theories of gender and women's interests through international conferences held in China, and they began to question and redefine the Marxist theory of women.

Critique

Marxist feminism has been the foundation of an influential economic theory of gender inequality that links the gendered division of labor in the family and in the workplace. Marxist feminism shows that women are locked into a condition of lesser economic resources whether they are wives of workers or workers themselves. If they marry economically successful men, they become dependents, and if they marry poor men or do not marry at all, they and their children can starve. The welfare-state solution—benefits to all mothers—is rooted in this analysis. There is, however, a negative side to state payments for child care (the equivalent of wages for housework); they are important in giving mothers independent economic resources, but they can also keep women out of the paid marketplace or encourage part-time work or work at low-paying jobs. These policies thus have the latent function of keeping women a reserve army of cheap labor in capitalist, state-owned, and welfare-state economies.

Women's economic inequality in the family division of labor has been somewhat redressed in countries that give all mothers paid leave before and after the birth of a child and that provide affordable child care. But that solution puts the burden of children totally on the mother and encourages men to opt out of family responsibilities altogether. To counteract that trend, feminists in the government of Sweden allocated a certain portion of paid child-care leave to fathers specifically.

Women in the former communist countries had what Marxist feminism in capitalist economies always wanted for women—full-time jobs with state-supported maternity leave and child-care services. But as Marxist feminists recognize, the state can be as paternalistic as any husband. They argue that male-dominated government policies put the state's interests before those of women. When the economy needs workers, the state pays for child-care leave; with a downturn in the economy, the state reduces the benefits. Similarly, when the state needs women to have more children, it cuts back on availability of abortions and contraceptive services. Thus, the Marxist feminist solution to women's economic inequality—full-time jobs and state-provided maternal and child welfare benefits—does not change women's status as primarily wives and mothers and men's status as the primary breadwinners. The gendered social order has been reformed but not significantly changed.

Summary

Marxist feminist theory emphasizes the economic and psychological differences between women and men, and men's power over women that emerges from their different statuses in the gendered division of labor. Marxist feminist theory is based on the division between work in the family (primarily women's work) and work in paid production (primarily men's work). Women are exploited because their work in the home is not recognized as work, but as care and nurturance done for love. The contribution of this work to the maintenance of the husband-worker or to the accumulation of the wealth of the husband-boss is invisible.

In state economies that provide maternal and child-care benefits, a woman with children is better off materially, but she is not economically independent. Instead of the private patriarchy of economic dependence on a husband, women are subject to the public patriarchy of a paternalistic state, which is more interested in using women as paid and unpaid workers and as child producers than in furthering gender equality in the home or in the workplace.

In all industrial economies, women and men have a different class consciousness because they do different work. Women have prime responsibility for child care, even though they may work full time outside the home. Thus, they live a significant part of their lives in a world of reciprocity and cooperation, personal responsibility and sharing, physical contact and affection, in contrast to the impersonal and abstract world of industrial production, the world of men's work. Men's work in the marketplace is rewarded according to time spent or product made. Women's work in the home is neverending; rewards depend on personalized standards, and others come first. It is emotional as well as intellectual and physical labor. Just as the economic positions of capitalists and the proletariat shape their class consciousness, women's daily material and emotional labor differentiates their consciousness from that of men.

A woman's class position, like that of a member of a disadvantaged racial ethnic group, is a mixed status—high in some respects, low in others. A single woman's occupation and income level are devalued by her gender. A married woman's class status is defined by her husband's occupation, income, and education. She may have a college education and he may not, but it is his social class that counts for the family. He may be a boss or an employee; in class terms, she is his subordinate in the home since he is considered the chief breadwinner. His salary is a "family wage," implicitly paid as well to his wife for her work in home and in the care of their children. But she may hire a woman to clean the house and another to care for her children. In that sense, she is an employer, in the "boss" class, especially if it is her income that goes to pay their salaries. If she is not employed, and her husband's income pays for the household help she has hired and directs, who is the boss?

Marxist feminism is important for making the invisible domestic work of women visible and for challenging its devaluation because it is not part of the monetary economy. While Marxism is a critique of capitalism, Marxist feminist analysis of the crucial contribution of women's domestic work applies to socialist and communist countries, too. In welfare states, women may garner generous children's benefits, but in turn, they provide the child care. In communist countries, women have been full-time paid workers and the primary domestic workers as well. Marxist feminism recognized the worth of women and their gender consciousness, but the remedies, wages for housework, subsidization for child care, or full-time jobs—do not go far to challenge the gendered social order and its division of labor. Conditions for women improve in welfare states or under state ownership of the means of production, but women's social status compared to men does not change.

SUGGESTED READINGS IN MARXIST FEMINISM

Acker, Joan. 1988. "Class, Gender, and the Relations of Distribution." *Signs* 13:473–497.

———. 1989. *Doing Comparable Worth: Gender, Class, and Pay Equity*. Philadelphia: Temple University Press.

———. 1999. "Rewriting Class, Race, and Gender: Problems in Feminist Rethinking." In Myra Marx Ferree, Judith Lorber, and Beth B. Hess, eds., *Revisioning Gender*. Thousand Oaks, CA: Sage.

———. 2006. *Class Questions: Feminist Answers*. Lanham, MD: Rowman & Littlefield/ AltaMira.

Bannerji, Himani. 1995. *Thinking Through: Essays on Feminism, Marxism, and Anti-Racism*. Toronto: Women's Press.

Barrett, Michèle. 1988. *Women's Oppression Today: The Marxist/Feminist Encounter*. Rev. ed. London: Verso.

Brenner, Johanna. 2000. *Women and the Politics of Class*. New York: Monthly Review Press.

Collins, Jane L., and Martha E. Gimenez, eds. 1990. *Work Without Wages: Comparative Studies of Domestic Labor and Self-Employment*. Albany: State University of New York Press.

Coontz, Stephanie, and Peta Henderson. 1986. *Women's Work, Men's Property: The Origins of Gender and Class*. London: Verso.

Eisenstein, Hester, ed. 2004. "Gender and Globalization: Marxist-Feminist Perspectives." Special section, *Socialism and Democracy*, 18, No. 1 (Winter/Spring).

———. 2006. "'Scouting Parties and Bold Detachments': Toward a Post-Capitalist Feminism." *Women's Studies Quarterly* 34:40–62.

Funk, Nanette, and Magda Mueller, eds. 1993. *Gender Politics and Post-Communism: Reflections from Eastern Europe and the Former Soviet Union*. New York: Routledge.

Glazer, Nona Y. 1993. *Women's Paid and Unpaid Labor: The Work Transfer in Retailing and Health Care*. Philadelphia: Temple University Press.

Glenn, Evelyn Nakano. 1992. "From Servitude to Service Work: Historical Continuities in the Racial Division of Paid Reproductive Labor." *Signs* 18:10–43.

Glenn, Evelyn Nakano. 1999. "The Social Construction and Institutionalization of Gender and Race: An Integrative Framework." In Myra Marx Ferree, Judith Lorber, and Beth B. Hess, eds., *Revisioning Gender*. Thousand Oaks, CA: Sage.

Hartsock, Nancy C. M. 1983. *Money, Sex, and Power: Toward a Feminist Historical Materialism*. New York: Longman.

Hennessy, Rosemary. 1993. *Materialist Feminism and the Politics of Discourse*. London: Routledge.

Holter, Harriet, ed. 1984. *Patriarchy in a Welfare Society*. Oslo, Norway: Universitetsforlaget.

Milkman, Ruth. 1987. *Gender at Work*. Urbana: University of Illinois Press.

Redclift, Nanneke, and Enzo Mingione, eds. 1985. *Beyond Employment: Household, Gender and Subsistence*. Oxford: Basil Blackwell.

Rueschemeyer, Marilyn, ed. 1994. *Women in the Politics of Postcommunist Eastern Europe*. Armonk, NY: M. E. Sharpe.

Sainsbury, Diane, ed. 1994. *Gendering Welfare States*. Thousand Oaks, CA: Sage.

Sargent, Lydia, ed. 1981. *Women and Revolution: A Discussion of the Unhappy Marriage of Marxism and Feminism*. Boston: South End Press.

Sayers, Janet, Mary Evans, and Nanneke Redclift, eds. 1987. *Engels Revisited: New Feminist Essays*. London: Tavistock.

Sokoloff, Natalie J. 1980. *Between Money and Love: The Dialectics of Women's Home and Market Work*. New York: Praeger.

Tax, Meredith. 1980. *The Rising of the Women: Feminist Solidarity and Class Conflict, 1880–1917*. New York: Monthly Review Press.

Walby, Sylvia. 1986. *Patriarchy at Work: Patriarchal and Capitalist Relations in Employment*. Minneapolis: University of Minnesota Press.

———. 1990. *Theorizing Patriarchy*. Oxford: Basil Blackwell.

Weigand, Kate. 2001. *Red Feminism: American Communism and the Making of Women's Liberation*. Baltimore, MD: Johns Hopkins University Press.

China

Chow, Esther Ngan-ling, Naihua Zhang, and Jinling Wang. 2009. "Promising and Contested Fields: Advancing Women's Studies and Sociology of Women/Gender in Contemporary China." In Christine E. Bose and Minjeong Kim, eds., *Global Gender Research: Transnational Perspectives*. New York: Routledge.

Croll, Elisabeth. 1978. *Feminism and Socialism in China*. New York: Schocken.

Gilmartin, Christina K. 1995. *Engendering the Chinese Revolution*. Berkeley: University of California Press.

Gilmartin, Christina K., Gail Hershatter, Lisa Rofel, and Tyrene White, eds. 1994. *Engendering China: Women, Culture, and the State*. Cambridge: Harvard University Press.

Johnson, Kay Ann. 1983. *Women, the Family and Peasant Revolution in China*. Chicago: University of Chicago Press.

Judd, Ellen. 2002. *The Chinese Women's Movement: Between State and Market*. Stanford, CA: Stanford University Press.

Stacey, Judith. 1983. *Patriarchy and Socialist Revolution in China*. Berkeley: University of California Press.

Wang, Zheng. 2005. "Research on Women in Contemporary China." In Xinrong Zheng and Fanquin Du, eds. *Women's Studies in China: Mapping the Social, Economic and Policy Changes in Chinese Women's Lives*. Seoul, South Korea: Ewha Womans University Press.

Zhang, Lixi. 2005. "Tradition and Change: Patriarchal Cultural Policy of Gender Equality, Division of Labor and Marital Conflicts in Modern Chinese Families." In Xinrong Zheng and Fanquin Du, eds. *Women's Studies in China: Mapping the Social, Economic and Policy Changes in Chinese Women's Lives*. Seoul, South Korea: Ewha Womans University Press.

Zheng, Xinrong, and Fanquin Du, eds. 2005. *Women's Studies in China: Mapping the Social, Economic and Policy Changes in Chinese Women's Lives*. Seoul, South Korea: Ewha Womans University Press.

3

Socialist Feminism

SOURCES OF GENDER INEQUALITY

- Complex inequality—intersecting and differential patterns of racial ethnic, class, and gender economic disadvantage
- Double and triple oppression of women in racial ethnic groups that suffer from economic and cultural discrimination
- Unequal pay scales that devalue women's caring and service occupations and professions, such as nursing and teaching

POLITICS

- Increased economic opportunities for women and disadvantaged men
- Upgrading women's jobs, especially caring and service work
- Redistribution of responsibilities in the family, equal sharing of family work
- Government support for care work in the home
- Universal entitlements to education, health care, income support

CRITIQUE

- Uneven effects of gender, racial ethnic status, and social class within groups divides loyalty and undercuts unified political action
- Generalized theories of inequality sometimes lose a gender focus, weakening feminist politics
- Women's issues are less likely to be addressed in political action

CONTRIBUTIONS

- Making visible the combined effects of gender, class, and racial ethnic discrimination

- Concept of complex inequality to describe and analyze the patterns of economic, educational, and cultural disadvantage
- Focus on the unequal pay scales for women's and men's jobs
- Analysis of the costs of child care and other forms of domestic labor to women

During the 1980s, socialist feminism expanded the ideas of Marxist feminism. Socialist feminism argues that gender inequality is not just the result of women's oppression as an unpaid worker for the family and as a low-paid worker in the economy. There are broader injustices from the intertwined effects of gender and class, gender and racial ethnic status, and all three combined. Gender discrimination devalues the status and income of women's jobs. Women in groups disadvantaged by race, ethnicity, and immigrant status suffer double or triple discrimination, but the interests of the men of their groups are more likely to prevail in political conflicts. Women's interests, socialist feminism argues, are not represented in class, racial ethnic, or national politics. When they suffer the accumulation of disadvantaged racial ethnic, class, and gender disadvantages, women are second-class citizens, but their multiple identities may undercut a unified feminist politics.

Intersectionality and Complex Inequality

Socialist feminism sees racial ethnic, gender, and class stratification as overlapping parts of a system of privilege and disadvantage. Each system is intertwined with the others in historically and regionally specific *complex inequalities*. Although the term *intersectionality* was not used widely until the 1990s, the concept of interlocked effects is an important contribution of socialist feminism. Social class, gender, and racial ethnic membership cannot be separated from each other, because each of those statuses affects others—a Black woman physician has a different status mix and social position than a physician who is a White woman or a Black man. Furthermore, privilege (and disadvantage) in any one status enhances or brings down the others. Wealth is a social good in its own right, but it can also be used to buy a good education for one's children and political candidacy for one's husband. It is less likely to foster a woman's political ambitions. The accumulation of advantages is not evenly distributed within groups; women and men of different racial ethnic groups vary in class, and class effects vary by gender and racial ethnic status. The result is *complex inequality*.

While gender, racial ethnic, and social class status are equally important in the theory of complex inequality, a gender analysis highlights its consequences for different groups of women. In the following excerpt from her book, *Complex Inequality: Gender, Class, and Race in the New Economy*, Leslie McCall, professor of sociology and women's studies, notes the complexities of inequality among women.

Gender and Complex Inequality

Leslie McCall

Rutgers University

In discussing the relevance of gender against a class-only approach, one has to begin by simply setting the record straight about current, and highly contradictory, perceptions of women workers and gender differences in the economy. Descriptive trends in gender inequality are quite distinct from trends in other forms of inequality and consequently are frequently misunderstood. While the 1980s brought increasing inequality within as well as between racial groups, gender inequality declined more in the 1980s than in any other decade of the twentieth century. At first, the decrease in gender inequality—the only form of inequality to decline—and the heightened visibility of managerial and professional women served to marginalize the interests of most working women and amplify the plight of working-class men, thus spawning the "angry white male" backlash and calls for class-based affirmative action. What lay below the surface of this polarizing rhetoric, however, was the fact that women were silently increasing their hours at work—even though their wages were not necessarily climbing—because their paychecks were becoming increasingly central to family survival. The contribution to family income by working mothers and wives was actually staving off declines in real median family income. And, unlike the 1930s, working women typically were not derided for stealing jobs from men (Milkman 1987). What had changed since then was the perception that women do indeed have a right to work, and indeed must work, and as a whole have made tremendous economic progress without much fanfare policy-wise.

Despite a lingering backlash against elite women, this perception of women's deserved and necessary economic progress is, I think, widely held and generally to be applauded. But what concerns me are the implications of the fact that this perception differs dramatically from perceptions of economic progress among minority racial groups. In the latter case, it is common to recognize the existence of a successful middle class within subordinate racial groups without assuming that the middle-class status of some members represents the social status of the entire group. In other words, the rise of the black middle class and the rise in inequality among blacks are each well-known and well-studied phenomena. In contrast, there is as yet little recognition of growing stratification among women.[a] Thus not only is gender

Reprinted from *Complex Inequality: Gender, Class, and Race in the New Economy*, 188–192. Copyright © 2001 by Routledge. Reprinted by permission.

inequality considered less pressing because of women's overall economic progress, but the problem of increasing class inequality among women is not on anyone's radar screen. If our goal is to diagnose and combat the new inequality, this rendering of women's economic experience and gender differences more generally is problematic for several reasons.

First, growing similarities between men and women mean, paradoxically, that a gendered analysis of the economy is perhaps more relevant now than ever. The job structure no longer privileges male jobs to the same extent it once did, particularly among the less-educated, and the working class has become increasingly feminized and majority female in service, clerical, and sales jobs (Clement and Myles 1994). This means that visions of reducing social inequality for the working class must take upgrading of women's jobs as seriously as the upgrading of men's jobs, for both men's and women's sake. Unions have increasingly recognized this and have worked in the services to organize not only women but a sector that is growing fast for both men and women (Cobble 1993; Kelley 1997). Similarly, in Europe, although policies aimed at enhancing the rights of workers in nonstandard jobs are undertaken in the name of gender equity, such policies are also meant to stave off the consequences of increasing insecurity for all workers (Ostner and Lewis 1995). But... if nonstandard jobs cannot be improved on the grounds of gender equity, other strategies should certainly be pursued. Paradoxically, then, even though empirically some gender barriers are clearly breaking down, a gendered analysis is needed because it is the most developed analysis of "new" forms of contingent and service employment. Those who have been concerned with gender inequality have been the most likely to recognize the strategic importance of certain kinds of "new" employment arrangements that have long been the domain of women.

Second, even though women and men are becoming more similar, gender remains important because certain remaining gender inequalities are still central to the debate on the causes of and remedies to the new inequality. The unintended effect of declining gender inequality—and the casting of women as winners against men as losers in the new economy—has been to make gender inequality appear irrelevant to policies advocated to counteract inequality. To take the most prominent example, the discussion of technology's role in causing and potentially solving the problem of inequality has had little mention of gender issues (Piore and Sabel 1984; Levy and Murnane 1992; Harrison 1994; Murnane and Levy 1996). When gender inequality itself appears to be a problem solved, it is absent from considerations of a new technological future invested with the power to level the playing field as long as everyone is properly schooled in the technological or information sciences. The perceived victims of restructuring, young non-college-educated men, are the presumed beneficiaries of a bright new technological order, without regard to the potential of reinstating gender and racial hierarchies (Jenson 1989). My research provides clear empirical evidence of greater gender and racial inequality in high-technology regions, especially high-technology manufacturing areas. While reindustrialization efforts involving technological transformations are to be applauded for delivering a new sense of hope to devastated communities, these efforts must simultaneously be construed as investments in gender and racial inequality. Economic policies must therefore be understood as organizers of multiple, and at times competing, dimensions of social inequality, especially when the implicit focus is on uplifting only particular groups of workers.

Finally, we need a new role for gender and attention to gender differences in order to distinguish between structures of inequality within gender groups. Attention to gender differences of this kind forces us to acknowledge that the sources of growing inequality among women may be different from those among men....Flexible and insecure economic conditions stemming from high rates of joblessness, casualization, and immigration are associated with high local levels of skills-based wage inequality for women but, for the most part, not for men. And postindustrial service economies are more likely to exhibit higher college wage gaps for men but not for women. Moreover, contrary to the economists' emphasis on technology, labor markets specializing in high-technology industries are not as strong as insecure employment conditions at explaining regional pockets of inequality.

Since the sources of stratification do vary by gender, inequality among women is actually higher than it is among men when the part-time labor force is counted, and women comprise nearly half the working population, addressing the new social inequality with only men in mind will fail to make significant headway in reversing the new inequality. Given these gender differences, the question of whether to target based on race or gender or to universalize based on class, a de facto form of targeting, misses the more strategic question of where to target and where to universalize. Although inequality is rising among blacks, Latinos, and women alike, this does not necessarily imply that the reasons are the same or that the industries or regions that are less unequal for one group are less unequal for other groups.[b]

The discussion of inequality must therefore be expanded from one revolving around a unitary term—the new inequality—to one involving an open question about the overlapping and conflicting manifestations of gender, race, and class inequality. This has important implications for the study of inequality but also for related issues, such as poverty, economic development, and education. For example, while I have focused on inequality as an outcome in this book, researchers often use family income inequality as an explanation of high poverty rates and adverse health effects. In fact, relocation services have been advocated as a way to connect the unemployed to labor markets that are growing, high-waged, and less unequal (Skocpol 1991; Weir 1992). Finally, it is common for different economic development strategies to be linked to their propensity to reduce or raise inequality. All these approaches rely on a single register of inequality and consequently have the potential to misrepresent the "opportunity structure" of regional economies which may offer economic benefits to some groups but not to others.

I have tried to expose only some of the inadequacies of a single, class-centered approach to the new social inequality through an analysis of gender inequality, inequality among women, and racial inequality. Framing the discussion in this way is a response to the resurgence of class-denominated thinking about matters of recognition and redistribution, but I could have just as easily reversed the tables and challenged feminists who prominently feature gender distinctions....My argument in either case is that the conditions and sources of inequality and the solutions put forward to halt and reverse it are not one and the same for every dimension of inequality. If the sources of inequality were universal, we would expect high-inequality regions to reflect high inequality between all groups. But I find conflicting patterns of inequality and therefore competing visions of equality. My research and that of others leads me to conclude that the new social inequality is not woven from the same cloth, except in the most general and therefore most misleading sense of the phrase. Given these realities, understanding and addressing inequality through the universalizing category of class will not suffice....

In one configuration, gender might present the starkest divisions, while in another it might be race or class, or in yet another it might be some combination. The presence of configurations of inequality, empirically, means that the politics of any single dimension of inequality must be informed by the broader context of inequality and the economic conditions underlying it.

Notes

a. Marta Tienda (1995) makes an analogous point about Latina/os.
b. For example, the adverse effects of rustbelt deindustrialization on blacks and Puerto Ricans is often contrasted to the effects of sunbelt reindustrialization in low-wage manufacturing industries on Mexicans and Asians (Lamphere et al. 1993; Moore and Pinderhughes 1993; Morales and Bonilla 1993; Tienda 1995).

References

Clement, Wallace, and John Myles. 1994. *Relations of Ruling: Class and Gender in Postindustrial Societies*. Buffalo, NY: McGill-Queens University Press.
Cobble, Dorothy Sue, ed. 1993. *Women and Unions*. Ithaca, NY: ILR Press.
Harrison, Bennett. 1994. *Lean and Mean*. New York: Basic Books.
Jenson, Jane. 1989. "The Talents of Women, the Skills of Men: Flexible Specialization and Women." In S. Wood, ed., *The Transformation of Work*. Winchester, MA: Unwin Hyman.

Kelley, Robin D. G. 1997. "The New Urban Working Class and Organized Labor." *New Labor Forum* (fall): 6–18.

Lamphere, Louise, Patricia Zavella, Felipe Gonzales, and Peter Evans. 1993. *Sunbelt Working Mothers*. Ithaca, NY: Cornell University Press.

Levy, Frank, and Richard Murnane. 1992. "U.S. Earnings Levels and Earnings Inequality: A Review of Recent Trends and Proposed Explanations." *Journal of Economic Literature* 30:1333–1381.

Milkman, Ruth. 1987. "Women Workers and the Labor Movement in Hard Times: Comparing the 1930s with the 1980s." In L. Beneria and C. Stimpson, eds., *Women, Households, and the Economy*. New Brunswick, NJ: Rutgers University Press.

Moore, Joan, and Raquel Pinderhughes, eds. 1993. *In the Barrios: Latinos and the Underclass Debate*. New York: Russell Sage Foundation.

Morales, Rebecca, and Frank Bonilla, eds. 1993. *Latinos in a Changing U.S. Economy*. Thousand Oaks, CA: Sage Publications.

Murnane, Richard, and Frank Levy. 1996. *Teaching the New Basic Skills*. New York: Free Press.

Ostner, Ilona, and Jane Lewis. 1995. "Gender and the Evolution of European Social Policies." In S. Leibfried and P. Pierson, eds., *European Social Policy*. Washington, DC: Brookings Institution.

Piore, Michael, and Charles Sabel. 1984. *The Second Industrial Divide: Possibilities for Prosperity*. New York: Basic Books.

Skocpol, Theda. 1991. "Targeting within Universalism: Politically Viable Policies to Combat Poverty in the United States." In C. Jencks and P. Peterson, eds., *The Urban Underclass*. Washington, DC: Brookings Institution.

Tienda, Marta. 1995. "Latinos and the American Pie: Can Latinos Achieve Economic Parity?" *Hispanic Journal of Behavioral Sciences* 17: 403–429.

Weir, Margaret 1992. *Politics and Jobs*. Princeton, NJ: Princeton University Press.

Gender Injustice

The demands of family on women are an additional aspect of complex inequality, with material and social penalties. Women are embedded into families in ways that men are not. Even if a woman can hire domestic help and child care, as a mother and wife in Western societies, she alone is responsible for the emotional, social, and physical well-being of her family. Compared to men and childless women, mothers make less money, are more likely to be fired, achieve fewer positions of authority and prestige, and have much less chance to wield social power. Those who cut back on hours or leave the workplace are socially downgraded and lose marital bargaining power. Working-class single mothers may end up on welfare.

In modern industrialized societies, it is acceptable for the husband's job to take precedence over his family responsibilities, and for the wife's family responsibilities to take precedence over her job. It is not acceptable for the husband who wants to advance in his career to routinely reduce his regular paid work time, his overtime, or his work-based travel because he has family duties.

Conversely, the wife who does not cover for her family duties before taking on routine or unusual job responsibilities is considered neglectful, and though she may advance in her career, the micropolitics of the workplace may eventually stigmatize her. The asymmetry of the husband's continued prime responsibility for economic support of the family and the wife's continued prime responsibility for family work overlays other aspects of gender inequality.

Although everyone in a society benefits from good parenting, mothers bear an unequal burden. Many Western industrial countries absorb some of the costs of child-rearing with child allowances, subsidized day care, free health care, and paid parental leave. But even if the workplace is family-friendly and governments or employers provide financial benefits for children, mothers have an extra job. This job does not bring public social rewards or economic success, rather it diminishes both. It is a privatized, disadvantaged status in Western industrialized societies.

Family caretaking is work that takes time, energy, thought, and skill, and that incurs costs and benefits to unpaid caretakers, paid workers, family members, and to the whole social order. All adult men and women are "caring citizens"; women, however, do most of the hands-on family work. To make caring citizenship gender-equal, the adults in a household, men as well as women, have to share family work and be able to balance it with their work time, and there has to be government support for this care work.

In the following excerpt from *The Invisible Heart: Economics and Family Values*, Nancy Folbre, a former president of the International Association for Feminist Economists and an economist who explores the interface between economics and feminist theory, lays out how care must be planned and paid for by governments, so that the burden does not continue to fall only on individual women.

The Invisible Heart

Nancy Folbre

University of Massachusetts, Amherst

Social democracy is about public commitment to meeting citizens' basic needs for health, education, and social welfare. It still exists in the United States, despite the efforts that many conservatives have made to dismantle it. But the Scandinavian countries of Sweden and Norway, as well as some other European countries, such as France and Germany, are better examples. All these countries offer universal health care and provide a sturdy social safety net. Their child poverty rates—as well as their overall

Reprinted from *The Invisible Heart: Economics and Family Values*, 225–232. Copyright © 2001 by Nancy Folbre. Reprinted with permission from The New Press.

poverty rates—are significantly lower than those of the United States. Wealth and income are distributed more equally.

Radicals sometimes dismiss European social democracy as "capitalism with a smiley face." To me, it has always seemed like a good place to start, partly because it has immediate implications for the development of children's capabilities. But if we want to successfully extend social democracy we will need to tend to several serious problems, even beyond...its dependence on the nation-state. Among these problems is bureaucracy, the nameless, faceless labyrinth of rules and procedures in which centralized service delivery usually gets bogged down. Large government institutions behave like monopolies, because they are protected from any disciplinary response from the customers they serve. Their managers are directly accountable to superiors, but not to citizens. We need to create new, positive incentives for better performance and introduce more direct democratic governance.[a] We should be willing to spend the money it will take to monitor and improve the quality of public services.

A second problem relates to gender inequality. The early theorists of social democracy, including Swedish feminist Alva Myrdal, recognized that the state could make it easier for women to combine paid work with family responsibilities.[b] But they were far more eager to expand women's opportunities than to modify men's roles. It never occurred to them that a division of labor based on breadwinner dads and homemaker moms was inherently unequal. Indeed, many public pension systems remain explicitly based on the obsolete bread winner/ homemaker model.

Feminists have traditionally been divided in their attitudes toward family policies, and with good reason. Policies aimed to support family work have often been designed to keep women in the home—giving mothers, for instance, but not fathers, paid leave from work. On the other hand, policies aimed to get women out of the home—such as making public assistance conditional on work for pay—have traditionally devalued nonmarket work. We should focus instead on policies that reward family care and promote gender equality at the same time. We should encourage both men and women to combine paid work with family and community work—a new division of labor that would develop men's capabilities for care along with women's capabilities for individual achievement.

This strategy has excited debate in the Netherlands, where feminist economist Marga Bruyn-Hundt became an early, outspoken advocate for egalitarian models of support for family care.[c] A Dutch Expert Committee has called for the elimination of breadwinners' subsidies in income tax and social security as well as an expansion of subsidized child care and home care for sick and elderly people. Greater "outsourcing" of some aspects of family care through the market and the state could be counterbalanced by a reduction in men's paid work time to enable their greater participation in the care economy.[d] One policy Alva Myrdal did suggest, years ago, was a reduction in the hours of paid employment to six hours a day, coinciding with the hours that children spend in school.[e]

In this country, many states are beginning to extend their public education system to meet the needs of children ages three to six. If we could provide the same level of public support as the French, who enroll virtually 95 percent of this age group in school, both children and parents would benefit. We also need to consider what happens to children when they get home from school and require adult attention and supervision. Changing school and work schedules so that they dovetail more efficiently would help. But we should also make it easier for both parents to spend less time in paid work, encouraging the kind of flexibility that families need to decide what is best for themselves and their children.

Other countries ensure plenty of parental attention for young infants by providing paid parental leaves. The Swedes offer a promising, if still somewhat gender-biased, example.[f] Parents there enjoy an eighteen-month paid, job-protected leave that can be prorated over the more extended period during which their children are under eight years of age. One month of this leave is assigned specifically to fathers, and about 50 percent of eligible fathers actually use it.

To provide stronger encouragement for gender equity, we could insist that paid benefits be set equal to wages (so that leaves are not more costly for higher-wage earners). Also, we could provide six months of paid leave for mothers and six for fathers, which each must "use or lose." Apart from that restriction, parents could distribute their leaves in a variety of ways. For instance, both parents could work part-time for two years at full pay.

The United States taxes families on their joint income, a practice that discourages the wife, usually a "second earner," from working more hours. Instead, we could tax individuals separately at a rate based on their individual market income, whether they are married or not. This is a much simpler approach to eliminating the so-called marriage penalty, because it would allow individuals to enjoy the benefits of pooling their income and sharing their expenses without moving themselves into a higher tax bracket. We could eliminate the tax deduction for a "dependent" who is an able-bodied adult (such as a full-time housewife or househusband) but provide a generous deduction (or allowance) for the care of a child, or an elderly, sick, or disabled person at home.[g]

A steeply progressive income tax rate on individuals would encourage people to spend less time on paid work and more on activities of direct use to their families and communities. We could also reduce the disincentives to part-time paid work by requiring companies to provide the same benefits (prorated by hours worked) to part-time as to full-time workers. At the same time, we could discourage individuals from specializing in family care by making rights to health and pension benefits conditional on some level of participation in market work. Individuals would no longer be able to gain benefits simply by marrying another adult who is covered. The costs of making these changes would partially countervail each other. For instance, the money that companies save by not automatically extending employee benefits to wives and husbands of employees could be spent on extending coverage to part-time employees.

A third problem concerns definitions of kinship. Our economic and legal system has not kept pace with changes in the types of caring relationships that individuals form. Marriage is the primary form of non-biological kinship that we recognize, yet marriage is, for many adults, a relatively short-term relationship. Rather than making divorce more difficult, which would probably discourage marriage, we could define simpler, more flexible domestic partnerships that set some guidelines for individuals who choose to live together. Gay and lesbian couples should be able to opt for these (or for marriage, if they so desire).

The state should be less concerned with the regulation of relationships between consenting adults, and more concerned with strengthening obligations to dependents such as young children and the elderly. More than improved child support enforcement is required: we need to rethink the ways that we define the responsibilities of kinship. Though it may pose difficulties for some families, joint custody of children in the absence of marriage or after divorce is far superior to an arrangement in which one parent cares, while the other parent pays. We need to devise new ways of promoting active and engaged fatherhood.

We need also to think beyond kinship itself. One category that seems to be entirely missing from our demographic vocabulary is "friend." Yet many single people, especially elderly people, rely on friends or neighbors, rather than relatives, to take them to the doctor, or to provide periodic home care. We should not limit the prerogatives of protected absences from work—such as those guaranteed by the Family and Medical Leave Act—to occasions that involve the needs of immediate family members. Workers should have the right to define their responsibilities for the care of others in broader terms. And we should encourage them to do so.

Extending family values to society as a whole requires looking beyond the redistribution of income to ways of strengthening cultural values of love, obligation, and reciprocity. Current welfare state policies have done little to encourage personal contact between rich and poor, skilled and unskilled, lucky and unlucky. Ironically, the warfare state has accomplished more than the welfare state in this respect: military service that entailed widespread participation in the defense of important democratic ideals, such as service in World War II, created enduring sentiments of social solidarity.

We could encourage greater civic participation, offering tax credits and other incentives for the provision of care services that develop long-term relationships between individuals and communities. We could discourage residential and cultural segregation by class and ethnicity. We could defend and enlarge our public spaces. Our educational institutions could encourage the development of caring skills and community involvement. Among other strategies, we might invite young people to repay the money invested in them through national service rather than simply through taxes.

Policies designed to promote care for other people appear unproductive only to those who define economic efficiency in cramped terms, such as increases in GDP. The weakening of family and social solidarity can impose enormous costs, reflected in educational failures, poor health, environmental degradation, high crime rates, and a cultural atmosphere of anxiety and resentment. The care and nurturance of human capabilities has always been difficult and expensive. In the past, a sexual division of labor based upon the subordination of women helped minimize both the difficulties and the expense. Today, however, the costs of providing care need to be explicitly confronted and fairly distributed....

In closing, I offer five guidelines for efforts to bring the invisible hand of the market into better balance with the invisible heart of care:

1. *Reject claims that women should be more altruistic than men, either in the home or in society as a whole.* Women may be naturally suited to some forms of care—such as breast-feeding. That's exactly why men should hustle to make up the difference elsewhere (changing diapers comes to mind). Assigning women primary responsibility for the care of others does more than let men off the hook. It separates care from power, and therefore reduces the overall level of social and economic support for caring work.

2. *Defend family values against the corrosive effects of self-interest.* Both men and women stand to gain from strengthening values of love, obligation, and reciprocity. These values create a cultural environment in which the individual pursuit of self-interest can lead to healthy outcomes. Carried too far, however, the individual pursuit of self-interest can degrade that environment, with particularly unfortunate consequences for future generations.

3. *Confront the difficulties of establishing democratic governance in families, communities, countries, and the world as a whole.* If we are to enforce social obligations to one another, we must do so in fair and equitable ways. On every level of society we need to figure out more effective ways of coordinating our activities without resorting to authoritarian rules or impersonal bureaucracies.

4. *Aim for a kinder and wiser form of economic development.* Calling attention to things that money can't buy doesn't require us to ignore the

things it can buy. We should try to improve global standards of living, defined in broader terms than the value of market production. We need to measure our success by the improvement of our capabilities, the flourishing of our families, and the health of our environment.

5. *Develop and strengthen ways of rewarding the work of care.* Care is not just another commodity. Personal, face-to-face, emotionally rich relationships are crucial to the delivery of high-quality child care, education, health, elder care, and many other social services. Whether they take place in families, communities, corporations, or other places of work, the services of care deserve public recognition and reward.

Notes

a. David Osborne and Ted Gaebler, Reinventing Government: How the Entrepreneurial Spirit Is Transforming the Public Sector (New York: Plume Books, 1993).

b. Alva Myrdal, Nation and Family: The Swedish Experiment in Democratic Family and Population Policy (London: Kegan Paul, Trench, Trubner and Co., 1945).

c. Marga Bruyn-Hundt, "Scenarios for a Redistribution of Unpaid Work in the Netherlands," Feminist Economics 2, no. 3 (1996), p. 129.

d. Ina Brouwer and Eelco Wiarda, "The Combination Model: Child Care and the Part Time Labour Supply of Men in the Dutch Welfare State," in J. J. Schippers, J. J. Siegers, and J. De Jong-Gierveld, eds, Child Care and Female Labour Supply in the Netherlands: Facts, Analyses, Policies (Amsterdam: Thesis Publishers, 1998).

e. Alva Myrdal and Viola Klein, Women's Two Roles: Home and Work (London: Routledge and Kegan Paul, 1956).

f. Clare Ungerson, "Gender, Cash, and Informal Care: European Perspectives and Dilemmas," Journal of Social Policy 24, no. 1 (1995), 31–52; Sheila B. Kamerman and Alfred J. Kahn, "Child and Family Policies in an Era of Social Policy Retrenchment and Restructuring," unpublished paper presented at the Luxembourg Income Study Conference on Child Well-Being in Rich and Transition Countries, September 30–October 2, 1999.

g. Julie Nelson, "Feminist Theory and the Income Tax," in Feminism, Objectivity, and Economics (New York: Routledge, 1996), 97–117.

Recognition and Redistribution

The redistribution of the costs and labor of caring work is not enough to redress gender inequality. Recognition of the devalued and powerless status of women, especially those of disfavored racial ethnic groups, is also needed (Fraser and Honneth 2003). Drucilla Cornell (1998) says that in the quest for equality, the question of who is compared with whom is crucial. If disadvantaged women achieve equality with the disadvantaged men of their group, they have not achieved very much. If they outperform them, as has happened for African American and Hispanic American women college and professional school graduates in the United States, then the men in the same groups are seen as endangered. Women may feel they are in a double bind and can't win if they raise themselves as women, leaving their men behind, but they don't want to subordinate themselves to their men, either.

Socialist feminist political action has gone beyond the sources of oppression that are specific to women. Without ignoring sexual exploitation and violence against women, socialist feminism has searched for ways to open access to economic resources, educational opportunities, and political power for all the disadvantaged. The focus is sometimes on gender, but women of different classes may not be interested in political action because their statuses are superior, or because they feel they have too much to lose from changes in the status quo. In some situations, it is necessary to reach out to subordinated men who are similarly oppressed and who want similar changes in the redistribution of resources and recognition of distinct racial ethnic cultures.

Socialist feminism has a pragmatic attitude towards reform of the gendered social order. It embeds the gender injustice of women's unpaid work for the family in the larger injustices of complex inequality produced by racial, class, and gender disadvantages. Thus, it addresses the problems that affect all women, as well as those that affect women and men at the bottom of the ladder.

Critique

Socialist feminism's expansion has turned into a general critique of late capitalist societies on domestic, economic, and political grounds. The feminism is evident in the prominent inclusion of gender, but otherwise the politics of socialist feminism is a struggle for economic and social equality for all the disadvantaged. In that politics, coalitions of women may be less important than class or racial ethnic coalitions. The question is whether women's interests tend to be put on the back burner in the fight for resources and recognition.

Women's work is still underpaid, although in postindustrial economies, it is often blue-collar men who are out of jobs. Whose interests should unions fight for? Progressive politicians are more likely to call for government-supported universal health care than government-supported child care. Both affect everyone, but child care is considered a woman's issue. Socialist feminism may downplay women's particular inequality in the fight against complex inequality.

Summary

Socialist feminism provides a general theory of inequality that combines the effects of gender, social class, and racial ethnic status. For women, inequality is embedded in their exploitation in the family and workplace. White upper- and upper-middle-class women do not have the same advantages as men of the same status. Men's lack of responsibility for social reproduction of the next generation frees them to pursue careers and political power. Their accumulation of advantages gives them wide-ranging social power and the means to dominate women. Working-class women and women of devalued racial ethnic statuses suffer double oppression compared to the men of the same class and status.

Politically, socialist feminism calls for a redistribution of responsibilities in the family, economic resources, and political power. Equal sharing of family work and government support for child care would give women the opportunity to accumulate the economic and social power now monopolized by men. Also necessary is gender-neutral access to high-paying jobs and positions of power. For all the disadvantaged, men as well as women, socialist feminism has fought for universal entitlements to education, health care, and income support as well as more open access to governmental and nongovernmental political power.

Socialist feminism's main contributions lay the groundwork for a structural analysis of the status of women within and beyond the family and the economy. They adopted the concept of complex inequality to make visible the combined effects of gender, class, and racial ethnic status. The accumulated economic, cultural, and political disadvantages turn women throughout the world into second-class citizens. While this concept breaks gender into heterogenous groups intersected by racial ethnic and social class status, it still maintains the underlying unequal gendered structure of the current social order. Socialist feminism's gender reforms are more concerned with redressing the inequalities of women's position within the complex inequality of racial, ethnic, class, and gender stratification than with changing the gendered social order.

SUGGESTED READINGS IN SOCIALIST FEMINISM

Adkins, Lisa. 2001. "Cultural Feminization: 'Money, Sex and Power' for Women." *Signs* 26: 669–695.

Armstrong, Chris. 2002. "Complex Equality: Beyond Equality and Difference," *Feminist Theories* 3: 67–82.

Britton, Dana M. 2000. "The Epistemology of the Gendered Organization." *Gender & Society* 14: 418–434.

Buhle, Mari Jo. 1983. *Women and American Socialism, 1870–1920*. Urbana: University of Illinois Press.

Cornell, Drucilla. 1998. *At the Heart of Freedom: Feminism, Sex and Equality*. Princeton, NJ: Princeton University Press.

Duffy, Mignon. 2005. "Reproducing Labor Inequalities: Challenges for Feminists Conceptualizing Care at the Intersections of Gender, Race, and Class." *Gender & Society* 19: 66–82.

———. 2007. "Doing the Dirty Work: Gender, Race, and Reproductive Labor in Historical Perspective." *Gender & Society* 21:313–336.

Eisenstein, Zillah, ed. 1978. *Capitalist Patriarchy and the Case for Socialist Feminism.* New York: Monthly Review Press.

Ferguson, Kathy E. 1984. *The Feminist Case Against Bureaucracy.* Philadelphia: Temple University Press.

Folbre, Nancy. 1994. *Who Pays for the Kids? Gender and the Structures of Constraint.* New York: Routledge.

———. 2001. *The Invisible Heart: Economics and Family Values.* New York: The New Press.

———. 2008. *Valuing Children: Rethinking the Economics of the Family.* Cambridge, MA: Harvard University Press.

Fraser, Nancy. 1989. *Unruly Practices: Power, Discourse and Gender in Contemporary Social Theory.* Minneapolis: University of Minnesota Press.

———. 1997. *Justice Interruptus: Critical Reflections on the "Postsocialist" Condition.* New York: Routledge.

Fraser, Nancy, and Axel Honneth. 2003. *Redistribution or Recognition? A Political-Philosophical Exchange.* Trans. Joel Golb, James Ingram, and Christiane Wilke. London: Verso.

Hansen, Karen V., and Ilene J. Philipson, eds. 1990. *Women, Class and the Feminist Imagination: A Socialist-Feminist Reader.* Philadelphia: Temple University Press.

Hochschild, Arlie Russell. 1983. *The Managed Heart: Commercialization of Human Feeling.* Berkeley: University of California Press.

Holmstrom, Nancy, ed. 2002. *The Socialist Feminist Project: A Contemporary Reader in Theory and Politics.* New York: Monthly Review Press.

Kruks, Sonia, Rayna Rapp, and Marilyn B. Young, eds. 1989. *Promissory Notes: Women in the Transition to Socialism.* New York: Monthly Review Press.

Lister, Ruth. 1997. *Citizenship: Feminist Perspectives.* London: Macmillan.

McCall, Leslie. 2001. *Complex Inequality: Gender, Class, and Race in the New Economy.* New York: Routledge.

———. 2005. "The Complexity of Intersectionality." *Signs* 30: 1771–1800.

Okin, Susan Moller. 1989. *Justice, Gender and the Family.* New York: Basic Books.

Walby, Sylvia. 1997. *Gender Transformations.* New York: Routledge.

Walby, Sylvia, Heidi Gottfried, Karin Gottschall, and Mari Osawa. 2007. *Gendering the Knowledge Economy: Comparative Perspectives.* New York: Palgrave Macmillan.

Walzer, Michael. 1983. *Spheres of Justice: A Defense of Pluralism and Equality.* New York: Basic Books.

Young, Iris Marion. 1990. *Justice and the Politics of Difference.* Princeton, NJ: Princeton University Press.

4

Postcolonial and Asian Feminism

SOURCES OF GENDER INEQUALITY

- Undercutting women's traditional economic base by restructuring and modernization
- Exploitation of women workers in the global economy
- Lack of education for girls
- Inadequate maternal and child health care
- Sexual exploitation
- Patriarchal family structures and cultural practices harmful to women and girls

POLITICS

- Protection of women's economic resources in modernization programs
- Education of girls
- Community-based health care, family planning services, and AIDS prevention and treatment
- Campaigns against genital cutting, child labor, and sex trafficking
- Community organizing of mothers
- National women's movements
- Empowerment of women in national politics

CRITIQUE

- Non-Western feminists argue that Western ideas of individualism and modernization undercut traditional cultures, but these cultures may be oppressive towards women
- Western feminist advocacy against female genital cutting has alienated feminists in countries with their own programs for change
- Western feminists have not recognized the accomplishments of national women's movements

- Globalization and its exploitation of women in developing countries has increased political differences between Western and non-Western feminists

CONTRIBUTIONS

- Gender analyses of modernization and economic restructuring programs
- Data on exploitation of women and children workers
- Documentation of the importance of economic resources to women's social status
- Laws against transnational sexual traffic and ritual female genital cutting
- Greater visibility of non-Western feminist perspectives
- Significant increases in women's political participation and leadership

Postcolonial feminism applies the socialist feminist analysis of gender, class, and racial ethnic inequality to what has been variously called the third world, the global south, postcolonial and nonindustrial societies, and developing countries. These refer to places like the Caribbean, parts of South America and Africa, India, Bangladesh, and Pakistan. These countries are linked to countries with developed industrial and postindustrial economies through globalization and transnational trade. Most of the developed countries are in North America and Europe, but also include Asian countries like Japan.

Income maldistributions in the developing countries are often made worse by the restructuring policies demanded by industrialized states as the price of economic aid and industrial development. Wages are low for most urban women and men. However, women workers in developing countries in Latin America, the Caribbean, Africa, and Asia are paid less than men workers, whether they work in factories or do piecework at home.

In rural areas, much of the agriculture is plantation farming for export or at the subsistence level, but there is an extensive "informal" economy of home-based manufacture and production of goods and foodstuffs for local markets that many women are engaged in. Women and girls are also responsible for finding and transporting clean water for household use. While women are usually significant food providers for their families, working at small farms and home-based businesses, they suffer from illiteracy and deaths in childbirth. Health care is poor, and there is a high rate of mortality in children before the age of five from diarrhea, malaria, infections, and other treatable or preventable illnesses. In both urban and rural areas, devastatingly high rates of early childbearing, sexual exploitation, prostitution, and HIV/AIDS add to women's oppression.

The family is a source of both exploitation and protection for women. Their labor is frequently used as a source of family income, but mothers also form grassroots service and community protest groups. In many countries, strong women's movements flourished, first as part of movements for national liberation and then for women's rights.

The gendered division of labor in developing countries is the outcome of centuries of European and American economic exploitation and cultural imperialism. Women's traditional contributions to food production were undermined in favor of exportable crops, such as coffee, and the extraction of raw materials, such as minerals. Men workers labored in mining and large-scale agriculture, where they were paid barely enough for their own subsistence. Women family members had to provide food for themselves and their children; however, good land was often confiscated for plantations, so women and children also lived at a survival level.

Since the end of World War II, many developing nations have sought financial capital and business investments from wealthier European and North American countries. The consequent economic restructuring and industrialization disadvantage women. Men workers, considered heads of families, are hired for the better-paying manufacturing jobs. Young single women, although they are working as much for their families as for themselves, are hired for jobs that pay much less than men's jobs. And married women, whose wages frequently go to feed their children, are paid the least of all. For example, in the *maquiladoras*, the Mexican border industries, where 85 to 90 percent of the workers are women, there is a division between the electronics industries, which offer somewhat better working conditions and higher pay but hire only young single women, and the smaller, less modern apparel factories, which employ older women supporting children.

Gender Inequality in the Global Economy

Postcolonial feminism uses theories of underdevelopment and socialist feminist theories of development to analyze the position of women in the global economy, with particular emphasis on newly industrializing countries. *The global economy* links wealthy countries whose economies focus on service, information, and finances with manufacturing sites and the sources of raw materials in poorer countries. Wealth, in the form of capital and profits, and legal and undocumented immigrants flow between them.

Men and women workers all over the world supply the labor for the commodities that end up in the stores in your neighborhood. Consumers want inexpensive food and clothing, which impacts on the workers in poorer areas. They are not paid according to their skills but according to the going wage, which varies enormously from country to country because it is dependent on the local standard of living.

Low-paid women workers in electronics factories produce most of the components of the world's televisions, computers, cell phones, and MP3 players. Women workers tend to be paid less than men workers throughout the world, whatever the wage scale, because they are supposedly supporting only themselves. However, in South Korea's economic development zone, many young single women factory workers live in crowded dormitories and eat one meal a day in order to send money home for a brother in college. In Mexico, many older married women's jobs are a significant source of their family's income.

Another important part of the global economy is the flow of immigrant labor from poor countries to wealthy countries. The jobs they do are low-paid "dirty work," but they pay more than work at home, so those who cannot get documents to work legally risk injury and death to get smuggled into wealthy countries. Men from the developing countries work in affluent areas as low-level service workers—dish washers, cleaners, gardeners, and other "invisible" labor. Women from these countries work as nannies and house-keepers. Whole families work as seasonal farm labor. There is also a thriving sex traffic, where young women are enticed with the promise of jobs and end up in brothels. Another form of exploitation is surrogacy—poor women having babies for rich Westerners.

Non-Western Feminism

Non-Western feminism is critical of Western concepts of gender relations and women's oppression, arguing that throughout much of the non-Western world, women are productive workers in their families, not just homemak-ers and child-care givers. The nuclear family that is seen as so oppressive by Western feminism is not the typical family structure in non-Western societ-ies—rather, the norm is the extended family where there are many adults to bring in income and do child care.

Non-Western women, like women in Western countries, vary in their social position; not all are low-status, powerless dependents, nor are all non-Western men authoritarian patriarchs. Well-educated and financially com-fortable Western feminists sometimes find that they are in a paradoxical position—their social class status resembles the women of the upper class in developing countries, who are the advantaged group in an oppressive social structure depriving lower-class women of education and decently paid jobs. Western feminists' sympathies are often with lower-class women in devel-oping countries, who may see them as upper-class interlopers.

In the mid-1980s, at the beginning of her professional life as a feminist the-orist and international activist, Chandra Talpade Mohanty published what became a famous challenge to Western feminists, "Under Western Eyes: Feminist Scholarship and Colonial Discourses." In it, she argued against a simplistic binary formula that ignores racial ethnic, national, and class dif-ferences: "Men exploit, women are exploited" (2003, 31). She also claimed that Western feminism too often portrayed non-Western women as differ-ent from themselves and more oppressed—traditional, religious, family-oriented, legally unsophisticated, illiterate, and embattled in nationalistic revolutions. In her latest book, *Feminism Without Borders*, Talpade Mohanty, Professor of Women's Studies, reprints this essay as the first chapter and rethinks it in the last chapter, "Under Western Eyes Revisited: Feminist Solidarity Through Anticapitalist Struggles." Now she argues that rather than focusing on differences, feminism should mount an antiglobalization struggle against "global economic and political processes [that] have become more brutal, exacerbating economic, racial, and gender inequalities" (230). Feminism's goal should be a solidarity that recognizes local differences, but is without borders, since globalization affects everyone.

Under Western Eyes at the Turn of the Century

Chandra Talpade Mohanty

Hamilton College and Union Institute and University, Cincinnati, Ohio

I wrote "Under Western Eyes" to discover and articulate a critique of "Western feminist" scholarship on Third World women via the discursive colonization of Third World women's lives and struggles. I also wanted to expose the power-knowledge nexus of feminist cross-cultural scholarship expressed through Eurocentric, falsely universalizing methodologies that serve the narrow self-interest of Western feminism. As well, I thought it crucial to highlight the connection between feminist scholarship and feminist political organizing while drawing attention to the need to examine the "political implications of our analytic strategies and principles." I also wanted to chart the location of feminist scholarship within a global political and economic framework dominated by the "First World."[a]

My most simple goal was to make clear that cross-cultural feminist work must be attentive to the micropolitics of context, subjectivity, and struggle, as well as to the macropolitics of global economic and political systems and processes. I discussed Maria Mies's study of the lacemakers of Narsapur as a demonstration of how to do this kind of multilayered, contextual analysis to reveal how the particular is often universally significant—without using the universal to erase the particular, or positing an unbridgeable gulf between the two terms. Implicit in this analysis was the use of historical materialism as a basic framework, and a definition of material reality in both its local and micro-, as well as global, systemic dimensions. I argued at that time for the definition and recognition of the Third World not just through oppression but in terms of historical complexities and the many struggles to change these oppressions. Thus I argued for grounded, particularized analyses linked with larger, even global, economic and political frameworks....

While my earlier focus was on the distinctions between "Western" and "Third World" feminist practices, and while I downplayed the commonalities between these two positions, my focus now ... is on what I have chosen to call an anticapitalist transnational feminist practice— and on the possibilities, indeed on the necessities, of cross-national feminist solidarity and organizing against capitalism. While "Under Western Eyes" was located in the context of the critique of Western humanism and Eurocentrism and of white, Western feminism, a similar essay written now would need to be located in the context of the critique of global capitalism (on antiglobalization), the naturalization of the values of capital, and the unacknowledged power of cultural relativism in cross-cultural feminist scholarship and pedagogies.

"Under Western Eyes" sought to make the operations of discursive power visible, to draw attention to what was left out of feminist theorizing, namely, the material complexity, reality, and agency of Third World women's bodies and lives. This is in fact exactly the analytic strategy I now use to draw attention to what is unseen, undertheorized, and left out in the production of knowledge about globalization. While globalization has always been a part of capitalism, and capitalism is not a new phenomenon, at this time I believe the theory, critique, and activism around antiglobalization has to be a key focus for feminists. This does not mean that the patriarchal and racist relations and structures that accompany capitalism are any less problematic at this time, or that antiglobalization is a singular phenomenon. Along with many other scholars and activists, I believe capital as it functions now depends on and exacerbates racist, patriarchal, and heterosexist relations of rule....

Antiglobalization Struggles

Although the context for writing "Under Western Eyes" in the mid-1980s was a visible and activist women's movement, this radical movement no longer exists as such. Instead, I draw inspiration from a more distant, but significant, antiglobalization movement in the United States and around the world. Activists in these movements are often women, although the movement is not gender-focused. So I wish to redefine the project of decolonization, not reject it. It appears more complex to me today, given the newer developments of global capitalism. Given the complex interweaving of cultural forms, people of and from the Third World live not only under Western eyes but also within them. This shift in my focus from "under Western eyes" to "under and inside" the hegemonic spaces of the One-Third World necessitates recrafting the project of decolonization.

My focus is thus no longer just the colonizing effects of Western feminist scholarship. This does not mean the problems I identified in the earlier essay do not occur now. But the phenomenon I addressed then has been more than adequately engaged by other feminist scholars. While feminists have been involved in the antiglobalization movement from the start, however, this has not been a major organizing locus for women's movements nationally in the West/North. It has, however, always been a locus of struggle for women of the Third World/South because of their location. Again, this contextual specificity should constitute the larger vision. Women of the Two-Thirds World have always organized against the devastations of globalized capital, just as they have always historically organized anticolonial and antiracist movements. In this sense they have always spoken for humanity as a whole.

I have tried to chart feminist sites for engaging globalization, rather than providing a comprehensive review of feminist work in this area. I hope this exploration makes my own political choices and decisions transparent and that it provides readers with a productive and provocative space to think and act creatively for feminist struggle. So today my query is slightly different although much the same as in 1986. I wish to better see the processes of corporate globalization and how and why they recolonize women's bodies and labor. We need to know the real and concrete effects of global restructuring on raced, classed, national, sexual bodies of women in the academy, in workplaces, streets, households, cyberspaces, neighborhoods, prisons, and social movements.

What does it mean to make antiglobalization a key factor for feminist theorizing and struggle? To illustrate my thinking about antiglobalization, let me focus on two specific sites where knowledge about globalization is produced. The first site is a pedagogical one and involves an analysis of the various strategies being used to internationalize (or globalize)[b] the women's studies curriculum in U.S. colleges and universities. I argue that this move to internationalize women's studies curricula and the attendant pedagogies that flow from this is one of the main ways we can track a discourse of global feminism in the United States. Other ways of tracking global feminist discourses include analyzing the documents and discussions flowing out of the Beijing United Nations conference on women, and of course popular television and print media discourses on women around the world. The second site of antiglobalization scholarship I focus on is the emerging, notably ungendered and deracialized discourse on activism against globalization.

Antiglobalization Pedagogies

Let me turn to the struggles over the dissemination of a feminist cross-cultural knowledge base through pedagogical strategies "internationalizing" the women's studies curriculum. The problem of "the (gendered) color line" remains, but is more easily seen today as developments of transnational and global capital. While I choose to focus on women's studies curricula, my arguments hold for curricula in any discipline or academic field that seeks to internationalize or globalize its curriculum. I argue that the challenge for "internationalizing" women's studies is no different from the one involved in "racializing" women's studies in the 1980s, for very similar politics of knowledge come into play here.[c]

So the question I want to foreground is the politics of knowledge in bridging the "local" and the "global" in women's studies. How we teach the "new" scholarship in women's studies is at least as important as the scholarship itself in the struggles over knowledge and citizenship in the U.S. academy. After all, the way we construct curricula and the pedagogies we use to put such curricula into practice tell a story—or tell many stories. It is the way we position historical narratives of experience in relation to each other, the way we theorize relationality as both historical and simultaneously singular and collective that determines how and what we learn when we cross cultural and experiential borders....

The Feminist Solidarity or Comparative Feminist Studies Model. This curricular strategy is based on the premise that the local and the global are not defined in terms of physical geography or territory but exist simultaneously and constitute each other. It is then the links, the relationships, between the local and the global that are foregrounded, and these links are conceptual, material, temporal, contextual, and so on. This framework assumes a comparative focus and analysis of the directionality of power no matter what the subject of the women's studies course is—and it assumes both distance and proximity (specific/universal) as its analytic strategy.

Differences and commonalities thus exist in relation and tension with each other in all contexts. What is emphasized are relations of mutuality, coresponsibility, and common interests, anchoring the idea of feminist solidarity. For example, within this model, one would not teach a U.S. women of color course with additions on Third World/South or white women, but a comparative course that shows the interconnectedness of the histories, experiences, and struggles of U.S. women of color, white women, and women from the Third World/South. By doing this kind of comparative teaching that is attentive to power, each historical experience illuminates the experiences of the others. Thus, the focus is not just on the intersections of race, class, gender, nation, and sexuality in different communities of women but on mutuality and coimplication, which suggests attentiveness to the interweaving of the histories of these communities. In addition the focus is simultaneously on individual and collective experiences of oppression and exploitation and of struggle and resistance.

Students potentially move away from the "add and stir" and the relativist "separate but equal" (or different) perspective to the coimplication/solidarity one. This solidarity perspective requires understanding the historical and experiential specificities and differences of women's lives as well as the historical and experiential connections between women from different national, racial, and cultural communities. Thus it suggests organizing syllabi around social and economic processes and histories of various communities of women in particular substantive areas like sex work, militarization, environmental justice, the prison/industrial complex, and human rights, and looking for points of contact and connection as well as disjunctures. It is important to always foreground not just the connections of domination but those of struggle and resistance as well.

In the feminist solidarity model the One-Third/Two-Thirds paradigm makes sense. Rather than Western/Third World, or North/South, or local/global seen as oppositional and incommensurate categories, the One-Third/Two-Thirds differentiation allows for teaching and learning about points of connection and distance among and between communities of women marginalized and privileged along numerous local and global dimensions. Thus the very notion of inside/outside necessary to the distance between local/global is transformed through the use of a One-Third/Two-Thirds paradigm, as both categories must be understood as containing difference/similarities, inside/outside, and distance/proximity. Thus sex work, militarization, human rights, and so on can be framed in their multiple local and global dimensions using the One-Third/Two-Thirds, social minority/social majority paradigm. I am suggesting then that we look at the women's studies curriculum in its entirety and that we attempt to use a comparative feminist studies model wherever possible.[d]

I refer to this model as the feminist solidarity model because, besides its focus on mutuality and common interests, it requires one to formulate questions about connection and disconnection between activist women's movements around the world. Rather than formulating activism and agency in terms of discrete and disconnected cultures and nations, it allows us to frame agency and resistance across the borders of nation and culture. I think feminist pedagogy should not simply expose students to a particularized academic scholarship but that it should also envision the possibility of activism and struggle outside the academy. Political education through feminist pedagogy should teach active citizenship in such struggles for justice.

My recurring question is how pedagogies can supplement, consolidate, or resist the dominant logic of globalization. How do students learn about the inequities among women and men around the world? For instance, traditional liberal and liberal feminist pedagogies disallow historical and comparative thinking, radical feminist pedagogies often singularize gender, and Marxist pedagogy silences race and gender in its focus on capitalism. I look to create pedagogies that allow students to see the complexities, singularities, and interconnections between communities of women such that power, privilege, agency, and dissent can be made visible and engaged with....

While feminist scholarship is moving in important and useful directions in terms of a critique of global restructuring and the culture of globalization, I want to ask some of the same questions I posed in 1986 once again. In spite of the occasional exception, I think that much of present-day scholarship tends to reproduce particular "globalized" representations of women. Just as there is an Anglo-American masculinity produced in and by discourses of globalization,[e] it is important to ask what the corresponding femininities being produced are. Clearly there is the ubiquitous global teenage girl factory worker, the domestic worker, and the sex worker. There is also the migrant/immigrant service worker, the refugee, the victim of war crimes, the woman-of-color prisoner who happens to be a mother and drug user, the consumer-housewife, and so on. There is also the mother-of-the-nation/religious bearer of traditional culture and morality.

Although these representations of women correspond to real people, they also often stand in for the contradictions and complexities of women's lives and roles. Certain images, such as that of the factory or sex worker, are often geographically located in the Third World/South, but many of the representations identified above are dispersed throughout the globe. Most refer to women of the Two-Thirds World, and some to women of the One-Third World. And a woman from the Two-Thirds World can live in the One-Third World. The point I am making here is that women are workers, mothers, or consumers in the global economy, but we are also all those things simultaneously. Singular and monolithic categorizations of women in discourses of globalization circumscribe ideas about experience, agency, and struggle. While there are other, relatively new images of women that also emerge in this discourse—the human rights worker or the NGO advocate, the revolutionary militant and the corporate bureaucrat—there is also a divide between false, overstated images of victimized and empowered womanhood, and they negate each other. We need to further explore how this divide plays itself out in terms of a social majority/minority, One-Third/Two-Thirds World characterization. The concern here is with whose agency is being colonized and who is privileged in these pedagogies and scholarship. These then are my new queries for the twenty-first century....[f]

Notes

a. Here is how I defined "Western feminist" then: "Clearly Western feminist discourse and political practice is neither singular or homogeneous in its goals, interests, or analyses. However, it is possible to trace a coherence of effects resulting from the implicit assumption of 'the West' (in all its complexities and contradictions) as the primary referent in theory and praxis. My reference to 'Western feminism' is by no means intended to imply that it is a monolith. Rather, I am attempting to draw attention to the similar effects of various textual strategies used by writers which codify Others as non-Western and hence themselves as (implicitly) Western." I suggested then that while terms such as "First" and "Third World" were problematic in suggesting oversimplified similarities as well as flattening internal differences, I continued to use them because this was the terminology available to us then. I used the terms with full knowledge of their limitations, suggesting a critical and heuristic rather than nonquestioning use of the terms....

b. In what follows I use the terms "global capitalism," "global restructuring," and "globalization" interchangeably to refer to a process of corporate global economic, ideological, and cultural reorganization across the borders of nation-states.

c. While the initial push for "internationalization" of the curriculum in U.S. higher education came from the federal government's funding of area studies programs during the cold war, in the post–cold war period it is private foundations like the MacArthur, Rockefeller, and Ford foundations that have been instrumental in this endeavor—especially in relation to the women's studies curriculum.

d. A new anthology contains some good examples of what I am referring to as a feminist solidarity or comparative feminist studies model. See Lay, Monk, and Rosenfelt 2002.

e. Discourses of globalization include the proglobalization narratives of neoliberalism and privatization, but they also include antiglobalization discourses produced by progressives, feminists, and activists in the antiglobalization movement.

f. There is also an emerging feminist scholarship that complicates these monolithic "globalized" representations of women. See Amy Lind's work on Ecuadorian women's organizations (2000), Aili Marie Tripp's work on women's social networks in Tanzania (2002), and Kimberly Chang and L. H. M. Ling's (2000) and Aihwa Ong's work on global restructuring in the Asia Pacific regions (1987 and 1991).

References

Chang, Kimberly, and L. H. M. Long. 2000. "Globalization and Its Intimate Other: Filipina Domestic Workers in Hong Kong." In Marianne Runyan and Anne Runyan, eds., *Gender and Global Restructuring: Sightings, Sites, and Resistances*. New York: Routledge.

Lay, Mary M., Janice Monk, and Deborah Silverton Rosenfelt, eds. 2002. *Encompassing Gender: Integrating International Studies and Women's Studies*. New York: Feminist Press.

Lind, Amy. 2000. "Negotiating Boundaries: Women's Organizations and the Politics of Restructuring in Ecuador." In Marianne Marchand and Anne Runyan, eds., *Gender and Global Restructuring: Sightings, Sites, and Resistances*. New York: Routledge.

Ong, Aihwa. 1991. "The Gender and Labor Politics of Postmodernity." *Annual Review of Anthropology* 20:279–309.

———. 1987. *Spirits of Resistance and Capitalist Discipline: Factory Women in Malaysia*. Albany, NY: State University of New York Press.

Tripp, Aili Marie. 2002. "Combining Intercontinental Parenting and Research: Dilemmas and Strategies for Women." *Signs* 27: 793–811.

Women's Linked Economic and Social Status

Postcolonial feminism links women's status to their contribution to their family's economy and their control of economic resources. To be equal with her husband, it is not enough for a married woman to earn money; she has to provide a needed portion of her family's income and also have control over the source of that income and over its distribution as well (Blumberg 1991). In a rural community, that means owning a piece of land, being able to market the harvest from that land, and deciding how the profit from the sale will be spent. In an urban economy, it may mean owning a store or small business, retaining the profit, and deciding what to spend it on or whether to put it back into the business (Blumberg 2004a, 2004b).

There are societies in Africa and elsewhere in the world where women control significant economic resources and so have a high status. In contrast, in societies with patriarchal family structures where anything women produce, including children, belongs to the husband, women and girls have a low value. Postcolonial feminism's theory is that in any society, if the food or income women produce is the main way the family is fed, and women also control the distribution of any surplus they produce, women have power and prestige. If men provide most of the food and distribute the surplus, women's status is low. Whether women or men produce most of the food or bring in most of the family income depends on the society's economy. When a woman is able to own the means of production (land, a store, a business) like a man, she has the chance to be economically independent. If her income is barely above subsistence level because the only job she can get is low-waged work in a factory, then the fact that she has an income does not give her a very high social status, especially if much of the money she earns is sent back home to her family. Thus, the mode of production and the kinship rules that control the distribution of any surplus are the significant determinants of the relative status of women in any society (Kandiyoti 1988).

Women's Grassroots Movements

Feminist research on women's economic and health problems in developing countries has been extensive, but even those who work for government organizations, United Nations agencies, or the World Bank have not had the power to make development or economic restructuring programs more women-friendly. Pooling resources through grassroots organizing, women of different communities have joined together to fight against exploitation and for social services. They do so as mothers for their children, and so have often been able to accomplish what more obvious political protest cannot, given the entrenchment of wealthy owners of land and factories.

One financial initiative that has been successful in helping women run small enterprises are microloans—a small amount of capital, averaging $200, lent at low interest rates. In 2006, Muhammad Yunus won the Nobel Peace Prize for his Grameen Bank's program of microcredit in Bangladesh. His bank is one of 3200 microcredit institutions serving more than 92 million clients, according to the 2005 State of the Microcredit Summit Campaign Report. Most of the loans are to women, and 98 percent pay them back.[1]

Rae Lesser Blumberg, a sociologist who developed a general theory of women's status linking production and control of economic resources within the family, has applied that theory to women in countries around the world. In the following excerpt, she compares women's chances for empowerment in three developing countries—Ecuador, El Salvador, and Nepal. She found "good, bad, and ugly" conditions for training, activism, and political power. Even in El Salvador, where conditions were ugly because of a 12-year civil war, women were able to form coalitions and get a domestic violence law passed.

Climbing the Pyramids of Power

Rae Lesser Blumberg
University of Virginia

This [excerpt] explores three routes to women's civic–political activism and empowerment in selected countries of Latin America and Asia— Ecuador, Nepal, and El Salvador. With apologies to Clint Eastwood's spaghetti western, I classify these routes as "the good, the bad, and the ugly." Much of my discussion concerns the extent to which women's economic empowerment facilitates political empowerment.[a] ...

Research in these countries has offered an exceptional opportunity for me to focus on the problem of political empowerment—an essential but underanalyzed component of my general theory of gender stratification[b] and still-evolving theory of gender and development.[c] In overview, my general theory, posits that the most important variable (although certainly not the only factor!) affecting the level of equality between women and men is economic power. I define economic power as the relative control of income and/or other economic resources by men versus women at various "nested" levels ranging from the most micro (the couple) to the most macro (the state). Then I hypothesize that as their economic power rises, women gain in self-confidence and in "voice and vote" in household-level decisions concerning fertility, economic allocation patterns, and domestic well-being (such as providing education and health care to sons versus daughters). I also hypothesize that with increasing economic power, women ultimately gain some degree of influence in spheres of power where they historically have been disadvantaged, including access to political power and avoidance of the power of force as manifested in male violence against them. Furthermore, I propose that with increasing economic power, women gain more self-confidence as well as more direct control over their own "life options." These I define as such basic aspects of one's destiny as one's relative say and freedom vis-à-vis marriage, divorce, sexuality, fertility, freedom of movement, access to education, and household power.[d]

The calculation of relative economic power is complicated by societal and structural considerations. One such element consists of macro- and microlevel "discount factors." At the level of the state, in today's world, macrolevel discount factors are always negative: they measure the extent to which the political, legal, economic, religious, and ideological arenas of a given country disadvantage women. (In this sense, a woman in Sweden, for example, will face a much lower discount rate than she would in Saudi Arabia.) Within couples, microlevel discounts can be negative or positive for both men and women. They derive from such factors as each partner's relative commitment to the relationship (by the "principle of least interest," the less committed person has more leverage); relative attractiveness; gender ideology; dependence on the other partner's income; and even such personality factors as relative assertiveness. In essence, these discount factors incorporate cultural and ideological factors into my framework.

A second broad consideration concerns the asymmetry of falling versus rising economic power. When women's relative economic power falls, I suggest that their overall position tends to drop rapidly, unless it is cushioned by a strong ideology supporting women's rights. Conversely, when women's relative economic power rises, their power tends to rise more slowly and less linearly. A third dimension relates to the asymmetry of surplus versus substance. Allocating surplus brings more economic power than allocating bare subsistence, which permits fewer degrees of freedom in spending money. This may be one reason why poor women, who tend to contribute a greater proportion of household subsistence than better-off counterparts, get so little leverage from their contributions. No society condones a mother's withholding food from hungry children to enhance the leverage of her economic contributions; in contrast, the wealthy can make their children jump through hoops to guarantee an inheritance....

I've explored these ideas through firsthand field research in more than thirty countries, on every continent except Antarctica. My first empirical research...has summarized the various routes for women to achieve enhanced political empowerment—that is, to climb the "pyramids of power" at all levels, from local to national. Some routes, however, seem better than others. The data from Ecuador, Nepal, and El Salvador have delineated what I termed the "good, bad, and ugly" ways to get there; however, any one observer can discern the common threads. Enhanced political empowerment seems to be promoted by, first, economic empowerment; and, second, practical training encompassing legal rights and responsibilities, gender awareness, leadership, and self-esteem. In turn, with a greater sense of political efficacy, women tend to advocate for ways to protect themselves from male violence and involve themselves in community-level activism.

What has varied has been whether the economic empowerment should precede or follow the training. The data from Ecuador and El Salvador tilt toward an "economic empowerment first" approach. The Nepali experience indicates that when one is "starting from zero," as is often the case in the Indo-Aryan–Hindu areas of the country, women may not be prepared to seize opportunities for economic empowerment unless their horizons are previously raised by some sort of "basic training" for citizenship and activism.

Regardless of the sequence, the findings discussed here seem to provide support for Luché's assertions that (1) the three constraints on women's political participation are lack of income, lack of information, and danger of male violence; and (2) the two factors galvanizing women's political activism are economic resources as well as training and information that are directly relevant to their lives.[e] These findings provide support for my own proposition about the critical role of economic power in overall gender equality. In addition, they show economic power's key role in promoting women's enhanced political activism, agency, and power.

It is interesting that violence against women (VAW) emerged as a crosscutting, relevant issue that galvanized women in all three countries. Laws against domestic violence were among the top priorities—and most unifying issues—of national-level women NGO leaders and politicians in Ecuador and El Salvador. In pushing these through, women in each country enhanced their position on the political "pyramid of power." Even in Nepal, grassroots women have focused on anti-alcohol campaigns (a somewhat disguised version of anti-VAW efforts) as their first and most popular activity in the public arena after receiving advocacy training.

Ecuador

Until the VAW issue surfaced in the early 1990s, the Ecuadorian women's movement had achieved only limited success vis-à-vis Kathleen Staudt's criterion for civic–political activism and empowerment for women: passage and implementation of policies aimed at increasing gender fairness and accountability to women as well as men.[f] Numerous national-level women's NGOs were established, as well as an active women's movement. Until the 1998 elections, however, Ecuador had the lowest proportion of women in parliament and in ministerial or subministerial positions in all of South America: the January 1998 averages for South America were 10 percent for woman in congress and 13 percent for women in cabinet-level posts; Ecuador's figures were 4 percent and 3 percent, respectively.

Then the women's movement took up VAW and began pressing for special tribunals to deal with domestic violence. Politicians who claimed that a law against domestic violence was not culturally acceptable finally agreed to the women's demands for the tribunals. In 1994, tribunals dealing exclusively with domestic violence—Comisarias de la Mujer—were opened in the five cities. Unexpectedly, they enjoyed immediate and spectacular popularity. As politicians saw the possible benefits of opposing wife beating and as pressure from women's groups intensified, draft legislation was introduced in congress for a law against violence to women and the family; the bill was passed in near-record time (June–December 1995). The caseload of the tribunals rose. During fiscal year 1997, "28,021 women victims of domestic violence received a just hearing and treatment of their cases and accessed decent legal, psychological, medical and social work services."[8]

The May 1998 elections more than tripled the proportion of women in congress, from 4 percent to 14.6 percent, which offered women activists the prospects of working with a "critical mass" of women politicians to promote further changes. Previously, they had had to climb that political "pyramid of power" from the outside, since they had so few potential women allies on the inside, in the formal political system. By focusing on VAW and raising their collective voice, the women of Ecuador achieved substantial progress.

El Salvador

The most conspicuous difference between Ecuador and El Salvador with respect to VAW is that in El Salvador it became the issue that broke through all the years of hostility and war and united women members of congress from both the Left (FMLN) and the Right (ARENA). To everyone's surprise, they formed a caucus; and helped by the strong women's NGOs discussed here, they pushed through a law prohibiting intrafamilial violence, as well as a new family code. Male politicians have yet to unite across El Salvador's great political divide. Following passage of these laws, teaching poor women about their new rights became the main activity of many of these women's NGOs.

Now, if they could form strategic alliances with the proliferating and donor-beloved microfinance programs, they could guarantee their own survival as well as the continued dissemination of their message. A well-run "best practices" microfinance entity should operate in the black, which means "minimalist" programs that focus only on credit, with or without a savings component. Throughout the world, women microfinance clients tend to be better at loan repayment than counterpart men. Consequently, the more a program focuses on the bottom line, the more it tends to seek out female clients—especially if it has not only a computerized management information system that provides timely data on clients' performance but also a system of bonuses for loan officers who maintain their portfolios below a target rate of arrears.[h] Women's NGOs in El Salvador—and elsewhere—could provide women clients of a microfinance program with nonfinancial services that would enhance the program's social impact. And although social impact is a major issue now among microfinance practitioners, their "best practices" model does not have a budget to be spent on social goals. Enter the women's NGOs. It's a win-win scenario for both types of organizations as well as for the women who gain access to microcredit-and-savings services that can empower them economically and transform their lives.

Nepal

The most common advocacy target of recently trained Nepali women was alcohol—in my opinion, as a stalking horse for VAW. Anti-alcohol campaigns were by far the most frequent choices of the women I interviewed who recently had received "rights, responsibilities and advocacy" training. In a country without any prohibitions on VAW, where a draft law against it has been widely denounced by women's groups as so flawed that it would be likely to make the problem worse, grassroots women may not be able to publicly campaign against wife battering. But much of this domestic violence is linked to male drinking, and it is socially acceptable in Indo-Aryan, Hindu-dominated Nepal to oppose the production and sale of liquor. The downside of this is that much of this liquor is home-brewed by poor Tibeto-Burman women. So the actions of the Indo-Aryan-Hindu majority women could jeopardize their minority sisters' livelihoods, should their anti-alcohol campaigns prove successful. So far, and not surprisingly, their victories have been scattered.

In summary, these findings yield two clear implications for policy. First, a combined strategy needs to be pursued that promotes economic empowerment as early in the process as structural and cultural factors allow. Second, this policy needs to be tied to practical training in how to climb the political pyramid of power. Underlying these findings are the theoretical and empirical studies about the centrality of economic power in affecting women's level of equality as well as their well-being. The strongest currents seem to flow from control of economic resources —or lack of it. With more economic power, one has the wherewithal and the confidence to go beyond the self and the household to the larger sociopolitical community; with more economic dependency, one is more likely to be a victim of violence and incapable of the kind of effective political leadership that can lead to policies that are both gender-fair and people-fair—that is, policies that provide voice as well as vote to the people on the lower slopes of the pyramid of power.

Notes

a. Research on these countries was carried out for a USAID Women in Politics program in 1998....

b. Rae Lesser Blumberg, "A General Theory of Gender Stratification," in *Sociological Theory* 1984, ed. Randall Collins (San Francisco: Jossey Bass, 1984); "Introduction: The 'Triple Overlap' of Gender Stratification, Economy, and the Family," in *Gender, Family, and Economy: The Triple Overlap*, ed. Rae Lesser Blumberg (Newbury Park, CA: Sage, 1991).

c. Rae Lesser Blumberg, *Making the Case for the Gender Variable: Women and the Wealth and Well-Being of Nations* (Washington, DC: Agency for International Development/Office of Women in Development, PN-ABC-454, 1989); Rae Lesser Blumberg, "Toward a Feminist Theory of Development," in *Feminism and Sociological Theory*, ed. Ruth A. Wallace (Newbury Park, CA: Sage, 1989); Rae Lesser Blumberg, "Engendering Wealth and Well-Being in an Era of Economic Transformation," in *Engendering Wealth and Well-Being: Empowerment for Global Change*, ed. Rae Lesser Blumberg, Michael Monteón, Catherine Rokowski, and Irene Tinker (Boulder, CO: Westview, 1995).

d. I also hypothesize that "mere work," even in a society's main production activities, does not enhance a woman's relative life options unless that work results in income under her control. Under certain conditions, however, "mere work" can be transformed into economic power. This is more likely (1) the higher the "strategic indispensability" of the women's labor; (2) the greater the extent to which the kinship system advantages women, especially vis-à-vis inheritance; and (3) the lower the level of socioeconomic stratification in the society. See Blumberg, "A General Theory of Gender Stratification."

e. Jenna Luché, "The Gender and Political Participation (GAPP) Study: The 1993 GAPP study of Women in Nepal, Bangladesh and Thailand" (Washington, DC: U.S. Agency for Development, Office of Women in Development, 1994)

f. Kathleen Staudt, "Political Representation: Engendering Democracy," in *Background Papers: Human Development Report 1995* (New York: United Nations Development Programme. 1996), 21.

g. USAID, "Results Review and Resource Request" (Quito: USAID, Ecuador, 1998).

h. Richard Roberts, Director of Microfinance Programs, Food and Agriculture of the United Nations (FAO), personal interview, Rome, March 1999.

Asian Feminism

The last 30 years has seen the rise in women's movements in many Asian countries. The activists in these women's movements often participated in national movements against dictators and hereditary leaders of repressive governments. Many of these struggles are still going on, and there are many heroes of these movements, such as Aung San Suu Kyi. Under house arrest and separated from her family since 1989, she was awarded the Nobel Peace Prize in 1991. She is fighting for Burmese democracy and freedom, not for women's rights. The movements that are more directly for women's rights are closely linked to women's studies as sources of theory and data that can be used in NGOs and governments to implement policies to change the status of women and empower them as political actors. That assumes that the governments are open to women's rights and that NGOs are free to organize for women's rights. In addition, women's studies scholars need to have the freedom to pursue studies on women's issues. So the two threads of activism—for supportive governments and for critical inquiries into the status of women—are often linked. This connection is frequently highlighted in Asian feminist publications.

Discussing the impact of the *Asian Journal of Women's Studies* on its tenth anniversary, Mala Khullar (2005) noted that the largest number of papers published from 1995 to 2005 were on women's participation in political processes in Japan, Korea, China, India, Malaysia, Singapore, Afghanistan, and the Philippines, and the second most popular topic was women's movements/ studies and feminism. The other frequently published topics were family, sexuality, religion, and education. She noted that state organs, such as the Ministry of Gender Equality in Korea and the Department of Women and Child Development in India, make use of the findings published in feminist journals and by feminist publishing houses to improve the status of women. Policies are likely to be based on gender mainstreaming, gender training, and gender sensitization rather than a critique of economic restructuring and modernization (Sobritchea 2005).

An important aspect of Asian feminist women's movements was the parallel rise of women's studies in universities. Feminists realized that research and publications were needed in order to influence governments and give women's organizations a data base to work from. Activism brought attention to gender discrimination and inequality, and women's studies produced a body of knowledge about women's lives from women's points of view. As Pooja Juyal (2005a) says about the development of Indian feminism in the 1970s:

> The critical link of women's studies with the women's movement makes this academic endeavour a bearer of the same normative concerns which were upheld by the movement, i.e., the concerns about equity, equality and social justice. It also incorporated within itself the same transformatory zeal. Women's studies may also be perceived as value-based knowledge with a humanist core. The nature and scope of its concern—documentation, study and research of women's lives from the women's view—was comprehensive and wide-ranging, as the discrimination practiced against women in society is endemic. (21)

In 2004 and 2005, Ewha Womans University Press[2] in South Korea published *Women's Studies in Asia*, a series of readers in English for upper-level undergraduate and graduate students on China, India, Indonesia, South Korea, the Philippines, Taiwan, and Thailand. Topics covered are family, work, sexuality, culture, law, women's movements, religion, the body, and health. The intent, according to the back covers, is to provide "access to knowledge produced by, about, and for Asian women." In addition to research reports, each of the books has at least one chapter on women's movements and political involvement.

These texts are but a few examples of the burgeoning literature on women's studies and feminism in Asian countries. The following overview will concentrate on India (Juyal 2005a, b), South Korea (Cho 2005, Kim 2005), and Japan (Gelb 2003, Mackie 2003), each of which have thriving women's movements.[3] Feminism in these countries reflects many of the themes of postcolonialism, especially campaigns against violence and the oppression of women by patriarchal traditions and economic deprivation.

India. The women's movement in India began around 1975, designated by the United Nations as International Women's Year. In India, a large number of autonomous groups were formed, which concentrated on violence against women, especially dowry murders and rapes, and also child marriages and the ill-treatment of widows. Other issues were education and access to health care. These issues were still salient by the 1990s, but within the movement, there was fragmentation by class, caste, and religion. Some religiously oriented personal laws on marriage, divorce, and inheritance affect women adversely, but reforming them would conflict with cultural traditions.

The policy of reserving one-third of the seats for women in governing bodies, as called for by a Constitutional Amendment in 1993, meant that poorer, rural women would need education and leadership training to be effective law makers. Increasingly, there were calls for quotas within the one-third to ensure diverse religious, class, and caste representation. Ultimately, the concept of "multiple patriarchies" replaced a unified vision of women's oppression and feminist politics.

South Korea. The South Korean women's movement had the opposite problem, one of too much homogeneity. Korean feminism and feminist studies had also begun in the 1970s. Right from the beginning, there was an emphasis on Korean identity in theories and practices. As Kim (2005) says,

> Throughout the culture, the discourse of "Korean feminism" has spawned the notion that Korean women have a different cultural outlook and values distinguishable from the cultural subjectivity characteristic to Western or American women in particular. (30)

The emphasis on Korean identity valorizes tradition and nationalism. The nationalistic discourse rejects what is Western and modern; "we" must be distinguished from "them." There is also a subtext of spiritual superiority. A Western-oriented feminist discourse would be more likely to valorize individuality, progress, modernization, and resistance to the imposed roles of family-oriented wife, mother, and daughter. A nationalist discourse Kim says, constructs "the archetypical Korean woman who preserves what is valuable through sacrifice and endurance" (46).

Feminist claims for a new vision of women have had to absorb cultural constructions of Korean femininity, but they have been adapted to a concept of "positive gender difference," what the advancement of women would bring to Korean society (Cho 2005). Cho notes, however, that the concept of "positive gender difference" implies a universalized, homogeneous "we, the women." Policies built on this concept, such as affirmative action, favor college graduates and middle-class women who seek employment in the public sector. What is needed, she argues, is a concept of gender that encompasses women in diverse social locations, with different paths to gender equality.

The trafficked and captured sexual prisoners of the Japanese during World War II (euphemistically called "comfort women") are an example of the contradictory pulls of nationalism and feminism. Feminism calls for these women to tell their stories in their own voices, but for many years they were rendered invisible by family shame and nationalistic dishonor. They were emblematic of the violated body of Korea under Japanese occupation, but they didn't have the purity and innocence to represent Korean victimhood. Only recently have they become a feminist cause in South Korea and Japan.

Japan. The Japanese women's movement has had a long history, with a first and second wave, and now a possibly third wave, with an influx of younger women. The first wave, at the end of the nineteenth and early twentieth century, was much like the first wave of feminism in the United States. The focus was on getting the vote, procreative freedom, and economic and political equality. It was an upper-middle-class movement and was suppressed before and during World War II. Under pressure from the United States during its occupation after Japan's defeat, a new constitution gave women the right to vote and run for political office, and civil code reform gave them equal rights in marriage and divorce. However, gendered expectations for middle-class men's intensive work habits and mother's responsibility for their children's education mean that a majority of Japanese women do not have full-time jobs. In the second wave, middle-class women organized locally to fight for consumer rights, environmental protection, and peace, and against militarism and nuclear power. These "housewife feminists" grouped in umbrella associations for greater impact.

Since the 1970s, one group of feminists has added violence against women, procreative rights, pornography, and sex tourism to their causes, while another group, affiliated with women members of government, has worked on issues of education, employment, and political representation. Japanese feminists have used international treaties and organizations that emerged from the 1975 International Women's Year and the 1995 United Nations Fourth World Women's Conference in Beijing to pressure the Japanese government into pro-woman policies. According to Joyce Gelb, "*Kansetsu gaiatsu*, the impact of international human and women's rights movements on Japanese policy and mobilization, cannot be overestimated" (2003, 29). It is a "politics of externality" and internationalism, the opposite of South Korean feminism's embrace of cultural traditions and nationalism.

Cultural Conflicts

The political issue of women's rights versus national and cultural traditions is a problematic area in many countries. In Beijing in 1995, the popular slogan was "human rights are women's rights and women's rights are human rights." The Platform for Action document that came out of the U.N. conference condemned particular cultural practices that are oppressive to women—infanticide, dowry, child marriage, and ritual genital cutting. The 187 governments that signed onto the platform agreed to abolish these practices. However, since they are integral parts of cultural and tribal traditions, giving them up could be seen as kowtowing to Western ideas. Postcolonial feminism is caught between a critique of Western cultural imperialism as too individualistic and materialistic and a critique of traditional patriarchy as oppressive of women.

One solution to this dilemma is community organizing around women's productive and procreative roles as mothers—so that what benefits them economically and physically is in the service of their families, not themselves alone. However, this same community organizing and family service can support the continuance of cultural practices that can be harmful to women, such as ritual female genital cutting. This issue has split feminists in the involved countries and also Western and non-Western feminists.

Ritual Female Genital Cutting

For more than two thousand years, in a broad belt across the middle of Africa, various forms of female genital cutting have been used to ensure women's virginity until marriage and to inhibit wives' desire for sexual relations after marriage, and also for aesthetic reasons. Girls undergo clitorectomies and removal of the outer lips of the vagina to be marriageable and feminine, according to their culture's views of chastity and how women's bodies should look. In many of the same cultural groups, boys undergo removal of the penile foreskin (circumcision) to become a man.

For women, childbirth becomes more dangerous because of tearing and bleeding, and there are risks of infection and urinary problems after the procedures and throughout life. Some anthropologists who have done interviews with African women argue that sexual pleasure after genital cutting is extremely variable. Some ritual genital cutting may increase the transmission of HIV infection for girls and women, but there have been no systematic studies. The data are clearer for boys and men and indicate that circumcision seems to protect against HIV transmission.

When done on children too young to consent, from the viewpoint of the West, female genital cutting seems like the ultimate in child abuse, but from the perspective of the societies where these practices are part of deeply held cultural beliefs, not to cut would be a serious breech of parental responsibility. In the parts of the world where these practices are imbued with religious, moral, and esthetic values, ritual genital cutting makes girls into marriageable woman.

Change is coming from within, through the influence of Islamic activists, the work of community health educators, and the efforts of educated African women. Western outrage and external efforts to stop female ritual genital cutting often provoke a strong backlash in the countries where these practices are common. This clash of cultural perspectives has led Carla Makhlouf Obermeyer, a German anthropologist, to question whether Western women could ever understand why African women would willingly undergo genital cutting and have it done on their young daughters, any more than African women who have been cut can understand how Western women can live with their ugly genitals. Although Westerners may be reluctant to criticize women's beliefs and practices in cultures not their own, feminist and human rights policies do condemn patriarchal social structures that control and oppress women, as well as practices such as ritual female genital cutting when they are part of women's subordination, just as they do Western body modification practices for the sake of idealized beauty.

Critique

Postcolonial feminism has developed a split between Western ideas of individualism and human rights and the power and values of local cultures. On the one hand, Western ideas support the rights of girls and women to an education that will allow them to be economically independent. They are also the source of a concept of universal human rights, which can be used to fight subordinating cultural practices. On the other hand, Western ideas undercut communal enterprises and traditional sharing of food production and child care as well as grassroots women's movements.

Non-Western postcolonial feminist scholars and activists in their own countries and in Western countries argue that all women cannot be subsumed into a universally oppressed "sisterhood." They show that concepts of individual rights and gender equality are embedded in the history, ideology, and political struggles of Westernized nation-states and cannot be imposed on people with different histories, ideologies, and politics. Postcolonial feminist politics has often split over transnational class and racial hierarchies in what Deborah Mindry (2001), an anthropologist, calls an invidious "politics of virtue"—advantaged urban, White, middle-class women "helping" poor, rural Black women.

Currently, postcolonial feminism advocates transnational activism, which seeks coalitions that recognize differences but band together over common issues of gender inequality—poverty, education, health care, reproductive rights, sexual exploitation, and AIDS.

Summary

Postcolonial feminism engages the global economy, with its competing state and private economic interests, and the capitalist drive for high production with cheap labor for maximum profits. Gender inequalities and politics are buried deep within class and racial ethnic divides, so that women's interests are intertwined with those of working-class and racially and ethnically disadvantaged men.

Postcolonial feminist research has shown that families all over the world need several workers in order to survive, often including children. Women and girls are doubly vulnerable—as workers and as family members. They are a prime source of low-paid wage workers whose earnings belong first to their families. They also work, often unpaid, in family businesses; they make things at home to sell to supplement their family's food supply; they become prostitutes at a young age, often sold as a source of family income. At the same time, women physically maintain households and have babies, and frequently bury them within a year of birth.

There is no doubt that in many parts of the world today, as postcolonial feminism has shown, women are living in dire conditions. To redress their situation, whole economic structures and family and kinship systems need to be overhauled.

Asian feminism has documented the uneven progress of women's rights movements in diverse Asian countries, as well as their linkages to nationalist liberation movements. Asian women's studies theorizing and data have been instrumental for gender policies in NGOs and governments supportive of women's rights.

Postcolonial feminism makes very evident the political dilemmas of gender reform feminisms. Throughout the world, men own most of the private property, monopolize the better jobs, and make the laws. The outcome of this inequality is men's double exploitation of women in the job market and in the home. Sex differences are not the cause of women's exploitation, but its justification. Women are subordinate in industrial and developing societies not because they are child bearers or child-minders but because economies depend on them as low-paid workers in the job market and nonpaid workers for the family. Each form of exploitation of women's work reinforces the other. Women's economic value as low-waged workers and as unpaid workers for the family are the *main* reasons for their subordination in industrialized and nonindustrialized modern societies.

Gender reform feminist politics is correct in pinpointing women's position in the world of paid work as the target for change. Postcolonial feminism, like Marxist and socialist feminism, has pointed out that the problem is that the entire global economy needs drastic change. If the global economy is not made more equal for everyone, women in general, and poor women in particular, suffer the most. But since the gendered social order as a whole is the source of gender inequality, economic changes alone will not necessarily put women on an equal footing with men. Cultural and ideological recognition of women's worth and the worth of their work as mothers of future generations is also necessary.

NOTES

1. http://news.nationalgeographic.com/news/2006/10/061013-nobel-peace.html.
2. Womans is the correct punctuation for Ewha Womans University.
3. For China, see the discussion in Marxist feminism.

SUGGESTED READINGS IN POSTCOLONIAL AND ASIAN FEMINISM

Basu, Amrita, Inderpal Grewal, Caren Kaplan, and Liisa Malkki, eds. 2001. "Globalization and Gender." Special Issue, *Signs* 26: Summer.

Benería, Lourdes. 2003. *Gender, Development, and Globalization: Economics as if All People Mattered.* New York: Routledge.

Bennholdt-Thomsen, Veronika, and Maria Mies. 2000. *The Subsistence Perspective: Beyond the Globalized Economy.* London: Zed.

Blumberg, Rae Lesser. 1991. *Gender, Family, and Economy: The Triple Overlap.* Newbury Park, CA: Sage.

————. 2004a. "Women's Rights, Land Rights and Human Rights: Dilemmas in East Africa." *Journal of Development Alternatives and Area Studies* 23: 17–32.

————. 2004b. "Extending Lenski's Schema to Hold Up Both Halves of the Sky—a Theory-Guided Way of Conceptualizing Agrarian Societies that Illuminates a Puzzle about Gender Stratification." *Sociological Theory* 22: 278–291.

Bose, Christine E., and Edna Acosta-Belén, eds. 1995. *Women in the Latin American Development Process.* Philadelphia: Temple University Press.

Bose, Christine E. and Minjeong Kim, ed. 2009. *Global Gender Research: Transnational Perspectives.* New York: Routledge.

Boserup, Ester. [1970] 1987. *Women's Role in Economic Development.* New York: St. Martin's Press.

Brah, Avtar, Helen Crowley, Lyn Thomas, and Merl Storr, eds. "Globalization." 2002. Special issue, *Feminist Review* 70.

Brydon, Lynne, and Sylvia Chant. 1989. *Women in the Third World: Gender Issues in Rural and Urban Areas.* New Brunswick, NJ: Rutgers University Press.

Chang, Grace. 2000. *Disposable Domestics: Immigrant Women Workers in the Global Economy.* Cambridge, MA: South End Press.

Charrad, Mounira. 2001. *States and Women's Rights: The Making of Postcolonial Tunisia, Algeria, and Morocco.* Berkeley: University of California Press.

Chow, Esther Ngan-ling, ed. 2003. "Gender, Globalization and Social Change in the 21st Century." Special Issue, *International Sociology* 18: September.

Chowdhry, Geeta, and Sheila Nair, eds. 2003. *Postcolonialism and International Relations: Race, Gender and Class.* New York: Routledge.

Christiansen-Ruffman, Linda, ed. 1998. *The Global Feminist Enlightenment: Women and Social Knowledge.* Madrid, Spain: International Sociological Association.

Davis, Kathy. 2007. *The Making of Our Bodies, Ourselves: How Feminism Travels Across Borders.* Durham, NC: Duke University Press.

Ehrenreich, Barbara, and Arlie Russell Hochschild, eds. 2002. *Global Woman: Nannies, Maids, and Sex Workers in the New Economy.* New York: Henry Holt.

Eschle, Catherine. 2001. *Global Democracy, Social Movements, and Feminism.* Boulder, CO: Westview.

————. 2005. "'Skeleton Women:' Feminism and the Antiglobalization Movement." *Signs* 30: 1741–1769.

Fernández-Kelly, María Patricia. 1983. *For We Are Sold, I and My People: Women and Industry in Mexico's Frontier.* Albany, NY: State University of New York Press.

Ferree, Myra Marx, and Aili Mari Tripp, eds. 2006. *Global Feminism: Transnational Women's Activism, Organizing, and Human Rights.* New York: New York University Press.

Grewal, Inderpal, and Caren Kaplan, eds. 1994. *Scattered Hegemonies: Postmodernity and Transnational Feminist Practice.* Minneapolis: University of Minnesota Press.

Harcourt, Wendy, ed. 1994. *Feminist Perspectives on Sustainable Development.* London: Zed.

Herzog, Hanna. 2004. "'Both an Arab and a Woman': Gendered, Racialised Experiences of Female Palestinian Citizens of Israel." *Social Identities* 10: 53–82.

———. 2008. "Re/visioning the Women's Movement in Israel." *Citizenship Studies* 12: 265–282.

Jaquette, Jane, ed. 1989. *The Women's Movement in Latin America: Feminism and the Transition to Democracy.* Winchester, MA: Unwin Hyman.

Kabeer, Naila, Agneta Stark, and Edda Magnus, eds. 2007. *Global Perspectives on Gender Equality: Reversing the Gaze.* New York: Routledge.

Kandiyoti, Deniz. 1988. "Bargaining with Patriarchy." *Gender & Society* 2: 274–290.

Leacock, Eleanor, and Helen I. Safa, eds. 1986. *Women's Work: Development and the Division of Labor by Gender.* South Hadley, MA: Bergin & Garvey.

Leyenaar, Monique, Najma Chowdhury, Thi Thuy Hang Truong, et al. 2008. "Comparative Perspectives Symposium: Challenges to Women's Leadership." *Signs* 34: 1–47.

Lionnet, Françoise, Obioma Nnaemeka, Susan Perry, and Celeste Schenck, eds. 2004. "Development Cultures: New Environments, New Realities, New Strategies." Special Issue, *Signs* 29: Winter.

Marchand, Marianne, and Anne Sisson Runyan, eds. 2000. *Gender and Global Restructuring: Sightings, Sites, and Resistances.* New York: Routledge.

Melhuus, Marit, and Kristi Anne Stølen, eds. 1997. *Machos, Mistresses, Madonnas: Contesting the Power of Latin American Gender Imagery.* London: Verso.

Mies, Maria. 1986. *Patriarchy and Accumulation on a World Scale: Women in the International Division of Labor.* London: Zed.

Mies, Maria, Veronika Bennholdt-Thomsen, and Claudia von Werlhof. 1988. *Women: The Last Colony.* London: Zed.

Mindry, Deborah. 2001. "Nongovernmental Organizations, 'Grassroots,' and the Politics of Virtue." *Signs* 26: 1187–1211.

Moghadam, Valentine M., ed. 1994. *Identity Politics and Women: Cultural Reassertions and Feminisms in International Perspective.* Boulder, CO: Westview Press.

———, ed. 1996. *Patriarchy and Development: Women's Positions at the End of the Twentieth Century.* Oxford, UK: Clarendon Press.

Mohanty, Chandra Talpade. 2003. *Feminism Without Borders: Decolonizing Theory, Practicing Solidarity.* Durham, NC: Duke University Press.

Mohanty, Chandra Talpade, Ann Russo, and Lourdes Torres, eds. 1991. *Third World Women and the Politics of Feminism.* Bloomington: Indiana University Press.

Morrissey, Marietta. 1989. *Slave Women in The New World: Gender Stratification in the Caribbean.* Lawrence: University of Kansas Press.

Naples, Nancy A. 1998. *Grassroots Warriors: Activist Mothering, Community Work, and the War on Poverty.* New York: Routledge.

Naples, Nancy A., and Manisha Desai, eds. 2002. *Women's Activism and Globalization: Linking Local Struggles and Transnational Politics.* New York: Routledge.

Narayan, Uma. 1997. *Dislocating Cultures: Identities, Traditions, and Third World Feminism.* New York: Routledge.

Narayan, Uma, and Sandra Harding, eds. 2000. *Decentering the Center: Philosophy for a Multicultural, Postcolonial, and Feminist World.* Bloomington: Indiana University Press.

Newell, Stephanie, ed. 1997. *Writing African Women: Gender, Popular Culture and Literature in West Africa*. London: Zed.

Nfah-Abbenyi, Juliana Makuchi. 1997. *Gender in African Women's Writing: Identity, Sexuality, and Difference*. Bloomington: Indiana University Press.

Nnaemeka, Obioma, ed. 1998. *Sisterhood, Feminisms, and Power: From Africa to the Diaspora*. Trenton, NJ: Africa World Press.

Oyewùmí, Oyèrónké. 1997. *The Invention of Women: Making an African Sense of Western Gender Discourses*. Minneapolis: University of Minnesota Press.

Parreñas, Rhacel Salazar. 2001. *Servants of Globalization: Women, Migration, and Domestic Work*. Stanford, CA: Stanford University Press.

Peterson, V. Spike. 1992. *Gendered States: Feminist Revisions of International Relations Theory*. Boulder, CO: Lynne Rienner.

Puri, Jyoti, Hyun Sook Kim, and Paola Bacchetta, eds. 2005. Special issue, "Gender-Sexuality-State-Nation: Transnational Feminist Analysis." *Gender & Society* 19: April.

Redclift, Nanneke, and M. Thea Sinclair, eds. 1991. *Working Women: International Perspectives on Women and Gender Ideology*. New York: Routledge.

Rodriguez, Robyn Magalit, ed. 2008. "Comparative Perspectives Symposium: Gendered Migrations." *Signs* 33: 761–807.

Sa'ar, Amalia. 2005. "Postcolonial Feminism, the Politics of Identification, and the Liberal Bargain." *Gender & Society* 19: 680–700.

Sassen, Saskia. 1998. *Globalization and Its Discontents: Essays on the New Mobility of People and Money*. New York: New Press.

Scheper-Hughes, Nancy. 1992. *Death Without Weeping: The Violence of Everyday Life in Brazil*. Berkeley: University of California Press.

Silliman, Jael, and Ynestra King, eds. 1999. *Dangerous Intersections: Feminist Perspectives on Population, Environment, and Development*. Boston: South End Press.

Smith, Peter H., Jennifer L. Troutner, and Christine Hunefeldt, eds. 2004. *Promises of Empowerment: Women in Asia and Latin America*. Lanham, MD: Rowman & Littlefield.

Sparr, Pam, ed. 1994. *Mortgaging Women's Lives: Feminist Critiques of Structural Adjustment*. London: Zed.

Spivak, Gayatri Chakravorty. 1988. *In Other Worlds: Essays in Cultural Politics*. New York: Routledge.

Tinker, Irene, ed. 1990. *Persistent Inequalities: Women and World Development*. New York: Oxford University Press.

Trinh, T. Minh-ha. 1989. *Woman, Native, Other: Writing Postcoloniality and Feminism*. Bloomington: Indiana University Press.

Visvanathan, Nalini, Lynn Duggan, Laurie Nisonoff, and Nan Wiegersma, eds. 1997. *The Women, Gender and Development Reader*. London: Zed.

Ward, Kathryn, ed. 1990. *Women Workers and Global Restructuring*. Ithaca, NY: ILR Books.

Young, Kate, Carol Wolkowitz, and Roslyn McCullagh, eds. 1981. *Of Marriage and the Market: Women's Subordination in International Perspective*. London: CSE Books.

Yuval-Davis, Nira. 1997. *Gender and Nation*. Thousand Oaks, CA: Sage.

Asian Feminism

Chang, Pilwha, and Eun-Shil Kim, eds. 2005. *Women's Experiences and Feminist Practices in South Korea*. Seoul, South Korea: Ewha Womans University Press.

Chow, Esther Ngan-ling, ed. 2002. *Transforming Gender and Development in East Asia.* New York: Routledge.

Chow, Esther Ngan-ling, Naihua Zhang, and Jinling Wang. 2009. "Promising and Contested Fields: Advancing Women's Studies and Sociology of Women/Gender in Contemporary China." In Christine E. Bose and Minjeong Kim, eds., *Global Gender Research: Transnational Perspectives.* New York: Routledge.

Gelb, Joyce. 2003. *Gender Policies in Japan and the United States: Comparing Women's Movements, Rights, and Politics.* New York: Palgrave Macmillan.

Hicks, George. 1995. *The Comfort Women: Japan's Brutal Regime of Enforced Prostitution in the Second World War.* New York: W.W. Norton.

Juyal, Pooja. 2005a. "Introduction." In Pooja Juyal et al., eds. 2005. *Women's Studies in India.* Seoul, South Korea: Ewha Womans University Press.

———. 2005b. "Women, Politics and the State in India: Reading Gender into the Indian State." In Pooja Juyal et al., eds. 2005. *Women's Studies in India.* Seoul, South Korea: Ewha Womans University Press.

Juyal, Pooja, and the Faculty of Isabella Thoburn College, eds. 2005. *Women's Studies in India: Some Contemporary Contours.* Seoul, South Korea: Ewha Womans University Press.

Khullar, Mala. 2005. *"Asian Journal of Women's Studies:* Ten Years and Beyond." Presented at International Symposium for 10th Anniversary of AJWS, "Theorizing the Experience of Asian Women's Studies in a Globalizing World." Asian Center for Women's Studies, Ewha Womans University, Seoul, South Korea, June 22.

Kim, Seung-Kyung. 1997. *Class Struggle or Family Struggle? The Lives of Women Factory Workers in South Korea.* Cambridge, UK: Cambridge University Press.

Kudva, Neema and Kajri Misra. 2008. "Gender Quotas, the Politics of Presence, and the Feminist Project: What Does the Indian Experience Tell Us?" *Signs* 34: 49–73.

Liddle, Joanna, and Sachiko Nakajima. 2000. *Rising Suns, Rising Daughters.* London, Zed Books.

Lin, Weihung, ed. 2005. *Gender, Culture and Society: Women's Studies in Taiwan.* Seoul, South Korea: Ewha Womans University Press.

Mackie, Vera. 2003. *Feminism in Modern Japan.* Cambridge, UK: Cambridge University Press.

Mies, Maria. 1982. *The Lace Makers of Narsapur: Indian Housewives Produce for the World Market.* London: Zed.

Misra, Kamal K., and Janet Huber Lowry, eds. 2007. *Recent Studies on Indian Women.* Jaipur, India: Rawat Publications.

Poerwandari, Kristi, Saparinah Sadli, and Tita Marlita, eds. 2005. *Indonesian Women in a Changing Society.* Seoul, South Korea: Ewha Womans University Press.

Rothchild, Jennifer. 2006. *Gender Trouble Makers: Education and Empowerment in Nepal.* New York: Routledge.

Satha-Anand, Suwanna, ed. 2004. *Women's Studies in Thailand: Power, Knowledge and Justice.* Seoul, South Korea: Ewha Womans University Press.

Schellstede, Sangmie Choi, ed. 2000. *Comfort Women Speak: Testimony of Sex Slaves of the Japanese Military.* New York: Holmes & Meier.

Schmidt, David Andrew. 2000. *Ianfu—The Comfort Women of the Japanese Imperial Army of the Pacific War: Broken Silence.* Lewiston, NY: Mellen.

Sobritchea, Carolyn I., ed. 2004. *Gender, Culture and Society: Selected Readings in Women's Studies in the Philippines.* Seoul, South Korea: Ewha Womans University Press.

———. 2005. "Representations of Gender Inequality and Women's Issues in Philippine Feminist Discourses." Presented at International Symposium for 10th Anniversary of AJWS, "Theorizing the Experience of Asian Women's Studies in a Globalizing World." Asian Center for Women's Studies, Ewha Womans University, Seoul, South Korea, June 22.

Subramaniam, Mangala. 2006. *The Power of Women's Organizing: Gender, Caste, and Class in India*. Lanham, MD: Lexington Books.

Ritual Genital Cutting

Abdalla, Raqiya Haji Dualeh. 1982. *Sisters in Affliction: Circumcision and Infibulation of Women in Africa*. London: Zed.

Abusharaf, Rogaia Mustafa. 2001. "Virtuous Cuts: Female Genital Mutilation in an African Ontology." *Differences: A Journal of Feminist Cultural Studies* 12: 112–140.

Bashir, L. Miller. 1997. "Female Genital Mutilation: Balancing Intolerance of the Practice with Tolerance of Culture." *Journal of Women's Health* 6: 11–14.

Boyle, Elizabeth Heger. 2002. *Female Genital Cutting: Cultural Conflict in the Global Community*. Baltimore: Johns Hopkins University Press.

Brady, M. 1999. "Female Genital Mutilation: Complications and Risk of HIV Transmission." *AIDS Patient Care and Sexually Transmitted Diseases* 13 (12): 709–716.

Denniston, George C., Frederick Mansfield Hodges, and Marilyn Fayre Milos, eds. 1999. *Male and Female Circumcision: Medical, Legal, and Ethical Considerations in Pediatric Practice*. New York: Kluwer.

El Dareer, Asma. 1982. *Woman, Why Do You Weep? Circumcision and Its Consequences*. London: Zed.

Ericksen, K. Paige. 1995. "Female Circumcision Among Egyptian Women." *Women's Health: Research on Gender, Behavior, and Policy* 1: 309–328.

Gruenbaum, Ellen. 2000. *The Female Circumcision Controversy: An Anthropological Perspective*. Philadelphia: University of Pennsylvania Press.

Hernlund, Ylva, and Bettina Shell-Duncan, eds. 2000. *Female "Circumcision" in Africa: Culture, Controversy, and Change*. Boulder, CO: Lynne Rienner.

James, Stephen A. 1994. "Reconciling Human Rights and Cultural Relativism: The Case of Female Circumcision." *Bioethics* 8(Nov. 1): 1–26.

———. 1998. "Shades of Othering: Reflections on Female Circumcision/Genital Mutilation." *Signs* 23: 1031–1048.

Korn, Fadumo, and Sabine Eichorst. 2006. *Born in the Big Rains. A Memoir of Somalia and Survival*. Tr. and Afterword by Tobe Levin. New York: Feminist Press.

Koso-Thomas, Olayinka. 1987. *The Circumcision of Women: A Strategy for Eradication*. London: Zed.

Lightfoot-Klein, Hanny. 1989. *Prisoners of Ritual: An Odyssey into Female Circumcision in Africa*. New York: Harrington Park Press.

Leonard, Lori. 2000a. "Interpreting Female Genital Cutting: Moving Beyond the Impasse." *Annual Review of Sex Research* 11: 158–191.

———. 2000b. "'We Did It for Pleasure Only:' Hearing Alternative Tales of Female Circumcision." *Qualitative Inquiry* 6: 212–228.

Mackie, Gerry. 1996. "Ending Footbinding and Infibulation: A Convention Account." *American Sociological Review* 61: 999–1017.

Njambi, Wairimu Ngaruiya. 2004. "Dualisms and Female Bodies in Representations of African Female Circumcision." *Feminist Theory* 5: 281–303. Responses and reply 305–328.

Obermeyer, Carla Makhlouf. 1999. "Female Genital Surgeries: The Known, the Unknown, and the Unknowable," *Medical Anthropology Quarterly* 13: 79–106.

O'Farrell, N., and M. Egger. 2000. "Circumcision in Men and the Prevention of HIV Infection: A 'Meta-analysis' Revisited." *International Journal of Sexually Transmitted Diseases and AIDS* 11: 137–142.

Rahman, Anika, and Nahid Toubia. 2000. *Female Genital Mutilation: A Guide to Laws and Policies Worldwide.* London: Zed.

Robertson, Claire. 1996. "Grassroots in Kenya: Women, Genital Mutilation, and Collective Action, 1920–1990." *Signs* 21: 615–641.

Shweder, Richard A. 2000. "What About 'Female Genital Mutilation'? And Why Understanding Culture Matters in the First Place." *Daedalus* 129(Fall): 209–232.

van der Kwaak, Anke. 1992. "Female Circumcision and Gender Identity: A Questionable Alliance?" *Social Science and Medicine* 35: 777–787.

Walker, Alice. 1992. *Possessing the Secret of Joy.* New York: Harcourt Brace Jovanovich.

Weiss, Helen A., Maria A. Quigley, and Richard J. Hayes. 2000. "Male Circumcision and Risk of HIV Infection in Sub-Saharan Africa: A Systematic Review and Meta-Analysis." *AIDS* 14(Oct. 20): 2361–2370.

Williams, Lindy, and Teresa Sobieszyzyk. 1997. "Attitudes Surrounding the Continuation of Female Circumcision in the Sudan: Passing the Tradition to the Next Generation." *Journal of Marriage and the Family* 59: 966–981.

Winter, Bronwyn. 1994. "Women, the Law, and Cultural Relativism in France: The Case of Excision." *Signs* 19: 939–974.

PART II

GENDER RESISTANCE FEMINISMS

I n the 1970s, in many countries, feminist ideas began to make inroads into the public consciousness, and women entered formerly all-men workplaces and schools. Derogatory remarks about women were no longer acceptable officially, but women became more and more aware of constant put-downs from men they saw every day—bosses and colleagues at work, professors and students in the classroom, fellow organizers in political movements, and worst of all, from boyfriends and husbands at home. These "microinequities" of everyday life—being ignored and interrupted, not getting credit for competence or good performance, being passed over for jobs that involve taking charge—crystallize into a pattern that insidiously wears women down.

Mary Rowe, a woman doctor using a pseudonym (because it was too dangerous even in the late 1970s to openly call attention to what men colleagues were doing to women), termed it the "Saturn's rings phenomenon" at a Conference on Women's Leadership and Authority in the Health Professions, held in California in 1977. The seemingly trivial sexist incidents, she said, are like the dust particles in the rings around the planet Saturn—separately they are tiny, but when they coalesce, they form a very visible pattern.

Younger women working in the civil rights, anti–Vietnam War, and student New Left movements in the late 1960s had realized even earlier that they were being used as handmaidens, bed partners, and coffee-makers by the men in their protest organizations. Despite the revolutionary rhetoric the young men were flinging in the face of Western civilization in many countries, when it came to women, they might as well have been living in the eighteenth century. Young women activists' realization of their sexual vulnerability to men's physical and emotional demands, to harassment and denigration of their bodies, and especially to rape, battering, and other forms of violence led to new feminisms.

Out of their awareness that sisters had no place in any brotherhood and that their activist brothers could be dangerous to them came the American and European gender resistance feminisms. Their watchword is *patriarchy*, or men's subordination of women. Gender resistance feminisms argue that patriarchy can be found wherever women and men are in contact with each other, in public life, in the family, and in face-to-face encounters. Patriarchy is very hard to eradicate because a sense of superiority to women is deeply embedded in the consciousness and subconsciousness of most men and is built into their privileges in Western society. These privileges are a sense of entitlement to the best jobs, claims on women's bodies, and domination of the cultural and media landscape.

Radical feminism emerged from the misogyny and objectification of women activists by their male colleagues in the civil rights and New Left movements of the 1960s. Tired of the constant degnigration, women began to vent to other women in consciousness-raising groups, where the topics of intense discussion came out of the commonalities of women's lives—emotional and sexual service to men, the constant sexual innuendoes and come-ons in workplaces and on college campuses, the lack of control over procreation, the fear of physical and sexual abuse. Politically, radical feminism took on the violence in women's oppression—rape and wife beating, the depiction of women as sex objects in the mass media and as pieces of meat in pornography, the global commerce in prostitution. This sexual exploitation of women is the worst effect of patriarchy, according to radical feminism, because its goal is social control of all women. Even if they are not directly attacked, the threat of sexual violence can be enough to keep women fearful and timid. Radical feminism fought back with "take back the night" rallies and campaigns against pornography and sex trafficking.

Lesbian feminism argues that sexual violence and exploitation are the common downside of romantic heterosexual love, which is itself oppressive to women, as is the assumption that everyone is heterosexual to lesbian women. The lesbian feminist perspective has been an important part of *cultural feminism*—the development of a woman's world perspective in the creation of women's knowledge and culture. Coming out became a political act, and women-only events a way to resist a culture dominated by men.

Psychoanalytic feminism provides a psychological theory of why men oppress women. Using Freudian concepts of personality development, psychoanalytic feminism argues that men's fear of castration by their mothers and repression of their primal attachment to her is sublimated in a *phallocentric* (sexually male) culture that symbolically subordinates and controls women. Politically, French feminism counters with cultural productions that celebrate women's bodies, sexuality, and maternality.

Standpoint feminism brought all these feminist theories and politics together in an agenda for research and culture. Science and social science have to formulate questions and gather data from a *woman's standpoint* and women have to produce their own culture. For standpoint feminists, it has been crucial for women to do research from their own point of view and thus to create new bodies of knowledge in biology, medicine, psychology, economics, sociology, and history. This knowledge starts from premises that put women, not men, at the center. At the same time, standpoint feminists encourage women to make their own culture: literature, arts, theater, classical and popular music, comedy, and crafts.

The important theoretical contribution of gender resistance feminisms has been in showing that women's devaluation and subordination are part of the ideology and values of Western culture, as represented in religion, the mass media, and cultural productions, and are built into the everyday practices of major institutions, such as medicine, the law, science, and social science. They also show how sexual exploitation and violence, especially rape and pornography, are a means of control of women.

Some political remedies—women-only consciousness-raising groups, alternative organizations, and lesbian separatism—are resistant to the gendered social order, but they are not able to transform it, as they stand apart from mainstream social institutions. They are vital in allowing women the "breathing space" to formulate important theories of gender inequality, to develop women's studies programs in colleges and universities, to form communities, and to produce knowledge, culture, ethics, and religions from a woman's point of view. The knowledge and culture produced by resistance feminism has greatly enriched Western societies, but it has sometimes alienated heterosexual White working-class women and women of disadvantaged racial or ethnic groups, who feel that their men are just as oppressed as they are by the dominant society. These women would not desert their brothers for a sisterhood they feel does not always welcome their point of view.

More effective have been the feminist campaigns against sexual harassment, rape, battering, incest, pornography, and prostitution. They have, however, led to head-on confrontations with some men's sense of sexual entitlement and have produced considerable antifeminist backlash. Despite the backlash, gender resistant feminisms continue to fight against the still-prevailing gender order that is permeated by men's patriarchal privileges. They may not have been able to transform it, but they haven't given up the fight.

5

Radical Feminism

SOURCES OF GENDER INEQUALITY

- Patriarchy—the system of men's oppression of women
- Legitimation of women's oppression in medicine, religion, science, law, and other social institutions
- Men's violence and control of women through rape, battering, and murder
- Objectification of women's bodies in advertisements, mass media, and cultural productions
- Sexual exploitation in pornography and prostitution
- Sexual harassment at work, in schools, and on the street

POLITICS

- Valorizing all kinds of women's bodies, women's sexuality, and maternal qualities
- Rape crisis centers and battered women's shelters
- Protection of women from international sex trafficking
- Sexual harassment guidelines and penalties for workplaces and schools
- Anti-pornography campaigns
- Campaigns against misogyny in the mass media

CRITIQUE

- Distrust of men as prone to sexual violence ignores differences among them
- Valorizing motherhood alienates women with careers
- Arguing that heterosexual relationships are intrinsically exploitative alienates heterosexual women
- Minimization of racial ethnic differences and loyalties erases differences among women

CONTRIBUTIONS

- Theory of patriarchy as the system that privileges men and exploits women sexually, emotionally, and physically
- Recognition of violence against women as a means of direct and indirect control through fear
- Identification of sexual harassment as part of the continuum of violence against women
- Tracing the global paths of sexual trafficking in women, raising public awareness of its harm to vulnerable young women
- Identification of rape as a weapon of war
- Establishment of accessible rape crisis centers and battered women's shelters
- Critique of hidden devaluation of women in science, medicine, law, and religion
- Linkage of environmental exploitation and women's exploitation in *ecofeminism*

The 1970s saw the growth of what has become a major branch of feminism. Originally used as a term for feminists who wanted to do away with the traditional family and motherhood, radical feminism became a perspective that makes motherhood into a valuable way of thinking and behaving. However, it continues to criticize the traditional family as a prime source of patriarchal oppression of women. Radical feminism condemns the violent aspects of heterosexuality in rape, sexual assaults, sexual harassment, pornography, and sex trafficking of prostituted women and girls.

Radical feminism expands the concept of *patriarchy* by defining it as a worldwide system of subordination legitimated by medicine, religion, science, law, and other social institutions. The values embedded in these major sectors of society favor men as a group over women as a group. For example, male qualities of objectivity, control, and individual achievement are lauded, while women's qualities of empathy, nurturance, and care of others are downplayed. Men's domination of the women of their racial ethnic group and social class gives them *patriarchal privileges*, so that even if they themselves are subordinated by other men, they feel superior to their women.

A prime means of control of women by men is through sexual and emotional exploitation. In the radical feminist view, because of Western society's encouragement of aggressiveness in men and sexual display in women, most men are capable of, if not prone to, violence against women, and most women are potential victims. Rape of the enemy's women is a common wartime strategy. Vulnerable young women are sold, forced, and recruited into global sex and pornography work.

Radical feminism sees sexual violence against women as a continuum from sexual harassment to rape to sexual murder. The constant threat of rape, battering, and murder is a powerful means of keeping women "in their place." Movies, TV, and stories and advertisements in all media sexualize women's bodies. The pervasive sexual objectification encourages men's use of women for their own needs. Also, if women are depicted as "sex objects," their intellectual and leadership capabilities disappear from view—they are just so much "meat." *Ecofeminism* equates the objectification, exploitation, and rape of women, animals, and the earth.

For radical feminists, the physical, political, and economic oppression of women reflects a society's inherent violence. In their view, the destruction of the World Trade Center and part of the Pentagon by suicidal plane hijackers on September 11, 2001, and the killing of thousands of people were a prime example of *masculine* violence. Post–September 11, many radical feminists deplored the hypocritical rhetoric of masculine protection that masked the violence of the bombing of Afghanistan and the invasion of Iraq, which killed many women and children.

One of the earliest statements of the radical feminist credo was the Redstockings Manifesto, written by a group of New York City women in 1969. It first appeared as a mimeographed flyer, designed for distribution at women's liberation events. According to the Redstockings website (http://www.redstockings.org),

> "Redstockings" was a name taken in 1969 by one of the founding women's liberation groups of the 1960s to represent the union of two traditions: the "bluestocking" label disparagingly pinned on feminists of earlier centuries—and "red" for revolution.
>
> Redstockings women would go on to champion and spread knowledge of vital women's liberation theory, slogans, and actions that have become household words such as consciousness-raising, the personal is political, the pro-woman line, sisterhood is powerful, the politics of housework, the Miss America Protest, and "speakouts" that would break the taboos of silence around subjects like abortion.
>
> Redstockings today is a new kind of grassroots, activist "think tank," established by movement veterans, for defending and advancing the women's liberation agenda. The Archives for Action is a project Redstockings established in 1989 to make the formative and radical 1960s experience of the movement more widely available for the taking stock needed for new understandings and improved strategies.

A current Redstockings project is a national health care system in the United States.

Redstockings Manifesto

I. After centuries of individual and preliminary political struggle, women are uniting to achieve their final liberation from male supremacy. Redstockings is dedicated to building this unity and winning our freedom.

II. Women are an oppressed class. Our oppression is total, affecting every facet of our lives. We are exploited as sex objects, breeders, domestic servants, and cheap labor. We are considered inferior beings, whose only purpose is to enhance men's lives. Our humanity is denied. Our prescribed behavior is enforced by the threat of physical violence.

Because we have lived so intimately with our oppressors, in isolation from each other, we have been kept from seeing our personal suffering as a political condition. This creates the illusion that a woman's relationship with her man is a matter of interplay between two unique personalities, and can be worked out individually. In reality, every such relationship is a class relationship, and the conflicts between individual men and women are political conflicts that can only be solved collectively.

III. We identify the agents of our oppression as men. Male supremacy is the oldest, most basic form of domination. All other forms of exploitation and oppression (racism, capitalism, imperialism, etc.) are extensions of male supremacy: men dominate women, a few men dominate the rest. All power structures throughout history have been male-dominated and male-oriented. Men have controlled all political, economic and cultural institutions and backed up this control with physical force. They have used their power to keep women in an inferior position. *All men* receive economic, sexual, and psychological benefits from male supremacy. *All men* have oppressed women.

IV. Attempts have been made to shift the burden of responsibility from men to institutions or to women themselves. We condemn these arguments as evasions. Institutions alone do not oppress; they are merely tools of the oppressor. To blame institutions implies that men and women are equally victimized, obscures the fact that men benefit from the subordination of women, and gives men the excuse that they are forced to be oppressors. On the contrary, any man is free to renounce his superior position provided that he is willing to be treated like a woman by other men.

We also reject the idea that women consent to or are to blame for their own oppression. Women's submission is not the result of brainwashing, stupidity, or mental illness but of continual, daily pressure from men. We do not need to change ourselves, but to change men.

The most slanderous evasion of all is that women can oppress men. The basis for this illusion is the isolation of individual relationships from their political context and the tendency of men to see any legitimate challenge to their privileges as persecution.

V. We regard our personal experience, and our feelings about that experience, as the basis for an analysis of our common situation. We cannot rely on existing ideologies as they are all products of male supremacist culture. We question every generalization and accept none that are not confirmed by our experience.

Our chief task at present is to develop female class consciousness through sharing experience and publicly exposing the sexist foundation of all our institutions. Consciousness-raising is not "therapy," which implies the existence of individual solutions and falsely assumes that the male-female relationship is purely personal, but the only method by which we can ensure that our program for liberation is based on the concrete realities of our lives.

The first requirement for raising class consciousness is honesty, in private and in public, with ourselves and other women.

VI. We identify with all women. We define our best interest as that of the poorest, most brutally exploited woman.

We repudiate all economic, racial, educational or status privileges that divide us from other women. We are determined to recognize and eliminate any prejudices we may hold against other women.

We are committed to achieving internal democracy. We will do whatever is necessary to ensure that every woman in our movement has an equal chance to participate, assume responsibility, and develop her political potential.

VII. We call on all our sisters to unite with us in struggle.

We call on all men to give up their male privileges and support women's liberation in the interest of our humanity and their own.

In fighting for our liberation we will always take the side of the women against their oppressors. We will not ask what is "revolutionary" or "reformist," only what is good for women.

The time for individual skirmishes has passed. This time we are going all the way.

July 7, 1969
REDSTOCKINGS
P.O. Box 748
Stuyvesant Station
New York, N.Y. 10009

Sexual Violence

To radical feminists, the struggle for women's liberation no longer means a good job and career advancement, but instead protection against sexual violence. Whether a woman is an executive, a waitress, a housewife, a nun, an old woman, or a pre-pubescent girl, she is vulnerable to a continuum of sexual assaults ranging from lewd comments on the street to rape. To some radical feminists, even romantic heterosexual relationships have the potential for sexual violence. They argue that since all men derive power from their dominant social status, any sexual and emotional relationship between women and men takes place in a socially unequal context. Consent by women to heterosexual intercourse is, by this definition, often forced by emotional appeals and threats to end the relationship. When a woman fears that a date or friend or lover or husband will use physical violence if she does not give in, and she feels forced to have sexual relations, it is *date-rape* or *marital-rape* and is as abusive as any other kind of rape.

Radical feminists argue that the fear and self-surveillance induced in women by the threat of sexual violence is a powerful means of social control. Women can't feel free to act assertively if they constantly have to worry about a sexual attack. As Catharine MacKinnon, a feminist lawyer and radical feminist theorist, says:

> It's threatening to one's takeability, one's rapeability, one's femininity, to be strong and physically self-possessed. To be able to resist rape, not to communicate rapeability with one's body, to hold one's body for uses and meanings other than that can transform what being a woman means. (1987, 122)

In the effort to combat sexual violence, radical feminism has mounted campaigns to raise awareness of rape victims and battered women and to condemn pornography and prostitution.

Sexual Harassment

Sexual harassment is the most common manifestation of sexual attacks against women in Western societies. Unwanted sexual invitations, sexually loaded remarks and jokes, and inappropriate comments on dress or appearance make it difficult for women and girls to do their work (or even to walk down the street) unmolested. When the response to a work-related request is, "Wow, that sweater really brings out your good points," the not-so-subtle intent is to turn a woman colleague into a "bimbo" and take her out of the running as a serious competitor. More obvious sexual harassment occurs when a boss or teacher threatens the loss of a job or a low grade if a worker or student will not "give a kiss" or if she responds to a grope with a slap. In the military and other hierarchical organizations, women feel that reporting a rape or coerced sex, let alone a pattern of demeaning comments, is useless when the higher-ups have the same sexist attitudes. Women who complain get tainted with a "troublemaker" label or are harassed by the person they complain to, but their harassers are let off with a mild talking to. Sexual harassment seems to get attention only when the media report a drunken attack on women in a public place, the same situation is found in army base after army base, or a high government official is involved.

As Catharine MacKinnon argued in *Sexual Harassment of Working Women* (1979), when sexual harassment adversely affects a worker's or student's concentration, or contaminates the environment in which they work or study, it becomes a form of discrimination. Radical feminism has made these patterns of sexual harassment and their discriminatory results visible. Its analysis is reflected in the sexual harassment guidelines and penalties of many schools and workplaces. In these guidelines, a sexual involvement of any kind between a subordinate and a person in a position of power is considered coercive and is explicitly forbidden. Also actionable is any situation where sexual remarks or uninvited attentions make employees or students so uncomfortable that they are unable to concentrate on their work. These guidelines set up formal processes for reports and complaints and rules for actions to be taken in cases of proven sexual harassment.

Misogyny

Men and boys who would not think of physically attacking a woman or girl and who understand the rationale behind the sexual harassment guidelines still may be guilty of misogyny. Hatred, dislike, or discomfort, especially of assertive women, are manifested in verbal and visual depictions of women and girls as dangerous, destructive, and bitchy.

In the early 1970s, fed up with the misogyny of the men of the New Left, Robin Morgan wrote what became a famous essay in radical feminism, "Goodbye to All That."[1] During the Hillary Rodham Clinton–Barack Obama primary fight preceding the 2008 U.S. presidential election, which divided feminists, Robin Morgan wrote "Goodbye to All That (#2)." It was posted on the Women's Media Center website[2] on Feb. 2, 2008, and immediately sped through the Internet via feminist lists and blogs. Morgan claimed that despite all the gains of women in the past 38 years, misogyny's virulence can still fill the media and the Internet. Robin Morgan is a co-founder of the Women's Media Center and author of twenty-one books, including the classic anthologies, *Sisterhood Is Powerful*, *Sisterhood Is Global*, and *Sisterhood Is Forever.*

Goodbye to All That (#2)

Robin Morgan

Women's Media Center

During my decades in civil-rights, anti-war, and contemporary women's movements, I've resisted writing another specific "Goodbye...". But not since the suffrage struggle have two communities—the joint conscience-keepers of this country—been so set in competition, as the contest between Hillary Rodham Clinton (HRC) and Barack Obama (BO) unfurls. *So.*

Excerpted from Women's Media Center, http://www.womensmediacenter.com/ex/020108.html. Printed by permission.

Goodbye to the double standard—

—Hillary is too ballsy but too womanly, a Snow Maiden who's emotional, and so much a politician as to be unfit for politics.

—She's "ambitious" but he shows "fire in the belly." (Ever had labor pains?)

—When a sexist idiot screamed "Iron my shirt!" at HRC, it was considered amusing; if a racist idiot shouted "Shine my shoes!" at BO, it would've inspired hours of airtime and pages of newsprint analyzing our national dishonor....

Goodbye to the toxic viciousness—

Carl Bernstein's disgust at Hillary's "thick ankles." Nixon-trickster Roger Stone's new Hillary-hating 527 group, "Citizens United Not Timid" (check the capital letters). John McCain answering "How do we beat the bitch?" with "Excellent question!" Would he have dared reply similarly to "How do we beat the black bastard?" *For shame.*

Goodbye to the HRC nutcracker with metal spikes between splayed thighs. If it was a tap-dancing blackface doll, we would be righteously outraged—and they would not be selling it in airports. *Shame.*

Goodbye to the most intimately violent T-shirts in election history, including one with the murderous slogan "If Only Hillary had married O.J. Instead!" *Shame.*

Goodbye to Comedy Central's "Southpark" featuring a storyline in which terrorists secrete a bomb in HRC's vagina. I refuse to wrench my brain down into the gutter far enough to find a race-based comparison. *For shame.*

Goodbye to the sick, malicious idea that this is funny. This is not "Clinton hating," not "Hillary hating." **This is sociopathic *woman-hating.*** If it were about Jews, we would recognize it instantly as anti-Semitic propaganda; if about race, as KKK poison. Hell, PETA would go ballistic if such vomitous spew were directed at *animals.* Where is our sense of outrage—as citizens, voters, Americans?...

Goodbye to pretending the black community is entirely male and all women are white—

Surprise! Women exist in all opinions, pigmentations, ethnicities, abilities, sexual preferences, and ages—not only African American and European American but Latina and Native American, Asian American and Pacific Islanders, Arab American and—hey, *every* group, because a group wouldn't be alive if we hadn't given birth to it. A few non-racist countries may exist—but sexism is everywhere. No matter how many ways a woman breaks free from other oppressions, she remains a female human being in a world still so patriarchal that it's the "norm."

So why should *all* women not be as justly proud of our womanhood and the centuries, even millennia, of struggle that *got* us this far, as black Americans, women and men, are justly proud of *their* struggles?

Goodbye to a campaign where he has to pass as white (which whites—especially wealthy ones—adore), while she has to pass as male (which both men and women demanded of her, and then found unforgivable). If she were black or he were female we wouldn't be having such problems, and I for one would be in heaven. But at present such a candidate wouldn't stand a chance....

So goodbye to conversations about this nation's deepest scar—slavery—which fail to acknowledge that labor- and sexual-slavery exist *today* in the US and elsewhere on this planet, and the majority of those enslaved are women.

Women have endured sex/race/ethnic/religious hatred, rape and battery, invasion of spirit and flesh, forced pregnancy; being the majority of the poor, the illiterate, the disabled, of refugees, caregivers, the HIV/AIDS afflicted, the powerless. *We have survived* invisibility, ridicule, religious fundamentalisms, polygamy, tear gas, forced feedings, jails, asylums, sati, purdah, female genital mutilation, witch burnings, stonings, and attempted gynocides. *We have tried* reason, persuasion, reassurances, and being extra-qualified, only to learn it never was about qualifications after all. *We know* that at this historical moment women experience the world differently from men—though not all the same as one another—and *can* govern differently, from Elizabeth Tudor to Michele Bachelet and Ellen Johnson Sirleaf....

Goodbye to the accusation that HRC acts "entitled" when she's worked intensely at everything she's done—including being a nose-to-the-grindstone, first-rate senator from my state.

Goodbye to her being exploited as a Rorschach test by women who reduce her to a blank screen on which they project their own fears, failures, fantasies.

Goodbye to the phrase "polarizing figure" to describe someone who embodies the transitions women have made in the last century and are poised to make in this one. It was the women's movement that quipped, *"We are becoming the men we wanted to marry."* She heard us, and she *has*.

Goodbye to some women letting history pass by while wringing their hands, because Hillary isn't as "likeable" as they've been warned *they* must be, or because she didn't leave him, couldn't "control" him, kept her family together and raised a smart, sane daughter....

And goodbye to the ageism—

Old woman are the one group that *doesn't* grow more conservative with age—and we are the generation of radicals who said "Well-behaved women seldom make history." *Goodbye to going gently into any goodnight any man prescribes for us.* We are the women who changed the reality of the United States. And though we never went away, *brace yourselves: we're back!*

We are the women who brought this country equal credit, better pay, affirmative action, the concept of a family-focused workplace; the women who established rape-crisis centers and battery shelters, marital-rape and date-rape laws; the women who defended lesbian custody rights, who fought for prison reform, founded the peace and environmental movements; who insisted that medical research include female anatomy, who inspired men to become more nurturing parents, who created women's studies and Title IX so we all could cheer the WNBA stars and Mia Hamm. We are the women who reclaimed sexuality from violent pornography, who put child care on the national agenda, who transformed demographics, artistic expression, language itself. We are the women who forged a worldwide movement. We are the proud successors of women who, though it took more than 50 years, won us the **vote**. *We are the women who now comprise the majority of US voters.*

Hillary said she found her own voice in New Hampshire....

So listen to *her* voice:

"For too long, the history of women has been a history of silence. *Even today, there are those who are trying to silence our words.*

"It is a violation of *human* rights when babies are denied food, or drowned, or suffocated, or their spines broken, simply because they are born girls. It is a violation of *human* rights when woman and girls are sold into the slavery of prostitution. It is a violation of *human* rights when women are doused with gasoline, set on fire and burned to death because their marriage dowries are deemed too small. It is a violation of *human* rights when individual women are raped in their own communities and when thousands of women are subjected to rape as a tactic or prize of war. It is a violation of *human* rights when a leading cause of death worldwide among women ages 14 to 44 is the violence they are subjected to in their own homes. It is a violation of *human* rights when women are denied the right to plan their own families, and that includes being forced to have abortions or being sterilized against their will.

"Women's rights are human rights. Among those rights are *the right to speak freely—and the right to be heard.*"

That was Hillary Rodham Clinton defying the US State Department and the Chinese Government at the 1995 UN World Conference on Women in Beijing.[a]...

And *this* voice, age 21, in "Commencement Remarks of Hillary D. Rodham, President of Wellesley College Government Association, Class of 1969."[b]

We are, all of us, exploring a world none of us understands...searching for a more immediate, ecstatic, and penetrating mode of living....[for the] integrity, the courage to be whole, living in relation to one another in the full poetry of existence. The struggle for an integrated life existing in an atmosphere of communal trust and respect is one with desperately important political and social consequences....Fear is always with us, but we just don't have time for it.

She ended with the commitment "to practice, with all the skill of our being: *the art of making possible.*"

And for decades, she's been learning *how.*

So goodbye to Hillary's second-guessing herself. The real question is deeper than her re-finding *her* voice. *Can we women find ours?* Can we do this for ourselves?

"Our President, Ourselves!" ...

As for the "woman thing"?

Me, I'm voting for Hillary not because she's a woman—but because *I* am.

Notes

a. Full, stunning speech: http://www.americanrhetoric.com/speeches/hillaryclintonbeijingspeech.htm.

b. Full speech: http://www.wellesley.edu/PublicAffairs/Commencement/1969/053169hillary.html.

Valorizing Mothering

Radical feminism turns male-dominated culture on its head. It takes all the characteristics that are valued by men in Western societies—objectivity, distance, control, coolness, aggressiveness, and competitiveness—and blames them for wars and poverty. It praises what women do—feed and nurture, cooperate and reciprocate, and attend to bodies, minds, and psyches.

The important values, radical feminism argues, are intimacy, persuasion, warmth, caring, and sharing—the characteristics that women develop in their hands-on, everyday experiences with their own and their children's bodies and with the work of daily living. Men could develop these characteristics, too, if they "mothered," but they are much more prevalent in women because women are usually the primary child-care givers and nurturers in a family. The political implications of "maternal thinking" are, according to Sara Ruddick, who has written on motherhood, peace, and feminism, that if men "mothered"—intensively cared for children—they would be less prone to the violence, aggression, and militarism radical feminists have deplored.

Ecofeminism

Long before the current environmental protection movement, radical feminists linked the exploitation of women's bodies to the exploitation of animals for fur and meat and the exploitation of natural resources in strip-mining and deforestation. Some ecofeminists link women's nurturance to caring for nature; others see men's exploitation of women's bodies as analogous to their exploitation of natural resources. Vandana Shiva takes a more materialist view of women's connection to the environment through their work with the land to produce food. She says,

> Women in subsistence economies, producing and reproducing wealth in part-
> nership with nature, have been experts in their own right of holistic and ecolog-
> ical knowledge of nature's processes. But these alternative modes of knowing,
> which are oriented to the social benefits and sustenance needs are not recog-
> nised by the [capitalist] reductionist paradigm, because it fails to perceive the
> interconnectedness of nature, or the connection of women's lives, work and
> knowledge with the creation of wealth. (1988, 24)

Whatever the feminist theoretical rationale, in these days of global warm-
ing and the need to protect the environment, ecofeminism resonates with
other movements to save the planet.

Feminist Religion

The radical feminist praise of the qualities of women that derive from their
nurturance and care of others, especially among those who speak of a woman's culture, has also led to feminist religions and ethics. Radical feminism
argues that while more women clergy and gender-neutral liturgical language
are very important in reforming religious practices, they do not make a religion less patriarchal unless there is also a place for women's prayers, rituals,
and interpretations of sacred texts. So, at Passover, Jewish feminists hold all-
women seders with specially written Haggadahs that tell of the Jews' exodus
from Egypt and wanderings in the desert from a woman's point of view.
They celebrate Miriam as well as Moses.

Feminist religious scholars have reinterpreted Judeo-Christian history
and texts showing the original influence of women spiritual leaders and
their gradual exclusion as Judaism became more patriarchal and, later, as
Christianity became institutionalized. Islamic feminists have found, in their
reading of the Qur'an, that Mohammed intended women and men to be
equal. Buddhism's many goddesses have been given a more important place
in the pantheon by feminists.

As an alternative to teachings of organized religions, Catholic and
Protestant feminist ethicists have developed an ethics that puts women's
experiences at the center of moral choices. In the United States, they work
through an umbrella organization called Women-Church that is composed
of feminist groups engaged in reconstructing ethics and sexual morality.
One of these groups, the Women's Alliance for Theology, Ethics, and Ritual
(WATER), argues for the importance of considering situational contexts in
moral judgments. Another group, Catholics for a Free Choice (CFFC), says
that the circumstances of a woman's life and that of her family should determine whether or not an abortion is justified. CFFC has broadened its activism beyond abortion rights into reproductive justice and are now involved in
Condoms for Life to prevent AIDS as well as conception.

Other radical feminists have discarded a traditional religious affiliation
altogether and have formed Wiccan covens. Some feminist spiritual circles

have derived their symbols and rituals from the earth and fertility god-
desses of pre-Judeo-Christian and pre-Islamic religions. They say that the
Virgin Mary is a cultural descendant of a fertility goddess, the Queen of
the May, and that three pre-Islamic fertility goddesses were transformed
into the daughters of Allah. The Teotihuacán Feathered Serpent of many
Mexican cultures originally represented a goddess, and the introduction of
Christianity by the Spaniards uprooted the native culture's Corn Mothers.
In reviving women-centered religions, radical spiritual feminism is reclaiming women's sexuality, pregnancy and childbirth, menstruation, and menopause from men who have made them into sins or illnesses.

Women's Health Care

In medicine, the women's health care movement has resisted medical practices dominated by men; at first, they did so outside of mainstream institutions, but then many of their recommended changes were incorporated into
the mainstream. Many women entered medical school in the 1960s and 1970s
in the United States and other countries where most of the physicians had
been men, but they found it very difficult to change curricula or training. At
that time, men's bodies were the norm in textbooks; women's bodies were
a deviation because they menstruated and gave birth and had a different
physiology. Standard medical practice has treated normal pregnancies as illnesses and has used monitors and machines routinely in normal childbirth,
distancing women from their own bodies. The new technologies for infertile
couples, such as in vitro fertilization, detach conception from sexual intimacy. In IVF, sperm produced by masturbation are mixed in a petri dish
with ova that are harvested surgically.

In the 1970s in the United States, the women's health movement tried to
take the control of women's bodies out of the hands of the medical system
because the care women patients were getting from men doctors took few
of their overall needs into consideration and allowed them very little control over their treatment. The solution was women-run clinics for women
patients. Nurses and other health care workers taught gynecological self-
examination, took a whole-person approach to diagnosis and treatment, and
dispensed alternative medicines. The women's health movement did not consider women physicians to be much better than men physicians, since they
had been trained in the same medical schools and hospitals. The activists in
the women's health movement thought that by educating women patients
to be more assertive and knowledgeable health consumers, they would put
pressure on the medical system to modify the way men and women physicians are taught to practice.

The women's health movement has encouraged the training and employment of midwives and the experience of family-oriented childbirth at home
and in birthing centers separated from hospitals. It has been critical of the
new procreative technologies, breast implants, and cosmetic surgery as violations of women's bodily integrity. The consumer movement in medicine has
taken over most of the women's health movement's demands that medicine

become more holistic and patient-oriented. Adapting the radical feminist critique and working within mainstream medicine, women physicians in the United States have, in the last few years, promoted research and held conferences on women's medical needs and have published medical journals devoted to research on women's health. They have pushed for women to be part of all clinical trials for new drugs and have collected statistics on the likelihood of women to contract "men's" illnesses, such as AIDS and heart disease. Female bodies are no longer seen as a deviation from a male norm; rather, the definition of "normal" has been altered.

Critique

Radical feminism's condemnation of patriarchal society's encouragement of men's violence and aggressive sexuality and its rejection of the unequal power in heterosexual relationships has alienated heterosexual women in relationships with men. Its defense of the value of mothering over paid work has led women with careers and childless women to feel ostracized.

Another divisive issue has been radical feminism's views on sexuality and pornography's harmfulness. Some feminists do not think pornography is that harmful to women. Radical feminism's stance against sadomasochism and other forms of "kinky" sex at the 1981 Barnard College conference, "The Scholar and the Feminist IX: Toward a Politics of Sexuality," opened a feminist "sex war" that has not died down to this day.

Yet it was radical feminism's extremism ("radical" means down to the roots) and fury at the throwaway use of women's bodies, sexuality, and emotions that made men and women realize how deeply misogynist our supposedly enlightened social world is. Radical feminism deserves much credit for bringing rape, sexual abuse of children, battering, sexual harassment, and global trafficking in women for prostitution to public attention. Those who try to raise the value of women by praising motherhood have been criticized by feminists who feel this strategy invokes traditional rationales for keeping women out of the public arena. But it does what some radical feminists want—to put women on the social map as different from men but worth just as much, if not more.

Summary

It may seem sometimes as if radical feminists' slogan could be, "Women are not just as good as men, they are *better*." (Others strongly repudiate such views.) If men are so violent and sexually aggressive, and women are so nurturing and emotionally sensitive, what the world needs is for women, not men, to run things. As leaders, women would be less hierarchical and authoritarian, more cooperative and consensual. They would respect the environment. Ethically, they would look out for others' needs, and spiritually, they would form loving, caring communities that included men. As many have pointed out, radical feminism's view of women is idealized and unrealistic.

Radical feminism's practical actions focus on setting up rape crisis centers and battered women's shelters, teaching women karate and other forms of self-defense, developing guidelines and penalties against sexual harassment, and educating people about date-rape. Radical feminist politics mounts campaigns against prostitution, pornography, and other forms of sex work, as well as against high-tech procreative technologies, breast implants, cosmetic surgery, and other types of demeaning objectification of women's bodies.

Radical feminism claims that women's ways of thinking have to be brought to the forefront in education and culture. Women's bodies, sexuality, and emotional relationships are different from men's, and so are women's literature, art, music, crafts, and rituals. If most of what is taught in schools is "men's studies," then what is needed is a separate focus on women's history, knowledge, and culture. These ideas helped to foster the formation of women's studies programs and departments in colleges and universities in many countries.

The same argument—that it is not enough to "add women and stir" but that women's experiences produce a radical rethinking—occurs in feminist ethics, religions, and medicine. Women's ethics are based on responsibility to others, not individual rights; women's religious rituals focus on their life cycles, not men's; and women's health care tends to the social as well as physical problems of girls and women.

Organizationally, radical feminists form nonhierarchical, supportive, women-only spaces where women can think and act and create free of constant sexist put-downs, sexual harassment, and the threat of rape and violence. The heady possibilities of creating woman-oriented health care facilities, safe residences for battered women, counseling and legal services for survivors of rape, a woman's culture, and a woman's religion and ethics forge the bonds of sisterhood.

Politically, radical feminism's primary mission is fighting for women and against men's social and cultural supremacy. Radical feminism, by refusing to go along with conventional assumptions, directly confronts the deep-seated denigration and control of women in the gendered social order. It pushes feminism into direct conflict with those in power. Rather than transform the gendered social order, radical feminism has tried to form a better woman-centered social order—more ethical, nurturant, respectful of the environment and women's bodies. The battle cry is no longer "Women deserve equal rights," but "Sisterhood is powerful."

NOTES

1. For an online version, see http://blog.fair-use.org/category/chicago/.
2. http://www.womensmediacenter.com/ex/020108.html.

SUGGESTED READINGS IN RADICAL FEMINISM

Theory and Politics

Bell, Diane, and Renate Klein, eds. 1996. *Radically Speaking: Feminism Reclaimed*. North Melbourne, AU: Spinifex.

Daly, Mary. 1973. *Beyond God the Father: Toward a Philosophy of Women's Liberation*. Boston: Beacon Press.

———. 1978. *Gyn/Ecology: The Metaethics of Radical Feminism*. Boston: Beacon Press.

———. 1984. *Pure Lust: Elemental Feminist Philosophy*. Boston: Beacon Press.

———. 1998. *Quintessence...Realizing the Archaic Future: A Radical Elemental Feminist Manifesto*. Boston: Beacon Press.

Daly, Mary, and Jane Caputi. 1987. *Webster's First New Intergalactic Wickedary of the English Language*. Boston: Beacon Press.

Echols, Alice. 1989. *Daring to Be Bad: Radical Feminism in America, 1967–1975*. Minneapolis: University of Minnesota Press.

Firestone, Shulamith. 1970. *The Dialectic of Sex: The Case for Feminist Revolution*. New York: William Morrow.

Frye, Marilyn. 1983. *The Politics of Reality: Essays in Feminist Theory*. Trumansburg, NY: The Crossing Press.

Fuss, Diane. 1989. *Essentially Speaking: Feminism, Nature, and Difference*. New York: Routledge.

Gilligan, Carol. 1982. *In a Different Voice: Psychological Theory and Women's Development*. Cambridge, MA: Harvard University Press.

Griffin, Susan. 1978. *Women and Nature: The Roaring Inside Her*. New York: Harper.

MacKinnon, Catharine A. 1979. *Sexual Harassment of Working Women*. New Haven, CT: Yale University Press.

———. 1987. *Feminism Unmodified: Discourses on Life and Law*. Cambridge, MA: Harvard University Press.

———. 1989. *Toward a Feminist Theory of the State*. Cambridge, MA: Harvard University Press.

———. 2007. *Are Women Human?: And Other International Dialogues*. Cambridge, MA: Belknap Press.

———. 2007. *Women's Lives, Men's Laws*. Cambridge, MA: Belknap Press.

Morgan, Robin, ed. 1970. *Sisterhood Is Powerful: An Anthology of Writings from the Women's Liberation Movement*. New York: Vintage.

———. 1984. *Sisterhood Is Global: The International Women's Movement Anthology*. New York: Doubleday. Reprint edition, 1996. New York: Feminist Press.

———. 2003. *Sisterhood is Forever: The Women's Anthology for a New Millennium*. New York: Washington Square Press.

O'Brien, Mary. 1981. *The Politics of Reproduction*. New York: Routledge.

———. 1989. *Reproducing the World: Essays in Feminist Theory*. Boulder, CO: Westview Press.

Pateman, Carole. 1988. *The Sexual Contract*. Stanford, CA: Stanford University Press.

Redstockings. 1979. *Feminist Revolution*. New York: Random House.

Rhodes, Jacqueline. 2005. *Radical Feminism, Writing, and Critical Agency: From Manifesto to Modern*. Albany, NY: State University of New York Press.

Willis, Ellen. 1992. *No More Nice Girls: Countercultural Essays*. Middletown, CT: Wesleyan University Press.

Bodies

Birke, Lynda. 2000. *Feminism and the Biological Body.* New Brunswick, NJ: Rutgers University Press.

Bordo, Susan R. 1993. *Unbearable Weight: Feminism, Western Culture, and the Body.* Berkeley: University of California Press.

Boston Women's Health Book Collective. 2005. *Our Bodies, Ourselves: A New Edition for a New Era.* 35th Anniversary Edition. New York: Simon and Schuster.

Buckley, Thomas, and Alma Gottlieb, eds. 1988. *Blood Magic: The Anthropology of Menstruation.* Berkeley: University of California Press.

Clarke, Adele, and Virginia L. Oleson, eds. 1999. *Revisioning Women, Health, and Healing: Feminist, Cultural, and Technoscience Perspectives.* New York: Routledge.

Davis, Kathy. 2007. *The Making of Our Bodies, Ourselves: How Feminism Travels Across Borders.* Durham, NC: Duke University Press.

———, ed. 1997. *Embodied Practices: Feminist Perspectives on the Body.* London: Sage.

Delaney, Janice, Mary Jane Lupton, and Emily Toth. 1977. *The Curse: A Cultural History of Menstruation.* New York: New American Library.

Donchin, Anne, and Laura M. Purdy, eds. 1999. *Embodying Bioethics: Recent Feminist Advances.* Lanham, MD: Rowman & Littlefield.

Grosz, Elizabeth. 1994. *Volatile Bodies: Toward a Corporeal Feminism.* Bloomington: Indiana University Press.

———. 1996. *Space, Time and Perversion: Essays on the Politics of the Body.* New York: Routledge.

Holmes, Helen Bequaert, and Laura M. Purdy, eds. 1992. *Feminist Perspectives in Medical Ethics.* Bloomington: Indiana University Press.

Knight, Chris. 1991. *Blood Relations: Menstruation and the Origins of Culture.* New Haven, CT: Yale University Press.

Laws, Sophie. 1990. *Issues of Blood: The Politics of Menstruation.* London: Macmillan.

Laws, Sophie, Valerie Hey, and Andrea Eagan. 1985. *Seeing Red: The Politics of Premenstrual Tension.* London: Hutchinson.

Luker, Kristin. 1984. *Abortion and the Politics of Motherhood.* Berkeley: University of California Press.

Martin, Emily. 1987. *The Woman in the Body: A Cultural Analysis of Reproduction.* Boston: Beacon.

Petchesky, Rosalind Pollack. 1984. *Abortion and Woman's Choice: The State, Sexuality, and Reproductive Freedom.* Boston: Northeastern University Press.

Rothman, Barbara Katz. [1982] 1991. *In Labor: Women and Power in the Birthplace.* New York: W. W. Norton.

———. 1986. *The Tentative Pregnancy: Prenatal Diagnosis and the Future of Motherhood.* New York: Viking.

———. 2001. *The Book of Life: A Personal and Ethical Guide to Race, Normality and the Human Gene Study.* Boston: Beacon Press.

Voda, Anne M., Myra Dinnerstein, and Sheryl R. O'Donnell, eds. 1982. *Changing Perspectives on Menopause.* Austin: University of Texas Press.

Zita, Jacquelyn N. 1998. *Body Talk: Philosophical Reflections on Sex and Gender.* New York: Columbia University Press.

Disability

Brownworth, Victoria, and Susan Raffo. 1999. *Restricted Access: Lesbians on Disability.* Seattle, WA: Seal Press.

Deegan, Mary Jo, and Nancy A. Brooks, eds. 1985. *Women and Disability: The Double Handicap*. New Brunswick, NJ: Transaction Books.

Fine, Michelle, and Adrienne Asch, eds. 1988. *Women with Disabilities: Essays in Psychology, Culture, and Politics*. Philadelphia: Temple University Press.

Hillyer, Barbara. 1993. *Feminism and Disability*. Norman: University of Oklahoma Press.

Lonsdale, Susan. 1990. *Women and Disability*. New York: St. Martin's Press.

Mairs, Nancy. 1986. *Plaintext*. Tucson: University of Arizona Press.

Wendell, Susan. 1996. *The Rejected Body: Feminist Philosophical Reflections on Disability*. New York: Routledge.

Ecofeminism

Adams, Carol J., ed. 1993. *Ecofeminism and the Sacred*. New York: Continuum.

Adams, Carol J., and Josephine Donovan, eds. 1995. *Animals and Women: Feminist Theoretical Explorations*. Durham, NC: Duke University Press.

Biehl, Janet. 1991. *Finding Our Way: Rethinking Ecofeminist Politics*. New York: Southend Press.

Birke, Lynda. 1994. *Feminism, Animals, Science: The Naming of the Shrew*. Philadelphia: Open University Press.

Diamond, Irene. 1994. *Fertile Ground: Women, Earth, and the Limits of Control*. Boston: Beacon Press.

Diamond, Irene, and Gloria Orenstein, eds. 1990. *Reweaving the World: The Emergence of Ecofeminism*. Berkeley: University of California Press.

Merchant, Carolyn. [1980] 1989. *The Death of Nature: Women, Ecology, and the Scientific Revolution*. New York: Harper & Row.

————. 1992. *Radical Ecology: The Search for a Livable World*. New York: Routledge.

————. 1995. *Earthcare: Women and the Environment*. New York: Routledge.

Mies, Maria, and Vandana Shiva, eds. 1993. *Ecofeminism: Reconnecting a Divided World*. London: Zed.

Ruether, Rosemary Radford. 1992. *Gaia and God: An Ecofeminist Theology of Earth Healing*. San Francisco: HarperSanFrancisco.

————, ed. 1996. *Women Healing Earth: Third World Women on Ecology, Feminism, and Religion*. Maryknoll, NY: Orbis Books.

Shiva, Vandana. 1996. *Biopiracy: The Plunder of Nature and Knowledge*. Boston: South End Press.

Warren, Karen, ed. 1994. *Ecofeminism: Multidisciplinary Perspectives*. Bloomington: Indiana University Press.

————. 1997. *Ecofeminism: Women, Culture, Nature*. Bloomington: Indiana University Press.

Ethics

Gatens, Moira. 1996. *Imaginary Bodies: Essays on Corporeality, Power and Ethics*. New York: Routledge.

Held, Virginia. 1993. *Feminist Morality: Transforming Culture, Society and Politics*. Chicago: University of Chicago Press.

————, ed. 1995. *Justice and Care: Essential Readings in Feminist Ethics*. Boulder, CO: Westview Press.

Irigaray, Luce. [1984] 1993. *An Ethics of Sexual Difference*. Trans. Carolyn Burke and Gillian C. Gill. London: Athlone Press.

Noddings, Nel. 2002. *Starting at Home: Caring and Social Policy.* Berkeley: University of California Press.

Sevenhuijsen, Selma. 1998. *Citizenship and the Ethics of Care: Feminist Considerations on Justice, Morality, and Politics.* New York: Routledge.

Tronto, Joan C. 1993. *Moral Boundaries: A Political Argument for an Ethic of Care.* New York: Routledge.

Walker, Margaret Urban. 1998. *Moral Understandings: A Feminist Study in Ethics.* New York: Routledge.

———. 2003. *Moral Contexts.* Lanham, MD: Rowman & Littlefield.

Gendered Global Violence

Enloe, Cynthia. 2000. *Maneuvers: The International Politics of Militarizing Women's Lives.* Berkeley: University of California Press.

———. 2001. *Bananas, Beaches and Bases: Making Feminist Sense of International Politics.* Updated ed. Berkeley: University of California Press.

"Forum: The Events of 11 September 2001 and Beyond." 2002. *International Feminist Journal of Politics* 4: 95–113.

Hawthorne, Susan, and Bronwyn Winter, eds. 2002. *September 11, 2001: Feminist Perspectives.* North Melbourne, AU: Spinifex.

"Roundtable: Gender and September 11." 2002. *Signs* 28: 432–479.

"Roundtable: September 11 and Its Aftermath: Voices from Australia, Canada, and Africa." 2004. *Signs* 29: 575–617.

Motherhood

Bobel, Chris. 2001. *The Paradox of Natural Mothering.* Philadelphia, PA: Temple University Press.

Hrdy, Sarah Blaffer. 1999. *Mother Nature: A History of Mothers, Infants, and Natural Selection.* New York: Pantheon.

Off Our Backs. 2006. *Feminism and Motherhood.* 36 (1): 8–65.

O'Reilly, Andrea. 2006. *Rocking the Cradle: Thoughts on Motherhood, Feminism and The Possibility of Empowered Mothering.* Toronto: Demeter Press.

———, ed. 2007. *Maternal Theory: Essential Readings.* Toronto: Demeter Press.

———. 2008. *Feminist Mothering.* Albany, NY: State University of New York Press.

Porter, Marie, Andrea O'Reilly, and Patricia Short, eds. 2005. *Motherhood: Power and Oppression.* Toronto: Women's Press.

Rich, Adrienne. 1977. *Of Woman Born: Motherhood as Experience and as Institution.* New York: W. W. Norton.

Rothman, Barbara Katz. 2000. *Recreating Motherhood: Ideology and Technology in a Patriarchal Society,* 2nd ed. New Brunswick, NJ: Rutgers University Press.

Ruddick, Sara. 1995. *Maternal Thinking: Toward a Politics of Peace.* Boston: Beacon Press.

Trebilcot, Joyce, ed. 1983. *Mothering: Essays in Feminist Theory.* Totowa, NJ: Rowman and Allenheld.

Religion

Ahmed, Leila. 1992. *Women and Gender in Islam.* New Haven, CT: Yale University Press.

Dame, Enid, Lily Rivlin, and Henny Wenkart. 1999. *Which Lilith?: Feminist Writers Re-Create the World's First Woman.* Northvale, NJ: Jason Aronson.

Eskinazi, Tamara Cohen, and Andrea L. Weiss, eds. 2008. *The Torah: A Women's Commentary.* New York: URJ Press.

Fiorenza, Elisabeth Schüssler. 1983. *In Memory of Her: A Feminist Theological Reconstruction of Christian Origins.* New York: Crossroad.

———. 1984. *Bread Not Stone: The Challenge of Feminist Biblical Interpretation.* Boston: Beacon Press.

———. 1992. *But She Said: Feminist Practices of Biblical Interpretation.* Boston: Beacon Press.

———. 1993. *Discipleship of Equals: A Critical Feminist Ekklesia-logy of Liberation.* New York: Crossroad.

———. 1995. *Jesus, Miriam's Child, Sophia's Prophet: Critical Issues in Feminist Christology.* New York: Continuum.

Frymer-Kensky, Tikva. 1992. *In the Wake of the Goddesses: Women, Culture and the Biblical Transformation of Pagan Myth.* New York: Fawcett Columbine.

———. 2002. *Reading the Women of the Bible: A New Interpretation of Their Stories.* New York: Schocken.

Gimbutas, Marija. 1989. *The Language of the Goddess.* San Francisco: Harper & Row.

———. 1999. *The Living Goddesses.* Edited and supplemented by Miriam Robbins Dexter. Berkeley: University of California Press.

Hiltebeitel, Alf, and Kathleen M. Erndl. 2000. *Is the Goddess a Feminist?: The Politics of South Asian Goddesses.* New York: New York University Press.

Jayakar, Pupul. 1990. *The Earth Mother: Legends, Ritual Arts, and Goddesses of India.* San Francisco: Harper & Row.

Kien, Jenny. 2000. *Reinstating the Divine Woman in Judaism.* Universal Publishers/ uPublish.com.

———. 2003. *The Battle Between the Moon and the Sun: The Separation of Women's Bodies From the Cosmic Dance.* Universal Publishers/uPublish.com.

Mernissi, Fatima. 1987. *Beyond the Veil: Male-Female Dynamics in Modern Muslim Society.* Bloomington: Indiana University Press.

———. 1991. *The Veil and the Male Elite: A Feminist Interpretation of Women's Rights in Islam.* Trans., Mary Jo Lakeland. Cambridge, MA: Perseus Books.

Pagels, Elaine. 1979. *The Gnostic Gospels.* New York: Vintage.

———. 1988. *Adam, Eve, and the Serpent.* New York: Vintage.

Plaskow, Judith. 1990. *Standing Again at Sinai: Judaism from a Feminist Perspective.* San Francisco: Harper and Row.

———. 2005. *The Coming of Lilith: Essays on Feminism, Judaism, and Sexual Ethics, 1972–2003.* Boston: Beacon Press.

Ruether, Rosemary Radford. 1983. *Sexism and God-talk: Toward a Feminist Theology.* Boston: Beacon Press.

———. 2005. *Goddesses and the Divine Feminine: A Western Religious History.* Berkeley: University of California Press.

Ruether, Rosemary Radford, and Eleanor McLaughlin, eds. 1979. *Women of Spirit: Female Leadership in the Jewish and Christian Traditions.* New York: Simon and Schuster.

Sabbah, Fatna A. 1984. *Woman in the Muslim Unconscious.* Trans., Mary Jo Lakeland. New York: Pergamon.

Starhawk. 1990. *Truth or Dare: Encounters with Power, Authority, and Mystery.* New York: HarperCollins.

———. [1979] 1999. *Spiral Dance: A Rebirth of the Ancient Religion of the Goddess.* 20th Anniversary Edition. New York: HarperCollins.

———. 2001. *The Twelve Wild Swans: A Journey to the Realm of Magic, Healing, and Action.* San Francisco: HarperSanFrancisco.

Wadud, Amina. 1999. *Qur'an and Woman: Rereading the Sacred Text from a Woman's Perspective.* New York: Oxford University Press.

Sexual Violence

Anderson, Irina, and Kathy Doherty. 2008. *Accounting for Rape: Psychology, Feminism and Discourse Analysis in the Study of Sexual Violence.* New York: Routledge.

Barry, Kathleen. 1979. *Female Sexual Slavery.* Englewood Cliffs, NJ: Prentice-Hall.

———. 1995. *Prostitution of Sexuality: Global Exploitation of Women.* New York: New York University Press.

Bart, Pauline B., and Eileen Geil Moran, eds. 1993. *Violence Against Women: The Bloody Footprints.* Thousand Oaks, CA: Sage.

Brownmiller, Susan. 1975. *Against Our Will: Men, Women and Rape.* New York: Simon and Schuster.

Caputi, Jane. 1987. *The Age of Sex Crime.* Bowling Green, OH: Bowling Green University Popular Press.

Dobash, R. Emerson, and Russell Dobash. 1979. *Violence Against Wives: A Case Against the Patriarchy.* New York: Free Press.

Dworkin, Andrea. 1974. *Woman Hating.* New York: NAL Penguin.

———. 1981. *Pornography: Men Possessing Women.* New York: Perigee (Putnam).

———. 1987. *Intercourse.* New York: Free Press.

Griffin, Susan. 1982. *Pornography and Silence: Culture's Revenge Against Nature.* San Francisco: Harper and Row.

Lederer, Laura, ed. 1980. *Take Back the Night: Women on Pornography.* New York: Morrow.

Russell, Diana E. H. 1998. *Dangerous Relationships: Pornography, Misogyny, and Rape.* Thousand Oaks, CA: Sage.

Yllö, Kersti, and Michele Bograd, eds. 1988. *Feminist Perspectives on Wife Abuse.* Thousand Oaks, CA: Sage.

6

Lesbian Feminism

SOURCES OF GENDER INEQUALITY

- Oppressive heterosexuality, subordinating women in emotional relationships
- The assumption that everyone is heterosexual (*heteronormativity*), reinforcing conventional gender binaries
- Men's domination of culture and other value-laden arenas

POLITICS

- Social acceptance of lesbian sexuality, relationships, motherhood
- Empowering women-identified women
- Fighting dual battles—for women's rights and for homosexual rights
- Movement for *marriage equality* for heterosexual and homosexual partners

CRITIQUE

- Expansion of lesbianism to woman-identified heterosexual women weakens the movement against oppressive heterosexuality
- Idealization of lesbian relationships as intrinsically nurturant, egalitarian, and harmonious is unrealistic
- Division of loyalties between feminist and homosexual activism creates a need for political bridges

CONTRIBUTIONS

- Creating lesbian feminist theory, research, and cultural productions
- Making lesbian women visible and valued
- Critically deconstructing heterosexual romantic love and sexual relationships
- Expanding lesbian perspectives to include community and culture

Lesbian feminism links sexual desire for other women, women's independent lifestyles, and women's friendships with the idea of women's culture and knowledge, producing a movement of resistance to a gendered social order that expects women to want more than anything else to fall in love with and marry a man.

Theoretically, lesbian feminism's core is a resistance to *heteronormativity*, the assumption that everyone is heterosexual. Chrys Ingraham, a lesbian feminist sociologist, argues that heteronormativity, or "thinking straight," the belief system underlying institutionalized heterosexuality, constitutes the dominant paradigm in Western society. She says,

> Gender is a central feature of heteronormativity, but it is institutionalized heterosexuality that is served by dominant or conventional constructions of gender, not the other way around. To critique the operation of gender as imbricated in racial, class, and sexual relations to the exclusion of institutionalized heterosexuality is to bracket off the ends served by prevailing and dominant gender constructions and practices. We need to revisit this question: Would gender exist were it not for its organizing relationship to institutionalized heterosexuality? (2006, 460)

Rather than challenging gender inequality directly, lesbian feminism attacks the oppression of women inherent in heterosexuality, which Ingraham claims is the basic building block of the gendered social order.

Lesbian feminism takes the radical feminist pessimistic view of men to its logical conclusion. If heterosexual relationships are intrinsically exploitative because of men's social, physical, and sexual power over women, why bother with men at all? If women are more loving, nurturing, sharing, and understanding, why not have them as emotional and sexual partners as well as friends? "Why not go all the way?" asks lesbian feminism. Stop sleeping with the "enemy" and turn to other women for sexual love as well as for intellectual companionship and emotional support.

Women's sexual desire for other women and lesbian relationships, like male homosexuality, while not illegal, had been underground in the United States and other Western countries until the mid-twentieth century. Fired by the social protest movements of the 1960s, men's and women's homosexuality became increasingly visible and acceptable. Up to the 1960s, many women professionals and activists, most of whom did not identify themselves as lesbian, were nonetheless able to break the mold of conventional women's roles because of their deeply emotional, supportive friendships with other women, which may or may not have been sexual.

The pre–Stonewall culture of lesbian resistance became defiantly visible in the years after the gay and lesbian riots in response to a police raid on the now-famous Greenwich Village nightclub, the Stonewall, on June 28, 1969. Stonewall Day is now celebrated in the United States and other Western countries with Gay Pride marches. With greater openness and acceptance, lesbian resistance shifted from sexual defiance to sexual and gender defiance. In recent years, lesbian feminists have argued over identification and community, gendered role behavior, biological motherhood, and now, in the debates over marriage equality, whether lesbian marriage is a sellout of radical resistance to the conventional nuclear family.

Lesbian Sexuality

Lesbian feminism's defining stance on sexuality is that heterosexuality is oppressive and therefore women are better off having sexual relationships with women. There are debates within lesbian feminism over the origin of women's sexual attraction to women—is it inborn and lifelong or can it develop at any time, perhaps beginning with an intense work relationship or political involvement? Another split in lesbian feminism is over sadomasochistic sexual relationships between women, which violate the egalitarian and nonviolent ethos of both feminism and lesbianism.

Still another area of contention is bisexuality, which challenges lesbian feminism behaviorally and politically. Bisexual women who have sexual relations with both women and men, sometimes simultaneously and sometimes serially, disturb the clear gender and sexual divisions that are the basis for woman-identification and lesbian separatism. Bisexuality may not undercut the identification with women as an oppressed social group, but it undermines the lesbian separatist solution.

Lesbian Identities, Lesbian Communities

As theory and in politics, lesbian feminism transforms love between women into an identity, a community, and a culture. Lesbian feminism praises women's sexuality and bodies, mother-daughter love, and the culture of women, thus expanding sexual and emotional relationships between women into a wholly engaged life.

Lesbians are not monolithic. In the 1950s, lesbians playing the "fem" role were extremely feminine in their dress, demeanor, and expressions of sexuality, while "butches" were cool, masculine-looking, and assertive. There were also butch-femme role exchangers ("roll overs" or "kikis") who played both parts. More open lifestyles encourage a range of sexual and gender behaviors, and a range of clothing, hairstyles, and cosmetic use. This variety is the surface reflection of a deeper sense of varied identity as a lesbian, and the recognition that lesbians who are identified with diverse racial ethnic and social class groups form their own communities. As a result, the social and sexual boundaries of lesbian communities have become more fluid. In the following excerpt, Arlene Stein, a sociologist, charts the history of lesbian feminism and discusses the ways it has become more various and decentered.

Decentering Lesbian Feminism

Arlene Stein

Rutgers University

Lesbian feminism emerged out of the most radical sectors of the women's movement in the early 1970s. Young women who "came out through feminism," as the saying went, attempted to broaden the definition of lesbianism, to transform it from a medical condition, or at best, a sexual "preference," into a collective identity that transcended rampant individualism and its excesses as well as compulsory gender and sex roles. It was a movement that spawned the most vibrant and visible lesbian culture that had ever existed in this country.

But by the mid-1980s, the vision of a Lesbian Nation which would stand apart from the dominant culture, as a sort of haven in a heartless (male/heterosexual) world, began to appear ever more distant. In contrast to the previous decade, lesbian culture and community seemed placeless. This complaint was common, particularly among women who came of age during the previous decade, when becoming a lesbian meant coming into a community committed to some shared values. Philosopher Janice Raymond sounded the call of alarm in a women's studies journal in 1989: "We used to talk a lot about lesbianism as a political movement—back in the old days when lesbianism and feminism went together, and one heard the phrase lesbian feminism. Today we hear more about lesbian sadomasochism, lesbians having babies and everything lesbians need to know about sex."[a] As she and others explained it, the 1980s and 1990s brought a retrenchment from the radical visions of the previous decade. A triumphant conservatism had shattered previously cohesive lesbian communities....

Reflecting this more decentered sense of community, today's lesbian "movement," if one can call it that, consists of a series of projects, often wildly disparate in approach, many of which incorporate radical and progressive elements. If the corner bar was once the only place in town, by the early 1990s in cities across the country there were lesbian parenting groups, support groups for women with cancer and other life-threatening diseases, new and often graphic sexual literature for lesbians, organizations for lesbian "career women" and lesbians of color, and mixed organizations where out lesbians played visible roles. What is new, I suggest, is the lack of any fundamental hegemonic logic or center to these projects.[b]

The once clear connection between lesbianism and feminism, in which the former was assumed to grow naturally out of the latter, is not all that clear today. Gone is the ideal of a culturally and ideologically unified Lesbian Nation. A series of challenges, largely from within lesbian communities themselves, has shaken many of the ordering principles of lesbian feminism. In the following, I want to explain this process of decentering. What does it mean? Why did it occur? And what might it tell us about the trajectory of identity-based movements?[c] ...

To my suggestion that lesbianism is becoming decentered, one could reply that the lesbian-feminist movement, consisting of hundreds of semi-autonomous small-scale efforts nationwide, was never centered. However, while it was never unified, it did have a hegemonic project. It was, first, an effort to reconstruct the category "lesbian," to wrest it from the definitions of the medical experts and broaden its meaning. It was, second, an attempt to forge a stable collective identity around that category and to develop institutions that would nurture that identity. And third, it sought to use those institutions as a base for the contestation of the dominant sex/gender system.

The medical model of homosexuality, dominant for most of the twentieth century, declared that sexuality is fixed at birth or in early childhood, an intractable property of the individual. The "old gay" prefeminist world, a series of semisecret subcultures located primarily in urban areas, formed in relation to the hegemonic belief that heterosexuality was natural and homosexuality an aberration. But for 1970s "new lesbians," the prefeminist world and the conviction that lesbians were failed women were no longer tenable or tolerable. In place of the belief in a lesbian essence or fixed minority identity signified by an inversion of gender, long synonymous with the image of lesbianism in the popular imagination, they substituted the universal possibility of "woman-identified" behavior.[d] As a popular saying went, "Feminism is the theory, lesbianism is the practice." ...

The movement could not have emerged without the second-wave feminist insight that gender roles are socially constructed, or without the gay liberationist application of that insight to sexuality. If the "exchange of women"—compulsory heterosexuality—was the bedrock of the sex/gender system, as Gayle Rubin and others argued, then women who made lives with other women were subverting the dominant order.[e] Jill Johnston and others declared that a "conspiracy of silence" insured that for most women "identity was presumed to be heterosextal unless proven otherwise....There was no lesbian identity. There was lesbian activity." Expressing the feelings of many middle-class women of her generation, Johnston wrote in 1973: "For most of us the chasm between social validation and private needs was so wide and deep that the society overwhelmed us for any number of significant individual reasons....We were all heterosexually identified and that's the way we thought of ourselves, even of course when doing otherwise."[f]

If homophobia on the part of heterosexual feminists and in society at large deterred many women from claiming a lesbian identity, collapsing the distinction between identification and desire minimized stigma and broadened the definition of lesbianism, transforming it into "female bonding," a more inclusive category, with which a larger number of middle-class women could identify. Indeed, there was historical precedent for this vision in the "passionate friendships" common among women of the eighteenth and nineteenth centuries.[g]

Lesbianism represented a sense of connectedness based on mutuality and similarity rather than difference. Ultimately, it was more than simply a matter of sex, poet Judy Grahn declared: "Men who are obsessed with sex are convinced that lesbians are obsessed with sex. Actually, like other women, lesbians are obsessed with love and fidelity."[h] The new, broadened definition of lesbianism resonated with many women who had long experienced their sexuality in relational rather than simply erotic terms, and who considered sexuality a relatively nonsalient aspect of identity and an insufficient basis upon which to organize a mass movement.

Centering lesbianism upon female relationality and identification, these "new lesbians" challenged medicalized conceptions that focused upon gender inversion and masculinized sexual desire. They blurred the boundary between gay and straight women and transformed lesbianism into a normative identity that over time came to have as much—and sometimes more—to do with lifestyle preferences (such as choice of dress or leisure pursuits) and ideological proclivities (anticonsumerist, countercultural identifications) as with sexual desires or practices.

This shift in meaning enabled many women who had never considered the possibility of claiming a lesbian lifestyle to leave their husbands and boyfriends—some for political reasons, others in expression of deeply rooted desires, many for both. It allowed many of those who lived primarily closeted lives to come out and declare their lesbianism openly. Never before had so much social space opened up so quickly to middle-class women who dared to defy deeply held social norms about their proper sexual place. As a result, the group of women who called themselves lesbians became increasingly heterogeneous, at least in terms of sexuality....

If lesbian feminism often presented itself as a totalizing identity that would subsume differences of race, class, and ethnicity and pose a united front against patriarchal society, these challenges pointed toward an understanding of lesbianism as situated in a web of multiple oppressions and identities. Lesbians of color and lesbian sex radicals questioned the belief that lesbian life could ever stand completely outside of or apart from the structures of the patriarchal culture. They problematized the once uncontested relationship between lesbianism and feminism. And they shifted lesbian politics away from its almost exclusive focus upon the "male threat," toward a more diffuse notion of power and resistance, acknowledging that lesbians necessarily operate in a society marked by inequalities of class and race as well as of gender and sexuality.

Notes

a. Janice Raymond, "Putting the Politics Back into Lesbianism," *Women's Studies International Forum* 12, no. 2 (1989).

b. Howard Winant makes a similar argument about the politics of race in "Post-modern Racial Politics: Difference and Inequality," *Socialist Review* 20 (January–March 1990).

c. These ideas are based on archival research and interviews conducted primarily in the San Francisco Bay Area. Parts of the analysis may not hold true for other parts of the country, particularly nonurban areas, where the pace of change may be slower.

d. Radicalesbians, "The Woman-Identified Woman," reprinted in Sarah Hoagland and Julia Penelope, eds., *For Lesbians Only* (London: Onlywoman Press, 1988); Adrienne Rich, "Compulsory Heterosexuality and Lesbian Existence," *Signs,* Summer 1980.

e. Gayle Rubin, "The Traffic in Women," in Rayna Reiter, ed., *Toward an Anthropology of Women* (New York: Monthly Review Press, 1975).

f. Jill Johnston, *Lesbian Nation: The Feminist Solution* (New York: Simon and Schuster, 1973), 58.

g. See Carole Smith-Rosenberg, *Disorderly Conduct* (New York: Knopf, 1985); "The Female World of Love and Ritual," in Nancy F. Cott and Elizabeth Pleck, eds., *A Heritage of Her Own* (New York: Simon and Schuster, 1979).

h. Judy Grahn, "Lesbians as Bogeywoman," *Women: A Journal of Liberation* 1, no. 4 (Summer 1970), 36.

Lesbian Identity Politics

Politically, lesbian feminists fight on two fronts—for all women's betterment and for the civil rights and social worth of homosexuals. Whether lesbians identify and act politically mostly as homosexuals or mostly as women varies. In the United States, lesbians first identified with homosexual men in their resistance to harassment and discrimination, but after experiencing the same gender discrimination as women in the civil rights and draft-resistance movements of the 1960s, they turned to feminist organizations. There, unhappily, they experienced hostility to their sexuality from heterosexual women. Subsequently, some lesbian feminists developed an oppositional, woman-identified, separatist movement. But many lesbian activist groups welcome heterosexual women in their work for women's issues. Other lesbians have joined with gay men in their battle with the AIDS epidemic, for civil rights, and for legal recognition of committed relationships.

Other potential sources of division among lesbians emerged with the visibility of lesbianism in working-class and racial ethnic communities. Lesbians who once would have left home to live in cities with a lesbian underground or would have closeted their sexuality now confront homophobia and antifeminist opposition in some working-class and racial ethnic groups. The politics of identity fragment their sense of self and their activism, as they try to fight for homosexual rights, women's rights, and for their class and racial ethnic group's rights.

Mignon Moore, professor of sociology and African American studies, has surveyed 100 African American, West Indian, Caribbean, and Latina lesbians in New York City about their presentations of self as women, lesbians, and members of their racial ethnic communities. Smaller groups were interviewed as couples and in focus groups. Her respondents ranged in age from 21 to 61 years old. Forty-five percent were working class; the others were middle and upper-middle class.

Lipstick or Timberlands? Gender Presentation in Black Lesbian Communities

Mignon R. Moore

University of California, Los Angeles

New York contains many distinct well-developed lesbian communities, and one consequence of these varied social groups is that women enter into a gay identity or form friendships among gay people who may not be lesbian-feminists. Women can become socialized into lesbian communities that are not based on specific feminist principles, which might be the case in neighborhoods and communities where the primary gay public organizations have a political focus. Moreover, many of these groups are segregated by race and ethnicity, facilitating the development of a gay identity in the context of a racially homogeneous environment. As a result, being gay is not experienced as an identity in and of itself that creates social distance from one's racial group or that is associated with a particular political ideology. In New York one can be gay and still remain connected to one's own ethnic and cultural groups (Hawkeswood 1997; Battle and Bennett 2005).

In the black lesbian communities of New York, demographic characteristics are insufficient markers of difference. Black gay women use specific modes of gender expression to organize their social relationships. Traditional demographic characteristics like age and education are only a small part in a series of other relevant characteristics. Physical representations of gender, indicated by clothing, hair, physical stance, the presence or absence of makeup, and various other symbols, are extremely important markers of identification. People's style of clothing lets others in the community know right away how they choose to represent their gender, as well as the type of physical representation they are attracted to: more feminine-looking women tend to partner with women who do not look as feminine....

This work finds that black lesbians in New York use gender display to structure social interactions, and the order of these social interactions maintains social control in the community. In order to attract a person with a certain gendered style, one must possess a complementary gender display. However, the structure imposed by these norms also grants women a certain agency or freedom to present themselves in a gendered way if they so desire, and that is different from the expectations in many lesbian-feminist social circles that encourage a look that is not overtly feminine or masculine. In black lesbian environments, lesbians...feel liberated by these categories of gender display, especially the gender-blender identity, because they allow for a way to express a nonfeminine gendered self and to have that identity valued by other gay women.

In today's society, women have a significant range of styles that are considered acceptable, so the categories of femme, gender-blender, and transgressive have the most meaning when they are presented in a context where lesbians are present. It is in the larger group of black lesbians that the subtleties that often accompany a femme or gender-blending presentation of self are made clear. Athletic jerseys and baggy jeans on women as they walk down 125th Street in Harlem or Flatbush Avenue in Brooklyn do not immediately mark them as lesbian but reveal their membership in a gender display category once they step into a convention center or nightclub filled with black lesbians....

Many black highly educated lesbians are reluctant to claim labels or membership in categories that are marked in larger society as deviant or are perceived in a negative way. Evelynn M. Hammonds (1997) argues that black women, in an effort to retaliate against the pathological image of black women's sexuality, have often promoted a public silence about sexuality and proper morality. In the case of nonfeminine lesbians, cultural notions of black female sexuality may inhibit their freedom of gender expression in certain contexts and disrupt the image of middle-class respectability they have achieved through other symbols of their socioeconomic mobility. As black women, many feel that they have to work harder to be accepted in mainstream society, and admitting a nonfeminine gender display categorizes them as "other" in yet another way by confirming pejorative conceptualizations of the black bulldagger and other stereotypes of black female sexuality (Collins 2000).

Particular transgressive presentations of self were harshly criticized, not only by larger society but also by black middle-class lesbians. At parties, women who wore athletic jerseys, do-rags on their heads, or baseball caps were said to lower the quality or status of the event, and other lesbians would react to their presence in a visibly negative way. Flyers announcing the latest party would often include the following warning: "No caps, do-rags, or athletic wear: Dress to impress." I once hosted a party for women of color at a lounge in Greenwich Village, and a few of the women who attended were dressed in athletic jerseys and fitted caps. Other than their style of dress, they did not stand out in any obvious way or behave differently from the other guests. However, throughout the night several women complained that I had "let those type of people" into the party. They said things like, "they bring the party down"; "we work so hard to get away from them, only to have them turn up at a classy event like this one." The harshest critics were usually middle-class gender-blending lesbians who wanted to be distinguished from this particular masculine expression of black sexuality.

When transgressive lesbians appropriate certain representations of masculinity owned by black and Latino men, they portray images that are raced, classed, and associated with violence and menace. Debra Wilson presents transgressive lesbians' experiences with this image in her 2003 award-winning documentary *Butch Mystique*. Some lesbians resent this presentation of self in other women because it is associated with an image of men who are disrespectful to women. Others with a disadvantaged background may be trying to distance themselves from a style that signifies membership or identification with lower-class life. But many feminine women are attracted to this type of masculinity on a female body, finding the image of a hip-hop "bad boy" alluring or cool when modified and transplanted on a woman.

There are dangers in representing black masculinity, particularly through the female form. First, transgressive women are rebelling against strong conventional norms, and their emphasis on self-expression above conformity attacks the core of male dominance and invites openly punitive responses from others. But more than that, a nonfeminine gender presentation in women may cause men to question the meaning of their own masculinity. Lexington (Lex), a thirty-nine-year-old working-class woman, said that on an almost daily basis she and other transgressives are discriminated against and denied their basic civil rights. "People call us out [of] our names, threaten us, all because of who we are and what we look like, what we represent." When I asked Lex why she thinks men respond to her and other transgressives in such a negative way, she paused, then said, "Because they've spent their whole lives with one idea of who they are, and then they look at us with our men's shirts, our men's shoes, and realize gender is something that is taught."

That black transgressives consistently partner with women who are more feminine and whose style is consistent with heterosexual standards of beauty also endangers male ownership of masculinity and the benefits that go along with it. Lex says that lesbians are threatening to all men but white men in particular because "they are the gold standard, the epitome of success, of what everyone in society aspires to have. We are a threat to them because we are not supposed to be able to get what they have. Not just aggressives but other women out there, too. How dare we own our own homes, have cars, raise families, and pull a woman that looks as good as theirs!" The raced and classed masculinity that exists simultaneously among black transgressive and gender-blending women can be dangerous because of the often hostile and untrusting environment that exists for black men in society. The enactment of dress and mannerisms that are consistent with particular male presentations of self are learned in disadvantaged environments or through images of male rappers and hip-hop performers and are also subject to harassment from police, distrust from strangers, and efforts by members of the middle class to distance themselves from the group.

Gender Presentation and Gender Ideologies

In trying to understand how black lesbians are negotiating the organization and meaning of gender display, I found that it is desire, not feminism or politics, that takes center stage. As I conducted this research, it became obvious to me that some feminist ideologies have profoundly influenced these women's lives, particularly with regard to how they have come to understand their own oppression based on their structural location as black women and as black lesbians. The calculated, nonrandom use of gender display suggests they are enacting a public, visible manifestation of women who are in control of their own sexuality, and it represents behavior that is at the very core of a philosophy of women's liberation. Nevertheless, their sexual identities, by and large, are not rooted in a particular feminist politics. When I asked Katrice Webster, a thirty-seven-year-old corporate attorney, if her lesbian identity is tied to feminism, she said that in her mind one has very little to do with the other. Most women, when asked if their sexuality was tied to feminism, said they had not consciously linked the two. Some women have a masculine presentation of self, are primarily attracted to feminine women, and also hold feminist beliefs about eradicating gender inequality. There are also transgressive, gender-blender, and femme women who would like their partners to take on some of the more traditionally female or male roles in relationships. Women who practice all three gender displays are able to distinguish between a gendered expression of self and their political beliefs about gender.

The lesbians in this study also make a distinction between style or mannerisms that define masculinity, on the one hand, and the gendered privileges and dominance that men tend to garner, on the other. The ability to appreciate or emulate a particular way of dressing that is masculine does not preclude transgressives or gender-blenders from seeing themselves as women in a society where men still have the greater advantage. They believe that men are constantly granted more status and authority because society continues to advance an ideology that privileges male leadership of important societal institutions and that awards men an earnings advantage that sometimes facilitates their partners' economic dependence. As women, lesbians do not benefit from either of these gendered structural advantages, so relationships organized around gender display do not provide a gendered economic advantage for the less feminine partner.

In the past, butch-femme roles eroticized and structured sexual interactions around the principle of gender difference. Gender presentation is defined more broadly now and is no longer primarily a means of structuring sexual interactions. However, it does continue to structure membership in and the organization of the lesbian social world. Black women take very careful pains to consistently present the same type of gender display because they are looking to create a particular aesthetic self and because the norms of the community require a consistency in their gender presentation. The structure imposed by community social norms becomes problematic when it impedes a person's freedom to partner with someone who has the "wrong" gender display. However, the use of gender display also liberates many lesbians by allowing a sense of freedom in their ability to express their individuality in a way that is specifically feminine or nonfeminine.

A closer examination of nonblack lesbian community life will most likely reveal similar patterns and meanings of gender presentation and similar organization of lesbian relationships, particularly among women who separate their political ideologies about gender and other issues from their identities as lesbians. A question that follows concerns how to relate differences in physical representations of gender and class to broader understandings of gender roles in same-sex relationships and gender expression in broader society. Connected to this point is a need to know how individuals conceptualize gay identity in the context of other important overlapping identities such as race, gender, and motherhood. The present study recognizes these points and initiates a dialogue between overlapping areas of study.

References

Battle, Juan J., and Natalie D. A. Bennett. 2005. "Striving for Place: Black Lesbian, Gay, Bisexual, and Transgender (LGBT) People in History and Society." In Alton Hornsby, ed., *A Companion to African American History*. Malden, MA: Blackwell.

Collins, Patricia Hill. 2000. *Black Feminist Thought: Knowledge, Consciousness, and the Politics of Empowerment*, 2nd ed. New York: Routledge.

Hammonds, Evelynn M. 1997. "Toward a Genealogy of Black Female Sexuality: The Problematic of Silence." In M. Jacqui Alexander and Chandra Talpade Mohanty, eds., *Feminist Genealogies, Colonial Legacies, Democratic Futures.* New York: Routledge.

Hawkeswood, William G. 1997. *One of the Children: Gay Black Men in Harlem* . Berkeley: University of California Press.

Marriage and Motherhood

Family issues are another potential minefield in lesbian feminism. Some lesbian women have biological children and raise them with a long-term lesbian partner. Others have been critical of sexual monogamy, with or without children, as imitative of the institution of heterosexual marriage. These lesbians prefer alternative household arrangements of several partners, which may include gay men. Lesbians who would like to have the legal benefits of marriage do not see why they, and not heterosexual feminists, have to give up the goal of legally recognized couple relationships to fight against the subordination of women in the traditional family.

In the fight for marriage equality and parental rights, lesbians are most likely to join homosexual men in a unified movement that often cuts across social class, racial ethnic, and gender lines. Feminists in general are frequently vocal supporters of the rights of homosexual women and men to marry the person of their choice, regardless of gender and sexual orientation, and to adopt children. In this fight, lesbian feminist politics is subordinated to gay rights politics.

Critique

Lesbian feminism expanded by including women who consider themselves lesbian in their emotional identification with women, even though they may be heterosexual or bisexual in their sexual relationships. This paradoxical identification runs counter to the lesbian feminist claim that their sexual relationships are more feminist than heterosexual relationships, because intimacy with a man undercuts a woman's independence. In addition, many lesbians feel that their sexual orientation is inborn, and not something you can adopt for political reasons.

A second unresolved argument is over marriage. Lesbian relationships have been idealized as sexually monogamous, emotionally nurturant, and egalitarian. Proponents of the right to marry build on such relationships, weakening the critical edge of the lesbian feminist argument against marriage as an oppressive institution. Lesbians argue that even if the structure of their relationships resembles that of heterosexual pairs, the quality of their relationships is entirely different. Free of male dominance, partners can be fully egalitarian and reciprocal in their behavior toward each other. However, research has shown that just like heterosexual couples, some lesbian couples have abusive relationships and split up acrimoniously. They also tend to exaggerate the extent to which they equally share domestic work. The more affluent partner often tends to do less of the work that maintains family life, and the partner in a lower-paid, lower-prestige occupation tends to do more. The partner doing less is likely to claim the division of labor as equal, since she is violating a gendered norm of woman as caretaker as well as the image of the egalitarian lesbian household.

Summary

As an offshoot of radical feminism, lesbian feminism pushes the critique of heterosexuality and conventional family life to its logical extreme. Theoretically, lesbian feminism argues that all heterosexual relationships, especially those that are romantic and sexual, are intrinsically coercive of women. Given men's dominant social position and tendency to oppress women in everyday interaction, it is better to have as little to do with them as possible. Women have to work with men and deal with them in many public arenas, but in their private lives and especially in sexual relationships, lesbian feminists feel that a woman is a far better partner.

Lesbian feminist separatists have created cultural communities, social lives, and political organizations that are for women only. Caring, nurturance, intimacy, and woman-to-woman love of all kinds are the ideals of these women's worlds. In recent years, however, the boundaries between lesbians and heterosexual feminists and between lesbians and gay men are giving way. Lesbians invite heterosexual women into their feminist political activities and vice versa, and lesbian and heterosexual women work with gay and straight men politically. With the advent of a men's feminist movement, lesbian feminism is less wary of even heterosexual men. In many political organizations today, neither gender nor sexual orientation is a significant marker of who sides with whom. Cross-cutting identification with racial ethnic communities has also decentered lesbian feminism.

Lesbian feminism at present seems to be going in two directions at once. Some coupled and parenting lesbians are mainstreaming into family-oriented communities, and fighting for the right to marry the person of their choice. Others are joining with gender-defiant queer communities of transgenders. The focus of lesbian feminism of the 1970s—woman-oriented separatism—seems to be fading fast.

By their varieties of gender presentations and relationships, lesbians challenge heteronormative assumptions that everyone is heterosexual, and that men are masculine and women are feminine. Their feminism may take second place to gay rights or racial ethnic activism, but their presence and visibility resist the conventionally gendered social order.

SUGGESTED READINGS IN LESBIAN FEMINISM

Abelove, Henry, Michèle Aina Barale, and David M. Halperin, eds. 1993. *The Lesbian and Gay Studies Reader*. New York: Routledge.

Akass, Kim, and Janet McCabe, eds. 2006. *Reading* The L Word: *Outing Contemporary Television*. London: I. B. Tauris.

Allen, Jeffner, ed. 1990. *Lesbian Philosophies and Cultures*. Albany, NY: State University of New York Press.

Battle, Juan J., and Natalie D. A. Bennett. 2005. "Striving for Place: Black Lesbian, Gay, Bisexual, and Transgender (LGBT) People in History and Society." In Alton Hornsby, ed., *A Companion to African American History*. Malden, MA: Blackwell.

Beemyn, Brett, ed. 1997. *Creating a Place for Ourselves: Lesbian, Gay, and Bisexual Community Histories*. New York: Routledge.

Bristow, Joseph, and Angelia R. Wilson, eds. 1993. *Activating Theory: Lesbian, Gay, and Bisexual Politics*. London: Lawrence & Wishart.

Faderman, Lillian. 1981. *Surpassing the Love of Men: Romantic Friendship and Love Between Women From the Renaissance to the Present*. New York: William Morrow.

———. 1991. *Odd Girls and Twilight Lovers: A History of Lesbian Life in Twentieth-Century America*. New York: Columbia University Press.

———. 2003. *Naked in the Promised Land: A Memoir*. Boston: Houghton Mifflin.

Feinberg, Leslie. 1993. *Stone Butch Blues*. Ithaca, NY: Firebrand Press.

Hemmings, Clare. 2002. *Bisexual Spaces: A Geography of Sexuality and Gender*. New York: Routledge.

Hoagland, Sarah, and Julia Penelope, eds. 1991. *For Lesbians Only: A Separatist Anthology*. London: Radical Feminist Lesbian Publishers.

Jeffreys, Sheila. 1996. "Heterosexuality and the Desire for Gender." In Diane Richardson, ed., *Theorising Heterosexuality*. Buckingham, UK: Open University Press.

———. 2003. *Unpacking Queer Politics: A Lesbian Feminist Perspective*. Cambridge, UK: Polity Press.

Johnston, Jill. 1973. *Lesbian Nation: The Feminist Solution*. New York: Simon and Schuster.

Kennedy, Elizabeth Lapovsky, and Madeline D. Davis. 1993. *Boots of Leather, Slippers of Gold: The History of a Lesbian Community*. New York: Routledge.

Kitzinger, Celia. 1987. *The Social Construction of Lesbianism*. Thousand Oaks, CA: Sage.

Leong, Russell, ed. 1996. *Asian American Sexualities: Dimensions of the Gay and Lesbian Experience*. New York: Routledge.

Lorde, Audre. 1984. *Sister Outsider*. Trumansburg, NY: The Crossing Press.

Phelan, Shane. 1989. *Identity Politics: Lesbian Feminism and the Limits of Community*. Philadelphia: Temple University Press.

———. 1994. *Getting Specific: Postmodern Lesbian Politics*. Minneapolis: University of Minnesota Press.

Ratti, Rakesh, ed. 1993. *A Lotus of Another Color: An Unfolding of the South Asian Gay and Lesbian Experience*. Boston: Alyson Publications.

Rich, Adrienne. 1980. "Compulsory Heterosexuality and Lesbian Existence." *Signs* 5: 631–660.

Rust, Paula C. Rodríguez. 1995. *Bisexuality and the Challenge to Lesbian Politics: Sex, Loyalty, and Revolution*. New York: New York University Press.

Snitow, Ann, Christine Stansell, and Sharon Thompson, eds. 1983. *Powers of Desire: The Politics of Sexuality*. New York: Monthly Review Press.

Stein, Arlene, ed. 1993. *Sisters, Sexperts, Queers: Beyond the Lesbian Nation*. New York: Plume.

———. 1997. *Sex and Sensibility: Stories of a Lesbian Generation.* Berkeley: University of California Press.

———. 2006. *Shameless: Sexual Dissidence in American Culture.* New York: New York University Press.

Storr, Merl, ed. 1999. *Bisexuality: A Critical Reader.* New York: Routledge.

Sullivan, Andrew, ed. 2004. *Same-Sex Marriage: A Reader.* New York: Vintage Books.

Taylor, Verta, and Leila Rupp. 1993. "Women's Culture and Lesbian Feminist Activism: A Reconsideration of Cultural Feminism." *Signs* 19: 32–61.

Trujillo, Carla, ed. 1991. *Chicana Lesbians: The Girls Our Mother Warned Us About.* Berkeley, CA: Third Woman.

Valverde, Mariana. 1985. *Sex, Power and Pleasure.* Toronto: Women's Press.

Vance, Carole S., ed. 1984. *Pleasure and Danger: Exploring Female Sexuality.* Boston: Routledge and Kegan Paul.

Walters, Suzanna Danuta. 2001. *All the Rage: The Story of Gay Visibility in America.* Chicago: University of Chicago Press.

Wittig, Monique. 1992. *The Straight Mind and Other Essays.* Boston: Beacon Press.

Zimmerman, Bonnie, and Toni A. H. McNaron, ed. 1996. *The New Lesbian Studies: Into the Twenty-First Century.* New York: Feminist Press.

Families

Bernstein, Mary, and Renate Reimann, eds. 2001. *Queer Families, Queer Politics: Challenging Culture and the State.* New York: Columbia University Press.

Carrington, Christopher. 1999. *No Place Like Home: Relationships and Family Life Among Lesbians and Gay Men.* Chicago: University of Chicago Press.

Dalton, Susan E., and Denise D. Bielby. 2000. "'That's Our Kind of Constellation': Lesbian Mothers Negotiate Institutionalized Understandings of Gender within the Family." *Gender & Society* 14: 36–61.

Dunne, Gillian A. 2000. "Opting into Motherhood: Lesbians Blurring the Boundaries and Transforming the Meaning of Parenthood and Kinship." *Gender & Society* 14: 11–35.

Hull, Kathleen. 2006. *Same-Sex Marriage: The Cultural Politics of Love and Law.* New York: Cambridge University Press.

Weeks, Jeffrey, Catherine Donovan, and Brian Heaphy. 2001. *Same-Sex Intimacies: Families of Choice and Other Life Experiments.* New York: Routledge.

Weston, Kathleen M. 1991. *Families We Choose: Lesbians, Gays, Kinship.* New York: Columbia University Press.

Heteronormativity

Farrell, Kathleen, Nisha Gupta, and Mary Queen, eds. 2007. *Interrupting Heteronormativity.* Syracuse, NY: Syracuse University Press.

Ingraham, Chrys. 2006. "Thinking Straight, Acting Bent: Heteronormativity and Homosexuality." In Kathy Davis, Mary Evans, and Judith Lorber, eds., *Handbook of Gender and Women's Studies.* London: Sage.

Jackson, Stevi. 2006. "Gender, Sexuality and Heterosexuality: The Complexity (and Limits) of Heteronormativity." *Feminist Theory* 7: 105–121.

———. 2003. "Heterosexuality, Heteronormativity and Gender Hierarchy: Some Reflections on Recent Debates." In Jeffrey Weeks, Janet Holland, and Matthew Waites, eds., *Sexualities and Society: A Reader.* Cambridge, UK: Polity Press.

Nielsen, Joyce McCarl, Glenda Walden, and Charlotte A. Kunkel. 2000. "Gendered Heteronormativity: Empirical Illustrations in Everyday Life." *Sociological Quarterly* 41: 283–296.

Sumara, Dennis, and Brent Davis. 1999. "Interrupting Heteronormativity: Toward a Queer Curriculum Theory." *Curriculum Inquiry* 29: 191–208.

Suter, Elizabeth A., and Karen L. Daas. 2007. "Negotiating Heteronormativity Dialectically: Lesbian Couples' Display of Symbols in Culture." *Western Journal of Communication* 71: 177–195.

Wiegman, Robyn. 2006. "Heteronormativity and the Desire for Gender." *Feminist Theory* 7: 89–103.

Yep, Gust A. 2003. "From Homophobia and Heterosexism to Heteronormativity: Toward the Development of a Model of Queer Interventions in the University Classroom." *Journal of Lesbian Studies* 6: 163–176.

7

Psychoanalytic Feminism

SOURCES OF GENDER INEQUALITY

- Gendered personality structures—ego-bound men and ego-permeable women
- Men's sublimated fear of castration by strong women
- Cultural domination by men's phallic-oriented perspective

POLITICS

- Correcting the male bias in psychoanalytic theory and practice
- Producing culture that features women's emotions, sexuality, and connectedness with the body
- Sharing parenting, so men as well as women parent intensively and children's personalities are degendered

CRITIQUE

- Replicates Freud's focus on the heterosexual nuclear family, failing to compare with the effects of single and same-sex parenting
- Neglects cross-national and racial ethnic comparisons of parenting
- Ignores non-Western, non-phallic cultures

CONTRIBUTIONS

- Building on the social implications of Freud's theory of personality development
- Stressing the importance of the greater involvement of fathers in child care
- Making evident the dominance of the phallus (symbol of masculine power) in Western culture
- Counteracting with cultural productions based on women's experiences of their bodies, sexualities, and emotions

In the 1970s, British, American, and French feminists began to reread and reinterpret Freud, focusing on his theories of personality development in boys and girls. Freud showed how the European patriarchal family structure of the early twentieth century produced boys whose personality structures were guarded and girls whose personality structures were open to others. Psychoanalytic feminism shows the extensive cultural and social effects of men's emotional repression, fear of castration, and ambivalence toward women, both needing and devaluing their emotional support.

Gendered Personality Structures

Psychoanalytic theory claims that the source of men's domination of women is men's ambivalent need for women's emotionality and their simultaneous rejection of women as potential castrators. Women submit to men because of women's desires for emotional connectedness. These gendered personality structures are the outcome of the child's attachment to the mother and psychological separation as the child develops a sense of individual identity.

Because the woman is the primary parent, infants bond with her. According to Freudian theory, boys have to separate from their mothers and identify with their fathers in order to establish their masculinity. This identification causes them to develop strong ego boundaries and a capacity for the independent action, objectivity, and rational thinking so valued in Western culture. Women are a threat to their independence and masculine sexuality because they remind men of their dependence on their mothers. However, men need women for the emotional sustenance and intimacy they rarely give each other. Their ambivalence toward women comes out in heterosexual love-hate relationships.

Girls continue to identify with their mothers, and so they grow up with fluid ego boundaries that make them sensitive, empathic, and emotional. It is these qualities that make them potentially good mothers and keep them open to men's emotional needs. But because the men in their lives have developed personalities that are emotionally guarded, women want to have children to bond with. Thus, psychological gendering of children is continually reproduced. Shared parenting would help to develop nurturing capabilities in men and would break the cycle of the reproduction of gendered personality structures.

Freud and Feminism

Psychoanalytic feminism has built on Freud's theories of gender and sexuality as intrinsically oppressive of women, relegating them to subordinate family roles. It argues that women's natural affiliation with other women is suppressed to make them handmaidens to men's emotional needs. In an essay, "Feminism, Femininity, and Freud," Nancy Chodorow, a sociologist and practicing psychoanalyst and the author of the influential book, *The Reproduction of Mothering*, lays out the reasons why Freud is important for feminism.

Freud and Feminism

Nancy J. Chodorow
University of California, Berkeley

First, Freud made gender and sexuality central to his theory. Psychoanalysis is first and foremost a theory of femininity and masculinity, a theory of gender inequality, and a theory of the development of heterosexuality. Freud did not develop just any theory or clinical practice, but this specific one. Moreover, psychoanalysis makes a feminist argument that women (and men) are made and not born, that biology is not enough to explain sexual orientation or gender personality.

Just as we cannot have a theory of the social organization of gender and sexuality apart from a psychological theory, so we cannot have a psychological theory of sex and gender apart from the social and political. Freud's theory is a social and political theory. The analysis of development that Freud puts forth is not the analysis of any development, but of development in a particular social situation which is intrinsic to the theory. That children develop in a family where women mother or perform primary parenting functions explains the development that Freud found; biology does not explain this development. Psychoanalysis shows that women and men and male dominance are reproduced in each generation as a result of a social division of labor in which women mother (recall the account of men's psychology and ideology of male superiority, of the nature of women's heterosexuality and connections to women and children, of women's self-valuation, of the development of attitudes toward women). That people develop in a society with a heterosexual norm and with parents who are heterosexual is also intrinsic to Freud's theory and explains development, whereas biology does not (otherwise, why should a girl turn from the mother whom she loves? Why should the mother experience her son and daughter differently and treat them differently? Why should father–daughter attraction develop?).

Further, Freud's theory assumes, and is founded on, "politics" in a wide sense. The inequality of child and adult, the child's powerlessness, is central to the explanation of character and neurosis development and of the formation of defenses. The inequality of women and men is central to the theory. Freud does not give us a theory which explains what is necessary for species survival or the survival of any society. He constructs his theory around what is necessary for the perpetuation of a male dominant social organization, for the restriction of women's sexuality to be oriented to men's, for the perpetuation of heterosexual dominance.

Reprinted from *Feminism and Psychoanalytic Theory*, 174–177. Copyright © 1989 by Nancy J. Chodorow. Reprinted by permission.

What about the second psychoanalytic objection, that psychoanalysis is a value-free science with no axe to grind, that psychoanalysis doesn't take sides about anything, whereas feminism is value-laden and by definition takes sides. I would give two kinds of answers to this objection. Most generally, I would say, psychoanalysis is not a behavioral or medical science; it cannot be, and should not be, a value-free positivistic description and explanation of behavior. Rather, it is an interpretive theory of mental processes, and with an interpretive theory, we can only say that an interpretation makes better or worse sense, not that it is true or false, right or wrong. Similarly, psychoanalysis is not founded on the objective description of someone out there about someone studied. It comes out of the transference situation, a mutually created interpersonal situation which in its turn reflexively informs the processes of free association, interpretation, and the further working through of the transference. "Observer" and "observed" together create psychoanalytic theory and clinical practice, through their interaction and the interpretation of that interaction.

On a completely different track, but in answer to the same objection, it must be pointed out that Freud himself made the "mistake" of constantly intertwining ideological positions with clinical interpretation and theory. Freud made an insistence on inequality central. There is nothing, for instance, inherently valuational in saying that women and men have differently formed superegos, or different modes of object-choice, or differently formed body images. But Freud insisted on introducing value and judgment, in arguing that men's mode of superego development and function, that men's mode of object choice, that men's body image, were better and more desirable.

Finally, we must recognize that Freud did not content himself with simply making *ad hominem* claims about women. He actively threw down the political gauntlet at feminists, in ways which make unclear whether it was he himself or feminists who first chose to make psychoanalysis a center of ideological struggle. In "The dissolution of the Oedipus complex," published in 1924, he claims that "the feminist demand for equal rights for the sexes does not take us far."[a] In 1925, in "Some psychical consequences of the anatomical distinction between the sexes," he argues that "we must not allow ourselves to be deflected from [conclusions about women's lesser sense of justice, their vanity, envy, etc.] by the denials of the feminists, who are anxious to force us to regard the two sexes as completely equal in position and worth."[b] When such criticism begins to creep into the psychoanalytic ranks themselves, and women psychoanalysts begin to object to his characterizations of women and claim that it may be biased, he responds with a more subtle anti-woman put-down: women psychoanalysts were not afflicted with the negative characteristics of femininity but were special and unlike other women. As he puts it in his lecture on femininity: "This doesn't apply to *you*. You're the exception; on this point you're more masculine than feminine."[c]

Let me try to bring my original query together, a query about the relation of femininity, feminism, and Freud. We started with the justifiable anger of past feminists. Freud does give us a prime example of an *ad hominem,* distorted ideology about women and women's inferiority, an ideology which feminists must confront, challenge, and transform.

But, more importantly, Freudian theory does not just oppress women. Rather, Freud gives us a theory concerning how people—women and men—become gendered and sexed, how femininity and masculinity develop, how sexual inequality is reproduced. With the exception of anthropological kinship theorists like Malinowski, Fortes, Lévi-Strauss, Schneider, and others, no major classical social theorist has made sex and gender central to his theory. In telling us how we come to organize sexuality, gender, procreation, parenting, according to psychological patterns, Freud tells us how nature becomes culture and how this culture comes to appear as and to be experienced as "second nature"—appears as natural. Psychoanalytic theory helps to demonstrate how sexual inequality and the social organization of gender are reproduced. It demonstrates that this reproduction happens in central ways via transformations in consciousness in the psyche, and not only via social and cultural institutions. It demonstrates that this reproduction is an unintended product of the structure of the sex–gender system itself—of a family division of labor in which women mother, of a sexual system founded on heterosexual norm, of a culture that assumes and transmits sexual inequality. Freud, or psychoanalysis, tells us how people become heterosexual in their family development (how the originally matrisexual girl comes to be heterosexual rather than lesbian); how a family structure in which women mother produces in men (and in women, to some extent) a psychology and ideology of male dominance, masculine superiority, and the devaluation of women and things feminine; how women develop maternal capacities through their relationship to their own mother. Thus, psychoanalysis demonstrates the internal mechanisms of the socio-cultural organization of gender and sexuality and confirms the early feminist argument that the "personal is political." It argues for the rootedness and basic-ness of psychological forms of inequality and oppression.

But psychoanalysis does not stop at this demonstration. Freud suggests that these processes do not happen so smoothly, that this reproduction of gender and sexuality is rife with contradictions and strains. People develop conflicting desires, discontents, neuroses. Psychoanalysis begins from psychic conflict; this is what Freud was first trying to explain. Thus, heterosexuality is not constituted smoothly for all time: Women still want relationships and closeness to women, and male heterosexuality is embedded in Oedipal devaluation, fear and contempt of women as well as a fear of the overwhelmingness of mother and of acknowledging emotional demands and needs. Male dominance on a psychological level is a masculine defense and a major psychic cost to men, built on fears and insecurity; it is not straightforward power. Psychoanalysis demonstrates, against theories of over-socialization and total domination, a lack of total socialization. It demonstrates discontent, resistance, and an undercutting of sexual modes and the institutions of sexual inequality.

Psychoanalysis is also a theory that people actively appropriate and respond to their life environment and experiences, make something of these psychologically, and, therefore, presumably can act to change them.

Notes

a. "The dissolution of the Oedipus complex," 1924, *New Introductory Lectures on Psychoanalysis, The Standard Edition of the Complete Psychological Works of Sigmund Freud*, ed. James Strachey (London: The Hogarth Press and the Institute of Psychoanalysis) (hereafter *SE*), vol. 19, p. 178.
b. "Some psychical consequences of the anatomical distinction between the sexes," 1925, *SE*, vol. 19, p. 258.
c. "Femininity," 1933, *SE*, vol. 22, pp. 116–117.

The Male Gaze

One of the manifestations of men's objectification of women is the *male gaze*, the cultural creation of women as the objects of men's sexual fantasies, feared as well as desired. Psychoanalytic feminism shows how Western culture represents men's sexualization of women and dread of emotional involvement in plays, operas, art, movies, rap music, and on MTV. These phallic cultural productions, according to psychoanalytic feminism, are full of men's aggression, competition between men, men's flight from women or domination of them. The underlying subtext is fear of castration—of becoming women. What women represent in phallic culture is the sexual desire and emotionality men must repress in order to become like their fathers—men who are self-controlled and controlling of others. No matter what role women play in cultural productions, the male gaze sees them as potentially castrating mothers and as potentially engulfing objects of desire. With the male gaze, men simultaneously create and control women either as madonnas (mothers) or whores (sexual objects). Madonnas can castrate, and whores have dangerous vaginas.

Performers like Madonna have not only resisted but turned the male gaze back on itself. As a media star, Madonna subverted both symbolic representations of women—as mothers (her name) and as whores (her clothes, gestures, language). Madonna created an aggressively feminized erotic vocabulary, selling herself sexually while symbolically parodying conventionally gendered sexuality. She countered the male gaze by making sexy clothing like her pointy-breasted bustiers into symbols of power. In her songs and films,

Madonna exaggerated and parodied femininity, turning the male gaze into an instrument of female power. In contrast, Marilyn Monroe, another highly sexualized star, did not distance herself from the male gaze and suffered for it. By taking the male gaze and using it to her own ends, Madonna has made female sexuality into in-your-face resistance.

French psychoanalytic feminism

In France, feminists took on the Freudian-oriented cultural critics Jacques Lacan and Jacques Derrida, who say that women cannot create culture because they lack a sense of difference (from the mother) and a phallus (identification with the powerful father). In French feminist psychoanalytic theory, a major part of patriarchal culture reflects the sublimation of men's suppressed infantile desire for the mother and fear of the loss of the phallus, the symbol of masculine difference from powerless women. Women's wish for a phallus and repressed sexual desire for their fathers is sublimated into wanting to give birth to a son; men's repressed sexual desire for their mothers and fear of the father's castration of them are sublimated into cultural creations.

These French feminists—Hélène Cixous, Luce Irigaray, Julia Kristeva, and others—developed "psych et po," psychoanalytically oriented feminist politics based on resistance to phallic thinking and phallic culture. To counter phallic cultural centrality with woman-centered culture, they called for women to write from their biographical experiences and their bodies—about menstruation, pregnancy, childbirth, intimacy with their mothers and their friends, their sexual desires for women as well as for men. Most of all, they need to experience and write about *jouissance*, exultant joy in their sexual bodies and emotions.

Rather than reassuring men of their masculinity by submitting to their symbolic sexual domination, Cixous says women must use their heads and their mouths for themselves. In "The Laugh of the Medusa," she transforms the image of the Medusa, the head whose look turns men to stone (a symbol of castration), into an icon of women's sexual strength. The Medusa's laughing mouth (women's sexuality) is liberating: "You have only to look at the Medusa straight on to see her. And she is not deadly. She is beautiful and she is laughing" (1976, 885). The article from which the following excerpt is taken was published in France in 1975 and translated and published in *Signs* in 1976, its first year.

The Laugh of the Medusa

Hélène Cixous

Centre de Recherches en Etudes Féminines

I shall speak about women's writing: about *what it will do*. Woman must write her self: must write about women and bring women to writing, from which they have been driven away as violently as from their bodies—for the same reasons, by the same law, with the same fatal goal. Woman must put herself into the text—as into the world and into history—by her own movement.

The future must no longer be determined by the past. I do not deny that the effects of the past are still with us. But I refuse to strengthen them by repeating them, to confer upon them an irremovability the equivalent of destiny, to confuse the biological and the cultural. Anticipation is imperative.

Since these reflections are taking shape in an area just on the point of being discovered, they necessarily bear the mark of our time—a time during which the new breaks away from the old, and, more precisely, the (feminine) new from the old (*la nouvelle de l'ancien*). Thus, as there are no grounds for establishing a discourse, but rather an arid millennial ground to break, what I say has at least two sides and two aims: to break up, to destroy; and to foresee the unforeseeable, to project.

I write this as a woman, toward women. When I say "woman," I'm speaking of woman in her inevitable struggle against conventional man; and of a universal woman subject who must bring women to their senses and to their meaning in history. But first it must be said that in spite of the enormity of the repression that has kept them in the "dark"— that dark which people have been trying to make them accept as their attribute—there is, at this time, no general woman, no one typical woman. What they have *in common* I will say. But what strikes me is the infinite richness of their individual constitutions: you can't talk about *a* female sexuality, uniform, homogeneous, classifiable into codes—any more than you can talk about one unconscious resembling another. Women's imaginary is inexhaustible, like music, painting, writing: their stream of phantasms is incredible.

I have been amazed more than once by a description a woman gave me of a world all her own which she had been secretly haunting since early childhood. A world of searching, the elaboration of a knowledge, on the basis of a systematic experimentation with the bodily functions, a passionate and precise interrogation of her erotogeneity. This practice, extraordinarily rich and inventive, in particular as concerns masturbation, is prolonged or accompanied by a production of forms, a veritable aesthetic activity, each stage of rapture inscribing a resonant vision, a composition, something beautiful. Beauty will no longer be forbidden.

I wished that that woman would write and proclaim this unique empire so that other women, other unacknowledged sovereigns, might exclaim: I, too, overflow; my desires have invented new desires, my body knows unheard-of songs. Time and again I, too, have felt so full of luminous torrents that I could burst—burst with forms much more beautiful than those which are put up in frames and sold for a stinking fortune. And I, too, said nothing, showed nothing; I didn't open my mouth, I didn't repaint my half of the world. I was ashamed. I was afraid, and I swallowed my shame and my fear. I said to myself: You are mad! What's the meaning of these waves, these floods, these outbursts? Where is the ebullient, infinite woman who, immersed as she was in her naiveté, kept in the dark about herself, led into self-disdain by the great arm of parental-conjugal phallocentrism, hasn't been ashamed of her strength? Who, surprised and horrified by the fantastic tumult of her drives (for she was made to believe that a well-adjusted normal woman has a...divine composure), hasn't accused herself of being a monster? Who, feeling a funny desire stirring inside her (to sing, to write, to dare to speak, in short, to bring out something new), hasn't thought she was sick? Well, her shameful sickness is that she resists death, that she makes trouble.

And why don't you write? Write! Writing is for you, you are for you; your body is yours, take it. I know why you haven't written. (And why I didn't write before the age of twenty-seven.) Because writing is at once too high, too great for you, it's reserved for the great—that is, for "great men"; and it's "silly." Besides, you've written a little, but in secret. And it wasn't good, because it was in secret, and because you punished yourself for writing, because you didn't go all the way; or because you wrote, irresistibly, as when we would masturbate in secret, not to go further, but to attenuate the tension a bit, just enough to take the edge off. And then, as soon as we come, we go and make ourselves feel guilty—so as to be forgiven; or to forget, to bury it until the next time.

Write, let no one hold you back, let nothing stop you: not man; not the imbecilic capitalist machinery, in which publishing houses are the crafty, obsequious relayers of imperatives handed down by an economy that works against us and off our backs; and not *yourself*. Smug-faced readers, managing editors, and big bosses don't like the true texts of women—female-sexed texts. That kind scares them.

I write woman: woman must write woman. And man, man. So only an oblique consideration will be found here of man; it's up to him to say where his masculinity and femininity are at: this will concern us once men have opened their eyes and seen themselves clearly.

Now women return from afar, from always: from "without," from the heath where witches are kept alive; from below, from beyond "culture"; from their childhood which men have been trying desperately to make them forget, condemning it to "eternal rest." The little girls and their "ill-mannered" bodies immured, well-preserved, intact unto themselves, in the mirror, Frigidified. But are they ever seething underneath! What an effort it takes—there's no end to it—for the sex cops to bar their threatening return. Such a display of forces on both sides that the struggle has for centuries been immobilized in the trembling equilibrium of a deadlock....

Write your self. Your body must be heard. Only then will the immense resources of the unconscious spring forth. Our naphtha will spread, throughout the world, without dollars—black or gold—nonassessed values that will change the rules of the old game.

To write. An act which will not only "realize" the decensored relation of woman to her sexuality, to her womanly being, giving her access to her native strength; it will give her back her goods, her pleasures, her organs, her immense bodily territories which have been kept under seal; it will tear her away from the superegoized structure in which she has always occupied the place reserved for the guilty (guilty of everything, guilty at every turn: for having desires, for not having any; for being frigid, for being "too hot"; for not being both at once; for being too motherly and not enough; for having children and for not having any; for nursing and for not nursing...)—tear her away by means of this research, this job of analysis and illumination, this emancipation of the marvelous text of her self that she must urgently learn to speak. A woman without a body, dumb, blind, can't possibly be a good fighter. She is reduced to being the servant of the militant male, his shadow. We must kill the false woman who is preventing the live one from breathing. Inscribe the breath of the whole woman.

Frida Kahlo, a twentieth-century Mexican artist, is an example of a woman artist who used her body as the central figure in allegories of birth, menstruation, and death. She had been in a tram accident as a girl and suffered all her life from the effects of multiple surgeries. She did many bold self-portraits portraying her unflinching stare at the viewer, as if to say, I am a woman and I am here. Another artist, Judy Chicago, created a gallery-sized table set with plates decorated with symbolic female genitalia, laid on an elaborately embroidered tablecloth showing the names of heroic women throughout history. Chicago's intent was to use women's crafts, pottery and embroidery, to visibly celebrate women's lives. *The Dinner Party*, now an icon of feminist art, is on permanent display at the Elizabeth A. Sackler Center for Feminist Art in the Brooklyn Museum of Art in New York City.

Critique

Freudian theories of gender and sexuality are based on the bourgeois Western nuclear family, in which the woman is the prime parent and the man is emotionally distant from his children. Feminist psychoanalytic theories are just as narrowly based in a family consisting of two heterosexual parents. The involvement of fathers in parenting varies enormously in societies throughout the world, but there are few tests of Freudian theories of each gender's personality development in single-parent, same-sex, and other types of households. Furthermore, it is not only heterosexual women who want the emotional attachment of mothering. Many lesbians who have deep and intense relationships with women also want children.

Psychoanalytic feminism has also been criticized for neglecting racial ethnic differences and colonial histories—not all fathers are powerful. Psychoanalytic feminism's theory of culture is also too generalized—it assumes that all men in Western culture are misogynist and emotionally repressed, and all women are oppressed by being portrayed as madonnas or whores.

Summary

In Freudian theory, gendered personality development comes out of the resolution of the Oedipus complex, in which the young boy represses his emotional attachment to his mother and identifies with his more powerful father because he is afraid that otherwise, like her, he will lose his penis. Western culture is the product of men's fear of losing the phallus, the symbol of masculine power. Since women do not have a penis to lose, they do not participate in the creation of this culture.

A little girl continues to be emotionally attached to her mother in the development of her feminine identity. When she grows up, she finds that men cannot fill her emotional needs because they are too detached, and the taboo against homosexuality turns her away from sexual relationships with women. The normal woman, in Freudian theory, will want to mother a child. Her attachment to her child, girl or boy, reproduces the cycle of gendered personality development all over again.

Psychoanalytic feminism's solution to these patterns of gendered personalities and phallic cultural productions is twofold. First, men have to be taught how to be emotionally attached parents to their sons and daughters. With a man as an intimate parent to bond with, a boy will not have to detach emotionally to develop a masculine identity, and a girl will be able to develop a strong ego.

Second, women have to create art, music, and literature out of their emotional and sexual experiences and their joy in their female bodies. Women's creativity can counteract the dominance of the phallus (symbolic masculinity) in Western culture. By encouraging women to produce woman-centered art and literature, psychoanalytic feminism has opened our eyes to the beauty and power of female bodies and sexualities. But it can lock women artists, musicians, and writers into a categorically female sensibility and emphasize their difference from men and the dominant culture even more. Women's emotional and erotic power is unleashed and made visible in women's cultural productions, but they are separated from men's culture, which is still dominant.

Psychoanalytic feminism, delving into the emotional and sexual base of Western society's gender order, uses woman-centered therapy, sexuality, and cultural productions to counter men's misogyny and phallic culture. Like radical and lesbian feminism, psychoanalytic feminism creates woman-centered social spaces in a male-dominated and gender-divided social order that they resist, but do not change.

SUGGESTED READINGS IN PSYCHOANALYTIC FEMINISM

Abel, Elizabeth, Barbara Christian, and Helene Moglen, eds. 1997. *Female Subjects in Black and White: Race, Psychoanalysis, Feminism.* Berkeley: University of California Press.

Baruch, Elaine Hoffman. 1991. *Women, Love, and Power: Literary and Psychoanalytic Perspectives.* New York: New York University Press.

Benjamin, Jessica. 1988. *The Bonds of Love: Psychoanalysis, Feminism, and the Problem of Domination.* New York: Pantheon.

Buhle, Mari Jo. 1998. *Feminism and Its Discontents: A Century of Struggle with Psychoanalysis.* Cambridge, MA: Harvard University Press.

Chancer, Lynn S. 1992. *Sadomasochism in Everyday Life: The Dynamics of Power and Powerlessness.* New Brunswick, NJ: Rutgers University Press.

Cheng, Anne Anlin. 2001. *The Melancholy of Race: Psychoanalysis, Assimilation, and Hidden Grief.* New York: Oxford University Press.

Chodorow, Nancy. 1978. *The Reproduction of Mothering.* Berkeley: University of California Press; updated edition, 1999.

——. 1989. *Feminism and Psychoanalytic Theory.* New Haven, CT: Yale University Press.

——. 1994. *Femininities, Masculinities, Sexualities: Freud and Beyond.* Lexington: University Press of Kentucky.

——. 1999. *The Power of Feelings: Personal Meanings in Psychoanalysis, Gender, and Culture.* New Haven, CT: Yale University Press.

Clough, Patricia Ticineto. 2000. *Autoaffection: Unconscious Thought in the Age of Teletechnology.* Minneapolis: University of Minnesota Press.

Dimen, Muriel, and Virginia Goldner, eds. 2002. *Gender in Psychoanalytic Space: Between Clinic and Culture.* New York: Other Press.

Flax, Jane. 1990. *Thinking Fragments: Psychoanalysis, Feminism, and Postmodernism in the Contemporary West.* Berkeley: University of California Press.

Gallop, Jane. 1982. *The Daughter's Seduction: Feminism and Psychoanalysis.* Ithaca, NY: Cornell University Press.

Mitchell, Juliet. 1975. *Psychoanalysis and Feminism: Freud, Reich, Laing and Women.* New York: Vintage.

Nair, Rukmini Bhaya. 2002. *Lying on the Postcolonial Couch: The Idea of Indifference.* Minneapolis: University of Minnesota Press.

O'Connor, Noreen, and Joanna Ryan. 1993. *Wild Desires and Mistaken Identity: Lesbianism and Psychoanalysis.* London: Virago.

Schwartz, Adria E. 1998. *Sexual Subjects: Lesbians, Gender, and Psychoanalysis.* New York: Routledge.

Walton, Jean. 2001. *Fair Sex, Savage Dreams: Race, Psychoanalysis, Sexual Difference.* Durham, NC: Duke University Press.

Worell, Judith. 2000. "Feminism in Psychology: Revolution or Evolution?" *Annals of the American Academy of Political and Social Science* 571: 183–196.

French Feminism

Cavallaro, Dani. 2006. *French Feminist Theory: An Introduction.* London: Continuum.

Cixous, Hélène. 1994. *The Hélène Cixous Reader.* Ed., Susan Sellers. New York: Routledge.

———. *Writing Notebooks.* Ed., Susan Sellers. London: Continuum.

Cixous, Hélène, and Catherine Clément. [1975] 1986. *The Newly Born Woman.* Trans., Betsy Wing. Minneapolis: University of Minnesota Press.

Irigaray, Luce. [1974] 1985. *Speculum of the Other Woman.* Trans., Gillian C. Gill. Ithaca, NY: Cornell University Press.

———. [1977] 1985. *This Sex Which Is Not One.* Trans., Catherine Porter with Carolyn Burke. Ithaca, NY: Cornell University Press.

———. 1992. *Je, Tu, Nous: Toward a Culture of Difference.* New York: Routledge.

Kristeva, Julia. 1986. *The Kristeva Reader.* Ed., Toril Moi. New York: Columbia University Press.

———. 2002. *Intimate Revolt.* Trans., Jeanine Herman. New York: Columbia University Press.

———. 2005. *Stigmata: Escaping Texts.* 2nd ed. New York: Routledge.

Marks, Elaine, and Isabelle de Courtivron, eds. 1981. *New French Feminisms.* New York: Schocken.

Mitchell, Juliet, and Jacqueline Rose, eds. 1985. *Feminine Sexuality: Jacques Lacan and the 'école freudienne'.* New York: W. W. Norton.

Moi, Toril. 1985. *Sexual/Textual Politics: Feminist Literary Theory.* New York: Methuen.

———, ed. 1987. *French Feminist Thought: A Reader.* New York: Basil Blackwell.

Oliver, Kelly, and Lisa Walsh, eds. 2005. *Contemporary French Feminism.* New York: Oxford University Press.

Women's Cultural Productions

Block, Adrienne Fried. 1998. *Amy Beach, Passionate Victorian: The Life and Work of an American Composer, 1867–1944.* New York: Oxford University Press.

Chicago, Judy. 1979. *The Dinner Party: A Symbol of Our Heritage.* New York: Doubleday.

Clément, Catherine. [1979] 1988. *Opera, or the Undoing of Women.* Trans., Betsy Wing. Minneapolis: University of Minnesota Press.

De Lauretis, Teresa. 1984. *Alice Doesn't: Feminism, Semiotics, Cinema.* Bloomington: Indiana University Press.

———. 1987. *Technologies of Gender.* Bloomington: Indiana University Press.

Garrard, Mary D. 1989. *Artemisia Gentileschi: The Image of the Female Hero in Italian Baroque Art.* Princeton, NJ: Princeton University Press.

Gilbert, Sandra M., and Susan Gubar. 1988. *No Man's Land: The Place of the Woman Writer in the Twentieth Century.* 2 vols. New Haven, CT: Yale University Press.

Harris, Anne Sutherland, and Linda Nochlin. 1976. *Women Artists: 1550–1950.* New York: Knopf.

Jackson, Buzzy. 2005. *A Bad Woman Feeling Good: Blues and the Women Who Sing Them.* New York: W.W. Norton.

Jackson, Irene V. 1981. "Black Women and Music: A Survey from Africa to the New World." In Filomina Chioma Steady, ed., *The Black Woman Cross-Culturally.* Cambridge, MA: Schenkman.

Jones, Amelia, and Laura Cottingham. 1996. *Sexual Politics: Judy Chicago's Dinner Party in Feminist Art History.* Berkeley: University of California Press.

Kingston, Maxine Hong. 1976. *The Woman Warrior.* New York: Vintage.

Levin, Gail. 2007. *Becoming Judy Chicago: A Biography of the Artist.* New York: Harmony Books.

Lowe, Sarah M. 1991. *Frida Kahlo.* New York: Universe Books.

Marcus, Jane. 1987. *Virginia Woolf and the Languages of Patriarchy.* Bloomington: Indiana University Press.

McClary, Susan. 1991. *Feminine Endings: Music, Gender, and Sexuality.* Minneapolis: University of Minnesota Press.

Moers, Ellen. 1977. *Literary Women: The Great Writers.* Garden City, NY: Doubleday Anchor.

Mulvey, Laura. 1989. *Visual and Other Pleasures.* Bloomington: Indiana University Press.

Nochlin, Linda. 1988. *Women, Art, and Power and Other Essays.* New York: Harper and Row.

Reckitt, Helena, and Peggy Phelan. 2001. *Art and Feminism.* New York: Phaidon Press.

Robinson, Hilary, ed. 1988. *Visibly Female: Feminism and Art Today.* New York: Universe Books.

Solie, Ruth A., ed. 1993. *Musicology and Difference: Gender and Sexuality in Music Scholarship.* Berkeley: University of California Press.

Standpoint Feminism

SOURCES OF GENDER INEQUALITY

- The neglect of women's perspective and experiences in the production of knowledge
- Women's exclusion from the sciences
- Male bias in science and social science research

POLITICS

- Making women central to research in the physical and social sciences, as researchers and as subjects
- Asking research questions from women's points of view
- Producing knowledge with diverse women's perspectives

CRITIQUE

- Women's bodies and sexualities are too varied for a unified perspective
- Women's social locations differ by social class, racial ethnic, and other statuses, so their perspectives will also differ
- Some men's perspectives are also marginalized

CONTRIBUTIONS

- Reframing research questions and priorities to include women and other marginalized people
- Challenging the universality and political neutrality of scientific "facts"
- Creating a feminist paradigm for the production of knowledge that is critical of conventional wisdom and consciously aware of social location
- Making women's perspectives or "voices" salient in the production of knowledge and culture

Radical, lesbian, and psychoanalytic feminist theories of women's oppression converge in standpoint feminism, which argues that knowledge must be produced from a woman's as well as a man's point of view. The main idea among the gender resistance feminisms is that in the production of knowledge, women's experiences and perspectives should be central, not invisible or marginal. This idea is the basis for standpoint feminism. Simply put, standpoint feminism says that because women's experiences are different from men's, so are their "voices"—and they must be heard.

Standpoint Theory

In the twentieth century, philosophers, psychologists, and physicists have argued that the social location, experiences, and point of view of the investigator or "looker," as well as those of the subjects or the "looked at," interact in producing what we know. A complete picture of a school, for instance, has to include the perspectives of the researcher, the teachers, students, their families, the school administrators, the bureaucrats of the department of education, and the politicians who set the school's budget.

The impact of the everyday world in its experiential reality and the structures that limit, shape, organize, and penetrate it are different for people in different social locations—but especially different for women and men because Western society is so gender-divided. Consider the school again—won't viewpoints be different if the teachers and involved parents are mostly women and the school and departmental administrators and politicians mostly men? Is a man or a woman researcher more likely to see the gendered concentration of power and its impact on curriculum and sports programs? Similarly, in a racially or ethnically divided community, it makes a lot of difference in the way research is done when the researcher is a member of the disadvantaged rather than the advantaged community.

Although men could certainly do research on and about women, and women on men, standpoint feminism argues that women are more sensitive to how other women see problems and set priorities and therefore would be better able to design and conduct research from their point of view. It is not enough, however, to just add more women to research teams or even to have them head a team—these women have to have a feminist viewpoint. They have to be critical of mainstream concepts that justify established lines of power, and they should recognize that "facts" often reflect stereotypical values and beliefs about women and men.

In addition to *phenomenology* (the philosophy that says that what we know comes out of our social location and experience), the grounding for standpoint feminism comes from Marxist feminist theory, which applies Marx's concept of class consciousness to women and men. Standpoint feminism argues that as physical and social producers of children—out of bodies, emotions, thought, and sheer physical labor—women are grounded in material reality in ways that men are not. Women are responsible for most of the everyday work, even if they are highly educated, while highly educated men concentrate on the abstract and the intellectual. Because they are closely connected to their bodies and their emotions, women's unconscious as well as conscious view of the world is unitary and concrete. If women produced knowledge, it would be much more in touch with the everyday, material world and with the connectedness among people, because that is what women experience.

Dorothy Smith, a feminist sociologist who has helped develop the ideas of standpoint feminism, says that knowledge has to be sought in "everyday/ everynight" local practices of individuals combined with institutional ethnography—mapping the practices of organizations and their members, which constrain individual actions by the relations of ruling. As she shows in the following excerpt from her 2005 book, *Institutional Ethnography: A Sociology for People,* women's standpoint injects mundane embodied actions into concentric systems of coordination and control. Research on an economic issue should go from the woman shopper to the organization of the store, the supply chain, food production, and the global economy, recognizing that each level has hierarchal relations of ruling that impact on the people involved and that this impact is likely to be gendered.

Women's Standpoint: Embodied Knowledge versus the Ruling Relations

Dorothy E. Smith
University of Toronto

It's hard to recall just how radical the experience of the women's movement was at its inception for those of us who had lived and thought within the masculinist regime against which the movement struggled. For us, the struggle was as much within ourselves, with what we knew how to do and think and feel, as with that regime as an enemy outside us. Indeed we ourselves had participated however passively in that regime. There was no developed discourse in which the experiences that were spoken originally as everyday experience could be translated into a public language and become political in the ways distinctive to the women's movement. We learned in talking with other women about experiences that we had and about others that we had not had. We began to name "oppression," "rape," "harassment," "sexism," "violence," and others. These were terms that did more than name. They gave shared experiences a political presence.

Starting with our experiences as we talked and thought about them, we discovered depths of alienation and anger that were astonishing. Where had all these feelings been? How extraordinary were the transformations we experienced as we discovered with other women how to speak with one another about such experiences and then how to bring them forward publicly, which meant exposing them to men. Finally, how extraordinary were the transformations of ourselves in this process. Talking our experience was a means of discovery. What we did not know and did not know how to think about, we could examine as we found what we had in common. The approach that I have taken in developing an alternative sociology takes up women's standpoint in a way that is modeled on these early adventures of the women's movement. It takes up women's standpoint not as a given and finalized form of knowledge but as a ground in experience from which discoveries are to be made.

It is this active and shared process of speaking from our experience, as well as acting and organizing to change how those experiences had been created, that has been translated in feminist thinking into the concept of a feminist standpoint—or, for me, women's standpoint. However the concept originated, Sandra Harding (1988) drew together the social scientific thinking by feminists, particularly Nancy Hartsock, Hilary Rose, and myself, that had as a common project taking up a standpoint in women's experience. Harding argued that feminist empiricists who claimed both a special privilege for women's knowledge and an objectivity were stuck in an irresolvable paradox. Those she described as "feminist standpoint theorists" moved the feminist critique a step beyond feminist empiricism by claiming that knowledge of society must always be from a position in it and that women are privileged epistemologically by being members of an oppressed group. Like the slave in Hegel's parable of the master–slave relationship, they can see more, further, and better than the master precisely because of their marginalized and oppressed condition. She was, however, critical of the way in which experience in the women's movement had come to hold authority as a ground for speaking, and claiming to speak truly, that challenged the rational and objectified forms of knowledge and their secret masculine subject (123). Furthermore, feminist standpoint theory, according to Harding, implicitly reproduced the universalized subject and claims to objective truth of traditional philosophical discourse, an implicit return to the empiricism we claimed to have gone beyond.

The notion of women's standpoint—or indeed the notion that women's experience has special authority—has also been challenged by feminist theorists. It fails to take into account diversities of class and race as well as the various forms and modulations of gender. White middle-class heterosexual women dominated the early phases of the women's movement in the 1960s and 1970s, but soon our, and I speak as one, assumptions about what would hold for women in general were challenged and undermined, first by working-class women and lesbians, then by African–North American, Hispanic, and Native women. The implicit presence of class, sexuality, and colonialism began to be exposed. Our assumptions were also challenged by women in other societies whose experience wasn't North American, by women such as those with disabilities and older women whose experience was not adequately represented and, as the women's movement evolved over time, by younger women who have found the issues of older feminists either alien or irrelevant.

The theoretical challenge to the notion of women's standpoint has been made in terms of its alleged essentialism. It has been seen as essentialist because it excludes other bases of oppression and inequity that intersect with the category "women." The critique of essentialism, however, assumes the use of the category "women" or "woman" to identify shared and defining attributes. While essentialism has been a problem in the theorizing of *woman,* it cannot be extended to all uses of such categories. In practice in the women's movement, the category has worked politically rather than referentially. As a political concept, it coordinates struggle against the masculinist forms of oppressing women that those forms themselves explicitly or implicitly universalize. Perhaps most important, it creates for women what had been missing, a subject position in the public sphere and, more generally, one in the political, intellectual, and cultural life of the society.

Claiming a subject position within the public sphere in the name of women was a central enterprise of the women's movement in its early days in the 1970s and 1980s. A powerful dynamic was created. While those making the claim first were white middle-class women, the new subject position in public discourse opened the way for others who had found themselves excluded by those who'd gone before. Their claims were positioned and centered differently, and their own experience became authoritative. It is indeed one of the extraordinary characteristics of the women's movement that its continual disruption, its internal struggles against racism and white cultural dominance, its internal quarrels and angers, have been far from destructive to the movement. On the contrary, these struggles in North America and Europe have expanded and diversified the movement as women other than those with whom it originated gave their own experiences voice.

Women's Standpoint and the Ruling Relations

Standpoint is a term lifted out of the vernacular, largely through Harding's innovative thinking and her critique (1988), and it is used for doing new discursive work. Harding identifies standpoint in terms of the social positioning of the subject of knowledge, the knower and creator of knowledge. Her own subsequent work develops an epistemology that relies on a diversity of subject positions in the sociopolitical-economic regimes of colonialism and imperialism. The version of standpoint that I have worked with, after I had adopted the term from Harding (previously I'd written of "perspective"; D. E. Smith 1974), is rather different. It differs also from the concept of a feminist standpoint that has been put forward by Nancy Hartsock (1998) in that it does not identify a socially determined position or category of position in society (or political economy).[a] Rather, my notion of women's (rather than feminist) standpoint is integral to the design of what I originally called "a sociology for women," which has necessarily been transformed into "a sociology for people." It does not identify a position or a category of position, gender, class, or race within the society, but it does establish as a subject position for institutional ethnography as a method of inquiry, a site for the knower that is open to anyone....

In general, instead of being ruled directly by individuals whom we've known (and perhaps hated) for years and who were known before us by our parents, we are ruled by people who are at work in corporations, government, professional settings and organizations, universities, public schools, hospitals and clinics, and so on and so on. Though they are, of course, individuals, their capacities to act derive from the organizations and social relations that they both produce and are produced by. The relations and organization in which they are active are also those that organize our lives and in which we in various ways participate. Watching television, reading the newspaper, going to the grocery store, taking a child to school, taking on a mortgage for a home, walking down a city street, switching on a light, plugging in a computer—these daily acts articulate us into social relations of the order I have called *ruling* as well as those of the economy; what we pick up when we're out shopping will likely have been produced by people living far away from us whom we'll never know. And so on. These transactions aren't with people we know as particular individuals, such as family members or neighbors. It doesn't matter whether the taxman or the supermarket clerk is someone we have a personal relationship with; it's their job that is the basis on which we interact with them. It doesn't matter that we'll never know—except as screen images—the people who tell us news stories on CNN or the Canadian Broadcasting Corporation. The functions of "knowledge, judgment, and will" have become built into a specialized complex of objectified forms of organization and consciousness that organize and coordinate people's everyday lives....

The concept of women's standpoint that I work with has evolved from the conjuncture of the local and embodied work of mothering, immediate subsistence, and household care and the locally transcending work of participating in the extralocal relations of sociological discourse and the institutional regime of the university. I recognize the historical specificity of this intersection in the lives of women like myself. It locates a contradiction fundamental to our society between, on the one hand, forms of ruling (including discourse) mediated by texts and organized extra- or translocally in objectified modes of the ruling relations and, on the other, the traditional particularizations of both locale and relationships that still characterize family households.

It has been the exclusion of women as subjects from the objectified relations of discourse and ruling that situate my formulation of women's standpoint. We do not have to look for it in what women otherwise may or may not have in common. "I think, therefore I am" has been spoken by men; "I do sex, I give birth, I care for children, I clean house, I cook, therefore I am not" has been the unspoken of women since the emergence of these extraordinary new forms of ruling—at least until the women's movement began our work of eroding the barriers excluding us from agency within these forms of organization. What has been repugnant, dangerous to the purity of the world of enlightened intellect[b] has been the presence of the mortal body that women's presence inserts, our breach of the divide that insulates mind's recognition that it has, dwells in, is not separable from, a body.

The concealed masculinity of the subject claiming the formal universality that is foundational to objectified forms of knowledge became visible in the women's movement somewhat indirectly. Perhaps it should have been obvious to us right off that when women claimed a subject position, it directly undermined the dichotomy of mind and discarded body on which universality depends. It wasn't just that subjects had bodies. Indeed phenomenology had been at work trying to ensure the cogency of a universal subject that was definitely embodied by bracketing embodiment. But women's claims to speak were not just as new members of the club; the starting point of the women's movement refused the separation of body and mind. Speaking from the experience of women, however diverse our experience and however refined and elaborated in feminist theory, was always and necessarily from sites of bodily being. Speaking from women's standpoint did not permit the constitutional separation between mind and body built into Western philosophy since Descartes and incorporated into sociology. Women's standpoint, as I've taken it up to remake sociology, does not permit that separation....

The strategy of beginning from women's standpoint in the local actualities of the everyday/everynight world does not bridge this division. It collapses it. The embodied knower begins in her experience. Here she is an expert. I mean by this simply that when it comes to knowing her way around in it, how things get done, where the bus stop for the B-line bus is, at which supermarket she can pick up both organic vegetables and lactate-reduced milk, and all the unspecifiables of her daily doings and the local conditions on which she relies—when it comes to knowing these matters, she is an expert. It is another matter altogether when it comes to the forms of organization that authenticate the organic status of the vegetables; that brings the supermarket or the bus company into daily existence; or that constitute the responsibility of the municipal government for the state of the streets, the sidewalks, the standards of waste disposal, and so on. And going deeper into the complex of relations into which these locally visible and effective forms are tied are the social relations of the economy.

Such are the ordinary realities of our contemporary world in North America. There are people at work elsewhere whom we don't know and will never know whose doings are coordinated with ours, whether it's when we go to the corner store to pick up a laundry detergent after hours, or when we turn on the television to listen to the latest news on the catastrophic present, or when we pick up a book about the cumulation of sociological theory to connect with the work of others done at who knows what times and places. Social relations coordinating across time and distance are present but largely unseen within the everyday/everynight worlds of people's experience. A sociology from women's standpoint makes this reality a problematic, a project of research and discovery.

Notes

a. Hartsock's concern is to reframe historical materialism so that women's experience and interests are fully integrated. Of particular importance to her is the adequate recognition of the forms of power that the women's movement has named "patriarchal." Women's marginal position, structured as it is around the work associated with reproduction and the direct production of subsistence, locates women distinctively in the mode of production in general. For her, taking a feminist standpoint introduces a dimension into historical materialism neglected by Marx and his successors. She designs a feminist standpoint that has a specifically political import. It might, I suppose, be criticized as essentialist, but, if we consider not just North America and not just white middle-class professional North America, it's hard to deny that Hartsock is characterizing a reality for women worldwide. In Canada a recent census report shows that while women's participation in the paid labor force has increased substantially over the past thirty years, "women remain more than twice as likely as men to do at least 30 hours a week of cooking and cleaning" (Andersen 2003, A7) and are more involved in child care than men, particularly care of younger children.

b. I am referring here to Mary Douglas's remarkable study, *Purity and Danger* (1966).

References

Anderson, E. 2003. "Women Do Lion's Share at Home." *Globe and Mail,* February 12, A7.

Douglas, M. 1966. *Purity and Danger.* New York: Penguin Books.

Harding, S. 1986. *The Science Question in Feminism.* Ithaca, NY: Cornell University Press.

Hartsock, Nancy C. M. 1998. *The Feminist Standpoint Revisited and Other Essays.* Boulder, CO: Westview Press.

Smith, D.E. 1974. "Women's Perspective as a Radical Critique of Sociology." *Sociological Inquiry* 44 (1): 1–13.

Feminist Science

While the theory that incorporation of women's standpoint would transform any area of knowledge production, it had its greatest impact through its application to scientific research. The sciences and social sciences are supposed to be universal in their research and data, but standpoint feminism argues that they present the world as it is seen through dominant men's eyes. This knowledge is not universally factual because it emerges from men's views of the world, and doesn't include the experiences or lives of women. Women see the world from a different angle, and they are still excluded from much of science.

In the social sciences, it is only in the last 25 years that questions have been asked from a woman's point of view. In anthropology, for example, men writing on evolution represented our early primate ancestors as chest-beating, aggressive male gorillas; women in the same field argued that humans were more like the gentler, cooperative male and female chimpanzees (Haraway 1989).

To create different knowledge takes more than adding women researchers and subjects. It takes choosing research projects that reflect women's lives and framing research questions in ways that don't assume conventional answers. The result is what Sandra Harding calls strong objectivity—getting beyond taken-for-granted categories and concepts. For example, standard biomedical research on menstruation and menopause treats them as illnesses, with negative physical and emotional symptoms—premenstrual tension, monthly cramps, hot flashes. Feminist researchers found that there was great diversity among women in what they experienced before and during menstruation and menopause and that for many, these body experiences were not negative, but positive. They described premenstrual surges of energy, pride in potential fertility, and postmenopausal wisdom and peace with one's body.

Standpoint feminism argues that our social location shapes our view of the world, but the viewpoints of marginalized "others," such as women, members of the working class, people in disadvantaged racial ethnic groups, and people in developing countries, do not enter the production of most scientific knowledge. The European colonial conquests of the past 300 years not only plundered native resources in North and South America and Africa, but also native agricultural and manufacturing processes, medicines, and maps. These were absorbed into Western science the way Greek, Roman, Chinese, and Islamic discoveries had been earlier, with little acknowledgment of their origin. Local sciences were co-opted for European needs; local scientists—farmers, artisans, healers—were denigrated as ignorant and unenlightened. Standpoint feminism claims that many of these local knowledge producers are women, so it is not just women educated in Western science whose work should be fostered, but also the scientific work of women who create a body of knowledge in their everyday lives as they grow food, make useful objects, and heal the sick.

Sandra Harding, Professor of Education and Women's Studies, has been one of the best known standpoint theorists in science studies. In the following excerpt from her 1998 book, *Is Science Multicultural?*, she answers the contention that scientific facts about "nature" are universal by arguing that what we know about natural phenomenon is shaped by the social locations of researchers and consumers of "facts."

Gendered Standpoints on Nature

Sandra Harding

University of California, Los Angeles

Women and men in the same culture have different "geographical" locations in heterogeneous nature, and different interests, discursive resources, and ways of organizing the production of knowledge.... Here the focus is on gender differences, on the reasons why it is more accurate and useful to understand women and men in any culture as having a different relationship to the world around them.

Many readers will find it strange and objectionable to consider the possibility that there are such things at all as gendered standpoints on nature—women's and men's distinctive relationships to the natural order. After all, don't women do the same science as men in biology, physics, and chemistry labs? Hasn't feminism taken a firm stand against the myth that women can't do "real science," or can't do it as rigorously and creatively as can men? However, the argument here will be that, nevertheless, analyses of how it is that women's lives can generate resources different from those arising from the men's lives upon which modern scientific and technological thought has been based deserve more appreciation than many of us, feminist and prefeminist alike, have given them. The issue is not only one about understanding women's past achievements, or only women's knowledge in premodern societies; it is also about the resources that starting off research from women's lives can provide for increasing human knowledge of nature's regularities and their underlying causal tendencies anywhere and everywhere that gender relations occur. It is also, in part, an issue about women making science policy, whether or not they are practicing scientists....

Most analyses that have focussed on "difference" have tended to focus on either "mere difference" or hierarchical differences, but not on both. On the one hand, focuses on power relations tend toward binarism, an overemphasis on discrete categories of "the powerful" and "the powerless," and the homogenization of differences within those categories. On the other hand, studies of different cultures often tend to lose sight of the global political economy and the unequal relations it creates between cultures, as well as of pervasive power relations such as gender relations that create similarities and alliances between, on the one hand, those who can exercise economic and political power and, on the other hand, those who are the object of others' power exercises. The standpoint of "others" is a good place to start thinking simultaneously about cultural difference and power relations. It can generate insights about how both kinds of difference contribute to enlarging and limiting knowledge of the natural world.

Feminist standpoint theory mapped the different scientific and epistemic resources that hierarchical gender relations create for starting off research or thought from women's lives as the latter have been understood in various feminist discourses. It showed how positions of political disadvantage can also be turned into sites of analytic advantage. This [excerpt] steps back for the moment from the gendered power relations that were the central concern of earlier standpoint theory to examine the distinctive resources that can be accessed by starting thought simply from whatever distinctions have been socially or biologically created between women's and men's lives. That is, women's lives would be valuable places from which to start off thought even if gender were not fundamentally a political relation, like, in this respect, class and race. Of course gender is indeed fundamentally a political relation..., so in everyday life mere gender difference does not exist; power relations are always in play here, subtly or not. Nevertheless, this analytic exercise seems interesting and valuable to pursue. It can be structured parallel to the "different cultures" arguments...in effect treating gender differences as if they were differences between cultures—as if women and men in the same historical and geographically located culture nevertheless lived in different cultures....

In order accurately to describe and explain women's lives and the meanings of womanliness we must look at the relations between women's and men's lives and between womanliness and manliness. In different cultures, gendered social structures and meanings take on distinctive characteristics: what is manly in one culture, such as engaging in public sphere economic relations, is womanly in another culture, such as west Africa where women are the market traders. Gender relations are to some extent or other always hierarchically organized since men tend to control more social resources and manliness is more closely identified with the admirably "human." Moreover, gender relations are always co-constituted by/with other hierarchically organized social relations such as class, ethnicity, race, and so on. An African American man's life is shaped by the gender relations peculiar to his position in racial as well as gender relations, and the class, ethnicity, sexuality, and other social relations that structure his particular society. Similarly, white women's opportunities and responsibilities are shaped by the way their gender location, meaning, and identity is co-constituted by class, racial, imperial, sexual, and other such organizing forces in a culture. Last, gender relations are never static or fixed; they are dynamic, historically changing ways of organizing access to scarce social resources. Thus, every other kind of social change offers opportunities for creating new forms of gender relations. To put the point another way, every kind of social change is always also a site for struggles over gender relations. Once we have in mind this richer and more accurate account of gender relations, it becomes easier to identify the ways in which women and men live in something like "gender cultures," and how gender struggles take place at moments of scientific and technological change....

Heterogeneous nature. First, women and men in any culture interact with partially different natural environments. In many ways they are exposed to different regularities of nature that offer them different possible resources and probable dangers and that can make some theories appear more or less plausible than they do to those who interact only with other environments. To start with, obviously females and males are "biologically" different,[a] though not in all those purported forms of such interest to biological determinists. Of course their reproductive systems differ. Menstruation, pregnancy, birthing, lactation, and menopause, to mention only the most obvious such processes, occur in women's bodies only. However, women differ from men biologically in other ways: in percent body fat (affecting, for example, their toleration for cold water in long-distance swimming), skeletal construction (affecting their abilities in sports, including their distinctive strengths and their distinctive susceptibility to injuries), susceptibility to the effects of drugs, and so on. Such biological differences expose them to different regularities of nature; they interact with some different aspects of nature than do men.

Moreover, socially assigned, gender-segregated activities—from tending children, the aged, and sick, to other unpaid domestic labor, local community maintenance, clerical work, factory work, service work (in social service agencies and health care, in paid domestic work, in the sex and tourist industries, etc.), gathering food, and maintaining subsistence agriculture, herding, and forestry—bring women into yet more distinctive interactions with natural environments. Women's biology and their culturally distinctive activities enable them to have some different interactions with natural environments than those their brothers have. Research that starts out from women's bodies and interactions with nature, too—not just men's—will arrive at more comprehensive and accurate descriptions and explanations of nature's regularities. So we could say that women and men are partly differently located in heterogeneous nature; or, to put the issue another way, heterogeneous nature is partly differently distributed in men's and and women's lives. Of course nothing forces women or men (or us) to interpret such situations in any particular ways. We have not yet arrived in this analysis at the ways that people are conscious of such differences, let alone at the production of knowledge, but only at an observation about distinctive sex- and gender-differentiated locations in nature "in themselves," so to speak.

Gendered interests. Three other kinds of gender-differing resources combine to enable and limit how people's locations in nature are turned into culturally distinctive objects of knowledge claims. First, women's and men's interests in their bodies and environments can differ. People tend to be interested in what they find around them. (Of course how they characterize and, thus, see "what they find around them" is discursively constituted as we shall see in a moment.) Clearly, women and men have at least partially different interests in and thus desires about the natural world to the extent that they are biologically different and that they are assigned activities that bring them into systematically different interactions with their environments. For example, women need and want to know how our bodies work, how drugs affect us, too, and how more effectively to interact with the environments on behalf of our own interests, including the well-being of the children, household members, kin, elderly, and sick, and the community networks that depend on women and for whom women usually are assigned responsibility.

Of course both men and women have children, other kin, sick and aged people around them, and live in communities; but they have at least partially gender-distinctive interests in and desires about these people's situations. These vary from culture to culture; each culture has norms for what are appropriate interests and desires for women and for men. These interests are most segregated where adult activities are maximally segregated. For example, there is geographic segregation in cases where men work in distant cities, in migrant agricultural labor, or in other countries as guest workers, only rarely returning to the areas where their wives and families live. Gender interests can even be highly geographically segregated where professional-managerial men spend long hours on the job downtown or travelling, and little time in domestic work or in the suburban communities where their wives and children live.

There are many other contexts for thinking about women's differing interests in nature. For example, recent reports show that the vast majority of fatalities in war are not military personnel, but civilian populations and, especially, women and children. Moreover, a much greater proportion of women's life work than men's is invested in birthing and raising the next generation, including the sons who will become soldiers. It is implausible to presume that women have the same interests and desires as their brothers to support militarism and the scientific and technological research agendas that service militaries. The point here is not that women's essential "natures" lead them to greater pacifism—that women are inherently more peaceful (they are not)—but rather that they bear more of the costs of warfare. The presumption that such sciences represent "human interests" is even more implausible when one considers how ideals of the warrior and the national hero are ideals of masculinity; women's compensation for the costs of war is far less than men's since they share only vicariously in the masculine glory that accrues from military victories. Successful military careers frequently generate "capital" that men can use to gain civil rights, public office, and other forms of political power. Women have fewer interests in research, basic and applied, that in fact services militarism and nationalism than do men, and more interests in research, basic and applied, that services sustainable domestic and local community activities. Basic research is also an issue here, not just applied research, since the part of heterogeneous nature that interests a research community can vary according to culturally differing interests. For example, the choice of which bodily processes a basic research project focusses on can predictably be useful for responding to the interests of militaries, population control councils, genetic engineering corporations, or women's health advocates. Thus, women are repositories of historically developed knowledge about what is of interest to them. This knowledge is not static or "premodern"....It always must be refined and developed in each generation as both nature and social relations, including gender relations, change over time. The environments that women interact with in their distinctive agricultural work, animal husbandry, trading, office and industrial work, child care, and responsibility for family health, for example, are all radically different now in many parts of the world than they were even two decades ago.

Of course interests and desires are not objectively given by any facts, natural or social. They are arrived at through culturally distinctive discourses—religious, national, ethnic, class, and are always historically specific. Thus, there is something artificial about separating out, as I have done, women's and men's locations in nature and different interests, as if these were in real life separable from the discursive traditions that generate interests and culturally distinctive ways of thinking, fearing, fantasizing, and caring about our locations in nature. Nevertheless, when one identifies interests as creating both resources and limits for the production of knowledge about the natural world, one can draw on the long and rich resources of sociology and political economy's discussions of historically differing interests. We know how to think about how people's different and often conflicting interests and desires result in different questions, problems, concerns. These kinds of analyses can also illuminate women's and men's different and often conflicting interests and desires with respect to environments.

Note

a. To speak of "biological differences" here of course ignores the impossibility biologists point out of distinguishing biological from social contributions to human bodies. Note that that not all males are men, nor are all females women. Sex and gender categories are far from securely attached to each other in many cultures and subcultures as, for example, in the transgender cultures of transvestism, gender- "passing," and "gender-bending" in parts of contemporary U.S. and European culture, or in the generous varieties of gender recognized in various Native American groups.

The Power of Social Location

In standpoint feminism, women's viewpoint is privileged in order to counteract the dominance of men's perspectives. The rationale is that whoever creates knowledge has the power to shape values and political agendas. Since men have dominated in these areas for so long, standpoint feminism insists that women's perspectives, women's ways of seeing the world, and women's experiences now be given precedence. But since women's social locations differ depending on where they live, their education, job, economic status, marital and parental status, religion, racial ethnic group, and sexual orientation, their perspectives will differ. Donna Haraway says that all knowledge is partial, dependent on social location, situated somewhere:

> Situated knowledges are about communities, not isolated individuals. The only way to find a larger vision is to be somewhere in particular. The science question in feminism is about objectivity as positioned rationality. Its images are not the products of escape and transcendence of limits (the view from above) but the joining of partial views and halting voices into a collective subject position that promises a vision of the means of ongoing finite embodiment, of living within limits and contradictions—of views from somewhere. (1988, 600)

Standpoint feminism argues for more than equal representation of all viewpoints. Setting the agendas for scientific and social scientific research is a form of power. *Hegemony* is the value base that legitimates a society's unquestioned assumptions. In Western society, the justifications for many of our ideas about women and men come from science. We believe in scientific "facts" and rarely question their objectivity. That is why standpoint feminism puts so much emphasis on demonstrating that scientific knowledge produced mostly by men and imbued with men's perspectives is not universal and general but partial and particular, and why woman's perspectives are so important.

However, knowledge produced from women's perspectives is not homogeneous. In addition to individual social positions, racial categories, ethnicity, religion, social class, age, and sexual orientation intersect with gender to produce varied life experiences and outlooks. There may be a common core to women's experiences, perhaps because they share similar bodies, but standpoint feminism cannot ignore the input from social statuses that are as important as gender.

Patricia Hill Collins (1997) points out that experiences are not just individual but also common to the members of a group that share a sense of identity. When a group's experiences frame the production of knowledge and set political agendas, that group has power. Most racial and ethnic groups in a heterogeneous society do not have such power; their experiential life-world views do not become part of the mainstream. Standpoint feminism needs to incorporate all of these perspectives into its production of knowledge. In order to include diverse perspectives in science, she suggests using *intersectional analyses*. "This approach means choosing a concrete topic that is already the subject of investigation and trying to find the combined effects of race, class, gender, sexuality, and nation, where before only one or two interpretive categories were used" (1999, 278).

Critique

A woman-centered perspective is a needed corrective to a gender-blind neutralism that erases women's experience. But the exclusive focus on "woman" is troublesome. Are women so much alike that they can be expected to always have similar experiences and a unitary perspective? Does standpoint feminism create a universal Woman who is actually middle-class, Western, heterosexual, and White? Does this universal Woman suppress other women's voices? How can they be heard? For that matter, don't men also differ by racial category, ethnicity, religion, social class, and sexual orientation? Not all of their voices are heard, either.

Standpoint feminism's answer to the diversity-sameness issue is that what binds all women together is their bodies and their connectedness to people through their work for their families and their nurturing. A strong critique of this view focuses on these claims of essential differences between men and women and the promotion of a separate and distinctive woman's perspective rooted in female bodies and nurturing abilities. Many feminists feel that these views are a throwback to biological justifications of women's inferiority.

However, if women's standpoint is not located in the female body but in their caretaking work and in their place in a gendered social order that allows them to be constantly threatened by violence, rape, and sexual harassment, then we can speak of a shared woman's standpoint without reverting to a direct biological cause. Standpoint feminism can legitimately argue that women's bodies are the source of their sexual oppression because of the ways they are used and abused by men, and that their consciousness is shaped by their family role as the primary caregiver. Similarly, it is not male biology that makes men dominant but their social power, which they get because they have a visible mark of identity that sets them off from women—a penis. Men in diverse social circumstances have something in common—the privileges of dominant status. (Its *symbol* is the *phallus*.) Social locations and experiences, such as growing up a girl or a boy in a poor Black community, create particular women's and men's identities and standpoints. These shared particular identities are like concentric circles within the larger circle of womanhood and manhood. Both the common and the diverse ways of thinking are needed for fully representative knowledge.

Summary

Standpoint feminism claims that what people think is universal, objective knowledge is biased because it does not include the life experiences of those who are not members of the dominant group. It challenges the claim that what is represented as "fact" is applicable to everyone. Phenomenologists and perception psychologists have argued that knowledge is produced out of experience. If that is so, then knowledge produced without women's experiences is not applicable to the universe but only to half of it. In order to balance out the dominance of men's experiences in most knowledge production, standpoint feminism elevates women's experience.

Using Marxist, socialist, psychoanalytic, and lesbian feminisms' analyses of how women's lives and work shape their conscious and unconscious thinking, standpoint feminism says that women's distinctive perspectives must be used in producing knowledge, especially in the sciences and social sciences.

We think that science is detached from the particulars of everyday life. That is not even true of astronomy and physics, which have a social impact in space travel and nuclear power, but it is especially false when it comes to research on people. When we want to know what makes people think and act the way they do, we are using the data of everyday life. The lives of women and of men of diverse racial categories, ethnicities, religions, social classes, and sexual orientations must be part of these data.

Similarly, the experiences of those in different positions need to be accounted for to arrive at a complete picture of an organization. This way of doing institutional ethnography allows us to more accurately map out the relations of ruling, the intersections and impact of different degrees of power on the people up and down the social scale. To the extent that an organization is stratified by gender, the relations of ruling will be gendered.

Standpoint feminism challenges the sciences and social sciences to take a more critical view of their basic assumptions, especially about women and men. It criticizes the research on sex/gender differences because women's social and experiential realities are ignored. Modern Western societies today believe in science as an explanation for the way things are; past generations believed life circumstances were God-given. Standpoint feminism claims that when it comes to sex and gender, there is as much faith as fact in men's science.

Standpoint feminism, as the culmination of resistance feminisms, offers an argument for privileging women's perspectives to counteract dominant men's perspectives that shape so much of Western scientific knowledge. Women's ways of knowing create another body of knowledge. Until this body of knowledge is incorporated into the mainstream, the gendered social order is enriched but not altered.

SUGGESTED READINGS IN STANDPOINT FEMINISM

Research and Knowledge

Alcoff, Linda, and Elizabeth Potter, eds. 1993. *Feminist Epistemologies.* New York: Routledge.

Belenky, Mary Field, Jill Mattuck Tarule, and Nancy Rule Goldberger, eds. 1986. *Women's Ways of Knowing: The Development of Self, Voice, and Mind.* New York: Basic Books.

Collins, Patricia Hill. 1997. "Comment on Hekman's 'Truth and Method: Feminist Standpoint Theory Revisited': Where's the Power?" *Signs* 22: 375–381.

DeVault, Marjorie. 1999. *Liberating Method: Feminism and Social Research.* Philadelphia: Temple University Press.

Embree, Lester, and Linda Fisher, eds. 1997. *Feminism and Phenomenology.* Boston: Kluwer.

Goldberger, Nancy Rule, and Jill Mattuck Tarule, eds. 1996. *Knowledge, Difference, and Power: Essays Inspired by* Women's Ways of Knowing. New York: Basic Books.

Hartsock, Nancy C. M. 1998. *The Feminist Standpoint Revisited and Other Essays.* Boulder, CO: Westview Press.

Hekman, Susan. 1997. "Truth and Method: Feminist Standpoint Theory Revisited." *Signs* 22: 341–365. Comments and Reply, 366–402.

Kelly, Joan. 1984. *Women, History, and Theory.* Chicago: University of Chicago Press.

Levesque-Lopman, Louise. 1988. *Claiming Reality: Phenomenology and Women's Experience.* Totowa, NJ: Rowman and Littlefield.

Reinharz, Shulamit. 1992. *Feminist Methods in Social Research.* New York: Oxford University Press.

Smith, Dorothy E. 1987. *The Everyday World as Problematic.* Toronto: University of Toronto Press.

———. 1990. *The Conceptual Practices of Power: A Feminist Sociology of Knowledge.* Toronto: University of Toronto Press.

———. 1990. *Texts, Facts, and Femininity: Exploring the Relations of Ruling.* New York: Routledge.

———. 1999. *Writing the Social: Critique, Theory, Investigations.* Toronto: University of Toronto Press.

———. 2005. *Institutional Ethnography: A Sociology for People.* Lanham, MD: Rowman & Littlefield/AltaMira.

Science and Technology

Bleier, Ruth. 1984. *Science and Gender.* New York: Oxford.

Collins, Patricia Hill. 1999. "Moving Beyond Gender: Intersectionality and Scientific Knowledge." In Myra Marx Ferree, Judith Lorber, and Beth B. Hess, eds., *Revisioning Gender.* Thousand Oaks, CA: Sage.

Fox, Mary Frank, Deborah G. Johnson, and Sue V. Rosser, eds. 2005. *Women, Gender, and Technology*. Urbana: University of Illinois Press.

Haraway, Donna. 1988. "Situated Knowledges: The Science Question in Feminism and the Privilege of Partial Perspective." *Feminist Studies* 14: 575–599.

———. 1989. *Primate Visions*. New York: Routledge.

———. 1991. *Simians, Cyborgs, and Women: The Reinvention of Nature*. New York: Routledge.

———. 1997. *Modest_Witness@Second_Millennium FemaleMan©_Meets_OncoMouse™: Feminism and Technoscience*. New York: Routledge.

Harding, Sandra. 1986. *The Science Question in Feminism*. Ithaca, NY: Cornell University Press.

———. 1991. *Whose Science? Whose Knowledge? Thinking from Women's Lives*. Ithaca, NY: Cornell University Press.

———. 1998. *Is Science Multicultural? Postcolonialisms, Feminisms, and Epistemologies*. Bloomington: Indiana University Press.

Hubbard, Ruth, Mary Sue Henifin, and Barbara Fried, eds. 1979. *Women Look at Biology Looking at Women: A Collection of Feminist Critiques*. Cambridge, MA: Schenkman.

Jacobus, Mary, Evelyn Fox Keller, and Sally Shuttleworth, eds. 1990. *Body/Politics: Women and the Discourses of Science*. New York: Routledge.

Keller, Evelyn Fox. 1983. *A Feeling for the Organism: The Life and Work of Barbara McClintock*. New York: W. H. Freeman.

———. 1985. *Reflections on Gender and Science*. New Haven, CT: Yale University Press.

Laslett, Barbara, Sally Gregory Kohlstedt, Helen Longino, and Evelynn Hammonds, eds. 1996. *Gender and Scientific Authority*. Chicago: University of Chicago Press.

Maddox, Brenda. 2002. *Rosalind Franklin: The Dark Lady of DNA*. New York: HarperCollins.

Parlee, Mary Brown. 1990. "The Social Construction of Premenstrual Syndrome: A Case Study of Scientific Discourse as Cultural Contestation." In M. G. Winkler and L. B. Cole, ed., The *Good Body: Asceticism in Contemporary Culture*. New Haven, CT: Yale University Press.

Roughgarden, Joan. 2004. *Evolution's Rainbow: Diversity, Gender and Sexuality in Nature and People*. Berkeley: University of California Press.

Sayre, Anne. 1975. *Rosalind Franklin and DNA*. New York: W. W. Norton.

Schiebinger, Londa L. 1989. *The Mind Has No Sex?: Women in the Origins of Modern Science*. Cambridge, MA: Harvard University Press.

———. 1999. *Has Feminism Changed Science?* Cambridge, MA: Harvard University Press.

Wyer, Mary, et al., eds. 2008. *Women, Science, and Technology: A Reader in Feminist Science Studies*. New York: Routledge.

PART III

GENDER REBELLION FEMINISMS

Since the late 1980s, a group of feminisms has focused on gender, not women. These feminisms challenge the foundations of many areas of knowledge by asking researchers and theorists to seriously address the question of gender. They critique the limits of gender resistance feminisms, especially the problems of the unity of women, the privileged perspective of women's standpoint, and the sources of identity in identity politics. They rebel against accepting the gendered social order as an unchanging given, to be reformed by treating women and men more equally or resisted by valorizing women and creating women's knowledge, culture, and communities. They question the unity of the binary gender categories, arguing that they are so intersected by other major social statuses that women and men cannot be considered homogeneous identities or statuses. Ultimately, gender rebellion feminisms question the stability and necessity of the whole gendered social order.

Gender rebellion feminisms have continued the development of feminist multiracial and multiethnic approaches. These perspectives pull apart gender as binary and oppositional. Gender is rather construed as a complex hierarchy of privileged and subordinated men and women, intersected by racial, ethnic, and social class statuses. Feminist studies of men take as their area of theory and politics the ways that men are gendered and how they might be influenced to be less violent and aggressive. Gender as performance, process, and practice are the mainstays of social construction feminist theory, which recognizes both the constraints and the possibilities for change in the gendered social order. As part of the postmodern questioning of assumptions underlying what we do, think, and believe, postmodern feminism deconstructs how gender is produced and maintained, and emphasizes its malleability and fluidity. Third-wave feminism picks and chooses among the performance aspects of gender, sometimes exaggerating and sometimes ironically parodying them, but always emphasizing women's and girls' agency. The politics of all the gender rebellion feminisms grow out of claims that the gendered social order is above all a human enterprise and so can be shaped, reshaped, and even dismantled by human agency.

Multiracial/multiethnic feminism, whose roots are in the history and politics of disadvantaged groups, argues that the major social statuses of a society produce a complex hierarchical stratification system. By teasing out multiple strands of oppression and exploitation, multiracial/multiethnic feminism shows that gender, racial categories, and ethnicity are intertwined social structures. How people are gendered differs according to whether they are members of dominant or subordinate racial ethnic groups. Social class is also an especially crucial dimension, given the wide differences between the poor and the rich throughout the world.

Multiracial/multiethnic feminism creates a politics that interweaves gender with the continuum of dominance and subordination derived from other social statuses. It argues that feminist political activism can no longer be based only on gender but must consider racial identifications, ethnicity, and social class as well. The battle for justice and recognition includes men, but the perspectives, politics, and cultural contributions of women of diverse racial ethnic groups take precedence.

Because other significant social statuses intersect gender as a social status, multiracial/multiethnic feminism challenges a strictly binary gendered social order.

Feminist studies of men, drawing on Marxist analyses of social class and gay and lesbian critiques of heteronormativity, have described the interlocking structures of power that make one group of men dominant and rank everyone else in a complex hierarchy of privilege and disadvantage. They document the gender practices that both exclude women from competition with men and determine which men are able to attain positions of great power.

The way men are drawn to violence in war, terrorism, and even sports is a major part of the theory and politics of feminist studies of men. This violence is both delegitimated (rape, battering) and legitimated (war, sports). The mixed messages to boys and men are confronted by feminist men in political action and education programs.

Like multiracial/multiethnic feminism, feminist studies of men use racial categories, ethnicity, religion, social class, and sexual orientation in analyses of men's social statuses, but focus on gender. Men vary in power and privilege, but within each group men have *patriarchal privilege* compared to the women of that group. Thus, although men are hardly a homogeneous grouping, feminist studies of men document the prevalence of *male hegemony* (dominance in values, knowledge, culture, and politics) and *patriarchal privilege* (men's advantages over the women of their group).

In a paradoxical turn, by making visible male hegemony and patriarchal privilege within diversity, feminist studies of men provide ammunition for a politics that could undermine the structure of gender. The rationale for the maintenance of the gender order is to perpetuate the dominance and privileges of men in power, and by extension, the power and privileges of all men. Thus, challenging men's dominance and privileges challenges the whole gender order.

Social construction feminism comes out of symbolic interaction in social psychology, which shows how people construct multiple meanings and identities in their daily encounters. Social construction feminism analyzes the processes and practices that create what we perceive to be the differences between women and men, *doing gender.* These processes also construct racial ethnic and social class stereotypes and beliefs about homosexuality as contrasted with heterosexuality, *doing difference.* Doing gender imposes categorical divisions on physiological and behavioral continuums and uses visible markers, such as skin color or genitals, as signs of supposedly inborn and essential behavioral characteristics. Because these physiological markers are usually hidden (people do not walk on the streets naked) and varied (some African Americans have pale skin), other identifiers of social status are needed: clothing, jewelry, and hair styles are the most common. In face-to-face encounters, visible cues of gender, class, ethnicity, sexual orientation, and other major social statuses pattern subsequent behavior—they act like team colors. Evident differences within categories of people and similarities between groups are repressed or ignored in doing gender.

Social construction feminism argues that multiple categories would better reflect the variety in people, but the gendered social order is built on a binary division of labor that uses differentiated categories of women and men for gender-typed roles in the family and the paid workforce. The gendered family and the gendered economy are mainstays of gender as a social institution. As a social institution, gender orders societies and assigns people to legal gender statuses, locking in a binary system that has no room for intersexual, transgendered, or gender-ambiguous people or for those who question sex, sexual, and gender binaries.

Crucial to social construction feminism's politics is the concept of gender as social structure that constrains people's choices and opportunities and that is built on men's exploitation of women's domestic labor and emotional and sexual services. Social construction feminism pushes for deep-seated change through *degendering*, rebellion against the institutionalized gendered social order by refusing to continue the practices and processes that construct and maintain it.

Postmodern feminism claims that gender and sexuality are performances and that individuals modify their displays of masculinity and femininity to suit their own purposes. Males can masquerade as women, and females can pass for men. Postmodern feminism argues that, like clothing, sexuality and gender can be put on, taken off, and transformed. Transgendered people display the fluidities of gender and sexuality, challenging normals to prove that they aren't also creating their gendered identities through their appearance and behavior. Queer theory, the postmodern focus of gay, lesbian, and transgender studies, turns the binaries of sex, sexuality, and gender inside out with "third terms"—intersexuality, bisexuality, transgendering.

Postmodern feminism and queer theories of gender go the furthest, politically, in undermining the gendered social order. Their rebellion against the stability and immutability of gendered categories—women, men, female,

male, homosexual, heterosexual—provide the lived experiences of a potentially degendered social order.

Third-wave feminism has most recently appeared on the scene. It has young adherents who do not see themselves as oppressed victims, but who rather reflect radical feminism in their body orientation and postmodern feminism in their gender displays. They can be outrageous and sexual in their behavior and cultural performances, but they are as serious in their political activism as their feminist foremothers, valorizing strong women and girl power.

Third-wave feminism doesn't destabilize the gendered social order the way postmodernism and queer theory does, so it seems like a throwback to radical feminism's resistance to the denigration of women and girls. However, third-wave feminism uses femaleness and femininity almost as a parody of gender typing, the way Madonna did early in her career. At the same time that young women are flaunting their sexual powers, they engage in political activism that includes their brothers and boyfriends and shows the strengths of women and girls. Third-wave feminism rebels against the binary gendered social order in action and politics, if not in theory.

Gender rebellion feminisms' theories destabilize what many people think is normal and natural and moral about gender, but they have only begun to develop new practices for work, family life, and intimate relationships. They need to translate multiple categories into everyday living, which could be revolutionary enough. But to fulfill their political potential, these feminisms need to spell out what precisely has to be done in all the gendered institutions and organizations of a society—family, workplace, government, the arts, science, and religion—to break the strangle-hold of oppressive gender practices and ensure equal participation and opportunity for every person in every group.

9

Multiracial/Multiethnic Feminism

SOURCES OF GENDER INEQUALITY

- The intersection of racial ethnic, social class, and gender discrimination
- Continued patterns of economic and educational privilege and disadvantage built into the social structure
- Cultural devaluation of women of subordinated racial ethnic groups

POLITICS

- Redistribution of privilege—equal access to education, good jobs, and political power
- Recognition—knowledge production that reflects the subordinate group's perspectives
- Revaluation of the cultural productions by women of varied racial ethnic heritages

CRITIQUE

- Traditional patriarchal racial ethnic cultures may create additional oppression for women of the group
- Women's independence and assertiveness may threaten their men's ego and sense of masculinity
- Competing racial ethnic and gender identities can undermine feminist consciousness and political activism

CONTRIBUTIONS

- The concept of *intersectionality*—the combined effects of racial ethnic, social class, and gender social statuses in producing a *matrix of domination*
- A complex politics of identity that includes but does not necessarily foreground gender

- Making multiple racial ethnic viewpoints visible in the production of knowledge and culture through the critical perspective of the *outsider within*
- Womanist culture, theology, and ethics that counters multiracial/multiethnic men's dominance with women's art, rituals, liturgy, and nurturant ethical practices

As part of a long line of critical theory and activist politics, multiracial/multiethnic feminism early in the second wave challenged White feminists to address the differences among women. It builds on standpoint feminism's theory and politics of social location, but does not always privilege women. Focusing on the *intersectionality* of gender, racial categories, ethnicity, and social class, multiracial/multiethnic feminism argues that you cannot look at one of these social statuses alone, nor can you add them one after another. Their interaction is synergistic—together they construct social locations that are oppressive because they are the result of multiple systems of domination. The entire matrix of domination must therefore be challenged.

Matrix of Domination

Gender, racial categories, ethnicity, and social class comprise a complex hierarchical stratification system in the United States, in which upper-class White men and women have privileges denied to lower-class women and men of disadvantaged racial ethnic groups, such as better schools, health care, job opportunities, and political access. In teasing out the multiple strands of oppression and exploitation, multiracial/multiethnic feminism has shown that gender is intertwined with and cannot be separated from other social statuses that confer advantage and disadvantage. People are caught in what Patricia Hill Collins, in her influential book *Black Feminist Thought,* calls a *matrix of domination.* The experiences of women and men in different social locations are the ground for their views of the world and their activist politics.

The social location of a man and woman of the same racial ethnic or social class status differs. Men of the subordinate group may be as oppressed as the women but often in different ways. For example, African American men in the United States are rewarded for aggressive behavior in sports, but are punished for it outside the sports arena; African American women are hired to take care of White children but are stigmatized for having many children of their own. If disadvantaged women achieve equality with the disadvantaged men of their group, they have not achieved very much. If they outperform them, as has happened with African American and Hispanic American women college and professional-school graduates in the United States, then the men in the same groups are seen as endangered.

Multiracial/multiethnic feminism thus has to juggle the sometimes competing battles for gender equality and for racial ethnic equality. It has its origins in the 1960s U.S. civil rights and Black power movements and the

Chicano, American Indian, and Asian American liberation movements. Out of these multiple groups came coalitions of women who felt that their issues were neglected, but who did not want to abandon entirely the fight against racial ethnic oppression. Today, multiracial/multiethnic feminism has a global theoretical, empirical, and political perspective.

Centering the Marginal

For both women and men, the dominant or hegemonic group sets the standards for what behavior is valued, what faces and bodies are considered beautiful, what cultural productions represent "everybody." The most advantaged group's values and ideas about the way people should behave usually dominate policies and social agendas. The subordinate group is always less influential unless it can turn the dominant values upside down, as standpoint feminism does when it says women's values and experiences have to be given as much credit as men's. The ascendance of a Black First Family into the White House after the 2008 election of President Barack Obama has similarly upended the racial social landscape of the United States. The same would have happened for gender if a woman president had been elected.

Multiracial/multiethnic feminism takes the standpoint perspective a step further. It is not enough to dissect a social institution or area of social thought from a woman's point of view; the viewpoint has to include the experiences of women of different racial ethnic groups and must also take into consideration social class and local economic conditions. As *outsiders within*, those from disadvantaged groups who have entry into higher education, the arts, and politics can critique and modify conventional knowledge. Multiracial/multiethnic feminism's politics focuses on this issue. For example, if the White, middle-class, two-parent family is taken as the norm, then the African American extended family of grandmothers, mothers, aunts, and "othermothers"—all responsible for the children of the household and pooling resources—is not seen as a strong kin group but as a deviant or problem family that needs changing.

Health care is another area where the dominant group's perspective translates into allocation of resources. If psychological stress is defined as resulting from pressure in a high-powered job, then the pressures of living in a ghetto are ignored. Eating disorders are a case in point. Among young White women, anorexia and bulimia are usually attributed to a desire for a thin, sexually attractive body because there is a culture of thinness in Western societies. For some African American and Hispanic women, however, binge eating and purging are ways of coping with the traumas of their lives—sexual abuse, poverty, racism, and injustice. In all these cases, the underlying cause of the eating disorder is social pressure, but the pressures differ enormously.

In the following excerpt from the second edition of *Black Feminist Thought*, Patricia Hill Collins, feminist theorist and 2009 president of the American Sociological Association, describes the processes of intersectionality in creating a matrix of domination, and lays out the ways that Black feminism can create transforming knowledge and power.

Black Feminism, Knowledge, and Power

Patricia Hill Collins

University of Maryland

Placing U.S. Black women's experiences in the center of analysis without privileging those experiences shows how intersectional paradigms can be especially important for rethinking the particular matrix of domination that characterizes U.S. society. Claims that systems of race, social class, gender, and sexuality form mutually constructing features of social organization foster a basic rethinking of U.S. social institutions. For example, using intersecting paradigms to investigate U.S. Black women's experiences challenges deeply held beliefs that work and family constitute separate spheres of social organization. Since U.S. Black women's experiences have never fit the logic of work in the public sphere juxtaposed to family obligations in the private sphere, these categories lose meaning. As the persistent racial discrimination in schooling, housing, jobs, and public services indicates, Black women's experiences certainly challenge U.S. class ideologies claiming that individual merit is all that matters in determining social rewards. The sexual politics of Black womanhood reveals the fallacy of assuming that gender affects all women in the same way—race and class matter greatly. U.S. Black women's activism, especially its dual commitment to struggles for group survival and to institutional transformation, suggests that understandings of the political should be rethought. Thus, by using intersectional paradigms to explain both the U.S. matrix of domination and Black women's individual and collective agency within it, Black feminist thought helps reconceptualize social relations of domination and resistance....

To maintain their power, dominant groups create and maintain a popular system of "commonsense" ideas that support their right to rule. In the United States, hegemonic ideologies concerning race, class, gender, sexuality, and nation are often so pervasive that it is difficult to conceptualize alternatives to them, let alone ways of resisting the social practices that they justify. For example, despite scant empirical research, beliefs about Black women's sexuality remain deeply held and widespread. Moreover, the sexual politics of Black womanhood reveals how important the controlling images applied to Black women's sexuality have been to the effective operation of domination overall.

School curricula, religious teachings, community cultures, and family histories have long been important social locations for manufacturing ideologies needed to maintain oppression. However, an increasingly important dimension of why hegemonic ideologies concerning race, class, gender, sexuality, and nation remain so deeply entrenched lies, in part, in the growing sophistication of mass media in regulating intersecting oppressions. It is one thing to encounter school curricula that routinely exclude Black women as bona fide subjects of study; religious teachings that preach equality yet are often used to justify Black women's submission to all men; Black community ideologies that counsel Black women to be more "feminine" so that Black men can reclaim their masculinity; and family histories that cover up patterns of physical and emotional abuse that blame Black women for their own victimization. It is quite another to see images of U.S. Black women as "hoochies" broadcast globally in seemingly infinite variation.

In the United States, one would think that the combination of a better-educated public and scholarship designed to shatter old myths would effectively challenge hegemonic ideologies. As the resurgence of White supremacist organizations with staunch beliefs about Black intellectual and moral inferiority suggest, this has not been the case. Instead, old ideas become recycled in new forms. Yesterday's welfare mother splits into social-class-specific images of the welfare queen and the Black lady. Yesterday's jezebel becomes today's "hoochie."

Racist and sexist ideologies, if they are disbelieved, lose their impact. Thus, an important feature of the hegemonic domain of power lies in the need to continually refashion images in order to solicit support for the U.S. matrix of domination. Not just elite group support, but the endorsement of subordinated groups is needed for hegemonic ideologies to function smoothly. Realizing that Black feminist demands for social justice threaten existing power hierarchies, organizations must find ways of appearing to include African-American women—reversing historical patterns of social exclusion associated with institutional discrimination—while disempowering us. Ideas become critical within this effort to absorb and weaken Black women's resistance. Regardless of their placement in social hierarchies, other groups also encounter these pressures. For example, White women are told that they become "race traitors" if they date Black men, a stigma that in effect asks them to calculate whether the gain of an interracial relationship is worth the loss of White privilege. Similarly, in the current reorganization of U.S. racial ideologies where Vietnamese, Cambodians, and other recent Asian immigrant groups jockey to find a racial identity between the fixed points of Blackness and Whiteness, Asians are encouraged to derogate Blacks. Taking one's place at the top of the "minority" ladder certainly provides better treatment than that dished out to the Blacks and Native Americans who are relegated to the bottom. Yet until the category of "Whiteness" is expanded to reclassify Asians as "White," becoming a "model minority" remains a hollow victory.

The significance of the hegemonic domain of power lies in its ability to shape consciousness via the manipulation of ideas, images, symbols, and ideologies. As Black women's struggles for self-definition suggest, in contexts such as these where ideas matter, reclaiming the "power of a free mind" constitutes an important area of resistance. Reversing this process whereby intersecting oppressions harness various dimensions of individual subjectivity for their own ends becomes a central purpose of resistance. Thus, the hegemonic domain becomes a critical site for not just fending off hegemonic ideas from dominant culture, but in crafting counter-hegemonic knowledge that fosters changed consciousness. Regardless of the actual social locations where this process occurs—families, community settings, schools, religious institutions, or mass media institutions—the power of reclaiming these spaces for "thinking and doing not what is expected of us" constitutes an important dimension of Black women's empowerment.

By emphasizing the power of self-definition and the necessity of a free mind, Black feminist thought speaks to the importance that African-American women thinkers place on consciousness as a sphere of freedom. Rather than viewing consciousness as a fixed entity, a more useful approach sees it as continually evolving and negotiated. A dynamic consciousness is vital to both individual and group agency. Based on their personal histories, individuals experience and resist domination differently. Each individual has a unique and continually evolving personal biography made up of concrete experiences, values, motivations, and emotions. No two individuals occupy the same social space; thus no two biographies are identical. Human ties can be freeing and empowering, as is the case with many Black women's heterosexual love relationships or in the power of motherhood in African-American families and communities. Human ties can also be confining and oppressive, as in cases of domestic violence or struggles to sustain mother-child families in inner-city neighborhoods.The same situation can look quite different depending on the consciousness one brings to interpret it.

The cultural context formed by those experiences and ideas that are shared with other members of a group or community give meaning to individual biographies. Each individual biography is rooted in several overlapping cultural contexts—for example, groups defined by race, social class, age, gender, religion, and sexual orientation. The most cohesive cultural contexts are those with identifiable histories, geographic locations, and social institutions. Some can be so tightly interwoven that they appear to be one cultural context, the situation of traditional societies with customs that are carried on across generations, or that of protracted racial segregation in the United States where

Blacks saw a unity of interests that necessarily suppressed internal differences within the category "Black." Moreover, cultural contexts contribute, among other things, the concepts used in thinking and acting.

Subjugated knowledges, such as U.S. Black women's thought, develop in cultural contexts controlled by oppressed groups. Dominant groups aim to replace subjugated knowledge with their own specialized thought because they realize that gaining control over this dimension of subordinate groups' lives simplifies control. While efforts to influence this dimension of an oppressed group's experiences can be partially successful, this level is more difficult to control than dominant groups would have us believe. For example, adhering to externally derived standards of beauty leads many African-American women to dislike their skin color or hair texture. Similarly, internalizing prevailing gender ideology leads some Black men to abuse Black women. These are cases of the successful infusion of dominant ideologies into the everyday cultural context of African-Americans. But the long-standing existence of Black women's resistance traditions as expressed through Black women's relationships with one another, the Black women's blues tradition, and the voices of contemporary African-American women writers all attest to the difficulty of eliminating the cultural context as a fundamental site of resistance.

In their efforts to rearticulate the standpoint of African-American women as a group, Black feminist thinkers potentially offer individual African-American women the conceptual tools to resist oppression. Empowerment in this context is twofold. Gaining the critical consciousness to unpack hegemonic ideologies is empowering. Coming to recognize that one need not believe everything one is told and taught is freeing for many Black women. But while criticizing hegemonic ideologies remains necessary, such critiques are basically reactive (Collins 1998, 187–96). Thus, the second dimension of empowerment within the hegemonic domain of power consists of constructing new knowledge. In this regard, the core themes, interpretive frameworks, and epistemological approaches of Black feminist thought can be highly empowering because they provide alternatives to the way things are supposed to be.

Reference

Collins, Patricia Hill. 1998. *Fighting Words: Black Women and the Search for Justice.* Minneapolis: University of Minnesota Press.

Identity Politics

Multiracial/multiethnic feminist politics sometimes unifies diverse women, sometimes is specific to different women, and sometimes links women of different groups to the men of that group. In the United States, African

American women, Latinas, and Asian American women all experience racial prejudice in social encounters, but they have markedly different experiences in schools and in the job market, and so their strategies for action have to be different. In some instances, the discrimination disadvantaged women experience is specific to them as women, and at other times they share class, racial, and ethnic oppression with their men. Since class, racial, ethnic, and gender identity are intertwined, political unity with the men of the same group can severely undermine a consciousness of their oppression as women.

Where, then, do a woman's loyalty, identification, and politics lie? It may not be with the men of their own racial or ethnic group, who may be oppressive to their own women because of a traditional patriarchal culture or because they themselves are oppressed by men at the top of the pyramid. Men's and women's standpoints within the same group may differ considerably, even though they may share a sense of injustice from their mutual racial or ethnic status. Within the African American community, feminists have developed *womanist culture, theology, and ethics* as a counter to male domination.

Womanist Culture, Theology, and Ethics

Alice Walker's book, *In Search of Our Mother's Gardens*, advocates a *womanist* perspective that is celebratory of women's culture. She defines womanist as:

> Usually referring to outrageous, audacious, courageous or *willful* behavior. Wanting to know more and in greater depth than is considered "good" for one....A woman who loves other women, sexually and/or nonsexually. Appreciates and prefers women's culture, women's emotional flexibility (values tears as natural counterbalance of laughter), and women's strength. Sometimes loves individual men, sexually and/or nonsexually. Committed to survival and wholeness of entire people, male *and* female. Not a separatist, except periodically, for health. Traditionally universalist....Traditionally capable....Loves music. Loves dance. Loves the moon. *Loves* the Spirit. Loves love and food and roundness. Loves struggle. *Loves* the Folk. Loves herself. *Regardless*....Womanist is to feminist as purple is to lavender. (1983, xi–xii)

Womanists find their symbolic language in the beauty of ritual and everyday objects—quilts, folk songs, wedding dances, food and the dishes to eat it from. In Africa and America, women's music accompanies rituals of birth, puberty, marriage, death, and also everyday activities, like preparing food. These are all part of women's culture that womanists celebrate.

Womanist theology is a movement that started in the 1980s and has burgeoned and flourished in African American churches. It incorporates Walker's woman-centeredness and sexual inclusiveness, is enriched by African American women's history and heroines, celebrates mothering, and reaches out to men in building and sustaining a just community. It is, in

Delores Williams' words, a "theology of the spirit informed by black women's political action" (1987). In its multiple strands, it is a

> multidialogical activity, [which] may, like a jazz symphony, communicate some of its most important messages in what the harmony-driven conventional ear hears as discord, as disruption of the harmony in both the black American and white American social, political, and religious status quo. (Williams, 1987)

Womanist humanism is an expansion of African American Christian womanist theology to embrace other religious traditions.

The womanist perspective reflects back on radical feminism's valorization of women and standpoint feminism's politics of location. It goes forward in its inclusion of multiracial/multiethnic cultures and history in feminism. It is a rebellion against multiracial/multiethnic men's domination in culture, theology, and ethics. The voices of women (and men) are richer, and liberation politics are stronger.

International Multiracial/Multiethnic Feminism

Multiracial/multiethnic feminist ideas of intersectionality and outsiders within have been used by global and transnational women's movements. The concept of outsiders within has a particular cogency in international feminism because feminists in developing countries have cautioned feminists from the United States and other Western countries not to impose their viewpoint on the world. Women's movements in different countries of necessity have to work within their own cultures and make their own international coalitions. Feminists in these societies have often found that working within the gender system can ultimately be more transformative than confrontational politics.

The 2004 winner of the Nobel Peace Prize, Wangari Muta Maathai, is a Kenyan biologist and activist who was head of the National Council of Women of Kenya from 1981 to 1987. In a confrontation with the police, she was knocked unconscious during a women's hunger strike in a city park. Dr. Maathai then engaged in another form of feminism—less confrontational and, in African politics, more successful. She started the Green Belt Movement in 1977. This movement gets tree nurseries throughout Africa to give seedlings to women to plant and pays them a small but useful amount of money if a tree takes root. Tens of millions of trees have been planted in Africa through the Green Belt Movement. By using women who cut brush for cooking fires to replace depleted forests, Dr. Maathai was able to help women and the environment—and also deflect criticism for feminist activism from patriarchal and dictatorial governments. Dr. Maathai was awarded the Nobel Peace Prize for the Green Belt Movement and other environmental activism.

The following excerpt from an article by Obioma Nnaemeka, an African feminist teaching French, Women's Studies, and African/African-Diaspora

Studies in the United States, lays out the theory and practice of doing feminism Africa's way.

Nego-Feminism

Obioma Nnaemeka

Indiana University, Indianapolis

But what is nego-feminism? First, nego-feminism is the feminism of negotiation; second, nego-feminism stands for "no ego" feminism. In the foundation of shared values in many African cultures are the principles of negotiation, give and take, compromise, and balance. Here, negotiation has the double meaning of "give and take/exchange" and "cope with successfully/go around." African feminism (or feminism as I have seen it practiced in Africa) challenges through negotiations and compromise. It knows when, where, and how to detonate patriarchal land mines; it also knows when, where, and how to go around patriarchal land mines. In other words, it knows when, where, and how to negotiate with or negotiate around patriarchy in different contexts. For African women, feminism is an act that evokes the dynamism and shifts of a process as opposed to the stability and reification of a construct, a framework. My use of space—the third space—provides the terrain for the unfolding of the dynamic process. Furthermore, nego-feminism is structured by cultural imperatives and modulated by ever-shifting local and global exigencies. The theology of nearness grounded in the indigenous installs feminism in Africa as a performance and an altruistic act.[a] African women do feminism; feminism is what they do for themselves and for others.[b] The rest of this section will examine how African women have negotiated disciplinary and pedagogical spaces and also address issues in gender, language, and practice.

The women's studies classroom in the West (in the United States, specifically) functions in a feminized (all/almost-all-female) environment as opposed to the gendered (a healthy mix of women and men) context operative in women's studies classrooms and conferences in Africa.[c] A homogeneous (in terms of sex, at least) classroom that is anesthetized by the comfort of the familiar/"home" needs the "foreignness" that challenges and promotes self-examination; it needs the different, the out of the ordinary, that defamiliarizes as it promotes the multiple perspectives and challenges rooted in heterogeneity....

The negotiations that are made at the level of gender and language are rooted in the indigenous as well: "African patterns of feminism can be seen as having developed within a context that views human life from a total, rather than a dichotomous and exclusive, perspective. For women, the male is not 'the other' but part of the human same. Each gender constitutes the critical half that makes the human whole. Neither sex is totally complete in itself. Each has and needs a complement, despite the possession of unique features of its own" (Steady 1987, 8). African women's willingness and readiness to negotiate with and around men even in difficult circumstances is quite pervasive. As the Cameroonian writer, Calixthe Beyala, puts it at the beginning of her book, *Lettre d'une Africaine à ses soeurs occidentales* (1995), "Soyons clairs: tous les hommes ne sont pas des salauds" (Let's face it, all men are not bastards; 1995, 7). I take that to mean that some men are bastards! But let us stick with Beyala's more benevolent phrasing of the issue. Another example is also by a Francophone African woman writer, Mariama Bâ of Senegal, who dedicated her fine novel, *Une si longue lettre* (1980), to many constituencies including "aux hommes de bonne volonté" (to men of goodwill). This, of course, excludes the bastards among them! By not casting a pall over men as a monolith, African women are more inclined to reach out and work with men in achieving set goals. Sexual politics were huge in Western feminism about two decades ago, but it would be inaccurate to suggest that the politics no longer exist; they are not passé. In my view, Western feminism has turned down the volume on sexual politics, but the residues are still a driving force. The resistance in institutions across the United States (including mine) against changing women's studies programs to gender studies programs is rooted principally in the argument that women's issues will be relegated to the back burner in a gender studies program.[d] I do not see a similar argument flourishing in Africa.[e] The language of feminist engagement in Africa (collaborate, negotiate, compromise) runs counter to the language of Western feminist scholarship and engagement (challenge, disrupt, deconstruct, blow apart, etc.) as exemplified in Amy Allen's excellent book on feminist theory, in which the author states that feminists are interested in "criticizing, challenging, subverting, and ultimately overturning the multiple axes of stratification affecting women" (1999, 2). African feminism challenges through negotiation, accommodation, and compromise....

Border Crossing and the Chameleon Walk

> They have disfigured the legacy of the sixties.... What I mean by the sixties legacies in traditional political terms are political activism and engagement on behalf of equality, democracy, tolerance. (Breines 1996, 114—no.z)

Nego-feminism in Africa is living those legacies in theory, practice, and policy matters. African women's engagement still nurtures the compromise and hopefulness needed to build a harmonious society.

As far as theory goes, Barbara Christian (1995) rightly noted that people of color theorize differently. But can feminist theory create the space for the unfolding of "different" theorizing not as an isolated engagement outside of feminist theory but as a force that can have a defamiliarizing power on feminist theory? In other words, seeing feminist theorizing through the eyes of the "other," from the "other" place, through the "other" worldview has the capacity to defamiliarize feminist theory as we know it and assist it not only in interrogating, understanding, and explaining the unfamiliar but also in defamiliarizing and refamiliarizing the familiar in more productive and enriching ways. Thus, the focus will be not on what feminist theory can do in terms of explicating other lives and other places but on how feminist theory is and could be constructed. In this instance, Westerners are led across borders so that they can cross back enriched and defamiliarized and ready to see the familiar anew. How do we deal with the theorizing emanating from other epistemological centers in the so-called third world? How do we come to terms with the multiplicity of centers bound by coherence and decipherment and not disrupted perpetually by endless differences?

In view of the issues about intervention, border crossing, turfism, intersectionality, compromise, and accommodation raised in this article, I will conclude with a piece of advice from my great-uncle. On the eve of my departure for graduate studies in *obodo oyibo* (land of the white people), my great-uncle called me into his *obi* (private quarters) and sounded this note of caution. "My daughter," he said, "when you go to *obodo oyibo*, walk like the chameleon."[a] According to my great-uncle, the chameleon is an interesting animal to watch. As it walks, it keeps its head straight but looks in different directions. It does not deviate from its goal and grows wiser through the knowledge gleaned from the different perspectives it absorbs along the way. If it sees prey, it does not jump on it immediately. First, it throws out its tongue. If nothing happens to its tongue, it moves ahead and grabs the prey. The chameleon is cautious. When the chameleon comes into a new environment, it takes the color of the environment without taking over. The chameleon adapts without imposing itself. Whatever we choose to call our feminism is our prerogative. However, in this journey that is feminist engagement, we need to walk like the chameleon—goal-oriented, cautious, accommodating, adaptable, and open to diverse views. Nego-feminists would heed the advice of my great-uncle.

Notes

a. Take, e.g., the Igbo proverb, *ife kwulu, ife akwudebie* (when something stands, something stands beside it). Sibdou Ouda's action during the "photo-shoot" (i.e., beckoning her children to stand beside her) is a vivid enactment of this proverb.

b. See Nnaemeka 1998a, 5. Also seen...where one of the African participants interjected "tell her [Nussbaum] that's not what we came here to do." An

African participant made a similar remark when the fight for supremacy erupted among feminists, womanists, and Africana womanists at the
first Women in Africa and the African Diaspora (WAAD) conference (see
Nnaemeka 1998a, 31, n. 3). [Note: Many African participants concurred with
interjections of "go on, my sister," "I agree with you one hundred percent,"
"speak for us, my dear," "tell her that's not what we came here to do," etc.]

c. At the first international WAAD conference I organized in Nsukka, Nigeria,
   in 1992, about 30 percent of the participants were male. About the same per-
   centage attended the third WAAD conference in Madagascar. The Women's
   World conference held in Kampala, Uganda, in 2002 also attracted many
   male participants/presenters. At the first WAAD conference, some foreign
   participants complained about the presence of men (see Nnaemeka 1998b,
   363–364). I heard the same complaint from the same constituency at the
   Kampala conference in 2002.

d. Some institutions have negotiated a compromise—women's/gender studies
   program.

e. One of the most prominent centers in Africa (Cape Town, South Africa) for
   the study of women assumed the name African Gender Institute, without
   equivocation.

f. It is important to note that he did not advise me to be like the chameleon but
   rather to walk like the chameleon. The indeterminacy implicated in being
   like a chameleon is not lost to my people (Igbo) who denounce chameleon-
   like behavior in humans—*ifu ocha icha, ifu oji ijie* (when you see white, you
   turn white; when you see black, you turn black). By advising me to walk
   like a chameleon, my great-uncle takes the chameleon metaphor in different
   directions.

References

Allen, Amy. 1999. *The Power of Feminist Theory: Domination, Resistance, Solidarity.*
Boulder, CO: Westview.

Bâ, Mariama. 1980. *Une si longue lettre.* Dakar: Nouvelles Editions Africaines.

Beyala, Calixthe. 1995. *Lettre d'une Africaine à ses surs occidentales.* Paris:
Spengler.

Breines, Wini. 1996. "Sixties Stories' Silences: White Feminism, Black Feminism,
Black Power." *National Women's Studies Association Journal* 8 : 101–121.

Christian, Barbara. 1995. "The Race for Theory." In Bill Ashcroft, Gareth Griffiths,
and Helen Tiffin, eds., *The Post-colonial Studies Reader.* London: Routledge.

Nnaemeka, Obioma. 1998a. "Introduction: Reading the Rainbow." In Obioma
Nnaemeka, ed., *Sisterhood, Feminisms, and Power: From Africa to the Diaspora.*
Trenton, NJ: Africa World Press.

———. 1998b. "This Women's Studies Business: Beyond Politics and History
(Thoughts on the First WAAD Conference)." In Obioma Nnaemeka, ed.,
Sisterhood, Feminisms, and Power: From Africa to the Diaspora. Trenton, NJ:
Africa World Press.

Steady, Filomina Chioma. 1987. "African Feminism: A Worldwide Perspective."
In Rosalyn Terborg-Penn, Sharon Harley, and Andrea Benton Rushing,
eds., *Women in Africa and the African Diaspora.* Washington, DC: Howard
University Press.

The Politics of Multiple Identities

For multiracial/multiethnic feminism, rebellion against the gender order is subtle and complex. It involves creating new knowledge, culture, theology, and ethics from a woman's point of view. It also involves actions that include and benefit the men of their group. Other actions encompass international issues and entail transnational coalitions of diverse multiracial/multiethnic women. Still other actions link up with similar men's political movements. Gender may not be in the foreground but rather shifting ground as a result of other aspects of political activism.

Critique

If racial ethnic and gender identity are as intertwined as multiracial/multiethnic feminism claims, then political unity with men of the same racial ethnic group could severely undermine a consciousness of oppression as women. For example, among African Americans, there has been a controversy over whether Black women's independence and assertiveness threaten their men's ego and sense of masculinity. When this view is adopted by White politicians, it becomes an agenda for family policies that make it extremely difficult for battered women to leave abusive men.

A politics based on identity is a complex of interlocking coalitions and oppositional groups. Consciousness of subordination and the forms of struggle may have to be different for women and men. The man who is Other may need to find the voice suppressed by the dominant men; the woman who is Other may need to find the voice suppressed by both dominant *and* subordinate men.

Summary

Throughout the twentieth century, social critics have argued about which aspect of inequality is the most damaging. In the United States, feminists have focused on women's oppression and civil rights activists on raising the status of the members of a particular disadvantaged racial ethnic group. Men and women together have been in the forefront of working-class political struggles. Internationally, postcolonial revolutions and nationalism add another focus. Multiracial/multiethnic feminism argues that all these aspects of subordination have to be fought at the same time.

The important point made by multiracial/multiethnic feminism is that a member of a subordinate group is not disadvantaged just by gender or racial ethnic status or social class, but by a multiple system or *matrix of domination*. Multiracial/multiethnic feminism is therefore critical of feminist theories that contrast two homogeneous groups—women and men. It argues that in racist societies, no one is just a woman or man; they are, in the United States, for example, a White woman or a Black woman, a White man or a Black man.

The combination of social statuses makes for a particular group standpoint on values, sense of appropriate behavior, and outlook on life (which may be completely distinctive or may overlap with that of other groups). The dominant group's standpoint is the one that prevails in the definition of social problems, in the attribution of their causes, and in allocation of resources to research and to political solutions. Dominant cultures tend to swamp native cultures, as witnessed by the spread of McDonald's and Starbucks. Popular culture may be imbued with the culture of subordinates, like Black music, but then it becomes mainstreamed. Members of disadvantaged racial ethnic and economic groups have fought to have their points of view heard, as have women. In the political arena, however, sometimes women band with other women and sometimes with men of their own social group. The politics of identity, as multiracial/multiethnic feminism is so aware, is a complex of shifting sides.

Multiracial/multiethnic feminism brings to feminism the tools of racial ethnic and class analysis. It gives us a powerful theory of the intersectionality of the multiple social statuses that shape individual lives and organize local communities and nations. Politically, however, multiracial/multiethnic feminism is often caught between the politics of race and ethnicity and that of gender. When they coalesce in the creation of new knowledge, viewpoints, and politics, the result is a major transformation of the gendered social order.

SUGGESTED READINGS IN MULTIRACIAL/MULTIETHNIC FEMINISM

African American

Breines, Wini. 2002. "What's Love Got to Do with It? White Women, Black Women, and Feminism in the Movement Years." *Signs* 27: 1095–1134.

Carby, Hazel. 1987. *Reconstructing Womanhood: The Emergence of the Afro-American Woman Novelist*. New York: Oxford University Press.

Cole, Johnnetta, and Beverly Guy-Sheftall. 2003. *Gender Talk: The Struggle for Women's Equality in African American Communities*. New York: Ballantine.

Collins, Patricia Hill. 1990. *Black Feminist Thought: Knowledge, Consciousness, and the Politics of Empowerment*. Boston: Unwin Hyman. 2nd ed., 2000. New York: Routledge.

———. 1998. *Fighting Words: Black Women and the Search for Justice*. Minneapolis: University of Minnesota Press.

———. 2004. *Black Sexual Politics: African Americans, Gender, and the New Racism*. New York: Routledge.

Combahee River Collective. 1986. *The Combahee River Collective Statement: Black Feminist Organizing in the Seventies and Eighties*. New York: Kitchen Table, Women of Color Press.

Davis, Angela Y. 1983. *Women, Race and Class*. New York: Vintage.

Durr, Marlese, and Shirley A. Hill, eds. 2006. *Race, Work, and Family in the Lives of African Americans*. Lanham, MD: Rowman & Littlefield.

Glenn, Evelyn Nakano. 2002. *Unequal Freedom: How Race and Gender Shaped American Citizenship and Labor*. Cambridge, MA: Harvard University Press.

Gubar, Susan. 1997. *Racechanges: White Skin, Black Face in American Culture*. New York: Oxford University Press.

Guy-Sheftall, Beverly, ed. 1995. *Words of Fire: An Anthology of African-American Feminist Thought*. New York: New Press.

hooks, bell. 1981. *Ain't I a Woman: Black Women and Feminism*. Boston: South End Press.

———. 1984. *Feminist Theory: From Margin to Center*. Boston: South End Press. 2nd ed., 2000.

———. 1989. *Talking Back: Thinking Feminist, Talking Black*. Boston: South End Press.

———. 1990. *Yearning: Race, Gender, and Cultural Politics*. Boston: South End Press.

———. 1994. *Outlaw Culture: Resisting Representations*. New York: Routledge.

———. 1996. *Bone Black: Memories of Girlhood*. New York: Henry Holt.

———. 2000. *Feminism Is for Everybody: Passionate Politics*. Boston: South End Press.

Hull, Gloria T., Patricia Bell Scott, and Barbara Smith, eds. 1982. *All the Women Are White, All the Blacks Are Men, But Some of Us Are Brave: Black Women's Studies*. New York: Feminist Press.

Jones, Jacqueline. 1986. *Labor of Love, Labor of Sorrow: Black Women, Work, and the Family from Slavery to the Present*. New York: Vintage.

King, Deborah. 1988. "Multiple Jeopardy, Multiple Consciousness: The Context of a Black Feminist Ideology." *Signs* 14: 42–72.

Landry, Bart. 2000. *Black Working Wives: Pioneers of the American Family Revolution*. Berkeley: University of California Press.

Moraga, Cherríe, and Gloria Anzaldúa, eds. 1981. *This Bridge Called My Back: Writings by Radical Women of Color*. Watertown, MA: Persephone Press.

Morrison, Toni. 2002. *Learning from Experience: Minority Identities, Multicultural Struggles*. Berkeley: University of California Press.

Omolade, Barbara. 1994. *The Rising Song of African American Women*. New York: Routledge.

Radford-Hill, Sheila. 2000. *Further to Fly: Black Women and the Politics of Empowerment*. Minneapolis: University of Minnesota Press.

Ruiz, Vicki L., ed. 2007. *Unequal Sisters: An Inclusive Reader in U.S. Women's History*, 4th ed. New York: Routledge.

Smith, Barbara, ed. [1983] 2000. *Home Girls: A Black Feminist Anthology*. New Brunswick, NJ: Rutgers University Press.

Spelman, Elizabeth. 1988. *Inessential Woman: Problems of Exclusion in Feminist Thought*. Boston: Beacon Press.

Thompson, Becky. 1994. *A Hunger So Wide and So Deep: A Multiracial View of Women's Eating Problems*. Minneapolis: University of Minnesota Press.

———. 2001. *A Promise and a Way of Life: White Antiracist Activism*. Minneapolis: University of Minnesota Press.

Thompson, Becky, and Sangeeta Tyagi, eds. 1996. *Names We Call Home: Autobiography on Racial Identity*. New York: Routledge.

Wall, Cheryl A., ed. 1989. *Changing Our Own Words: Essays on Criticism, Theory, and Writing by Black Women*. New Brunswick, NJ: Rutgers University Press.

Wallace, Michele. [1978] 1990. *Black Macho and the Myth of the Superwoman*. London: Verso.

Wiegman, Robyn. 1995. *American Anatomies: Theorizing Race and Gender*. Durham, NC: Duke University Press.

Williams, Patricia J. 1991. *The Alchemy of Race and Rights*. Cambridge, MA: Harvard University Press.

———. 1995. *The Rooster's Egg*. Cambridge, MA: Harvard University Press.

———. 1998. *Seeing a Color-Blind Future: The Paradox of Race*. New York: Noonday Press.

Wyatt, Jean. 2004. *Risking Difference: Identification, Race, and Community in Contemporary Fiction and Feminism*. Albany, NY: State University of New York Press.

Asian American

Bow, Leslie. 2001. *Betrayal and Other Acts of Subversion: Feminism, Sexual Politics, Asian American Women's Literature*. Princeton, NJ: Princeton University Press.

Espiritu, Yen Le. 1997. *Asian American Women and Men*. Thousand Oaks, CA: Sage.

Glenn, Evelyn Nakano. 1986. *Issei, Nisei, War Bride*. Philadelphia: Temple University Press.

Shah, Sonia. 1997. *Dragon Ladies: Asian American Feminists Breathe Fire*. Boston: South End Press.

Song, Young I. and Ailee Moon, eds. 1998. *Korean American Women: From Tradition to Modern Feminism*. Westport, CT: Greenwood Publishing.

Yamada, Mitsuye, Merle Woo, and Nellie Wong. 2003. *Three Asian American Writers Speak Out on Feminism*. Saddle River, NJ: Red Letter Press.

Yamamoto, Traise. 1999. *Masking Selves, Making Subjects: Japanese American Women, Identity, and the Body*. Berkeley: University of California Press.

Chicana/Latina

Anzaldúa, Gloria E. [1987] 1999. *Borderlands/La Frontera: The New Mestiza*. San Francisco, CA: Spinsters/Aunt Lute.

———. 1990. *Making Face, Making Soul Haciendo Caras: Creative and Critical Perspectives by Women of Color*. San Francisco, CA: Spinsters/Aunt Lute.

Anzaldúa, Gloria E., and AnaLouise Keating, eds. 2002. *This Bridge We Call Home: Radical Visions for Transformation*. New York: Routledge.

Arredondo, Gabriela F., Aida Hurtado, Norma Klahn, and Olga Najera-Ramirez, eds. 2003. *Chicana Feminisms: A Critical Reader*. Durham, NC: Duke University Press.

Davalos, Karen Mary. 2008. "*Sin Vergüenza*: Chicana Feminist Theorizing." *Feminist Studies* 34: 151–171.

De la Torre, Adela, and Beatríz M. Pesquera. 1993. *Building with Our Hands: New Directions in Chicana Studies*. Berkeley: University of California Press.

Garcia, Alma, ed. 1997. *Chicana Feminist Thought: The Basic Historical Writings*. New York: Routledge.

Hurtado, Aída. 1996. *The Color of Privilege: Three Blasphemies on Race and Feminism*. Ann Arbor: University of Michigan Press.

———. 2003. *Voicing Chicana Feminisms: Young Women Speak Out on Sexuality and Identity*. New York: New York University Press.

Romero, Mary, Pierrette Hondagneu-Sotelo, and Vilma Ortiz, eds. 1997. *Challenging Fronteras: Structuring Latina and Latino Lives in the U.S.: An Anthology of Readings*. New York: Routledge.

Saldívar-Hull, Sonia. 2000. *Feminism on the Border: Chicana Gender Politics and Literature*. Berkeley: University of California Press.

Sandoval, Anna Marie. 2009. *Toward a Latina Feminism of the Americas: Repression and Resistance in Chicana and Mexicana Literature*. Austin, TX: University of Texas Press.

Sandoval, Chela. 2000. *Methodology of the Oppressed*. Minneapolis: University of Minnesota Press.

Trujillo, Carla, ed. 1998. *Living Chicana Theory*. Berkeley, CA: Third Woman.

Transnational

Cruz María e Silva, Teresa, and Ari Sitas, eds. 1996. *Gathering Voices: Perspectives on the Social Sciences in Southern Africa*. Proceedings of the International Sociological Association Regional Conference for Southern Africa, Durban, South Africa.

Nnaemeka, Obioma, ed. 1998. *Sisterhood, Feminisms, and Power: From Africa to the Diaspora*. Trenton, NJ: Africa World Press.

———. 2004. "Nego-Feminism: Theorizing, Practicing, and Pruning Africa's Way." *Signs* 29: 357–385.

Womanist Culture, Ethics, Theology

Brown, Elsa Barkley. 1989. "African-American Women's Quilting." *Signs* 14: 921–929.

Cannon, Katie G. 1988. *Black Womanist Ethics*. Atlanta, GA: Scholars Press.

Floyd-Thomas, Stacey M. 2006a. *Mining the Motherlode: Methods in Womanist Ethics*. Cleveland, OH: Pilgrim Press.

———. 2006b. *Deeper Shades of Purple: Womanism in Religion and Society*. New York: New York University Press.

Gilkes, Cheryl Townsend. 2001. *"If It Wasn't for the Women…": Black Women's Experience and Womanist Culture in Church and Community*. Maryknoll, NY: Orbis Books.

Grant, Jacquelyn, ed. 1995. *Perspectives on Womanist Theology*. Atlanta: ITC Press.

Harris, Melanie L. 2006. "Womanist Humanism: A New Hermeneutic." In Stacey Floyd-Thomas, ed., *Deeper Shades of Purple: Womanism in Religion and Society*. New York: New York University Press.

Hayes, Diana L. 1995. *Hagar's Daughters: Womanist Ways of Being in the World*. Mahwah, NJ: Paulist Press.

Hollies, Linda H. 2003. *Bodacious Womanist Wisdom*. Cleveland, OH: Pilgrim Press.

Mitchem, Stephanie Y. 2002. *Introducing Womanist Theology*. Maryknoll, NY: Orbis Books.

Phillips, Layli. 2006. *The Womanist Reader: The First Quarter Century of Womanist Thought*. New York: Routledge.

Riggs, Marcia Y. 1994. *Awake, Arise and Act: A Womanist Call for Black Liberation*. Cleveland, OH: Pilgrim Press.

Townes, Emilie M. 1995. *In a Blaze of Glory: Womanist Spirituality as Social Witness*. Nashville, TN: Abingdon Press.

———. 2006. *Womanist Ethics and the Cultural Production of Evil*. Basingstoke, UK: Palgrave Macmillan.

———, ed. 1997. *Embracing the Spirit: Womanist Perspectives on Hope, Salvation, and Transformation*. Maryknoll, NY: Orbis Books.

Walker, Alice. 1983. *In Search of Our Mothers' Gardens: Womanist Prose*. New York: Harcourt Brace.

Williams, Delores S. 1987. "Womanist Theology: Black Women's Voices." *Christianity and Crisis*, March 2:66–70. Reprinted at http://www.religion-online.org/showarticle.asp?title=445.

———. 1995. *Sisters in the Wilderness: The Challenge of Womanist God-Talk*, new ed. Maryknoll, NY: Orbis Books.

10

Feminist Studies of Men

SOURCES OF GENDER INEQUALITY

- Hegemonic masculinity—dominance of economic and political power and cultural values by elite men
- Legitimation of men's violence and sexual exploitation of women
- Socialization that encourages boys' aggressiveness and unemotionality

POLITICS

- Working for greater economic, educational, and political equality
- Enhancing the status of disadvantaged men, including gay and transgendered men
- Making men responsible for controlling their own violent behavior

CRITIQUE

- Politics to change values and behavior need to come from men themselves
- Feminist men need a movement to challenge hegemony and patriarchal privileges
- Research and activism have to turn a gender lens on hegemonic men in all the areas where they still dominate, especially corporations and politics

CONTRIBUTIONS

- Concept of masculine hegemony
- Analysis of men's gender as part of a set of institutionalized relationships of dominance and subordination, nationally and internationally
- Recognition of men's dominance of other men as well as of women
- Identification of a range of masculinities
- Condemnation of war, pornography, rape, and violence as aspects of men's gendering

Feminist studies of men treat men as well as women as a gender and scrutinize masculinity as carefully as femininity. Its perspective is that genders—men's and women's—are relational and embedded in the structure of the social order. The original object of analysis in feminist studies of men was masculinity in its oppositional relationship to femininity, since much of masculinity is a careful avoidance of the appearance of femininity. What is valued and socially encouraged in men is their difference from women. Men and boys are therefore encouraged to be aggressive, cool, and physically strong. Violence, especially in sports, is condoned. The ability to fight, on the street, in the sports arena, and in wars, is always valorized. Feminist studies of men have studied the ways that boys are socialized to develop masculine characteristics and how their behavior as teens and adults reflect these characteristics. They particularly focus on how masculinity imbues cultural, social, and political values and behavior.

Other research in feminist studies of men homes in on the stratification of men within societies. Because of the range of men's social positions, masculinity is better construed as masculinities—dominant, subordinate, intersected with the norms of social class, nationalities, religion, racial ethnic status, and sexual orientations. Feminist studies of men argue that although a pattern of social dominance over women is prevalent, there are many subordinate men, as studies of working-class men and men under colonial domination make very clear.

Men vary in status and power, but what maintains gender inequality is *male hegemony* (men's dominance in values, knowledge, culture, and politics) and *patriarchal privileges* (better jobs and higher salaries, women's emotional care, sexual availability, and domestic labor). Feminist studies of men examine the extent to which groups of men participate in the creation of hegemonic values, knowledge, and culture. Another area of research is how much different groups of men benefit from patriarchy. For example, African American and Hispanic working-class women outstrip the men of their group in educational attainment and in the job market, since there are more opportunities in health care and service work, which are women's occupations, than in blue-collar industries. Disadvantaged men may try to shore up their weakened masculine status by violence against their wives and girlfriends. Those who are successful in sports can become phenomenally wealthy and famous. Hegemonic men vicariously participate in the sports played by upwardly mobile disadvantaged men. In this web of masculinity, women are marginalized and sexualized.

Feminist studies of men provide the concepts and empirical data for a politics that could subvert the gendered social order built on masculine hegemony and patriarchal privilege.

Hegemonic Men, Hegemonic Masculinity

The main concept used in feminist studies of men is *hegemony* (pervasive dominance in values, knowledge, culture, and politics). Hegemony is inter-gendered (men as a group are hegemonic compared to women) and intra-gendered (some men are considered superior). Hegemonic men are economically successful, from racially and ethnically privileged groups, and visibly heterosexual; they are well-educated and work at the most prestigious and lucrative occupations. In the United States, many are of poor or working-class origins, but most have been educated at good colleges and universities and have professional or managerial careers or go into politics. Their hegemonic status is produced and legitimated by these valued attributes: Whiteness, wealth, education, social position, heterosexuality. Hegemonic men are both born to these characteristics (e.g., Whiteness) and achieve them (education). Attaining a position of power often counteracts a lesser status, like membership in a devalued racial or ethnic group. Sometimes events propel men of lesser status to a more glorified status. Since September 11, 2001, New York City firefighters have become the symbol of American strength in the face of adversity. Their valorization as heroes has become international, but their economic and political status in New York City is not quite hegemonic. They are still working-class.

Hegemonic men within a society monopolize privileges, resources, and power. They control national politics, set policies, impose their view of what is valuable, virtuous, and moral on the rest of society, and marshal legitimacy for their views through the media, education, religion, and law, which they also dominate. Because newly independent countries are still suffering from the effects of colonization, hegemonic men in the Western societies that have been economically and socially dominant for the past 500 years have a double advantage—national and global hegemony. According to R. W. Connell (2005), a major theorist and researcher in feminist studies of men, Western masculinity may become the hegemonic worldwide form of masculinity, creating a global gender hierarchy of dominance and subordination that places hegemonic men at the top, coalescing their power.

The premises and development of the concept of hegemonic masculinity are laid out in the following excerpt by Connell and James Messerschmidt, sociologists and feminists. They suggest that as hegemonic values and gender relations change, so do ideas about masculinity.

Hegemonic Masculinity

R. W. Connell

University of Sydney, Australia

James W. Messerschmidt

University of Southern Maine

Hegemonic masculinity was understood as the pattern of practice (i.e., things done, not just a set of role expectations or an identity) that allowed men's dominance over women to continue.

Hegemonic masculinity was distinguished from other masculinities, especially subordinated masculinities. Hegemonic masculinity was not assumed to be normal in the statistical sense; only a minority of men might enact it. But it was certainly normative. It embodied the currently most honored way of being a man, it required all other men to position themselves in relation to it, and it ideologically legitimated the global subordination of women to men.

Men who received the benefits of patriarchy without enacting a strong version of masculine dominance could be regarded as showing a complicit masculinity. It was in relation to this group, and to compliance among heterosexual women, that the concept of hegemony was most powerful. Hegemony did not mean violence, although it could be supported by force; it meant ascendancy achieved through culture, institutions, and persuasion.

These concepts were abstract rather than descriptive, defined in terms of the logic of a patriarchal gender system. They assumed that gender relations were historical, so gender hierarchies were subject to change. Hegemonic masculinities therefore came into existence in specific circumstances and were open to historical change. More precisely, there could be a struggle for hegemony, and older forms of masculinity might be displaced by new ones. This was the element of optimism in an otherwise rather bleak theory. It was perhaps possible that a more humane, less oppressive, means of being a man might become hegemonic, as part of a process leading toward an abolition of gender hierarchies....

We argue that the concept of hegemonic masculinity is in need of reformulation in four main areas: the nature of gender hierarchy, the geography of masculine configurations, the process of social embodiment, and the dynamics of masculinities. In the following subsections, we offer a line of thought, and some research suggestions, about each of these issues.

Reprinted from "Hegemonic Masculinity: Rethinking the Concept." *Gender & Society* 19: 832–833, 847–853. Copyright © 2005 by Sociologists for Women in Society. Reprinted by permission of Sage Publications.

Gender Hierarchy

Compared with original formulations of the concept, contemporary research has shown the complexity of the relationships among different constructions of masculinity. The recent research in discursive psychology indicates how different constructions of masculinity at the local level may serve as tactical alternatives. Structured relations among masculinities exist in all local settings, motivation toward a specific hegemonic version varies by local context, and such local versions inevitably differ somewhat from each other. Demetriou's (2001) notion of dialectical pragmatism captures the reciprocal influence of masculinities on each other; hegemonic masculine patterns may change by incorporating elements from the others.

Analyses of relations among masculinities now more clearly recognize the agency of subordinated and marginalized groups—often conditioned by their specific location (as discussed below). "Protest masculinity" (Poynting, Noble, and Tabar 2003) can be understood in this sense: a pattern of masculinity constructed in local working-class settings, sometimes among ethnically marginalized men, which embodies the claim to power typical of regional hegemonic masculinities in Western countries, but which lacks the economic resources and institutional authority that underpins the regional and global patterns.

Research has also documented the durability or survivability of non-hegemonic patterns of masculinity, which may represent well-crafted responses to race/ethnic marginalization, physical disability, class inequality, or stigmatized sexuality. Hegemony may be accomplished by the incorporation of such masculinities into a functioning gender order rather than by active oppression in the form of discredit or violence. In practice, both incorporation and oppression can occur together. This is, for instance, the contemporary position of gay masculinities in Western urban centers, where gay communities have a spectrum of experience ranging from homophobic violence and cultural denigration to toleration and even cultural celebration and political representation. Similar processes of incorporation and oppression may occur among girls and women who construct masculinities (Messerschmidt 2004).

The concept of hegemonic masculinity was originally formulated in tandem with a concept of hegemonic femininity—soon renamed "emphasized femininity" to acknowledge the asymmetrical position of masculinities and femininities in a patriarchal gender order. In the development of research on men and masculinities, this relationship has dropped out of focus. This is regrettable for more than one reason. Gender is always relational, and patterns of masculinity are socially defined in contradistinction from some model (whether real or imaginary) of femininity.

Perhaps more important, focusing only on the activities of men occludes the practices of women in the construction of gender among men. As is well shown by life-history research, women are central in many of the processes constructing masculinities—as mothers; as schoolmates; as girlfriends, sexual partners, and wives; as workers in the gender division of labor, and so forth. The concept of emphasized femininity focused on compliance to patriarchy, and this is still highly relevant in contemporary mass culture. Yet gender hierarchies are also affected by new configurations of women's identity and practice, especially among younger women—which are increasingly acknowledged by younger men. We consider that research on hegemonic masculinity now needs to give much closer attention to the practices of women and to the historical interplay of femininities and masculinities.

We suggest, therefore, that our understanding of hegemonic masculinity needs to incorporate a more holistic understanding of gender hierarchy, recognizing the agency of subordinated groups as much as the power of dominant groups and the mutual conditioning of gender dynamics and other social dynamics. We think this will tend, over time, to reduce the isolation of men's studies and will emphasize the relevance of gender dynamics to the problems—ranging from effects of globalization to issues of violence and peacemaking—being explored in other fields of social science.

The Geography of Masculinities

Change in locally specific constructions of hegemonic masculinity has been a theme of research for the past two decades. But with growing attention to globalization, the significance of transnational arenas for the construction of masculinity has also been argued. Hooper (1998, 2000) describes the deployment of hegemonic and other masculinities in the arenas of international relations, and Connell (1998) proposed a model of "transnational business masculinity" among corporate executives that was connected with neoliberal agendas of globalization.

Whether, or how far, such processes override more local and regional gender dynamics is still being debated. Pease and Pringle (2001), in a recent international collection, argue for a continued focus on understanding masculinities regionally and comparatively. At the least, we must understand that regional and local constructions of hegemonic masculinity are shaped by the articulation of these gender systems with global processes. In this vein, Kimmel (2005) has recently examined how the effects of a global hegemonic masculinity are embedded in the emergence of regional (white supremacists in the United States and Sweden) and global (al Qaeda from the Middle East) "protest" masculinities.

We consider these issues are now unavoidable for studies of masculinity and suggest the following simple framework. Empirically existing hegemonic masculinities can be analyzed at three levels:

1. Local: constructed in the arenas of face-to-face interaction of families, organizations, and immediate communities, as typically found in ethnographic and life-history research;

2. Regional: constructed at the level of the culture or the nation-state, as typically found in discursive, political, and demographic research; and

3. Global: constructed in transnational arenas such as world politics and transnational business and media, as studied in the emerging research on masculinities and globalization.

Not only do links between these levels exist; they can be important in gender politics. Global institutions pressure regional and local gender orders; while regional gender orders provide cultural materials adopted or reworked in global arenas and provide models of masculinity that may be important in local gender dynamics.

Let us consider specifically the relation between regional and local masculinities. Hegemonic masculinity at the regional level is symbolically represented through the interplay of specific local masculine practices that have regional significance, such as those constructed by feature film actors, professional athletes, and politicians. The exact content of these practices varies over time and across societies. Yet regional hegemonic masculinity shapes a society-wide sense of masculine reality and, therefore, operates in the cultural domain as on-hand material to be actualized, altered, or challenged through practice in a range of different local circumstances. A regional hegemonic masculinity, then, provides a cultural framework that may be materialized in daily practices and interactions....

Social Embodiment

That hegemonic masculinity is related to particular ways of representing and using men's bodies has been recognized from the earliest formulations of the concept. Yet the pattern of embodiment involved in hegemony has not been convincingly theorized.

The importance of masculine embodiment for identity and behavior emerges in many contexts. In youth, skilled bodily activity becomes a prime indicator of masculinity, as we have already seen with sport. This is a key way that heterosexuality and masculinity become linked in Western culture, with prestige conferred on boys with heterosexual partners and sexual learning imagined as exploration and conquest. Body practices such as eating meat and taking risks on the road also become linked with masculine identities. This logically results in health promotion strategies that work by degendering—contesting hegemonic masculinity, or moving men in a more androgynous direction. But the difficulties of degendering strategies also are partly based in embodiment, for instance, in the commitment to risk-taking practices as means of establishing masculine reputation in a peer group context.

The common social scientific reading of bodies as objects of a process of social construction is now widely considered to be inadequate. Bodies are involved more actively, more intimately, and more intricately in social processes than theory has usually allowed. Bodies participate in social action by delineating courses of social conduct—the body is a participant in generating social practice. It is important not only that masculinities be understood as embodied but also that the interweaving of embodiment and social context be addressed.

The need for a more sophisticated treatment of embodiment in hegemonic masculinity is made particularly clear by the issue of transgender practices, which are difficult to understand within a simple model of social construction. This issue has been reframed by the rise of queer theory, which has treated gender crossing as a subversion of the gender order or at least as a demonstration of its vulnerability. Sharp debates over transsexualism have arisen, with some psychiatrists' questioning the very possibility of gender change. It is therefore not easy to be confident about the implications of transgender practice for hegemony. With Rubin (2003) and Namaste (2000), we consider that the masculinities constructed in female-to-male transsexuals' life courses are not inherently counterhegemonic. "Self-made men" can pursue gender equality or oppose it, just like nontranssexual men. What the transsexual experience highlights is modernity's treatment of the body as the "medium through which selves interact with each other" (Rubin 2003, 180).

To understand embodiment and hegemony, we need to understand that bodies are both objects of social practice and agents in social practice (Connell 2002). There are circuits of social practice linking bodily processes and social structures—many such circuits, which add up to the historical process in which society is embodied. These circuits of social embodiment may be very direct and simple, or they may be long and complex, passing through institutions, economic relations, cultural symbols, and so forth—without ceasing to involve material bodies. This can readily be illustrated by thinking about the gender patterns in health, illness, and medical treatment.

Among dominant groups of men, the circuits of social embodiment constantly involve the institutions on which their privileges rest. This is dramatically shown in a pioneering study by Donaldson and Poynting (2004) of the daily lives of ruling-class men. This study shows, for instance, how their characteristic sports, leisure, and eating practices deploy their wealth and establish relations of distance and dominance over other men's bodies. A rich field of research opens up here, especially when we consider how expensive technologies—computer systems, global air travel, secure communications—amplify the physical powers of elite men's bodies.

The Dynamics of Masculinities

Although long acknowledged, the internal complexity of masculinities has only gradually come into focus as a research issue. As indicated by our earlier discussion of the subject in gender practice, we must now explicitly recognize the layering, the potential internal contradiction, within all practices that construct masculinities. Such practices cannot be read simply as expressing a unitary masculinity. They may, for instance, represent compromise formations between contradictory desires or emotions, or the results of uncertain calculations about the costs and benefits of different gender strategies.

Life-history research has pointed to another dynamic of masculinities, the structure of a project. Masculinities are configurations of practice that are constructed, unfold, and change through time. A small literature on masculinity and aging, and a larger one on childhood and youth, emphasize this issue. The careful analysis of life histories may detect contradictory commitments and institutional transitions that reflect different hegemonic masculinities and also hold seeds of change.

Hegemonic masculinities are likely to involve specific patterns of internal division and emotional conflict, precisely because of their association with gendered power. Relationships with fathers are one likely focus of tension, given the gender division of labor in child care, the "long hours culture" in professions and management, and the preoccupation of rich fathers with managing their wealth. Ambivalence toward projects of change on the part of women are likely to be another, leading to oscillating acceptance and rejection of gender equality by the same men. Any strategy for the maintenance of power is likely to involve a dehumanizing of other groups and a corresponding withering of empathy and emotional relatedness within the self (Schwalbe 1992). Without treating privileged men as objects of pity, we should recognize that hegemonic masculinity does not necessarily translate into a satisfying experience of life.

Change over time, while certainly shaped by contradictions within masculinities, may also be intentional. Children as well as adults have a capacity to deconstruct gender binaries and criticize hegemonic masculinity, and this capacity is the basis of many educational interventions and change programs. At the same time, bearers of hegemonic masculinity are not necessarily "cultural dopes"; they may actively attempt to modernize gender relations and to reshape masculinities as part of the deal. A good example is the "new public management" in public-sector organizations, which rejects old-style bureaucracy and believes in "flatter" organizations, equal opportunity, and family-friendly employment policies. Yet even the modernization of masculinities may not solve problems. This too, as Meuser (2001) argues, generates contradictions that may lead to further change.

Gender relations are always arenas of tension. A given pattern of hegemonic masculinity is hegemonic to the extent that it provides a solution to these tensions, tending to stabilize patriarchal power or reconstitute it in new conditions. A pattern of practice (i.e., a version of masculinity) that provided such a solution in past conditions but not in new conditions is open to challenge—is in fact certain to be challenged.

Such contestation occurs continuously, through the efforts of the women's movement (at the local, regional, and global levels), among generations in immigrant communities, between models of managerial masculinity, among rivals for political authority, among claimants for attention in the entertainment industry, and so on. The contestation is real, and gender theory does not predict which will prevail—the process is historically open. Accordingly, hegemony may fail. The concept of hegemonic masculinity does not rely on a theory of social reproduction.

Put another way, the conceptualization of hegemonic masculinity should explicitly acknowledge the possibility of democratizing gender relations, of abolishing power differentials, not just of reproducing hierarchy. A transitional move in this direction requires an attempt to establish as hegemonic among men ("internal hegemony" in Demetriou's [2001] sense) a version of masculinity open to equality with women. In this sense, it is possible to define a hegemonic masculinity that is thoroughly "positive" (in Collier's [1998] sense). Recent history has shown the difficulty of doing this in practice. A positive hegemony remains, nevertheless, a key strategy for contemporary efforts at reform.

References

Collier, R. 1998. *Masculinities, Crime and Criminology: Men, Heterosexuality and the Criminal(ised) Other.* London: Sage.

Connell, R. W. 1998. "Masculinities and Globalization." *Men and Masculinities* 1: 3–23.

———. 2002. *Gender.* Cambridge, UK: Polity Press.

Demetriou. D. Z. 2001. "Connell's Concept of Hegemonic Masculinity: A Critique." *Theory and Society* 30: 337–361.

Donaldson, M. 1991. *Time of Our Lives: Labor and Love in the Working Class.* Sydney, AU: Allen and Unwin.

Hooper, C. 1998. "Masculinist Practices and Gender Politics: The Operation of Multiple Masculinities in International Relations." In M. Zalewski and J. Parpart, eds., *The "Man" Question in International Relations.* Boulder, CO: Westview.

———. 2000. "Masculinities in Transition: The Case of Globalization." In M. H. Marchand and A. S. Runyan, eds., *Gender and Global Restructuring*. London: Routledge.

Kimmel, M. S. 2005. "Globalization and Its Mal(e)contents: The Gendered Moral and Political Economy of Terrorism. In M. S. Kimmel, J. Hearn, and R. W. Connell, eds., *Handbook of Studies on Men & Masculinities*. Thousand Oaks, CA: Sage.

Messerschmidt, J. W. 2004. *Flesh & Blood: Adolescent Gender Diversity and Violence*. Lanham, MD: Rowman & Littlefield.

Meuser, M. 2001. "This Doesn't Really Mean She's Holding a Whip": Transformation of the Gender Order and the Contradictory Modernization of Masculinity." *Diskurs* 1: 44–50.

Namaste, V. K. 2000. *Invisible Lives: The Erasure of Transsexual and Transgendered People*. Chicago: University of Chicago Press.

Poynting, S., G. Noble, and P. Tabar. 2003. "'Intersections' of Masculinity and Ethnicity: A Study of Male Lebanese Immigrant Youth in Western Sydney. Unpublished manuscript, University of Western Sydney.

Rubin, H. 2003. *Self-made Men: Identity and Embodiment among Transsexual Men*. Nashville, TN: Vanderbilt University Press.

Schwalbe, M. 1992. "Male Supremacy and the Narrowing of the Moral Self." *Berkeley Journal of Sociology* 37:29–54.

Sports and Masculinity

One of the arenas for the display of masculinity is sports. Sport is a deeply gendered social institution, dominated by men and masculine values. The focus is men athletes; the popular games are built on men's bodies; the cultural ambience is masculine; the values are violence, aggression, and extreme competitiveness. Players of team sports are often from disadvantaged groups, while the owners are upper-class men. The audiences are men and boys who vicariously adopt sports values and build sports metaphors into a locker-room mentality—aggressive towards male peers and misogynistic towards girls and women. The gendering is so skewed to men that women's sports have almost no place in it. In the institution of sport, they seem to be irrelevant.

The consumers of sport in Western-oriented societies use the language, imagery, and metaphors of popular sports in corporation board rooms, political chambers, courtrooms, and science laboratories. Clients are wooed while playing golf or from expensive seats at games. The consumers are usually far removed from the physical life of sport, so their engagement is vicarious, but wherever men are the majority of workers, the locker-room is never far away. Sport talk is so prevalent in the United States that any woman in corporate life—or politics—has to join in. During the 2008 U.S. Democratic primary campaigns, both Hillary Clinton and Barack Obama were criticized for not being jocks. She needed a sport; he couldn't bowl—but he could shoot hoops, so his display of masculinity was not diminished.

Sports play a particularly important part in corporate culture. They are the source of the metaphors in everyday language; last night's game is the subject of water-cooler talk; the golf course is the place to entertain clients; tickets to the big games are the deal sweeteners. Not being able to talk the language, share the postgame analysis, play golf with the guys, and be a proper audience are all grounds for informal devaluation on the job. Vicarious participation in sports demonstrates not just masculinity, but the values that supposedly make for success in the corporate world—aggressive competitiveness and no-holds-barred individual or team effort. The ideological subtext of sport in Western culture is that physical strength is men's prerogative, and it justifies men's physical and sexual domination of women.

According to Michael Messner, there is a televised manhood sports formula that virtually trains a young male audience to the locker-room mentality that will govern their cultural lives—a version of masculinity "grounded in bravery, risk taking, violence, bodily strength, and heterosexuality" (2002, 126). The telecasts, announcers' commentaries, and commercials glorify violence, denigrate men who don't appear tough enough, and show women as sexy prizes for the truly masculine, winning guys. According to Messner, the connection between audience, athletes, and corporations is tightly woven:

> The televised sports manhood formula is a master narrative that is produced at the nexus of the institutions of sport, mass media, and corporations that hope to sell products and services to boys and men. As such, this formula appears well suited to discipline boys' and men's bodies, minds, and consumption choices.... The perpetuation of these commercial interests appears to be predicated on boys and men accepting—indeed, glorifying and celebrating—a set of bodily and relational practices that resist and oppose a view of women as fully human and place boys' and men's long-term health prospects in jeopardy. (2002, 126)

Men athletes suffer the effects of concussions, torn muscles, broken bones, and illegal body-enhancing drugs. The undermining of the glorification of aggressive competition and violence in men's sports may come from men athletes, their corporate sponsors, and their fans—football players who are openly talking about the long-term deleterious effects of concussions suffered on the field, U.S. baseball fans who are booing Barry Bonds' home runs now because of his suspected body-building drug use in the past, and corporate financiers who are dumping dope-positive Tour de France cyclists. But until men are more openly critical of the worst aspects of sport, it will remain an arena where hegemonic masculinity is rampant.

Fatherhood

Much of the research and policy in feminist studies of men has been critical of men's aggressiveness and violence, but there is a domain where men are showing nurturing capabilities and willingness to share domestic responsibilities with the women in their lives—fatherhood. In most Western countries, fathers at least "give a hand," by changing diapers, putting children to bed, and comforting crying babies during the day and when they wake at night. Michael Lamb (1987), in assessing the amount of child care performed by fathers throughout the world, described three levels of involvement with children: *child-minding*—being on call near the child but not directly engaged in care; *one-on-one care*—holding, feeding, bathing, dressing, playing with, helping with homework, reading to the child, and so on; and *responsibility*—thinking about the child's emotional, social, and physical development and welfare and making arrangements for nonparental care, sick care, doctor visits, school visits, and playtime. In the last 25 years, more Western men have been willing to be intimately involved in their children's care.

Many of the men who share parenting start early—sharing the decision to have children and getting involved in fertility issues, prenatal checkups, preparation for birth, birthing, and infant care. Scott Coltrane (1996) found that co-parenting fathers liked the way they were able to develop their caring skills, and some became closer to their own fathers. Diane Ehrensaft (1987) said that in the course of fathering, men who shared parenting fell in love with their children and wanted to be with them because they were so fascinating and lovable. The intensity of the men's feelings for their children reversed the conventional parental triangle; instead of the fathers being jealous of the time the mothers spent with the children, mothers felt left out of the father-child "couple."

The skills of parenting are learned, usually "on the job," so men who are single fathers or who do a significant amount of child care become good at it. Barbara Risman (1987) interviewed men who became single parents out of necessity because their wives had died or left them with the children. These single fathers did not have previous beliefs about their capacity for intimate parenting, but they developed fully nurturing relationships with their children. Even men who did not have good role models become good fathers. Leonard Pitts, Jr., a *Miami Herald* journalist who interviewed African American men about their troubled relationships with their fathers, says that for him and others, there are always role models: "fathers, black men, *family* men who came up on hard streets, sired by disappointing dads, yet get up every morning and do the hard work of raising and supporting their children" (1999, 198).

Sweden gives fathers a "daddy month" to stay home with newborn or newly adopted children. These fatherhood policies have been actively promoted by men's and women's feminist groups as part of an ideological commitment to gender equality and have been strengthened by government commissions and media campaigns. But they have run up against a gendered labor market and wage scales and the persistence of the cultural assumption that men will be the primary breadwinners. As a result, men in Sweden frequently convert their "daddy month" into long weekends or extended vacations instead of using it to bond intensively with their new children.

How widespread is shared parenting likely to be among heterosexual couples in the United States? African American fathers are more likely to share parenting than White fathers, because of the need for two incomes. For more couples to share parenting equally, women have to give up being the chief child-care expert, and men have to learn how to be one. Also necessary are "family-friendly policies" in workplaces and encouragement of their use, so that neither fathers nor mothers get penalized for spending time with their children. Hegemonic masculinity has involved being a father who supports his children economically and confers his high social position on them. Perhaps with changing values, it will mean intensive fathering.

Sexual Stratification

Feminist studies of men overlap with gay studies in analyzing the social dimensions of male homosexuality. Examining homosexuality from a gender perspective shows that homosexual men are *men*, not a third gender, and partake of the privileges (or lack of them) and lifestyle of men of the same racial ethnic group and social class. Nonetheless, because homosexual men do not have sexual relationships with women—an important marker of manhood in Western society—they are considered not-quite-men. Thus, like other men who do not have the marks of dominant status (being White, economically successful, heterosexual), homosexual men are lower on the scale of privilege and power in Western society. Homosexual men, however, do not subvert the gender order, because they retain some of the patriarchal privileges of men's status.

Endangered and Dangerous Men

Not all men are privileged and powerful. In many countries, young working-class urban men's impoverished environment and "taste for risk" have made them an endangered species. They put their bodies on the line in confronting seeming slurs on their manhood, and they incur physical traumas in their work, in recreation, and especially when they become professional athletes and soldiers.

Men and boys in any social strata engage in gang rape as a way of showing off their sexual prowess to their friends. Feminist studies of men blame sports, the military, fraternities, and other places where men bond for encouraging physical and sexual violence and misogyny. They deplore the social pressure on men to identify with but not be emotionally close to their fathers, and to be "cool" and unfeeling toward the women in their lives and distant from their own children.

Although feminist studies of men use psychoanalytic theories of the need to detach from the mother to explain men's emotional repression, they do not feel that the answer are men's movements that foster a search for the inner primitive, or "wild man." The men-only retreats of these movements in many ways replicate other types of stag events—they foster men bonding with each other, not with the women and children in their lives. Feminists also regard religiously oriented men's organizations, such as Promise Keepers, as dangerous to women's autonomy because they link responsibility to family with patriarchal concepts of manhood that want submission from women. Feminist studies of men argue that these movements seek to change individual attitudes and do not address the structural conditions of inequality among men.

These power differences emerge from different men's places in gender regimes, and they change as the regimes change. Successful religious revolutions in Islamic countries have downgraded college-educated, middle-class men and upgraded religious mullahs and martyrs. High birth rates and slow economic development have provided few well-paid jobs for college-educated men. An alternative route to valued masculinity is to die heroically as a martyr. Many terrorists have been college-educated men who became embittered by being locked out of middle-class careers. Michael Kimmel, author of a history of masculinity in America and many other works in feminist studies of men, compared the terrorists of September 11 to the American White supremacist Timothy McVeigh, who bombed a federal building in Oklahoma in 1995, killing 168 people. In the following excerpt, Kimmel describes the terrorists' and White supremacists' path from loss of middle-class male privilege to anger toward and resentment of those more successful, to a violent restoration of masculine pride.

Gender, Class, and Terrorism

Michael S. Kimmel

State University of New York, Stony Brook

The events of September 11 [2001] have sent scholars and pundits alike scrambling to make sense of those seemingly senseless acts. While most analyses have focused on the political economy of globalization or the perversion of Islamic teachings by Al Qaeda, several commentators have raised gender issues.

Some have reminded us that in our haste to lionize the heroes of the World Trade Center collapse, we ignored the many women firefighters, police officers, and rescue workers who also risked their lives. We've been asked to remember the Taliban's vicious policies toward women; indeed, even Laura Bush seems to be championing women's emancipation.

A few have asked us to consider the other side of the gender coin: men. Some have rehearsed the rather tired old formulae about masculine bloodlust or the drive for domination and conquest, with no reference to the magnificent humanity displayed by so many on September 11.

In an article in *Slate*, the Rutgers anthropologist Lionel Tiger trotted out his old male-bonding thesis but offered no understanding of why Al Qaeda might appeal to some men and not others. Only the journalist Barbara Ehrenreich suggests that there may be a link between the misogyny of the Taliban and the masculinity of the terrorists.

As for myself, I've been thinking lately about a letter to the editor of a small, upstate–New York newspaper, written in 1992 by an American GI after his return from service in the Gulf War. He complained that the legacy of the American middle class had been stolen by an indifferent government. The American dream, he wrote, has all but disappeared; instead, most people are struggling just to buy next week's groceries.

That letter writer was Timothy McVeigh from Lockport, N.Y. Two years later, he blew up the Murrah federal building in Oklahoma City in what is now the second-worst act of terrorism ever committed on American soil.

What's startling to me are the ways that McVeigh's complaints were echoed in some of the fragmentary evidence that we have seen about the terrorists of September 11, and especially in the portrait of Mohammed Atta, the suspected mastermind of the operation and the pilot of the first plane to hit the World Trade Center.

Looking at these two men through the lens of gender may shed some light on both the method and the madness of the tragedies they wrought.

McVeigh was representative of the small legion of white supremacists—from older organizations like the John Birch Society, the Ku Klux Klan, and the American Nazi Party, to newer neo-Nazi, racist skinhead, white-power groups like Posse Comitatus and the White Aryan Resistance, to radical militias.

These white supremacists are mostly younger (in their early 20s), lower-middle-class men, educated at least through high school and often beyond. They are the sons of skilled workers in industries like textiles and tobacco, the sons of the owners of small farms, shops, and grocery stores. Buffeted by global political and economic forces, the sons have inherited little of their fathers' legacies. The family farms have been lost to foreclosure, the small shops squeezed out by Wal-Marts and malls. These young men face a spiral of downward mobility and economic uncertainty. They complain that they are squeezed between the omnivorous jaws of global capital concentration and a federal bureaucracy that is at best indifferent to their plight and at worst complicit in their demise.

As one issue of *The Truth at Last*, a white-supremacist magazine, put it:

> Immigrants are flooding into our nation willing to work for the minimum wage (or less). Superrich corporate executives are flying all over the world in search of cheaper and cheaper labor so that they can lay off their American employees.

...Many young White families have no future! They are not going to receive any appreciable wage increases due to job competition from immigrants.

What they want, says one member, is to "take back what is rightfully ours."

Their anger often fixes on "others"—women, members of minority groups, immigrants, gay men, and lesbians—in part because those are the people with whom they compete for entry-level, minimum-wage jobs. Above them all, enjoying the view, hovers the international Jewish conspiracy.

What holds together these "paranoid politics"—antigovernment, antiglobal capital but pro-small capitalist, racist, sexist, anti-Semitic, homophobic—is a rhetoric of masculinity. These men feel emasculated by big money and big government—they call the government "the Nanny State"—and they claim that "others" have been handed the birthright of native-born white men.

In the eyes of such downwardly mobile white men, most white American males collude in their own emasculation. They've grown soft, feminized, weak. White supremacists' Web sites abound with complaints about the "whimpering collapse of the blond male"; the "legions of sissies and weaklings, of flabby, limp-wristed, nonaggressive, nonphysical, indecisive, slack-jawed, fearful males who, while still heterosexual in theory and practice, have not even a vestige of the old macho spirit."

American white supremacists thus offer American men the restoration of their masculinity—a manhood in which individual white men control the fruits of their own labor and are not subject to emasculation by Jewish-owned finance capital or a black- and feminist-controlled welfare state. Theirs is the militarized manhood of the heroic John Rambo, a manhood that celebrates their God-sanctioned right to band together in armed militias if anyone, or any government agency, tries to take it away from them. If the state and the economy emasculate them, and if the masculinity of the "others" is problematic, then only "real" white men can rescue America from a feminized, multicultural, androgynous melting pot.

Sound familiar? For the most part, the terrorists of September 11 come from the same class, and recite the same complaints, as American white supremacists.

Virtually all were under 25, educated, lower middle class or middle class, downwardly mobile. The journalist Nasra Hassan interviewed families of Middle Eastern suicide bombers (as well as some failed bombers themselves) and found that none of them had the standard motivations ascribed to people who commit suicide, such as depression.

Although several of the leaders of Al Qaeda are wealthy—Osama bin Laden is a multimilionaire, and Ayman al-Zawahiri, the 50-year-old doctor thought to be bin Laden's closest adviser, is from a fashionable suburb of Cairo—many of the hijackers were engineering students for whom job opportunities had been dwindling dramatically. (Judging from the minimal information I have found, about one-fourth of the hijackers had studied engineering.) Zacarias Moussaoui, who did not hijack one of the planes but is the first man to be formally charged in the United States for crimes related to September 11, earned a degree at London's South Bank University. Marwan al-Shehhi, the chubby, bespectacled 23-year-old from the United Arab Emirates who flew the second plane into the World Trade Center, was an engineering student, while Ziad Jarrah, the 26-year-old Lebanese who flew the plane that crashed in Pennsylvania, had studied aircraft design.

Politically, these terrorists opposed globalization and the spread of Western values; they opposed what they perceived as corrupt regimes in several Arab states (notably Saudi Arabia and Egypt), which they claimed were merely puppets of American domination. "The resulting anger is naturally directed first against their rulers," writes the historian Bernard Lewis, "and then against those whom they see as keeping those rulers in power for selfish reasons."

Central to their political ideology is the recovery of manhood from the emasculating politics of globalization. The Taliban saw the Soviet invasion and westernization of Afghanistan as humiliations. Bin Laden's October 7 videotape describes the "humiliation and disgrace" that Islam has suffered "for more than 80 years." And over and over, Nasra Hassan writes, she heard the refrain: "The Israelis humiliate us. They occupy our land, and deny our history."

Terrorism is fueled by a fatal brew of antiglobalization politics, convoluted Islamic theology, and virulent misogyny. According to Ehrenreich, while these formerly employed or self-employed males "have lost their traditional status as farmers and breadwinners, women have been entering the market economy and gaining the marginal independence conferred by even a paltry wage." As a result, "the man who can no longer make a living, who has to depend on his wife's earnings, can watch Hollywood sexpots on pirated videos and begin to think the world has been turned upside down."

The Taliban's policies thus had two purposes: to remasculinize men and to refeminize women. Another journalist, Peter Marsden, has observed that those policies "could be seen as a desperate attempt to keep out that other world, and to protect Afghan women from influences that could weaken the society from within." The Taliban prohibited women from appearing in public unescorted by men, from revealing any part of their body, and from going to school or holding a job. Men were required to grow their beards, in accordance with religious images of Muhammad, yes; but also, perhaps, because wearing beards has always been associated with men's response to women's increased equality in the public sphere, since beards symbolically reaffirm biological differences between men and women, while gender equality tends to blur those differences.

The Taliban's policies removed women as competitors and also shored up masculinity, since they enabled men to triumph over the humiliations of globalization and their own savage, predatory, and violently sexual urges that might be unleashed in the presence of uncovered women.

All of these issues converged in the life of Mohammed Atta, the terrorist about whom the most has been written and conjectured. Currently, for example, there is much speculation about Atta's sexuality. Was he gay? Was he a repressed homosexual, too ashamed of his sexuality to come out? Such innuendoes are based on no more than a few circumstantial tidbits about his life. He was slim, sweet-faced, neat, meticulous, a snazzy dresser. The youngest child of an ambitious lawyer father and a pampering mother, Atta grew up shy and polite, a mama's boy. "He was so gentle," his father said. "I used to tell him, 'Toughen up, boy!' "

When such revelations are offered, storytellers seem to expect a reaction like "Aha! So that explains it!" (Indeed, in a new biography of Adolf Hitler, *The Hidden Hitler,* Lothar Machtan offers exactly that sort of explanation. He argues that many of Hitler's policies—such as the killing of longtime colleague and avowed homosexual Ernst Rohm, or even the systematic persecution and execution of gay men in concentration camps—were, in fact, prompted by a desire to conceal his own homosexuality.)

But what do such accusations actually explain? Do revelations about Hitler's or Atta's possible gay propensities raise troubling connections between homosexuality and mass murder? If so, then one would also have to conclude that the discovery of Shakespeare's "gay" sonnet explains the Bard's genius at explicating Hamlet's existential anguish, or that Michelangelo's sexuality is the decisive factor in his painting of God's touch in the Sistine Chapel.

Such revelations tell us little about the Holocaust or September 11. They do, however, address the consequences of homophobia—both official and informal—on young men who are exploring their sexual identities. What's relevant is not the possible fact of Hitler's or Atta's gayness, but the shame and fear that surround homosexuality in societies that refuse to acknowledge sexual diversity.

Even more troubling is what such speculation leaves out. What unites Atta, McVeigh, and Hitler is not their repressed sexual orientation but gender—their masculinity, their sense of masculine entitlement, and their thwarted ambitions. They accepted cultural definitions of masculinity, and needed someone to blame when they felt that they failed to measure up. (After all, being called a mama's boy, a sissy, and told to toughen up are demands for gender conformity, not matters of sexual desire.) Gender is the issue, not sexuality.

All three failed at their chosen professions. Hitler was a failed artist—indeed, he failed at just about every job he ever tried except dictator.

McVeigh, a business-college dropout, found his calling in the military during the Gulf War, where his exemplary service earned him commendations; but he washed out of Green Beret training—his dream job—after only two days. And Atta was the odd man out in his family. His two sisters both became doctors—one a physician and one a university professor. His father constantly reminded him that he wanted "to hear the word 'doctor' in front of his name. We told him, your sisters are doctors and their husbands are doctors and you are the man of the family."

Atta decided to become an engineer, but his degree meant little in a country where thousands of college graduates were unable to find good jobs. After he failed to find employment in Egypt, he went to Hamburg, Germany, to study architecture. He was "meticulous, disciplined, and highly intelligent, an ordinary student, a quiet, friendly guy who was totally focused on his studies," according to another student in Hamburg.

But his ambitions were constantly undone. His only hope for a good job in Egypt was to be hired by an international firm. He applied and was continually rejected. He found work as a draftsman—highly humiliating for someone with engineering and architectural credentials and an imperious and demanding father—for a German firm involved with razing low-income Cairo neighborhoods to provide more scenic vistas for luxury tourist hotels.

Defeated, humiliated, emasculated, a disappointment to his father and a failed rival to his sisters, Atta retreated into increasingly militant Islamic theology. By the time he assumed the controls of American Airlines Flight 11, he evinced a hysteria about women. In the message he left in his abandoned rental car, he made clear what mattered to him in the end. "I don't want pregnant women or a person who is not clean to come and say good-bye to me," he wrote. "I don't want women to go to my funeral or later to my grave." Of course, Atta's body was instantly incinerated, and no burial would be likely.

The terrors of emasculation experienced by lower-middle-class men all over the world will no doubt continue, as they struggle to make a place for themselves in shrinking economies and inevitably shifting cultures. They may continue to feel a seething resentment against women, whom they perceive as stealing their rightful place at the head of the table, and against the governments that displace them. Globalization feels to them like a game of musical chairs, in which, when the music stops, all the seats are handed to others by nursemaid governments.

The events of September 11, as well as of April 19, 1995 (the Oklahoma City bombing), resulted from an increasingly common combination of factors—the massive male displacement that accompanies globalization, the spread of American consumerism, and the perceived corruption of local political elites—fused with a masculine sense of entitlement. Someone else—some "other"—had to be held responsible for the terrorists' downward mobility and failures, and the failure of their fathers to deliver their promised inheritance. The terrorists didn't just get mad. They got even.

Such themes were not lost on the disparate bands of young, white supremacists. American Aryans admired the terrorists' courage and chastised their own compatriots. "It's a disgrace that in a population of at least 150 million White/Aryan Americans, we provide so few that are willing to do the same [as the terrorists]," bemoaned Rocky Suhayda, the chairman of the American Nazi Party. "A bunch of towel heads and niggers put our great White Movement to shame."

It is from such gendered shame that mass murderers are made.

Critique

Feminist studies of men, done by both women and men, have amply documented the structure and processes that establish and maintain men's hegemonic dominance and patriarchal privileges. The politics to change values and behavior need to come from men themselves, because feminist women's long efforts against gender discrimination, misogyny, sexual harassment, rape, battering, and male violence have often created backlash and stubborn resistance.

Feminist men's politics of educating young men about date rape and fraternity gang rape are important, as are athletes who have written and lectured about the violent values in sport. Black and Hispanic men feminists have analyzed the dangers of risk taking and machismo. Gay men have analyzed and documented the recent history of homosexuality and its path from the headiness of the Greenwich Village Stonewall riot to the tragedies of AIDS. A thriving men's health movement is developing a body of knowledge about how men's risky lifestyles cause illness.

These political efforts are addressed to individuals. Mass movements of men are more along the lines of Iron Johns and Promise Keepers, who offer versions of masculinity that are not much different from the conventional beliefs in men's intrinsic "wildness" or need to be the "head of the house." Another strand in the nonfeminist politics of masculinity is the argument that says that men's power is a myth because so many men's roles are dangerous. They, and not women, are exploited—fighting wars, fires, criminals, and terrorists. Women feminists, not men, have countered this argument with studies of women in the military, law enforcement, and other occupations where formerly only men showed they had the "right stuff." (Women could not enter such occupations until fairly recently.) A woman feminist has documented men's rapid rise up the "glass escalator" to the top positions in women's occupations. Both types of data—that women can do the dangerous work men do and that men doing women's work have the advantage of their dominant gender status—are analyses that came from women, not men.

If feminist studies of men are to add the dimension of the insider's view of the structure and institutionalization of masculinity, men have to turn the gender lens on themselves in all the areas where they still dominate—not only sport, which has been amply criticized, but also traditional religions, science, the higher echelons of finance, and the capitalist markets of the global economy, and most especially, politics. As Michael Messner said in the Sociologists for Women in Society Feminist Lecture:

> What we need is a renewed movement of ordinary women and men working side by side to push assertively for an ideal of the public that is founded first and foremost on compassion and caring. The seeds of such a movement currently exist—in feminist organizations, in the peace movement, in religious-based immigrant rights organizations, in union-based organizing for the rights of workers. A coalition of these progressive organizations can succeed in infusing local and national politics with the values of public compassion. This will not happen easily, or without opposition. We need to expect that such a movement will have to be tough and will have to fight—against entrenched privilege and against the politics of fear—to place compassion and care at the top of the public agenda. Out of such a movement, we can generate and support women and men who will lead with love and compassion and follow with muscle. (2007, 479)

And that would also be the seeds a new gender order.

Summary

Feminist studies of men focus on men and masculinity, with overlaps in research on the body, sexuality, violence, personality development, health, and family relationships. These overlaps make feminist studies of men an increasingly valuable part of feminist studies.

Feminist studies of men have brought attention to the fact that men as well as women have a gender status. Men's gender status is dominant in most societies, although there is a hierarchy of hegemonic and subordinate men. Even though disadvantaged men may be lower on the status scale than hegemonic men, they are usually dominant over the women of their own group, giving them patriarchal privileges. Men's hegemonic status in the structure of privilege, as well as the sexist practices and violent behavior that maintain all men's dominance over women in their group, have been dissected and deplored by feminist studies of men.

Another important focus of feminist studies of men is the analysis of violence in men in sport, war, and terrorism. In sport, racial and economic stratification and a culture of violence take a high toll on the players and on aspiring teenagers. A few professional athletes have careers that are rewarding financially and in popularity, but for the most part, the money in sport is made by White, middle-class men. In the health field, the high death rate of young men from poor urban centers and the short life expectancy of older men have been attributed to gendered, racial, ethnic, and economic pressures.

Feminist studies of men should be distinguished from the men's movements that focus on individual change. Bonding with symbolic brothers and fathers and dancing to drums in the woods may make men more emotionally expressive, but it does nothing to change men's inability to bond with the women and children in their lives. Feminist studies of men also criticize movements that offer men a rightful place as heads of their families in exchange for the promise of taking responsibility for the welfare of their wives and children. Feminist men would rather see men and women sharing family work and economic support as equal partners. Feminist men have also undertaken an active program of anti-rape and anti-battering education.

In its perspectives on men and masculinities as part of the gendered social order and the processes that reproduce and maintain it, feminist studies of men have offered a challenge to their perpetuation. Feminist men's calls for redistribution of hegemonic men's advantages and their questioning men's control over politics, the media, education, law, religions, and cultural productions, undercut men's superiority. Without the values and control of hegemonic men and the patriarchal privileges men of all groups still have, the gender order would be close to collapsing. The research and critique of feminist studies of men could be used for a political movement that rebels against the current gender order, but it needs a concerted effort that includes hegemonic men who are willing to give up their dominance.

SUGGESTED READINGS IN FEMINIST STUDIES OF MEN

Abalos, David T. 2001. *The Latino Male: A Radical Redefinition.* Boulder, CO: Lynne Rienner.

Adams, Rachel, and David Savran, eds. 2002. *The Masculinity Studies Reader.* Malden, MA: Blackwell.

Ashe, Fidelma. 2007. *The New Politics of Masculinity: Men, Power and Resistance.* New York: Routledge.

Beasley, Christine. 2008. "Rethinking Hegemonic Masculinity in a Globalizing World." *Men and Masculinities* 11: 86–103. Commentaries and response, 104–115.

Bourdieu, Pierre. 2001. *Masculine Domination.* Stanford, CA: Stanford University Press.

Boyarin, Daniel. 1997. *Unheroic Conduct: The Rise of Heterosexuality and the Invention of the Jewish Man.* Berkeley: University of California Press.

Brownell, Susan, and Jeffrey N. Wasserstrom, eds. 2002. *Chinese Femininities/Chinese Masculinities: A Reader.* Berkeley: University of California Press.

Byrd, Rudolph, and Beverly Guy-Sheftall, eds. 2001. *Traps: African American Men on Gender and Sexuality.* Bloomington: Indiana University Press.

Carby, Hazel V. 2000. *Race Men.* Cambridge, MA: Harvard University Press.

Cleaver, Frances, ed. 2002. *Masculinities Matter! Men, Gender and Development.* London: Zed.

Collier, Richard. 2008. *Essays on Law, Men and Masculinities.* New York: Routledge.

Connell, R. W. 1995. *Masculinities.* Berkeley: University of California Press.

———. 2000. *The Men and the Boys.* Berkeley: University of California Press.

———. 2005. "Change among the Gatekeepers: Men, Masculinities, and Gender Equality in the Global Arena." *Signs* 30: 1801–1825.

Connell, R. W. and James W. Messerschmidt. 2005. "Hegemonic Masculinity: Rethinking the Concept." *Gender & Society* 19: 829–859.

Cornwall, Andrea, and Nancy Lindisfarne, eds. 1994. *Dislocating Masculinity: Comparative Ethnographies*. New York: Routledge.

Digby, Tom, ed. 1998. *Men Doing Feminism*. New York: Routledge.

Edwards, Tim. 2006. *Cultures of Masculinity*. New York: Routledge.

Ehrenreich, Barbara. 1983. *Hearts of Men: American Dreams and the Flight from Commitment*. New York: Anchor Doubleday.

Eng, David L. 2001. *Racial Castration: Managing Masculinity in Asian America*. Durham, NC: Duke University Press.

Ferguson, Ann Arnett. 2000. *Bad Boys: Public Schools in the Making of Black Masculinity*. Lansing, MI: University of Michigan Press.

Flood, Michael, Judith Kegan Gardiner, Bob Pease, and Keith Pringle, eds. 2007. *International Encyclopedia of Men and Masculinities*. New York: Routledge.

Gardiner, Judith Kegan, ed. 2002. *Masculinity Studies and Feminist Theory*. New York: Columbia University Press.

Ghoussoub, Mai, and Emma Sinclair-Webb, eds. 2000. *Imagined Masculinities: Male Identity and Culture in the Modern Middle East*. London: Saqi Books.

Gutmann, Matthew C. 1996. *The Meanings of Macho: Being a Man in Mexico City*. Berkeley: University of California Press.

Haywood, Chris, and Máirtín Mac an Ghaill. 2003. *Men and Masculinities: Theory, Research and Social Practice*. Milton Keynes, UK: Open University Press.

Hearn, Jeff. 1987. *The Gender of Oppression: Men, Masculinity and the Critique of Marxism*. New York: St. Martin's Press.

———. 1992. *Men in the Public Eye: The Construction and Deconstruction of Public Men and Public Patriarchies*. London: Routledge.

———. 2004. "From Hegemonic Masculinity to the Hegemony of Men." *Feminist Theory* 5:49–72.

Hearn, Jeff, and David Morgan, eds. 1990. *Men, Masculinities and Social Theory*. London: Unwin Hyman.

Herdt, Gilbert. 1981. *Guardians of the Flutes: Idioms of Masculinity*. New York: McGraw-Hill.

hooks, bell. 2003. *We Real Cool: Black Men and Masculinity*, new ed. New York: Routledge.

———. 2004. *The Will to Change: Men, Masculinity, and Love*. New York: Atria.

Hooper, Charlotte. 2001. *Manly States: Masculinities, International Relations, and Gender Politics*. New York: Columbia University Press.

Howson, Richard. 2005. *Challenging Hegemonic Masculinity*. New York: Routledge.

Janssen, Diederik F., ed. 2008. *International Guide to Literature on Masculinity: A Bibliography*. Harriman, TN: Men's Studies Press.

Kimmel, Michael S., ed. 1991. *Men Confront Pornography*. New York: Meridian.

———. 1996. *Manhood in America: A Cultural History*. New York: Free Press.

———. 2003. "Globalization and Its Mal(e)contents: The Gendered Moral and Political Economy of Terrorism." *International Sociology* 18:603–620.

———. 2005a. *The History of Men: Essays on the History of American and British Masculinities*. Albany, NY: State University of New York Press.

———. 2005b. *The Gender of Desire: Essays on Male Sexuality*. Albany, NY: State University of New York Press.

———. 2008. *Guyland: The Perilous World Where Boys Become Men*. New York: Harper.

Kimmel, Michael S., and Amy Aronson, eds. 2004. *Men and Masculinities: A Social, Cultural, and Historical Encyclopedia*. Santa Barbara: ABC-Clio.

Kimmel, Michael S., Jeff Hearn, and R. W. Connell, eds. 2004. *Handbook of Studies on Men and Masculinities*. Thousand Oaks, CA: Sage.

Kimmel, Michael S., and Michael A. Messner, eds. 2006. *Men's Lives*, 7th ed. Boston: Allyn and Bacon.

Mac an Ghaill, Máirtín, ed. 1996. *Understanding Masculinities: Social Relations and Cultural Arenas*. Milton Keynes, UK: Open University Press.

Majors, Richard, and Janet Mancini Billson. 1992. *Cool Pose: The Dilemmas of Black Manhood in America*. New York: Lexington Books.

Messerschmidt, James W. 1993. *Masculinities and Crime: Critique and Reconceptualization of Theory*. Lanham, MD: Rowman & Littlefield.

Messner, Michael A. 1997. *Politics of Masculinities: Men in Movements*. Newbury Park, CA: Sage.

———. 2007. "The Masculinity of the Governator: Muscle and Compassion in American Politics." *Gender & Society* 21:461–80.

Mirande, Alfredo. 1997. *Hombres y Machos: Masculinity and Latino Culture*. Boulder, CO: Westview.

Nardi, Peter M., ed. 1992. *Men's Friendships*. Thousand Oaks, CA: Sage.

———. 2000. *Gay Masculinities*. Thousand Oaks, CA: Sage.

Ouzgane, Lahoucine, ed. 2006. *Islamic Masculinities*. London: Zed Books.

Pease, Bob. 2000. *Recreating Men: Postmodern Masculinity Politics*. London: Sage.

Pease, Bob, and Keith Pringle, eds. 2002. *A Man's World? Changing Men's Practices in a Globalized World*. London: Zed.

Petersen, Alan 1998. *Unmasking the Masculine: 'Men' and 'Identity' in a Sceptical Age*. London: Sage.

Sabo, Donald F., Terry A. Kupers, and Willie London, eds. 2001. *Prison Masculinities*. Philadelphia, PA: Temple University Press.

Schacht, Steven P., and Doris Ewing, eds. 1998. *Feminism and Men: Reconstructing Gender Relations*. New York: New York University Press.

Schwalbe, Michael. 1996. *Unlocking the Iron Cage: The Men's Movement, Gender Politics, and American Culture*. New York: Oxford University Press.

Segal, Lynne. 1990. *Slow Motion: Changing Masculinities, Changing Men*. New Brunswick, NJ: Rutgers University Press.

———. 1994. *Unreasonable Men: Masculinity and Social Theory*. New York: Routledge.

Seidler, Vic. 2005. *Transforming Masculinities: Men, Cultures, Bodies, Power, Sex and Love*. New York: Routledge.

Srivastava, Sanjay, ed. 2004. *Sexual Sites, Seminal Attitudes: Sexualities, Masculinities and Culture in South Asia*. Thousand Oaks, CA: Sage.

Stoltenberg, John. 1990. *Refusing to Be a Man: Essays on Sex and Justice*. New York: Meridian.

———. 1993. *The End of Manhood: A Book for Men of Conscience*. New York: Plume.

Tarrant, Shira, ed. 2007. *Men Speak Out: Views on Gender, Sex, and Power*. New York: Routledge.

Whitehead, Stephen M. 2002. *Men and Masculinities: Key Themes and New Directions*. Cambridge, UK: Polity Press.

Whitehead, Stephen M. ed. 2006. *Men & Masculinities: Critical Concepts in Sociology.* Vols. 1–5. New York: Routledge.

Bodies and Health

Bordo, Susan R. 1999. *The Male Body: A New Look at Men in Public and in Private.* New York: Farrar, Straus and Giroux.

Friedman, David M. 2003. *A Mind of Its Own: A Cultural History of the Penis.* New York: Penguin USA.

Loe, Meika. 2004. *The Rise of Viagra: How the Little Blue Pill Changed Sex in America.* New York: New York University Press.

Luciano, Lynne. 2001. *Looking Good: Male Body Image in Modern America.* New York: Hill and Wang.

McLaren, Angus. 2007. *Impotence: A Cultural History.* Chicago: University Of Chicago Press.

Moore, Lisa Jean. 2007. *Sperm Counts: Overcome by Man's Most Precious Fluid.* New York: New York University Press.

Oudshoorn, Nelly. 2003. *The Male Pill: A Biography of a Technology in the Making.* Durham, NC: Duke University Press.

Pope, Harrison G., Jr., Katharine A. Phillips, and Roberto Olivardia. 2000. *The Adonis Complex: The Secret Crisis of Male Body Obsession.* New York: Free Press.

Riska, Elianne. 2004. *Masculinity and Men's Health: Coronary Heart Disease in Medical and Public Discourse.* Lanham, MD: Rowman & Littlefield.

Rosenfeld, Dana, and Christopher Faircloth, eds. 2006. *Medicalized Masculinities.* Philadelphia, PA: Temple University Press.

Sabo, Don, and David Frederick Gordon, eds. 1995. *Men's Health and Illness: Gender, Power and the Body.* Thousand Oaks, CA: Sage.

Watson, Jonathan. 2000. *Male Bodies: Health, Culture and Identity.* Buckingham, UK: Open University Press.

Fatherhood

Coltrane, Scott. 1996. *Family Man: Fatherhood, Housework, and Gender Equity.* New York: Oxford University Press.

Deutsch, Francine M. 1999. *Halving It All: How Equally Shared Parenting Works.* Cambridge, MA: Harvard University Press.

Dienhart, Anna. 1998. *Reshaping Fatherhood: The Social Construction of Shared Parenting.* Thousand Oaks, CA: Sage.

Ehrensaft, Diane 1987. *Parenting Together: Men and Women Sharing the Care of Their Children.* Urbana, IL: University of Illinois Press.

Gerson, Kathleen. 1993. *No Man's Land: Men's Changing Commitments to Family and Work.* New York: Basic Books.

Haney, Lynne, and Miranda March. 2003. "Married Fathers and Caring Daddies: Welfare Reform and the Discursive Politics of Paternity," *Social Problems* 50: 461–481.

Hobson, Barbara, ed. 2002. *Making Men into Fathers: Men, Masculinities and the Social Politics of Fatherhood.* Cambridge, UK: Cambridge University Press.

Lamb, Michael E., ed. 1987. *The Father's Role: Cross-Cultural Perspectives.* Hillsdale, NJ: Lawrence Erlbaum.

Pitts, Leonard, Jr. 1999. *Becoming Dad: Black Men and the Journey to Fatherhood.* Atlanta, GA: Longstreet Press.

Risman, Barbara J. 1987. "Intimate Relationships from a Microstructural Perspective: Men Who Mother." *Gender & Society* 1: 6–32.

———. 1998. *Gender Vertigo: American Families in Transition.* New Haven, CT: Yale University Press.

Smith, Calvin D. 1998. " 'Men Don't Do This Sort of Thing:' A Case Study of the Social Isolation of Househusbands." *Men and Masculinities* 1: 138–172.

Wall, Glenda, and Stephanie Arnold. 2007. "How Involved Is Involved Fathering? An Exploration of the Contemporary Culture of Fatherhood." *Gender & Society* 21: 508–527.

Sport

Aitchison, Cara, ed. 2006. *Sport and Gender Identities: Masculinities, Femininities and Sexualities.* New York: Routledge.

Anderson, Eric. 2005. *In the Game: Gay Athletes and the Cult of Masculinity.* Albany, NY: State University of New York Press.

———. 2008. " 'I Used to Think Women Were Weak': Orthodox Masculinity, Gender Segregation, and Sport." *Sociological Forum* 23:257–280.

Grasmuck, Sherri. 2005. *Protecting Home: Class, Race, and Masculinity in Boys' Baseball.* New Brunswick, NJ: Rutgers University Press.

Klein, Alan. 1993. *Little Big Men: Bodybuilding Subculture and Gender Construction.* Albany, NY: State University of New York Press.

McKay, Jim, Michael A. Messner, and Donald Sabo, eds. 2000. *Masculinities, Gender Relations, and Sport.* Thousand Oaks, CA: Sage.

Messner, Michael A. 1992. *Power at Play: Sports and the Problem of Masculinity.* Boston: Beacon Press.

———. 2002. *Taking the Field: Women, Men and Sports.* Minneapolis: University of Minnesota Press.

Messner, Michael A., and Donald F. Sabo, eds. 1990. *Sport, Men, and the Gender Order: Critical Feminist Perspectives.* Champaign, IL: Human Kinetics.

———. 1994. *Sex, Violence, and Power in Sports: Rethinking Masculinity.* Freedom, CA: Crossing Press.

Wacquant, Loïc. 2003. *Body and Soul: Notebooks of an Apprentice Boxer.* New York: Oxford University Press.

Woodward, Kath. 2006. *Boxing, Masculinity and Identity: The 'I' of the Tiger.* New York: Routledge.

Violence, Rape, and War

Bowker, Lee H., ed. 1997. *Masculinities and Violence.* Thousand Oaks, CA: Sage.

Braudy, Leo. 2003. *From Chivalry to Terrorism: War and the Changing Nature of Masculinity.* New York: Knopf.

Breines, Ingeborg, R. W. Connell, and Ingrid Eide, eds. 2000. *Male Roles, Masculinities and Violence: A Culture of Peace Perspective.* Paris: UNESCO.

Dudink, Stefan, Josh Tosh, and Karen Hagemann, eds. 2004. *Masculinities in Politics and War: Gendering Modern History.* Manchester, UK: Manchester University Press.

Gibson, J. William. 1994. *Warrior Dreams: Paramilitary Culture in Post-Vietnam America.* New York: Hill and Wang.

Hatty, Suzanne E. 2000. *Masculinities, Violence and Culture.* Thousand Oaks, CA: Sage.

Higate, Paul, ed. 2003. *Military Masculinities: Identity and the State*. Westport, CT: Praeger.

Kaplan, Danny. 2003. *Brothers and Others in Arms: The Making of Love and War in Israeli Combat Units*. New York: Harrington Press.

Lefkowitz, Bernard. 1997. *Our Guys: The Glen Ridge Rape and the Secret Life of the Perfect Suburb*. Berkeley: University of California Press.

Messerschmidt, James W. 2000. *Nine Lives: Adolescent Masculinities, the Body, and Violence*. Boulder, CO: Westview.

Sanday, Peggy Reeves. 1990. *Fraternity Gang Rape: Sex, Brotherhood, and Privilege on Campus*. New York: New York University Press.

Scully, Diana. 1990. *Understanding Sexual Violence: A Study of Convicted Rapists*. Boston: Unwin Hyman.

Work

Chalmers, Lee V. 2001. *Marketing Masculinities: Gender and Management Politics in Marketing Work*. Westport, CT: Greenwood Press.

Cockburn, Cynthia. 1983. *Brothers: Male Dominance and Technological Change*. London: Pluto Press.

Collinson, David L., and Jeff Hearn, eds. 1996. *Men as Managers, Managers as Men: Critical Perspectives on Men, Masculinities and Managements*. London: Sage.

Gregory, Michele R. 2009. "Inside the Locker Room: Male Homosociability in the Advertising Industry." *Gender, Work and Organization*. In press.

———. 2009. "'Talking Sports': Sports and the Construction of Hegemonic Masculinities at Work." In Mustafa F. Özbilgin, ed., *Equality, Diversity and Inclusion at Work: A Research Companion*. Cheltenham, UK: Edward Elgar.

Jackson, Cecile, 2001. *Men at Work: Labour, Masculinities, Development*. Newbury Park, UK: Frank Cass.

McDowell, Linda. 2003. *Redundant Masculinities: Employment Change and White Working Class Youth*. Hoboken, NJ: Wiley.

Simpson, Ruth. 2004. "Masculinity at Work: The Experiences of Men in Female Dominated Occupations." *Work, Employment & Society* 18: 349–368.

Snyder, Karrie Ann, and Adam Isaiah Green. 2008. "Revisiting the Glass Escalator: The Case of Gender Segregation in a Female Dominated Occupation." *Social Problems* 55: 271–299.

Williams, Christine L., ed. 1993. *Doing "Women's Work": Men in Nontraditional Occupations*. Thousand Oaks, CA: Sage.

———. 1995. *Still a Man's World: Men Who Do Women's Work*. Berkeley: University of California Press.

Wingfield, Adia Harvey. 2009. "Racializing the Glass Escalator: Reconsidering Men's Experiences with Women's Work." *Gender & Society* 23: in press.

11

Social Construction Feminism

SOURCES OF GENDER INEQUALITY

- Practices and processes of gendering in everyday life
- Gendering children
- Gendering bodies and sexualities
- Gendered division of labor in the family
- Gendered work organizations
- Cultural values built into gendering and gender as a social status

POLITICS

- Making the processes of gender construction visible
- Minimizing the gendering of children
- Counteracting the power of gender norms at work and in the family
- Breaking down the binaries of sex, sexuality, and gender
- Challenging the cultural valuations of gender binaries

CRITIQUE

- Changing gendered behavior does not necessarily change gendered organizations
- Legal gender equality does not erase informal sexism, discrimination, and misogyny
- Gendering in the family and in work organizations are so closely linked that each must be modified simultaneously
- Gendering is pervasive, so *degendering* needs to be constant and multileveled

CONTRIBUTIONS

- A theory of gender that connects gendered processes with gendered social structures

- Evidence of the ways supposedly natural sex differences are socially constructed
- Showing how bodies are socially gendered
- Analysis of the social construction of sexuality and its social control
- Documentation of how the gendered social order can be changed by changing gendered practices and processes

Multicultural/multiracial feminism focuses on how women suffer from the effects of a system of racial ethnic disadvantage, and feminist studies of men focus on the hierarchical relationships of men to other men and to women. Social construction feminism looks at the structure of the gendered social order as a whole and at the processes that construct and maintain it. Social construction feminism sees gender as a society-wide institution because it is built into all the major social organizations—family, work, law, religion, education, government, medicine, the military, and so on. As a social institution, gender determines the distribution of power, privileges, and economic resources. Other major social statuses, especially racial, ethnic, and social class, combine with gender to produce an overall stratification system, but men are privileged over women in most social groups.

Through parenting, the schools, and the mass media, gendered norms and expectations get built into children's bodies, behavior, and sense of self as a certain kind of human being. Other social statuses are similarly socially constructed and reproduced, but gendering is so deeply embedded that it is rarely examined or resisted. Those who rebel against their assigned gender are stigmatized. By the time people get to be adults, alternative or non-gendered ways of behaving and arranging work and family life are literally unthinkable.

Doing Gender, Doing Difference

Social construction feminism demonstrates that gender is a constant part of who and what we are, how others treat us, and our general standing in society. Our bodies, personalities, and ways of thinking, acting, and feeling are gendered. Early and constant gendering gives the illusion of inborn sex differences, but social construction feminism argues that gender differences are not sex differences.

Sex differences are derived from male and female bodies, physiologies, and procreative systems. They are modified by social processes, such as diet, sports, and control over childbearing. Gender differences are manifest in myriad aspects of behavior, emotions, relationships, and the organization of work and family. They are produced and maintained by social processes. As an organizing principle of social orders, gender divides people into two major categories: men and women. They are expected to be different, are treated differently, and so become different. Without these socially produced differences, the whole gender order would collapse.

Social construction feminism explains the historical and cross-cultural variability of gender differences by power imbalances between women and men. Where men are oppressively dominant, the divide between women and men is strictly enforced. In more equal societies, the differences between women and men tend to be minimized, but they are never entirely erased because a gendered social order depends on gender differences.

The social construction of gender not only produces the differences between men's and women's characteristics and behavior, it also produces gender inequality. Although societies can insure that differences are not used to legitimate unequal legal rights or discriminatory practices, there is always debate over how equal women and men can be, given what seems to be a substantially wide and unbridgeable gap between female and male "natures." In the evaluation of gender differences, women are ranked lower than men. Even valued characteristics of women, such as the capacity for empathy, nurturance, and care for others, are ranked lower in Western societies than men's characteristics for assertion, competitiveness, and individual achievement. Because men and boys are held in higher social regard than women and girls and are granted advantages and rights, gender differences produce gender inequality. Although gender is intertwined with other unequal statuses, remedying the gendered part of these structures of inequality may be the most difficult, because gendering is so pervasive.

If, as social construction feminism claims, the gendered social order and its constant reproduction and maintenance are the outcome of people's actions and interactions, the gendering processes could be altered, reversed, diminished, or halted. Yet we cannot stop "doing gender" because it is part of our basic identity. In a social order based on gender divisions, everyone "does gender" almost all the time. That was the insight in "Doing Gender" by Candace West and Don Zimmerman (1987) that has become a classic of social construction feminism. It lays out the interconnections between "doing gender" in the course of everyday life and the build-up of both gendered self-identity and gendered social structures that congeal men's dominance and women's subordination. Feminist research has documented this gendering and its consequences in the social construction of gendered bodies, sexuality, families, and work.

While the social construction perspective allows for changes in gendered practices, change does not come easily, because many of the foundational assumptions of the gendered social order and its ubiquitous processes are legitimated by religion, taught by education, upheld by the mass media, and enforced by systems of social control. The strongest element in the continued conventional construction of gender is its invisibility. Put simply, we are gendered because we do gender, and we do gender because we are constantly subject to gendered social processes and structures. Throughout our lives, we dance a gendered dance, and through the dance we are gendered.

The Social Construction of "Sex Differences"

It is the pervasiveness of gendering that leads so many people to believe that the differences between women and men are "natural." In this belief, there are two and only two genders, and bodies, sexualities, and personalities are lined up on one side or the other. Intersexed and transgendered people are supposed to have a "true gender" buried in ambiguously sexed bodies or cross-gender identities. The belief in categorically binary genders has been legitimated by the constant scientific search for sex differences in the body and brain.

Much of the research on the biological sources of gendered behavior compares genetically identified females and males (sex differences) to explain social behavior (gender differences). In biology, the hypothesized source of sex differences has been XX and XY chromosomes, then testosterone and estrogen, and now it is the prenatal "hardwiring" of the brain through genetic and/or hormonal input. Thus, a girl's choice of a career in elementary school teaching and a boy's selection of engineering are attributed to genes, chromosomes, hormones, and brain organization. Socialization, family and peer pressure, the advice of school counselors, and the gender typing of jobs are omitted from the picture.

Even though there has been experimental evidence since the 1930s that the so-called male and female hormones are equally important to the development of both sexes, and we know from sex testing at sports competitions that people with XY chromosomes can have female anatomy and physiology, all of the research efforts in the twentieth century were geared to finding clear male-female differences, preferably with an easily identifiable physiological source. Before the intensive criticism of feminist scientists and social scientists, there was very little effort to document how the biases in science both reflect and construct stereotypes of masculinity and femininity in Western societies.

The feminist social construction perspective on sex differences is that genes and hormones have a loop-back effect with physical environments and individual life experiences.

The Social Construction of Gendered Bodies

Gender is one of the most significant factors in the transformation of physical bodies into social bodies. Bodies have a material reality but their meaning, value, and uses are social and cultural. Social construction feminism asks, which women's and men's bodies are considered beautiful? How are the physical capacities of human men and women enhanced in physical labor and sports? What physical aspects of women and men are valued in different societies? Social construction feminism focuses on the ways that masculine and feminine bodies are literally made through physical labor, exercise, sports, and cosmetic surgery.

In Western culture, dieting, breast enhancement, and face-lifts are ways that women have changed their appearance to fit ideals of feminine beauty.

Men lift weights, take muscle-building drugs, get hair transplants, and undergo cosmetic surgery to mold their bodies and faces to a masculine ideal. These practices may lead to illnesses, such as eating disorders, and to lifelong physical damage. To social construction feminists, the larger damage is to young people's self-confidence caused by these culturally idealized views of how women's and men's bodies should look.

The physiology and anatomy of female and male bodies do not determine the ways women's and men's bodies look and are used. According to feminist social construction theory, the "ideal types" of bodies are the product of a society's gender ideology, practices, and stratification systems. Western societies expect men to be aggressive initiators of action and protectors of women and children; therefore, their bodies should be muscular and physically strong. Women are expected to be nurturant and emotionally giving, willing to subordinate their own desires to please men and their own interests to take care of children. Therefore, women's bodies should be yielding and sexually appealing to men when they are young and plump and maternal when they are older.

The ideas and practices that shape bodies do not just produce visible differences between women and men (one major reason for them); they also reproduce the gender stratification system, in which men's bodies are viewed as superior to women's bodies.

Sport is a prime cultural arena for the social construction of men's and women's bodies. In sport, men's bodies have an extremely high value, paying off in prestige and income. Women's sports do not pay off as well, even though the bodies of women athletes have physical capabilities most ordinary men and women could not emulate.

Another area in which gender norms affect bodies is health and illness. Here, men are more disadvantaged. Young men put themselves at risk for accidents, homicides, and drug and alcohol abuse, which cut down their life span. Young women with eating disorders also put themselves at risk, but the death rates are not so high. When it comes to risk of HIV/AIDS, young women are becoming even more vulnerable than young men.

Both women and men are disadvantaged by physical disability, but gender norms affect them in somewhat different ways. Men are expected to be assertive and competitive, even if they are in a wheelchair; they retain their masculinity. Physically damaged women lose their femininity. Ironically, a man may rely heavily on a woman for care, while a woman may have no one to look out for her.

There is agency and intention in how we shape our bodies, but whether we conform to or rebel against conventional models of how female and male bodies should look and function, we are constrained by gendered expectations.

Gendering Intersexuality

As social construction feminism points out, there cannot be a gender-neutral or androgynous or "unisex" body in deeply gendered societies, because bodies (and the way they are dressed and adorned) signal a major identity. Parents of intersexed children are urged to have their genitalia surgically altered to look "normal" at an early age. Children can be dressed in gender-neutral clothes, but parents are warned that they will be mocked and ostracized if other children see their ambiguous genitalia. In order to fit into the gender binaries, intersexed bodies are surgically and hormonally reshaped. Doctors urge parents to let them create "normal-looking" genitalia as quickly as possible, even though "normal" genitalia vary widely in size and shape.

The current political goal of many intersexual adults is to have the legal status of intersexual, not male or female. Anti-surgery activists urge parents not to allow the "clarifying" genital surgery that transforms ambiguous genitalia into "normal," gender-identifiable clitorises, vaginas, penises, and scrotums. Unaltered intersexual bodies would not only undercut gender categories but would also undermine Western societies' putative foundational source of gender—naturally sexed bodies.

In what could become a landmark case, Australia issued a gender-neutral passport in 2003 to Alex MacFarlane, who has a 47XXY chromosomal structure, a form of androgyny shared by about one in every 1500 to 2000 babies. Now 48 years old, Alex has been fighting bureaucratic misrepresentation since reaching adulthood. Alex says, "Intersex individuals should not have to break the law, by pretending to be male or female, in order to vote, marry, hold a license, or own property" (Butler 2003).

As long as Western social orders are built on two and only two genders, and everyone must have one or the other legal identity, those who are not female and not male don't exist socially.

Gendering Sexuality

Social construction feminism has paid as much attention to the gendering of sexuality as it has to the gendering of bodies. Sexual scripts differ for women and for men whether they are heterosexual, homosexual, or bisexual. Linking the experience of physical sex and gendered social prescriptions for sexual feelings, fantasies, and actions are individual bodies, desires, and patterns of sexual behavior, which coalesce into gendered sexual identities. These identities, however various and individualized, are categorized and patterned into socially recognized gendered sexual statuses—heterosexual man, heterosexual woman, homosexual man, lesbian woman, bisexual man, bisexual woman. The relationships and sexual practices of women and men in each sexual category differ, with gender as much of an influence as sexual orientation. For example, bisexual women and men prefer women partners for emotional intimacy and men partners for physical assertiveness (Weinberg, Williams, and Pryor, 1994).

Gendered norms influence ideals of feminine and masculine sexual attractiveness and the kinds of sexual behavior acceptable for women and men of different social classes, racial ethnic groups, religions, and ages. These norms are most starkly seen in aging women and men and those with visible disabilities. Many economically secure and powerful older men retain their sexuality; few women of the same status do. In most societies, permitted and tabooed sexual behavior is embedded in gendered hierarchies of power, prestige, and social class.

Gendering Children

One of the reasons that gender differences are so deep-seated is that children are gendered from a very early age. Experimental studies have shown that adults respond differently to an infant depending on whether they are told it is a girl or a boy (regardless of the actual sex). They offer the child what they think are gender-appropriate toys and are gentler with "girls" and more likely to rough-house with "boys."

Although teachers today are attuned to the dangers of treating boys and girls differently, they still separate them in class teams and do not encourage their playing together in games or sports. Children who behave in gender-appropriate ways are considered normal; anything else (girls insulting, threatening, and physically fighting boys and other girls; boys who do not like sports and who cry a lot) is considered gender deviance.

It is extremely difficult for parents to counteract the gendering in schools, among peers, and in the mass media. Barbara Risman (1997) assessed the children in gender-egalitarian families as "growing up to be happy, healthy, and well adjusted" but not especially gender-free. In interviews and observation of 21 children ranging in age from 4 to 15, Risman found a complex combination of gender-egalitarian values and gendered identities. The children, like their parents, believed that women and men were equal in capabilities and should be equal socially, but from their experiences at school and with their peers, they got the message that boys and girls were totally different.

What are the effects of gay and lesbian parenting? In a careful review of studies that claimed few or no differences between children raised by heterosexual and "lesbigay" parents, Judith Stacey and Timothy Biblarz (2001) found that children with same-gender parents, especially co-mothers, develop in less gender-stereotypical ways than do children with heterosexual parents. They are also more open to homoerotic relationships, and the girls are more sexually experimental. They are, however, no more likely to become gay or lesbian as adults than children raised by heterosexual parents.

The Family as a Producer of Gender

For adults as well as children, the family is a prime site for the maintenance of gender differences. In most households, women do most of the daily cooking, cleaning, and laundry. Men's primary family role is earning enough money to support the family economically. Married women may earn as much or even more than their husbands, but to be a good woman, they need to care for family members physically and emotionally. In dual-earner families, women do more housework than the men they live with even if they work longer hours or make more money. Work for the family not only maintains the household, it also reinforces gender distinctions.

The fluid households of divorced parents, poor and working-class single mothers, two-income African American families, immigrant families, stepfamilies, and lesbian and gay co-parents are considered deviant family forms in Western postindustrial societies. Although some governments have extended the legal benefits of marriage to cohabiting heterosexual and non-heterosexual couples in domestic partnerships, the complexities of second-parent adoption and other ways of ensuring that adults who are not related by blood can have legal permanent relationships with children are only beginning to be explored. A group of adults and children living together could legitimately be a family if there were a way of sharing legal responsibility for each other in a non-gendered civil union, but Western society's model of the family is the heterosexual nuclear family, with its gendered division of labor.

Doing Gender at Work

The organization of work reflects the gendered assumptions that a husband will be the prime breadwinner and the wife will be the prime parent. The idealized worker is a man—someone who does not have daily responsibility for the maintenance of a home or care of children. The structure of work—hours, overtime, travel—as well as pay scales and promotion ladders reflect the assumption that the ideal worker is a man and not a woman. In addition, workers are subject to gendered expectations about their abilities that influence the kind of job they will have, how much they will be paid, and their chances for promotion.

Assumptions that women and men workers are significantly different underlie the gendered organization of work. Workplaces are more or less gendered on several levels. Women and men usually do different jobs, or they do the same jobs with different names and salaries. Men usually boss women and men, but women usually supervise only women.

When workers are recruited, gendered characteristics influence the search process for candidates who are "masculine," "feminine," or "neutral." In Westernized cultures, "masculine" implies physical strength, rationality, objectivity, aggressiveness; "feminine" connotes dexterity, emotional sensitivity, psychological perceptivity, ability to mediate and compromise. Intelligence, honesty, experience, and mental agility seem to be gender-neutral. The gender designation of the attributes are culturally contingent, and the skills needed for a job are frequently re-gendered as the gender composition of the workforce changes. Thus, when most bankers were men, it was argued that only men knew how to handle large sums of money. Now, bank tellers, branch managers, and financial-services providers are routinely women because it is believed that they are good with customers and clients, but global financiers are almost all men.

Workplaces are organized by gender, jobs within workplaces are gendered as "men's work" and "women's work," so recruitment is for " feminine" women or "masculine" men. Whatever way you consider gender, the economic outcome seems to advantage men. Salaries are highest in jobs where men are the predominant workers, whether the worker is a woman or a man, and lowest in jobs where women are the predominant workers, again whether the worker is a man or a woman. Looked at from the perspective of the worker, men have the advantage no matter what the gender composition of the job or workplace. Men earn more than women in jobs where men are the majority, in jobs where women are the majority, and in gender-neutral jobs.

The extent of gendering depends on the decisions, policies, and history of the particular workplace. These factors produce a structure: allocation of jobs, salary scales, advancement criteria, evaluation of workers, leave and return policies, type of control (rule-based, top-down, collegial). This structure is maintained through the interactions of the workers and through their decisions and choices as they evaluate and work within the organizational system.

Discriminatory practices persist even with equal opportunity guidelines because so much of recruitment and evaluation is interactive, and interaction between women and men is steeped in gendered beliefs and ideologies. Gender is a "superschema," an "invisible hand," a set of cultural rules that pattern face-to-face encounters. This taken-for-granted frame works as long as the participants live by gendered rules, as they generally do. The workplace is the least acceptable place for a man to be noncompetitive or a woman to be overtly aggressive. For a man to be a father first and a worker second or a woman to be a worker first and a mother second are major workplace transgressions. Even an equal commitment to work and to family goes against gender norms.

The working mother is suspected of divided attention and insufficient career commitment, even though research shows that women who work full-time and take care of families are more productive than men who only do one of those jobs (Bielby and Bielby 1988). Mothers who ask for a temporary flexible or part-time work schedule jeopardize their chances for advancement on resuming full-time work. Men who might want to take parental leave or cut back on their work to spend more time with their children are even more discouraged by "parent track" stigma and negative responses from colleagues, relatives, and friends.

Against these gendered assumptions about men and women workers with children is the postindustrial phenomenon of married mothers who have small children and husbands in the work force and are working full-time because the family needs the income or because they are committed to careers. Despite the cultural lag in public opinion and unchanged workplaces, most of these women don't opt out. They organize their work and family life to be able to do both.

Changing Gender

Since we are deeply embedded in gendered patterns and structures and continue to build them, like bees in a hive, how does change take place?

We know it does. In Western societies, women have achieved formal, legal equality with men in many areas. But we also know it doesn't, because in many informal settings and activities, sexual harassment, gender discrimination, and covert misogyny are still evident.

In the following excerpt from her Sociologists for Women in Society Feminist Lecture, Barbara Risman explores the conditions for change. She conceptualizes gender as a structure with three dimensions:

> (1) At the individual level, for the development of gendered selves; (2) during interaction as men and women face different cultural expectations even when they fill identical structural positions; and (3) in institutional domains where explicit regulations regarding resource distribution and material goods are gender specific. (2004, 433)

She then lays out the constraints of gender structures and also the "wiggle room" that allows change to occur.

Gender as a Social Structure

Barbara J. Risman
University of Illinois at Chicago

When we conceptualize gender as a social structure, we can begin to identify under what conditions and how gender inequality is being produced within each dimension. The "how" is important because without knowing the mechanisms, we cannot intervene. If indeed gender inequality in the division of household labor at this historical moment were primarily explained (and I do not suggest that it is) by gendered selves, then we would do well to consider the most effective socialization mechanisms to create fewer gender-schematic children and resocialization for adults. If, however, the gendered division of household labor is primarily constrained today by cultural expectations and moral accountability, it is those cultural images we must work to alter. But then again, if the reason many men do not equitably do their share of family labor is that men's jobs are organized so they cannot succeed at work and do their share at home, it is the contemporary American workplace that must change (Williams 2000). We may never find a universal theoretical explanation for the gendered division of household labor because universal social laws may be an illusion of twentieth-century empiricism. But in any given moment for any particular setting, the causal processes should be identifiable empirically. Gender complexity goes beyond historical specificity, as the particular causal processes that constrain men and women to do gender may be strong in one institutional setting (e.g., at home) and weaker in another (e.g., at work).

The forces that create gender traditionalism for men and women may vary across space as well as time. Conceptualizing gender as a social structure contributes to a more postmodern, contextually specific social science. We can use this schema to begin to organize thinking about the causal processes that are most likely to be effective on each dimension. When we are concerned with the means by which individuals come to have a preference to do gender, we should focus on how identities are constructed through early childhood development, explicit socialization, modeling, and adult experiences, paying close attention to the internalization of social mores. To the extent that women and men choose to do gender-typical behavior cross-situationally and over time, we must focus on such individual explanations. Indeed, much attention has already been given to gender socialization and the individualist presumptions for gender. The earliest and perhaps most commonly referred to explanations in popular culture depend on sex-role training, teaching boys and girls their culturally appropriate roles. But when trying to understand gender on the interactional/cultural dimension, the means by which status differences shape expectations and the ways in which in-group and out-group membership influence behavior need to be at the center of attention. Too little attention has been paid to how inequality is shaped by such cultural expectations during interaction.... On the institutional dimension, we look to law, organizational practices, and formal regulations that distinguish by sex category. Much progress has been made in the post–civil rights era with rewriting formal laws and organizational practices to ensure gender neutrality. Unfortunately, we have often found that despite changes in gender socialization and gender neutrality on the institutional dimension, gender stratification remains.

What I have attempted to do here is to offer a conceptual organizing scheme for the study of gender that can help us to understand gender in all its complexity and try to isolate the social processes that create gender in each dimension. This is necessary before we can begin to imagine how to change these processes and thus to change the way we socially construct gender....

I begin with an example from my own work of how conceptualizing gender as a social structure helps to organize the findings and even push forward an understanding of the resistance toward an egalitarian division of family work among contemporary American heterosexual couples. This is an area of research that incorporates a concern with nurturing children, housework, and emotional labor. My own question, from as early as graduate school, was whether men could mother well enough that those who care about children's well-being would want them to do so. Trained in the warfare model of science, my dissertation was a test of structural versus individualist theories (Kanter 1977) of men's mothering. As someone who considered herself a structuralist of some generic sort, I hypothesized (Risman 1983) that when men were forced into the social role of primary parent, they could become just like mothers: The parenting role (e.g., a measure of family structure) would wipe out the effects of individual gendered selves in my models. What I found was, alas, more complicated. At the time, I concluded that men could "mother" but did not do so in ways identical to women (Risman 1983). After having been influenced by studies showing that tokenism worked differently when men were the tokens (Williams 1992; Zimmer 1988) and that money could not buy power in marriage for women quite as it seemed to for men (Brines 1994; Ferree 1990), I came to the realization that gender itself was a structure and would not disappear when men and women were distributed across the variety of structural positions that organize our social world.

To ask the question, Can men mother, presuming that gender itself is a social structure leads us to look at all the ways that gender constrains men's mothering and under what conditions those change. Indeed, one of my most surprising, and unanticipated, findings was that single fathers who were primary caretakers came to describe themselves more often than other men with adjectives such as "nurturant," "warm," and "child oriented," those adjectives we social scientists use to measure femininity. Single fathers' identities changed based on their experiences as primary parents. In my research, men whose wives worked full-time did not, apparently, do enough mothering to have such experiences influence their own sense of selves. Most married fathers hoard the opportunity for leisure that frees them from the responsibilities of parenting that might create such identity change. My questions became more complicated but more useful when I conceptualized gender as a social structure. When and under what conditions do gendered selves matter? When do interactional expectations have the power to overcome previous internalized predispositions? What must change at the institutional level to allow for expectations to change at the interactional level? Does enough change on the interactional dimension shift the moral accountability that then leads to collective action in social organizations? Could feminist parents organize and create a social movement that forces workplaces to presume that valuable workers also have family responsibilities? . . .

Feminist scholarship must seek to understand how and why gender gets done, consciously or not, to help those who hope to stop doing it. I end by focusing our attention on what I see as the next frontier for feminist change agents: A focus on the processes that might spur change at the interactional or cultural dimension of the gender structure. We have begun to socialize our children differently, and while identities are hardly postgender, the sexism inherent in gender socialization is now widely recognized. Similarly, the organizational rules and institutional laws have by now often been rewritten to be gender neutral, at least in some nations. While gender-neutral laws in a gender-stratified society may have short-term negative consequences (e.g., displaced homemakers who never imagined having to support themselves after marriage), we can hardly retreat from equity in the law or organizations. It is the interactional and cultural dimensions of gender that have yet to be tackled with a social change agenda. . . .

Feminist scholarship always wrestles with the questions of how one can use the knowledge we create in the interest of social transformation. As feminist scholars, we must talk beyond our own borders. This kind of theoretical work becomes meaningful if we can eventually take it public. Feminist sociology must be public sociology (Burawoy 2004). We must eventually take what we have learned from our theories and research beyond professional journals to our students and to those activists who seek to disrupt and so transform gender relations. We must consider how the knowledge we create can help those who desire a more egalitarian social world to refuse to do gender at all, or to do it with rebellious reflexiveness to help transform the world around them. For those without a sociological perspective, social change through socialization and through legislation are the easiest to envision. We need to shine a spotlight on the dimension of cultural interactional expectations as it is here that work needs to begin.

We must remember, however, that much doing gender at the individual and interactional levels gives pleasure as well as reproduces inequality, and until we find other socially acceptable means to replace that opportunity for pleasure, we can hardly advocate for its cessation. The question of how gender elaboration has been woven culturally into the fabric of sexual desire deserves more attention. Many of our allies believe that "viva la difference" is required for sexual passion, and few would find a postgender society much of a feminist utopia if it came at the cost of sexual play. No one wants to be part of a revolution where she or he cannot dirty dance.

In conclusion, I have made the argument that we need to conceptualize gender as a social structure, and by doing so, we can analyze the ways in which gender is embedded at the individual, interactional, and institutional dimensions of our society. This situates gender at the same level of significance as the economy and the polity. In addition, this framework helps us to disentangle the relative strength of a variety of causal mechanisms for explaining any given outcome without dismissing the possible relevance of other processes that are situated at different dimensions of analysis. Once we have a conceptual tool to organize the encyclopedic research on gender, we can systematically build on our knowledge and progress to understanding the strength and direction of causal processes within a complicated multidimensional recursive theory. I have also argued that our concern with intersectionality must continue to be paramount but that different structures of inequality have different infrastructure and perhaps different influential causal mechanisms at any given historical moment. Therefore, we need to follow a both/and strategy, to understand gender structure, race structure, and other structures of inequality as they currently operate, while also systematically paying attention to how these axes of domination intersect. Finally, I have suggested that we pay more attention to doing research and writing theory with explicit attention to how our work can come to be "fighting words" (Collins 1998) to help transform as well as inform society. If we can identify the mechanisms that create gender, perhaps we can offer alternatives to them and so use our scholarly work to contribute to envisioning a feminist utopia.

References

Brines, Julie. 1994. "Economic Dependency, Gender, and the Division of Labor at Home." *American Journal of Sociology* 100: 652–688.

Burawoy, Michael. 2004. "Public Sociologies: Contradictions, Dilemmas and Possibilities." *Social Forces.* 80: 1603–18.

Collins, Patricia Hill. 1998. *Fighting Words: Black Women and the Search for Justice.* Minneapolis: University of Minnesota Press.

Ferree, Myra Marx. 1990. "Beyond Separate Spheres: Feminism and Family Research." *Journal of Marriage and the Family* 53: 866–884.

Kanter, Rosabeth. 1977. *Men and Women of the Corporation.* New York: Basic Books.

Risman, Barbara J. 1983. "Necessity and the Invention of Mothering." Ph.D. diss., University of Washington.

Williams, Christine. 1992. "The Glass Escalator: Hidden Advantages for Men in the 'Female' Professions. *Social Problems* 39: 253–267.

Williams, Joan. 2000. *Unbending Gender: Why Family and Work Conflict and What to Do About It.* New York: Oxford University Press.

Zimmer, Lynn. 1988. "Tokenism and Women in the Workplace: The Limits of Gender-Neutral Theory." *Social Problems* 35: 64–77.

Degendering

If gender is socially constructed within individuals as part of their identity in interaction with gendered others and within the constraining structures of the gendered social order, how do we create change that will occur on all levels simultaneously? In *Breaking the Bowls* (Lorber, 2005), I argued for *degendering*. It means not doing gender, as an individual, a social other, or a member of a family or work organization.

Degendering is a recognition of the myriad ways that we do gender—and deliberately not continuing these practices. Degendering means not assigning tasks in the home and workplace by gender. It means not grouping children by gender in schools. Degendering means confronting gender expectations in face-to-face interaction and underplaying gender categories in language (not saying "ladies and gentlemen" but "colleagues and friends"). Where language itself is built on gender categories, developing gender-neutral ways of addressing and referring to people will be a major and revolutionary enterprise, but its accomplishment would go a long way towards degendering.

As degendering agents in our everyday lives, we can confront the ubiquitous bureaucratic and public gender binaries just as intersexual people do—by thinking about whether we want to conform or challenge. We could stop ticking off the M/F boxes at the top of every form we fill out or ask about the need for them. Shannon Faulkner, a girl, got into the Citadel, an all-boys military school, because the admission form did not have an M/F check-off box; it was assumed that only boys would apply. All her credentials and biographical information qualified her for admission, but when the Citadel administration found out she was a girl, she was immediately disqualified. The person didn't change; her qualifications remained the same. The legal status—and all the stereotypical baggage about capabilities that comes with it—changed. It was on that basis that she successfully claimed gender discrimination and challenged the all-male status of the Citadel (Kimmel 2000). That is precisely what degendering would do.

The feminist task of gaining citizenship rights and economic equality for most of the world's women is undeniably of first priority, but a second task can be done in Western societies where women are not so terribly unequal—challenging the binary structures just a little bit more by asking why they are necessary at all. Degendering means freedom from gender restrictions, but it does not mean anarchy. Gradual degendering would be preferable, until all taken-for-granted gender practices are replaced with degendered practices in bureaucracies and work organizations and in informal interaction in everyday life. Gendering is taken for granted now, done without reflection. Without awareness of how much we do gender, we cannot degender. Degendering is disruptive, but that is the point of it—to call attention to what is done without thinking, think about it, and not do it. In order to have a positive goal, I offer a thought experiment—imagining a world without gender.

Imagining a World without Gender

Judith Lorber

Brooklyn College and Graduate Center, CUNY

Love and sexuality, friendships and intimacies revolve around people with a mutual attraction to each other's bodies, intellects, interests, and personalities. Males inseminate willing females through copulation or provide sperm for insemination. Females who want to, give birth to infants. These infants become part of families of different kinds of kinship groups and households composed of a variety of responsible adults. They are breast-fed by lactating females and cared for by competent child minders. They receive love and affection from the older children and adults in their circles of relationships. Their favorites and role models vary over time, but there is at least one legally responsible adult for every child.

Children are not sexed at birth—their genitalia are irrelevant in the choice of names, blankets, and clothing. "A child is born to...," the announcements read. In play groups and schools, children are organized by age, size, talents, skills, reading ability, math competence, whatever the needs of the group. Children's talents, skills, and interests shape their choices of further education and job training.

If we can assume nonassortment by other invidious categories, such as racial ethnic group, people would be hired on the basis of their credentials, experience, interviewing skills, and connections. The salary scales and prestige value of occupations and professions depend on various kinds of social assessments, just as they do now, but the positions that pay best and are valued most are not monopolized by any one type of person. Science is done by scientists, teaching by teachers, cultural productions by writers, artists, musicians, dancers, singers, actors, and media producers. The beliefs and values and technologies of the time and place govern the content.

Positions of public authority in corporations, bureaucracies, and governments are attained by competition, sponsorship and patronage, networking, and other familiar forms of mobility. Charity, honesty, and competence are as evident as corruption, double-dealing, and shoddy work—people are people.

So there are still murders, wars, and other forms of violence, although perhaps through an ethical evolution, societies might develop in which people are taught how to handle anger and conflict in positive ways. But rules are made to be broken, so there is still a need for police and soldiers, judges and prison guards.

Games and sports are played for fitness and fun. New games have been devised that put less emphasis on body shapes and more on skill. In competitions, people of different levels of body functioning and abilities compete against one another in a variety of "Olympics."

In the major and minor religions, new liturgies and rituals are in use, but old ones are turned to for their historical cultural value, as are the old novels, plays, songs, and operas. Those who have the calling and the talent lead congregations and prayer services and speak for the god(s).

New language forms have developed that do not mark or categorize the speaker or the spoken about.[a] The old forms of language and literature are studied for their archaic beauty and what they tell us about the way people used to live and behave and think.

People group and identify themselves on the basis of all sorts of similarities and disdain others on the basis of all sorts of differences. Sometimes those who identify with each other wear similar clothing or hair styles or jewelry or cosmetics. Sometimes these displays become fashions for all who consider themselves chic. Group and individual ways of speaking, dressing, and behaving serve as cues for interaction and distancing.

There are no women or men, boys or girls—just parents and children, siblings and cousins, and other newly named kin, and partners and lovers, friends and enemies, managers and workers, rulers and ruled, conformers and rebels. People form social groups and have statuses and positions and rights and responsibilities—and no gender. The world goes on quite familiarly but is radically changed—gender no longer determines an infant's upbringing, a child's education, an adult's occupation, a parent's care, an economy's distribution of wealth, a country's politicians, the world's power brokers.

Note

a. Oyěwùmí, commenting on the genderization of Yorùbá by English colonials, says, "Genderlessness in language is not necessarily a futuristic undertaking; sadly, it could well be passé." Oyèrónké Oyewùmí, *The Invention of Women: Making an African Sense of Western Gender Discourses*. Minneapolis: University of Minnesota Press, 1997, 175.

Critique

Social construction feminism is faced with a political dilemma. Getting people to understand the constrictions of gender norms and expectations and encouraging rebellion against them in daily life will not necessarily change social structures. Couples who have set up egalitarian households and who scrupulously share parenting run into work-scheduling problems. Men are still supposed to put work before family, and women are supposed to put family before work. Conversely, getting work organizations to hire men for women's jobs and women for men's jobs has not changed gender norms. Women bosses are criticized for being too assertive, while men teachers, social workers, and nurses are quickly pushed ahead into administration or specialty areas considered appropriate for men.

The dilemma of structure and action is built into the theory of social construction. Socially patterned individual actions and institutional structures construct and reinforce each other. People constantly re-create and maintain the gender norms and expectations and patterns of behavior that are built into work and family structures. They may rebel, but the main patterns of the gendered social order are very slow to change.

In addition to challenging the ideological underpinnings of gender divisions and gendered behavior as natural, long-lasting change of the deeply gendered social order would have to mean a conscious reordering of the gendered division of labor in the family and at work, and at the same time, challenging the assumptions about the capabilities of women and men that justify the status quo. Such change is unlikely to come about unless the pervasiveness of the social institution of gender and its social construction are openly confronted. Since the processes of gendering end up making them invisible, where are we to start? With individual awareness and attitude change, or with restructuring social institutions and behavioral change? Certainly, both individuals and institutions need to be altered to achieve gender equality, but it may be impossible to do both at once.

Summary

Social construction feminism focuses on the processes that both create gender differences and render the construction of gender invisible. One of the most common gendered social practice is the division of labor in the home that allocates child care and housework to women. Another process that supports this gender differentiation is the insistence in two-earner families that the man is the breadwinner, even if the woman brings in more income. The other side of this process is the woman's continued responsibility for care of the household and family members. The work force is constantly gendered through gender typing of occupations so that women and men do not do the same kind of work, and women are paid less. Regendering is common—occupations go from men's work to women's work and the gender typing is justified both ways by "natural" masculine and feminine characteristics. In general, women and men are compared in ways that ignore similarities and differences attributable to other social statuses.

Gender-inappropriate behaviors and appearances that could challenge conventional gendering are suppressed. Deviations from what is considered normal for boys and girls are subject to disapproval and punishment by parents, teachers, and peers. In adults, attempts at gender rebellion are controlled by laws, religions, and psychiatry. The beliefs about gender norms are legitimated by the constant scientific search for biologically based sex differences. This search replicates gender divisions by downplaying overlaps and similarities between male and female physiology and men's and women's behavior.

For the most part, people act in approved ways because the whole gendered social order is set up for men and women to feel different and act differently. Even when social institutions change, as when girls are admitted to an all-boys' school or men are hired for a "woman's" job, such as nurse, gender boundaries are not erased. Ways are found for the girls to be distinguishable from the boys (skirts, longer hair), and for the men to do more masculine work (nursing men patients, becoming administrators).

The gendered social order constructs not only differences but gender inequality. Appropriately gendered behavior builds up men's dominance and women's subordination. The gendered structure of family work puts more of the burden of housework and child care on the wife, even if she is a high earner in a prestigious career. The gendered division of the labor market reserves better-paying jobs and positions of authority for men. All this has been well documented by earlier feminisms. What social construction feminism reveals is how we all collude in maintaining the unequal gendered social order, most of the time without even realizing we are "doing gender." In addition, social construction feminism has analyzed the multiple ways that gender is built into the social structure of all the institutions in a society. In this feminist theory, gender itself is a social institution.

Social construction feminist research has produced extensive evidence of how gendered differences are created and reinforced, how gendered bodies, sexualities, and identities are constructed, how families and workplaces are the source of processes and structures of gendering, and how these all add up to continued gender inequality because of the continued devaluation of the female, feminine, woman side of the binary. A rebellion rooted in refusal to do gender would have truly earth-shaking consequences for the gendered social order we continue to live in.

SUGGESTED READINGS IN SOCIAL CONSTRUCTION FEMINISM

Cameron, Deborah. 2007. *The Myth of Mars and Venus: Do Men and Women Really Speak Different Languages?* New York: Oxford University Press.

Connell, R. W. 1987. *Gender and Power.* Stanford, CA: Stanford University Press.

Deutsch, Francine M. 2007. "Undoing Gender." *Gender & Society* 21:106–127.

Goffman, Erving. 1976. *Gender Advertisements.* New York: Harper Colophon.

Harrison, Wendy Cealey, and John Hood-Williams. 2002. *Beyond Sex and Gender.* Thousand Oaks, CA: Sage.

Kessler, Suzanne J., and Wendy McKenna. 1978. *Gender: An Ethnomethodological Approach.* Chicago: University of Chicago Press.

Kimmel, Michael S. 2000. "Saving the Males: The Sociological Implications of the Virginia Military Institute and the Citadel." *Gender & Society* 14: 494–516.

Lorber, Judith. 1994. *Paradoxes of Gender*. New Haven, CT: Yale University Press.

———. 1996. "Beyond the Binaries: Depolarizing the Categories of Sex, Sexuality, and Gender," *Sociological Inquiry* 66: 143–159.

———. 2000. "Using Gender to Undo Gender: A Feminist Degendering Movement." *Feminist Theory* 1:101–118.

———. 2001. "It's the 21st Century—Do You Know What Gender You Are?" In Vasilikie Demos and Marcia Texler Segal, eds., *International Feminist Challenges to Theory*. Greenwich, CT: JAI Press.

———. 2005. *Breaking the Bowls: Degendering and Feminist Change*. New York: W. W. Norton.

Lucal, Betsy. 1999. "What It Means to Be Gendered Me: Life on the Boundaries of a Dichotomous Gender System." *Gender & Society* 13: 781–797.

Martin, Patricia Yancey. 2004. "Gender as Social Institution." *Social Forces* 82: 1249–1275.

Ridgeway, Cecilia L., and Shelley J. Correll. 2004. "Unpacking the Gender System: A Theoretical Perspective on Gender Beliefs and Social Relations." *Gender & Society* 4: 510–531.

Risman, Barbara. 2004. "Gender as Social Structure: Theory Wrestling with Activism." *Gender & Society* 18: 429–450.

Silver, Catherine B. 2003. "Gendered Identities in Old Age: Toward (De)gendering?" *Journal of Aging Studies* 17: 379–397.

West, Candace, and Sarah Fenstermaker. 1995. "Doing Difference." *Gender & Society* 9: 8–37.

West, Candace, and Don Zimmerman. 1987. "Doing Gender." *Gender & Society* 1: 125–151.

Bodies

Brumberg, Joan Jacobs. 1997. *The Body Project: An Intimate History of American Girls*. New York: Vintage.

Davis, Kathy. 1995. *Reshaping the Female Body: The Dilemma of Cosmetic Surgery*. New York: Routledge.

Deutsch, Helen, and Felicity Nussbaum, eds. 2000. *"Defects": Engendering the Modern Body*. Ann Arbor: University of Michigan Press.

Dowling, Collette. 2000. *The Frailty Myth: Redefining the Physical Potential of Women and Girls*. New York: Random House.

Dworkin, Shari L. and Faye Linda Wachs. 2008. *Body Panic: Gender, Health, and the Selling of Fitness*. New York: New York University Press.

Fausto-Sterling, Anne. 2000. *Sexing the Body: Gender Politics and the Construction of Sexuality*. New York: Basic Books.

Fine, Michelle and Adrienne Asch, eds. 1988. *Women with Disabilities: Essays in Psychology, Culture, and Politics*. Philadelphia: Temple University Press.

Gerschick, Thomas J. and Adam Stephen Miller. 1994. "Gender Identities at the Crossroads of Masculinity and Physical Disability." *Masculinities* 2: 34–55.

Gimlin, Debra L. 2002. *Body Work: Beauty and Self-Image in American Culture*. Berkeley: University of California Press.

Haiken, Elizabeth. 1999. *Venus Envy: A History of Cosmetic Surgery*. Baltimore: Johns Hopkins.

Hatoum, Ida Jodette, and Deborah Belle. 2004. "Mags and Abs: Media Consumption and Bodily Concerns in Men." *Sex Roles* 51: 397– 407.

Heywood, Leslie, and Shari Dworkin. 2003. *Built to Win: The Female Athlete as Cultural Icon*. Minneapolis, MN: University of Minnesota.

Hobson, Janell. 2005. *Venus in the Dark: Blackness and Beauty in Popular Culture*. New York: Routledge.

Klein, Alan. M. 1993. *Little Big Men: Bodybuilding Subculture and Gender Construction*. Albany, NY: State University of New York Press.

Kudlick, Catherine. 2005. "The Blind Man's Harley: White Canes and Gender Identity in America." *Signs* 30: 1549–1606.

Laqueur, Thomas W. 1990. *Making Sex: Body and Gender from the Greeks to Freud*. Cambridge, MA: Harvard University Press.

Lorber, Judith, and Lisa Jean Moore. 2002. *Gender and the Social Construction of Illness*, 2nd ed. Lanham, MD: Rowman & Littlefield/AltaMira.

———. 2007. *Gendered Bodies: Feminist Perspectives*. New York: Oxford University Press.

McCabe, Marita, and Lina Ricciardelli. 2004. "Body Image Dissatisfaction Among Males Across the Lifespan: A Review of Past Literature." *Journal of Psychosomatic Research* 56: 675–685.

O'Brien, Ruth. 2005. *Bodies in Revolt: Gender, Disability, and an Alternative Ethic of Care*. New York: Routledge.

Oudshoorn, Nelly. 1994. *Beyond the Natural Body: An Archeology of Sex Hormones*. New York: Routledge.

Smith, Bonnie G., and Beth Hutchison, eds. 2004. *Gendering Disability*. New Brunswick, NJ: Rutgers University Press.

van den Wijngaard, Marianne. 1997. *Reinventing the Sexes: The Biomedical Construction of Femininity and Masculinity*. Bloomington: Indiana University Press.

Weitz, Rose, ed. 2002. *The Politics of Women's Bodies: Sexuality, Appearance and Behavior*, 2nd ed. New York: Oxford University Press.

Wendell, Susan. 1996. *The Rejected Body: Feminist Philosophical Reflections on Disability*. New York: Routledge.

Children

Bem, Sandra Lipsitz. 1983. "Gender Schema Theory and Its Implications for Child Development: Raising Gender-Aschematic Children in a Gender-Schematic Society." *Signs* 8: 598–616.

Lamb, Sharon, and Lyn Mikel Brown. 2006. *Packaging Girlhood: Rescuing Our Daughters from Marketers' Schemes*. New York: St. Martin's Press.

Martin, Karin A., 1998. "Becoming a Gendered Body: Practices of Preschools." *American Sociological Review* 63: 494–511.

Stacey, Judith, and Timothy Biblarz. 2001. "(How) Does the Sexual Orientation of Parents Matter?" *American Sociological Review* 66: 159–183.

Thorne, Barrie. 1993. *Gender Play: Girls and Boys at School*. New Brunswick, NJ: Rutgers University Press.

Families

Bem, Sandra Lipsitz. 1998. *An Unconventional Family*. New Haven, CT: Yale University Press.

Berk, Sarah Fenstermaker. 1985. *The Gender Factory: The Apportionment of Work in American Households*. New York: Plenum.

Bernstein, Mary, and Renate Reimann, eds. 2001. *Queer Families, Queer Politics: Challenging Culture and the State.* New York: Columbia University Press.

Bielby, Denise D., and William T. Bielby. 1988. "She Works Hard for the Money: Household Responsibilities and the Allocation of Work Effort," *American Journal of Sociology* 93: 1031–1059.

Carrington, Christopher. 1999. *No Place Like Home: Relationships and Family Life Among Lesbians and Gay Men.* Chicago: University of Chicago Press.

Dalton, Susan E., and Denise D. Bielby, 2000. "'That's Our Kind of Constellation': Lesbian Mothers Negotiate Institutionalized Understandings of Gender within the Family." *Gender & Society* 14: 36–61.

DeVault, Marjorie L. 1991. *Feeding the Family: The Social Organization of Caring as Gender Work.* Chicago: University of Chicago Press.

Dunne, Gillian A. 2000. "Opting into Motherhood: Lesbians Blurring the Boundaries and Transforming the Meaning of Parenthood and Kinship." *Gender & Society* 14: 11–35.

Fineman, Martha Albertson. 1995. *The Neutered Mother, the Sexual Family and Other Twentieth Century Tragedies.* New York: Routledge.

Hertz, Rosanna, and Nancy L. Marshall, eds. 2001. *Working Families: The Transformation of the American Home.* Berkeley: University of California Press.

Malone, Kareen, and Rose Cleary. 2002. "(De)Sexing the Family: Theorizing the Social Science of Lesbian Families." *Feminist Theory* 3: 271–293.

Potuchek, Jean L. 1997. *Who Supports the Family? Gender and Breadwinning in Dual-Earner Marriages.* Stanford, CA: Stanford University Press.

Risman, Barbara J. 1987. "Intimate Relationships from a Microstructural Perspective: Men Who Mother." *Gender & Society* 1: 6–32.

———. 1998. *Gender Vertigo: American Families in Transition.* New Haven, CT: Yale University Press.

Sullivan, Oriel. 2004. "Changing Gender Practices Within the Household," *Gender & Society* 18: 207–222.

Williams, Joan. 2000. *Unbending Gender: Why Family and Work Conflict and What to Do About It.* New York: Oxford University Press.

Sexualities

Foucault, Michel. 1978. *The History of Sexuality: An Introduction.* Trans., Robert Hurley. New York: Pantheon.

Greenberg, David F. 1988. *The Construction of Homosexuality.* Chicago: University of Chicago Press.

Kitzinger, Celia. 1987. *The Social Construction of Lesbianism.* Thousand Oaks, CA: Sage.

Laqueur, Thomas W. 2003. *Solitary Sex: A Cultural History of Masturbation.* New York: Zone Books.

Ortner, Sherry B., and Harriet Whitehead, eds. 1981. *Sexual Meanings: The Cultural Construction of Gender and Sexuality.* Cambridge, UK: Cambridge University Press.

Rubin, Gayle. 1975. "The Traffic in Women: Notes on the Political Economy of Sex." In Rayna Rapp Reiter, ed., *Toward an Anthropology of Women.* New York: Monthly Review Press.

———. 1984. "Thinking Sex: Notes for a Radical Theory of the Politics of Sexuality." In Carole S. Vance, ed., *Pleasure and Danger: Exploring Female Sexuality.* Boston: Routledge & Kegan Paul.

Rust, Paula C. Rodríguez, ed. *Bisexuality in the United States.* New York: Columbia University Press, 2000.

Seidman, Steven. 2003. *The Social Construction of Sexuality.* New York: W.W. Norton.

Schwartz, Pepper, and Virginia Rutter. *The Gender of Sexuality.* Thousand Oaks, CA: Pine Forge Press.

Storr, Merl, ed. 1999. *Bisexuality: A Critical Reader.* New York: Routledge.

Tucker, Naomi, ed. 1995. *Bisexual Politics: Theories, Queries, and Visions.* Binghamton, NY: Harrington Park Press.

Weinberg, Martin S., Colin J. Williams, and Douglas W. Pryor. 1994. *Dual Attraction: Understanding Bisexuality.* New York: Oxford University Press.

Intersexuality

Butler, Julie. 2003. "X Marks the Spot for Intersex Alex." West Australian Newspapers Limited, January 11. Retrieved from http://www.bodieslikeours.org/intersexalex.html.

Chase, Cheryl. 1998. "Hermaphrodites with Attitude: Mapping the Emergence of Intersex Political Activism." *GLQ: A Journal of Lesbian and Gay Studies* 4:189–211.

———. 2000. "Genital Surgery on Children Below the Age of Consent: Intersex Genital Mutilation." In Lenore Szuchman and Frank Muscarella, eds., *Psychological Perspectives on Human Sexuality.* New York: Wiley.

Dreger, Alice Domurat. 1998. *Hermaphrodites and the Medical Invention of Sex.* Cambridge, MA: Harvard University Press.

———, ed. 1999. *Intersexuality in the Age of Ethics.* Hagerstown MD: University Publishing Group.

Foucault, Michel. 1980. *Herculine Barbin: Being the Recently Discovered Memoirs of a Nineteenth-Century French Hermaphrodite.* Trans., Richard McDougall. New York: Pantheon.

Hird, Myra J. 2000. "Gender's Nature: Intersexuals, Transsexuals, and the 'Sex'/'Gender' Binary." *Feminist Theory* 1: 347–364.

———. 2003. "Considerations for a Psychoanalytic Theory of Gender Identity and Sexual Desire: The Case of Intersex." *Signs* 28: 1067–1092.

Kessler, Suzanne J. 1998. *Lessons from the Intersexed.* New Brunswick, NJ: Rutgers University Press.

Preves, Sharon E. 1998. "For the Sake of the Children: Destigmatizing Intersexuality." Special Issue on Intersex, *Journal of Clinical Ethics* 9: 411–420.

———. 2003. *Intersex and Identity: The Contested Self.* New Brunswick, NJ: Rutgers University Press.

———. 2004. "Out of the O.R. and into the Streets: Exploring the Impact of Intersex Activism." *Research in Political Sociology* 13: 179–223.

Turner, Stephanie S. 1999. "Intersex Identities: Locating New Intersections of Sex and Gender" *Gender & Society* 13: 457–479.

Zucker, Kenneth J. 1999. "Intersexuality and Gender Identity Differentiation." *Annual Review of Sex Research* 10: 1–69.

Work Organizations

Acker, Joan. 1990. "Hierarchies, Jobs, and Bodies: A Theory of Gendered Organizations." *Gender & Society* 4: 139–158.

Britton, Dana M. 2000. "The Epistemology of the Gendered Organization." *Gender & Society* 14: 418–434.

Gherardi, Silvia. 1995. *Gender, Symbolism and Organizational Cultures.* Thousand Oaks, CA: Sage.

Hearn, Jeff R., and Wendy Parkin. 2002. *Gender, Sexuality and Violence in Organizations: The Unspoken Forces of Organization Violations.* Thousand Oaks, CA: Sage.

Martin, Patricia Yancey. 2001. "'Mobilizing Masculinities': Women's Experiences of Men at Work." *Organization* 8: 587–618.

———. 2003. "'Said and Done' versus 'Saying and Doing': Gendering Practices, Practicing Gender at Work." *Gender & Society* 17: 342–366.

Mennino, Sue Falter, and April Brayfield. 2002. "Job-Family Trade-Offs: The Multidimensional Effects of Gender." *Work & Occupations* 29: 226–256.

Rantalaiho, Liisa, and Tula Heiskanen, eds. 1997. *Gendered Practices in Working Life.* New York: St. Martin's Press.

Ridgeway, Cecilia L. 1997. "Interaction and the Conservation of Gender Inequality: Considering Employment." *American Sociological Review* 62: 218–235.

Wajcman, Judy. 1998. *Managing Like a Man: Women and Men in Corporate Management.* University Park: Pennsylvania State University Press.

12

Postmodern Feminism and Queer Theory

SOURCES OF GENDER INEQUALITY

- The belief that gender and sexuality are fixed and inevitable
- Constraints of gender and sexual "normality"
- Cultural and individual replication of normative gender and sexual behavior

POLITICS

- Constantly questioning what is supposedly normal about gender and sexuality
- Demonstrating the fluidity of gender and sexual boundaries
- Queering—subverting binary gender and sexual categories
- Fighting for gay and transgender rights

CRITIQUE

- Postmodern free agency and queering have a narrow, individualistic scope
- Too little attention is paid to structural and institutional controls over behavior
- Emphasis on individual acts of transgression does not change gender constraints

CONTRIBUTIONS

- The concept of *performativity*—gender does not exist without gender display
- Deconstruction—making visible the gender and sexual performances in what is considered normal and natural
- Queer theory—challenging the gender, sex, and sexual binaries with multiple sexualities and transgendering

- Making visible and destigmatizing diverse sexualities and gender performances

Postmodern feminism theoretically builds on social construction feminism, but it emphasizes agency, not structure, and takes its examples from culture rather than the social sciences. It focuses on gender identities, body displays, and sexualities, arguing that these can be shaped and manipulated by individuals. Postmodern feminism strips away the façade of the normal and natural, showing that what we don't see is the *performativity* of heterosexuality, femininity, masculinity. Postmodern feminism claims that it is the constant performance of normative gender and sexuality that maintains the gendered social order.

Those who "queer" gender and sexuality rebel against the strictures of oppositional and fixed categories. They construct ambiguities and blur borders in order to undermine the social foundations of physical, sexual, and gender binaries. Change will come, they argue, when there are so many sexes, sexualities, and genders that one cannot be played against the other as normal and deviant, valued and stigmatized.

Postmodernism and Feminism

Postmodernism undermines foundational categories by insisting that bodies, identities, and statuses are contingent—time-bound, situational, and culturally shaped. Feminism has been a movement for and about women. If woman and man, male and female, heterosexuality and homosexuality are not clear oppositional categories, then how can we have feminist research and politics? Where will the data that show inequality come from? How will activists fight for the rights of the oppressed if the oppressed are constantly shape-shifting? Some feminists have rejected postmodernism, claiming it undermines the whole feminist enterprise. Others have called for using postmodern ideas to advance feminism's project of challenging the gender order.

Postmodern feminists insist that postmodernism can free feminism from the constraints of gender norms, conventional body ideals, and heteronormativity. Using postmodern methods of deconstructing the ways that cultures produce symbolic social worlds of images and values, postmodern feminism shows how gender and sexual norms and expectations are produced and reproduced.

Deconstruction

Postmodern feminism examines the ways societies create beliefs about gender at any time (now and in the past) with *discourses* embedded in cultural representations or *texts*. Not just art, literature, and the mass media, but anything produced by a social group, including newspapers, political pronouncements, and religious liturgy, is a *text*. A text's *discourse* is what it says, does not say, and hints at (sometimes called a *subtext*). The historical and social context and the material conditions under which a text is produced become part of the text's discourse. If a movie or newspaper is produced in a time of conservative values or under a repressive political regime, its discourse is going to be different from what is produced during times of openness or social change. Who provides the money, who does the creative work, and who oversees the managerial side all influence what a text conveys to its audience. The projected audience also shapes any text, although the actual audience may read quite different meanings from those intended by the producers. *Deconstruction* is the process of teasing out all these aspects of a text.

The concepts of deconstruction and texts derived from cultural studies may sound quite esoteric, but we are all familiar with these processes. The coverage of Princess Diana's death and funeral created discourses about her—as wife, mother, divorcée, and benefactor. The days before the funeral were full of discourses on the meaning of royalty. Her funeral became a public ritual with a subtext on the proper expression of grief. As spectators, we read ourselves into the text of her life, using parallels with our own lives or fantasies about how we would like to live.

Soap operas, romance novels, and the public and private behavior of media stars are "read" by women the way Diana's life was; action films, war novels, and the public and private behavior of sport stars are the stuff of men's spectatorship. Postmodern feminism deconstructs cultural representations of gender, as seen in movies, videos, TV, popular music, advertising—whether aimed at adults, teenagers, or children—as well as paintings, operas, theater productions, ballet, and the Olympics. These are all discourses that overtly and subliminally tell us something about female and male bodies, sexual desire, and gender roles. A romantic song about the man who got away glorifies heterosexuality; a tragedy deploring the death of a salesman tells us that men's hard work should pay off. These discourses influence the way we think about our world, without questioning the underlying assumptions about gender and sexuality. They encourage approved-of choices about work, marriage, and having children by showing them as normal and rewarding and by showing what is disapproved of as leading to a "bad end."

By unpacking the covert as well as more obvious meanings of texts, postmodern deconstruction reveals their messages. We can then accept or reject them, or use them for our own purposes. The memoirs and life histories of transgendered people, and the activities of gay men and lesbian women, as depicted in the media, create a different discourse.

Performativity

Judith Butler's concept of *performativity* encompasses the process of making gendered selves. Reiteration of conventional behavior and gender displays reproduce acceptable social norms of femaleness and maleness, femininity and masculinity, and heterosexual sexuality. This process also produces gendered selves, bodies, and identities. Performativity means that you cannot separate the doer of gender from the doing. Self and social are one and the same; one does not precede the other.

In reiteration lies the possibility for "gender trouble." Gendering has to be done over and over, almost ritualistically, to reproduce the social norms. But different ways of gendering produce differently gendered people. So, with deliberation, one might create oneself differently gendered, and indeed, transgendered people and gender queers do just that.

The concept of performativity comes from Judith Butler's *Gender Trouble*. First published in 1990, when her ideas were almost incomprehensible, *Gender Trouble* has become the classic of postmodern feminism, and Butler is now an internationally acclaimed feminist philosopher. She is Professor of Rhetoric, Comparative Literature, and Women's Studies, which indicates the breadth of her work.

By 1993, Butler was rethinking the aspects of gender performativity. In *Bodies That Matter*, she takes up the materiality or bodiedness of gender performativity and discusses how doing gender is "doing bodies," constructing materialized persons, some of whom matter and others who don't.

Gender, Sex, and Sexual Performativity

Judith Butler
University of California, Berkeley

If gender is a construction, must there be an "I" or a "we" who enacts or performs that construction? How can there be an activity, a constructing, without presupposing an agent who precedes and performs that activity? How would we account for the motivation and direction of construction without such a subject? As a rejoinder, I would suggest that it takes a certain suspicion toward grammar to reconceive the matter in a different light. For if gender is constructed, it is not necessarily constructed by an "I" or a "we" who stands before that construction in any spatial or temporal sense of "before." Indeed, it is unclear that there can be an "I" or a "we" who has not been submitted, subjected to gender, where gendering is, among other things, the differentiating relations by which speaking subjects come into being. Subjected to gender, but subjectivated by gender, the "I" neither precedes nor follows the process of this gendering, but emerges only within and as the matrix of gender relations themselves.

This then returns us to the second objection, the one which claims that constructivism forecloses agency, preempts the agency of the subject, and finds itself presupposing the subject that it calls into question. To claim that the subject is itself produced in and as a gendered matrix of relations is not to do away with the subject, but only to ask after the conditions of its emergence and operation. The "activity" of this gendering cannot, strictly speaking, be a human act or expression, a willful appropriation, and it is certainly *not* a question of taking on a mask; it is the matrix through which all willing first becomes possible, its enabling cultural condition. In this sense, the matrix of gender relations is prior to the emergence of the "human." Consider the medical interpellation which (the recent emergence of the sonogram notwithstanding) shifts an infant from an "it" to a "she" or a "he," and in that naming, the girl is "girled," brought into the domain of language and kinship through the interpellation of gender. But that "girling" of the girl does not end there; on the contrary, that founding interpellation is reiterated by various authorities and throughout various intervals of time to reenforce or contest this naturalized effect. The naming is at once the setting of a boundary, and also the repeated inculcation of a norm.

Such attributions or interpellations contribute to that field of discourse and power that orchestrates, delimits, and sustains that which qualifies as "the human." We see this most clearly in the examples of those abjected beings who do not appear properly gendered; it is their very humanness that comes into question. Indeed, the construction of gender operates through *exclusionary* means, such that the human is not only produced over and against the inhuman, but through a set of foreclosures, radical erasures, which are, strictly speaking, refused the possibility of cultural articulation. Hence, it is not enough to claim that human subjects are constructed, for the construction of the human is a differential operation that produces the more and the less "human," the inhuman, the humanly unthinkable. These excluded sites come to bound the "human" as its constitutive outside, and to haunt those boundaries as the persistent possibility of their disruption and rearticulation.[a]

As a result of this reformulation of performativity, (a) gender performativity cannot be theorized apart from the forcible and reiterative practice of regulatory sexual regimes; (b) the account of agency conditioned by those very regimes of discourse/power cannot be conflated with voluntarism or individualism, much less with consumerism, and in no way presupposes a choosing subject; (c) the regime of heterosexuality operates to circumscribe and contour the "materiality" of sex, and that "materiality" is formed and sustained through and as a materialization of regulatory norms that are in part those of heterosexual hegemony; (d) the materialization of norms requires those identificatory processes by which norms are assumed or appropriated, and these identifications precede and enable the formation of a subject, but are not, strictly speaking, performed by a subject; and (e) the limits of constructivism are exposed at those boundaries of bodily life where abjected or delegitimated bodies fail to count as "bodies." If the materiality of sex is demarcated in discourse, then this demarcation will produce a domain of excluded and delegitimated "sex." Hence, it will be as important to think about how and to what end bodies are constructed as it will be to think about how and to what end bodies are *not* constructed and, further, to ask after how bodies which fail to materialize provide the necessary "outside," if not the necessary support, for the bodies which, in materializing the norm, qualify as bodies that matter.

How, then, can one think through the matter of bodies as a kind of materialization governed by regulatory norms in order to ascertain the workings of heterosexual hegemony in the formation of what qualifies as a viable body? How does that materialization of the norm in bodily formation produce a domain of abjected bodies, a field of deformation, which, in failing to qualify as the fully human, fortifies those regulatory norms? What challenge does that excluded and abjected realm produce to a symbolic hegemony that might force a radical rearticulation of what qualifies as bodies that matter, ways of living that count as "life," lives worth protecting, lives worth saving, lives worth grieving?...

Note

a. For different but related approaches to this problematic of exclusion, abjection, and the creation of "the human," see Julia Kristeva, *Powers of Horror: An Essay on Abjection*, tr. Leon Roudiez (New York: Columbia University Press, 1982); John Fletcher and Andrew Benjamin, eds., *Abjection, Melancholia and Lover: The Work of Julia Kristeva* (New York and London: Routledge, 1990); Jean-Francois Lyotard, *The Inhuman: Reflections on Time,* tr. Geoffrey Bennington and Rachel Bowlby (Stanford: Stanford University Press, 1991).

Butler ended the first edition of *Gender Trouble* by arguing for the subversive political possibilities inherent in gender performativity. She said, "The task is not whether to repeat, but how to repeat, and through a radical proliferation of gender, to *displace* the very gender norms that enable the repetition itself" (1990, 148). In the preface to the tenth anniversary edition, she says that she was somewhat too elated about these possibilities, forgetting normative gender's deep tentacles into our psyches. In *Undoing Gender,* she says:

> The genders I have in mind have been in existence for a long time, but they have not been admitted into the terms that govern reality. So it is a question of developing within law, psychiatry, social, and literary theory a new legitimating lexicon for the gender complexity that we have been living for a long time. (2004, 31)

That would mean creating a new gendered reality.

Queer Theory

In queer theory, doing gender, body, or sexuality differently—"queering"— can be subversive. What we wear and how we use and mark our bodies are signs of gender and sexual orientation. These can be parodied, flaunted, played with, and mixed up any way we want. Recently, seated in the audience at an academic lecture I gave in Germany was a young man with a conventional haircut but with orange hair, one long earring, dark red lipstick, blue nail polish on fingers and toes, a unisex black T-shirt, a yellow sarong skirt of the kind worn by men and women in tropical resorts, and clunky, open-toed sandals. Queer theorists claim such mixed gender displays create a freer social space for gender rebels and transgenders.

Western societies have a long history of parodying gender by *travesti* actors and singers. Today, people who usually live and dress conventionally play with queered gender and sexuality at costume parties and in Mardi Gras and gay pride parades.

Drag

Drag performances by male "queens" and female "kings" also queer gender and sexuality. In the sense that it openly and deliberately confronts and plays with gender, drag can be subversive. In the following excerpt, Leila Rupp, a historian, and Verta Taylor, a sociologist, discuss the ways that drag performances can be part of a social movement to subvert the gendered social order. Their conclusions are based on three years of research at the 801 Cabaret in Key West, Florida. They interviewed dozens of drag queens, attended performances, and were photographed in female drag. They suggest three criteria that make a cultural performance like a drag show oppositional and political.

Thinking about Drag as Social Protest

Leila J. Rupp

University of California, Santa Barbara

Verta Taylor

University of California, Santa Barbara

We argue that the drag queens are performing protest, are part of the gay and lesbian movement's efforts to make the world a better place for those of us with same-sex desires. Through their dress, gestures, routines, dancing, talk, comedy, and interaction with the audience, they make understandable the concept that people and desires and sexual acts and emotions cannot always be simply categorized into one of two or three possibilities. In making this argument, we are suggesting that cultural forms such as drag performances are political, and that the fact that they are cast as entertainment may make them especially effective in reaching people and changing the ways they think.

Finally, we see the consequences of the drag queens' performance of protest. In a very complicated way, they affirm gay/lesbian/bisexual/ transgender identities in contrast to heterosexual ones; but they also break down those differences and assert the common interests of all people. That they do indeed make people think and that they do indeed have the potential to change minds, if not immediately the world, are confirmed by what audience members take away from the shows.

What happens at an evening at the 801 is, we think, a story about more than one particular bar. That is partly because of the sharing of drag queen repertoires across the county, including through such major national events as Wigstock, the annual New York drag extravaganza that ended a seventeen-year run in 2001, and the multitude of local and regional drag queen contests and competitions.[a] The 801 Girls even announced one year a plan to sponsor "Drag Queen University" in Key West. An article in *Celebrate!* describes familiar scenes at Diva's, where Inga and Gugi went to perform:

> It is a place where gender blurs and reality is relative....Straight men clamor to press dollar bills into Inga's cleavage or rush to the stage to offer homage to Vogue, whose flawless rendition of Tina Turner's stage moves makes your heart pound. Lesbian ladies find themselves all fired up by Gugi Gomez's spicy Latina sensuality and straight women ignore their dates to steal a kiss and run their hands along Colby's taunt [sic] thighs. Somehow, the talents of these performers take the audience outside of themselves. At Diva's, you can be anyone you want to be.[b]

You can be anyone you want to be—and you are challenged to think differently about what you thought you were.

This is more than the story of the 801 Cabaret in yet another sense....[W]e think that what happens onstage has implications for the larger question of what makes certain types of cultural expressions political. Drag shows are entertaining, as we have seen. They attract a whole slew of people who might never venture out to watch, much less join, a gay pride celebration or a demonstration. Yet they elicit strong emotions, even sexual responses, which are likely to have a powerful impact on people. Such visceral moments make change possible. We suggest that what makes drag shows—as well as other cultural performances—political is that they subvert the traditional (in this case, gender and sexual) order, that the performers intend them to have these consequences, and that they build and affirm a gay/lesbian collective identity and also broaden the meaning of community by linking diverse audience members to the performers and to each other. Drag shows help us to see how social movements have an effect, how social movements matter.

Notes

a. See www.wigstock.nu/what is/what is.html.
b. Kate Reynolds, "The Naked Eye Review: Diva's: A Divine Diversion," *Celebrate!*, April 13, 2001, 2.

Queer theory argues that we can all be gender rebels by queering gender, sexuality, and sex in everyday life. Transgendered people live these queer gender politics.

Transgendering: Doing or Undoing Gender?

Transgendering both challenges and reifies gender binaries. Many of those who change genders feel there are two clearly marked and separated gender categories, and they deeply desire to be in the one their birth sex category did not put them into. They feel they are in the wrong body, living as the wrong gender. Even if they continue to do the same work, they want to do it as a woman, if they are male-to-female, or as a man, if they are female-to-male.

The goal of many transgendered people is to "pass" as a "normal" gendered person, a goal that is necessary for solving problems of daily life in their desired gender, but not one that disrupts the gendered social order. Those who successfully construct their gender as different from their birth assignment in order to live as a member of their chosen gender reaffirm the conventional categories of man and woman even as their behavior subtly sabotages the solidity of the categories. A transgendered male-to-female changes her body, name, legal status, relationships, clothing, hair, cosmetics, voice, speaking style, and personality, but not her education, occupation, racial ethnic status, or social class. She declares that she is now the person she always felt she was, a "woman." What does that mean?

Deirdre McCloskey (1999), an economist, claims that women make better economists than the men who dominate the field, because women take social factors into consideration, especially family relationships. McCloskey thought economics was more rhetoric than abstract mathematics when she was man. Was that because she was, deep down inside, a woman? Or can men as well as women think "like a woman"?

What is the core of gender? Transgender transformations indicate that it is legal status, body shape, and gender display. The genitalia need not be surgically altered, as long as they remain hidden. If the legal status of gender was removed, would trans people need to change genders? In "The Empire Strikes Back," Sandy Stone (1991) admits complicity with the conventionalizing gender order and its medical control agents. She felt it was necessary to pass as "normal" to mitigate the dangers of visibility as a "post-transexual." She admits that *not* passing as "normal" would be more transformative:

> This is a treacherous area, and were the silenced groups to achieve voice we might find, as feminist theorists have claimed, that the identities of individual,

embodied subjects were far less implicated in physical norms, and far more diversely spread across a rich and complex structuration of identity and desire, than is now possible to express. (298)

Transgendered people who live openly as transgendered, rather than "passing," do challenge the gender order. When a transgendered male-to-female wants to be "read" as a woman, she wears a demure dress, stockings, and high-heeled shoes, and often passes successfully. Non-conformers are much more problematic. Someone whose looks are unconventionally gendered, whose body has ambiguous sex markers, and whose sexuality is fluid belongs nowhere in our constantly gendered social world. Even transgendered people who pass cannot get appropriate health care and are in danger of violence from homophobic people. With transgendering, the free agency of postmodern feminism and queering runs head-on into the iron cage of gendered laws and bureaucracies.

But what postmodern feminism has made evident is that no one is safely "normal." The tall, hefty biological woman with short hair who dresses in jeans and t-shirts can be kicked out of women's bathrooms. To be safely "normal," one must do gender appropriately in many, many ways. Or, one can bravely choose to rebel against gendering, challenging the assumptions of "normality" and the clearness of the binary sex, sexual, and gender categories.

Critique

If social construction feminism puts too much emphasis on institutions and structures and not enough on individual actions or agency, postmodern feminism has just the opposite problem. Its emphasis is on agency, impression management, and presentation of the self in the guise and costume most likely to produce or parody conformity. Postmodern feminism is mainly concerned with deconstructing cultural productions, neglecting the controlling discourses embedded in organizational, legal, religious, and political texts.

Social construction feminism's analyses of the institutional and organizational practices that maintain the gender order could be combined with postmodern feminist analyses of gender performance and deconstruction of how high- and pop-culture representations of women and men produce gender and sexual "normality." Social construction feminism argues that the gendered social order is constantly restabilized by individual action, but postmodern feminism has shown how individuals can consciously and purposefully create disorder and gender instability, opening the way to social change.

However, postmodern free agency has a narrow, individualistic scope, and the politics of queering does not make much of a dent in the constraints of gendered legal, health, educational, economic, and other social institutions.

Summary

Postmodern feminism questions all the conventional assumptions about gender, sex, and sexuality, arguing that the categories of "man," "woman," "heterosexual," "homosexual," "male," "female" are names for performances and displays. Like social construction feminism, postmodern feminism claims that gender is created in the doing—the way we dress, use our bodies, talk, behave. Postmodern feminists recognize but do not focus on the social structures that are built up out of repeated gender performances. They write about the fluidity and multiplicity of genders, sexes, and sexualities.. There are no permanent identities, making identity politics questionable.

Politically, postmodern feminists deconstruct the messages we get about gender, bodies, and sexuality in the mass media, popular culture, sport, and the arts. These messages or texts are subliminal sermons on how to be a man or a woman, how male and female bodies should look, and how to be heterosexually sexy. If we can see through these messages, we can rebel against them.

Queer theory goes even further in destabilizing gender, sex, and sexuality. In queer theory, a body can be female and male at the same time, as when a transgendered person uses hormones to grow breasts but does not have surgery to remove the penis. Drag queens and kings parody femininity and masculinity. Queering the way you look in everyday life can play with gendered bodies, sexualities, and identities. Queer politics turns what we think is normal and natural inside out by showing how genders, bodies, and sexualities are created for conformity—and how they could be different.

Postmodern feminism is playful but has the serious intent of making us think about what we take for granted—that men and women, homosexuals and heterosexuals, males and females are totally different creatures, and that we can't make and remake ourselves. Genders, sexes, and sexualities can be as numerous and varied as the imagination can dream up. Politically, postmodern feminism's subtext is gender rebellion.

SUGGESTED READINGS IN POSTMODERN FEMINISM

Postmodern Feminist Theory

Benhabib, Seyla. 1992. *Situating the Self: Gender, Community and Postmodernism in Contemporary Ethics.* Cambridge: Polity Press.

Butler, Judith. 1990. *Gender Trouble: Feminism and the Subversion of Identity*, 10th Anniversary Edition, 1999. New York: Routledge.

———. 1993. *Bodies That Matter: On the Discursive Limits of "Sex."* New York: Routledge.

———. 2004. *Undoing Gender.* New York: Routledge.

Epstein, Julia. 1990. "Either/Or—Neither/Both: Sexual Ambiguity and the Ideology of Gender." *Genders* 7: 100–142.

Garber, Marjorie. 1992. *Vested Interests: Cross-Dressing and Cultural Anxiety.* New York: Routledge.

———. 1995. *Vice Versa: Bisexuality and the Eroticism of Everyday Life.* New York: Simon and Schuster.

———. 1998. *Symptoms of Culture.* New York: Routledge.

Herdt, Gilbert, ed. 1994. *Third Sex, Third Gender: Beyond Sexual Dimorphism in Culture and History.* New York: Zone Books.

Ingraham, Chrys. 2008. *White Weddings: Romancing Heterosexuality in Popular Culture,* 2nd ed. New York: Routledge.

Jacobs, Sue-Ellen, and Jason Cromwell. 1992. "Visions and Revisions of Reality: Reflections of Sex, Sexuality, Gender, and Gender Variance." *Journal of Homosexuality* 23: 43–69.

Mann, Patricia S. 1994. *Micro-Politics: Agency in a Post-Feminist Era.* Minneapolis: University of Minnesota Press.

Nicholson, Linda J., ed. 1990. *Feminism/Postmodernism.* New York: Routledge.

Queen, Carol. 1997. *Real Live Nude Girl: Chronicles of a Sex-Positive Culture.* San Francisco: Cleis Press.

Queen, Carol, and Lawrence Schimel, eds. 1997. *PoMoSexuals: Challenging Assumptions About Gender and Sexuality.* San Francisco: Cleis Press.

Richardson, Diane, ed. 1996. *Theorizing Heterosexuality: Telling It Straight.* Buckingham, UK: Open University Press.

Rubin, Gayle. 1992. "Of Catamites and Kings: Reflections on Butch, Gender and Boundaries." In Joan Nestle, ed., *The Persistent Desire: A Femme-Butch Reader.* New York: Alyson Books.

Walters, Suzanna Danuta. 1995. *Material Girls: Making Sense of Feminist Cultural Theory.* Berkeley: University of California Press.

———. 1996. "From Here to Queer: Radical Feminism, Postmodernism, and the Lesbian Menace (Or, Why Can't a Woman Be More Like a Fag?)" *Signs* 21: 830–869.

Wilchins, Riki Anne. 1997. *Read My Lips: Sexual Subversion and the End of Gender.* New York: Firebrand Books.

Queer Theory

Atkins, Dawn, ed. 1998. *Looking Queer: Image and Identity in Lesbian, Bisexual, Gay and Transgendered Communities.* Binghamton, NY: Haworth.

Beemyn, Brett, and Mickey Eliason, eds. 1996. *Queer Studies: A Lesbian, Gay, Bisexual and Transgender Anthology.* New York: New York University Press.

Damsky, Lee, ed. 2000. *Sex and Single Girls: Straight and Queer Women on Sexuality.* Seattle, WA: Seal Press.

Jagose, Annamarie. 1996. *Queer Theory (Interpretations).* Melbourne, AU: Melbourne University Press.

Muñoz, José. 1999. *Disidentifications: Queers of Color and the Performance of Politics.* New York: New York University Press.

Namaste, Ki. 1994. "The Politics of Inside/Out: Queer Theory, Poststructuralism, and a Sociological Approach to Sexuality." *Sociological Theory* 12: 220–231.

Nestle, Joan, Riki Wilchins, and Clare Howell, eds. 2002. *GenderQueer: Voices from Beyond the Sexual Binary.* New York: Alyson Books.

Sedgwick, Eve Kosofsky. 1990. *Epistemology of the Closet.* Berkeley: University of California Press.

———. 1993. *Tendencies.* Durham, NC: Duke University Press.

———, ed. 1997. *Novel Gazing: Queer Readings in Fiction.* Durham, NC: Duke University Press.

Seidman, Steven. 1997. *Difference Troubles: Queering Social Theory and Sexual Politics.* Cambridge, UK: Cambridge University Press.

Stein, Arlene, and Ken Plummer. 1994. "'I Can't Even Think Straight.' 'Queer' Theory and the Missing Sexual Revolution in Sociology." *Sociological Theory* 12: 178–187.

Sullivan, Nikki. 2003. *A Critical Introduction to Queer Theory*. New York: New York University Press.

Thomas, Calvin, ed. 2000. *Straight With a Twist: Queer Theory and the Subject of Heterosexuality*. Urbana: University of Illinois Press.

Valocchi, Stephen. 2005. "Not Yet Queer Enough: The Lessons of Queer Theory for the Sociology of Gender and Sexuality." *Gender & Society* 19: 750–770.

Warner, Michael, ed. 1993. *Fear of a Queer Planet: Queer Politics and Social Theory*. Ann Arbor: University of Michigan Press.

Weed, Elizabeth, and Naomi Senor, eds. 1997. *Feminism Meets Queer Theory*. Bloomington: Indiana University Press.

Whisman, Vera. 1996. *Queer by Choice: Lesbians, Gay Men and the Politics of Difference*. New York: Routledge.

Wilchins, Riki. 2004. *Queer Theory, Gender Theory: An Instant Primer*. New York: Alyson Books.

Body Modification

Blum, Virginia. 2003. *Flesh Wounds: The Culture of Cosmetic Surgery*. Berkeley, CA: University of California Press.

Caplan, Jane, ed. 2000. *Written on the Body: The Tattoo in European and American History*. Princeton, NJ: Princeton University Press.

Chen, Nancy N., and Helene Moglen, eds. 2006. *Bodies in the Making: Transgressions and Transformations*. Santa Cruz, CA: New Pacific Press.

Davis, Kathy. 2003. *Dubious Equalities and Embodied Differences: Cultural Studies on Cosmetic Surgery*. Lanam, MD; Rowman and Littlefield.

Featherstone, Mike, ed. 2000. *Body Modification*. London: Sage.

Inckle, Kay. 2007. *Writing on the Body? Thinking Through Gendered Embodiment and Marked Flesh*. Newcastle, UK: Cambridge Scholars Publishing.

Pitts, Victoria. 2003. *In the Flesh: The Cultural Politics of Body Modification*. New York: Palgrave Macmillan.

Drag

Newton, Esther. 1979. *Mother Camp: Female Impersonators in America*. Chicago: University of Chicago Press.

Rupp, Leila J., and Verta Taylor. 2003. *Drag Queens at the 801 Cabaret*. Chicago: University of Chicago Press.

Schacht, Steven. 2000. "Paris is Burning: How Society's Stratification System Makes Drag Queens of Us All." *Race, Gender & Class* 7: 147–166.

———. 2002a. "Lesbian Drag Kings and the Feminine Embodiment of the Masculine" In Donna Troka, Kathleen Lebesco, and Jean Noble, eds., *The Drag King Anthology*. New York: Harrington Park Press.

———. 2002b. "Four Renditions of Doing Female Drag: Feminine Appearing Conceptual Variations of a Masculine Theme." In Patricia Gagné and Richard Tewksbury, eds., *Gendered Sexualities*. Greenwich, CT: JAI.

Schacht, Steven, with Lisa Underwood, eds. 2004. *The Drag Queen Anthology: The Absolutely Fabulous and Flawlessly Customary World of Female Impersonators*. New York: Haworth Press.

Troka, Donna Jean, Kathleen LeBesco, and Jean Bobby Noble, eds. 2002. *The Drag King Anthology*, New York: Haworth Press.

Volcano, del La Grace, and Judith Halberstam. 1999. *The Drag King Book*. London: Serpent's Tail.

Transgender

Bettcher, Talia and Ann Garry. 2009. Transgender Studies and Feminism: Theory, Politics, and Gendered Realities. Special Issue, *Hypatia* 24: Summer.

Bornstein, Kate. 1994. *Gender Outlaw: On Men, Women, and the Rest of Us*. New York: Vintage.

Boylan, Jennifer Finney. 2003. *She's Not There: A Life in Two Genders*. New York: Broadway Books.

Bullough, Bonnie, Vern Bullough, and James Elias, eds. 1997. *Gender Blending*. Amherst, NY: Prometheus.

Califia, Pat. 1997. *Sex Changes: The Politics of Transgenderism*. San Francisco, CA: Cleis Press.

Cromwell, Jason. 1999. *Transmen and FTMs: Identities, Bodies, Genders, and Sexualities*. Chicago: University of Chicago Press.

Currah, Paisley. 2006. "Gender Pluralisms Under the Transgender Umbrella." In Paisley Currah, Richard M. Juang, and Shannon Price Minter, eds., *Transgender Rights*. Minneapolis: Minnesota University Press.

Currah, Paisley, and Shannon Minter, eds. 2004. *Transgender Rights: Culture, Politics, and Law*. Minneapolis: University of Minneapolis Press.

Denny, Dallas, ed. 1997. *Current Concepts in Transgender Identity*. New York: Garland Publishing.

Devor, Holly. 1989. *Gender Blending: Confronting the Limits of Duality*. Bloomington: Indiana University Press.

———. 1997. *FTM: Female-to-Male Transsexuals in Society*. Bloomington: Indiana University Press.

Ekins, Richard. 1997. *Male Femaling: A Grounded Theory Approach to Cross-Dressing and Sex-Changing*. New York: Routledge.

Ekins, Richard, and Dave King, eds. 1996. *Blending Genders: Social Aspects of Cross-Dressing and Sex-Changing*. New York: Routledge.

———. 2006. *The Transgender Phenomenon*. London: Sage.

Epstein, Julia, and Kristina Straub, eds. 1991. *Body Guards: The Cultural Politics of Gender Ambiguity*. New York: Routledge.

Feinberg, Leslie. 1996. *Transgender Warriors: Making History from Joan of Arc to Dennis Rodman*. Boston: Beacon Press.

Gagné, Patricia, and Richard Tewksbury. 1998. "Rethinking Binary Conceptions and Social Constructions: Transgender Experiences of Gender and Sexuality." In Marcia Texler Segal and Vasilikie Demos, eds., *Advances in Gender Research*, Vol. 3. Greenwich, CT: JAI.

———. 1999. "Knowledge and Power, Body and Self: An Analysis of Knowledge Systems and the Transgendered Self." *Sociological Quarterly* 40: 59–83.

Gagné, Patricia, Richard Tewksbury, and Deanna McGaughey. 1997. "Coming Out and Crossing Over: Identity Formation and Proclamation in a Transgender Community." *Gender & Society* 11: 478–508.

———. 1998. "Conformity Pressures and Gender Resistance Among Transgendered Individuals." *Social Problems* 45: 81–101.

Halberstam, Judith. 1998. *Female Masculinity*. Durham, NC: Duke University Press.

Heyes, Cressida J. 2003. "Feminist Solidarity After Queer Theory: The Case of Transgender." *Signs* 28: 1093–1120.

Hird, Myra J. 2000. "Gender's Nature: Intersexuals, Transsexuals, and the 'Sex'/ 'Gender' Binary." *Feminist Theory* 1: 347–364.

Jacobs, Sue-Ellen, Wesley Thomas, and Sabine Lang. 1997. *Two-Spirit People: Native American Gender Identity, Sexuality, and Spirituality.* Urbana: University of Illinois Press.

Kates, Gary. 1995. *Monsieur d'Eon Is a Woman: A Tale of Political Intrigue and Sexual Masquerade.* New York: Basic Books.

Kulick, Don. 1998. *Travesti: Sex, Gender, and Culture Among Brazilian Transgendered Prostitutes.* Chicago: University of Chicago Press.

McCloskey, Deirdre. 1999. *Crossing: A Memoir.* Chicago: University of Chicago Press.

Meyerowitz, Joan. 2002. *How Sex Changed: A History of Transsexuality in the United States.* Cambridge, MA: Harvard University Press.

Middlebrook, Diane Wood. 1998. *Suits Me: The Double Life of Billy Tipton.* Boston: Houghton Mifflin.

Namaste, Viviane. 2000. *Invisible Lives: The Erasure of Transsexual and Transgendered People.* Chicago: The University of Chicago Press.

Roen, Katrina. 2002. "'Either/Or' and 'Both/Neither': Discursive Tensions in Transgender Politics." *Signs* 27: 501–522.

Rubin, Henry. 2003. *Self-Made Men: Identity, Embodiment and Recognition Among Transsexual Men.* Nashville, TN: Vanderbilt University Press.

Schilt, Kristen. 2006. "Just One of the Guys?: How Transmen Make Gender Visible at Work." *Gender & Society* 20: 465–490.

Scott-Dixon, Krista, ed. 2006. *Trans/forming Feminisms: Transfeminist Voices Speak Out.* Toronto: Sumach Press.

Stone, Sandy. 1991. "The *Empire* Strikes Back: A Posttranssexual Manifesto." In Julia Epstein and Kristina Straus, eds., *Body Guards: The Cultural Politics of Gender Ambiguity.* New York: Routledge.

Stryker, Susan, and Stephen Whittle, eds. 2006. *The Transgender Studies Reader.* New York: Routledge.

Valentine, David. 2006. *Imagining Transgender.* Durham, NC: Duke University Press.

Vidal-Ortiz, Salvador. 2008. "Gender and the Hybrid Identity: On Passing Through." In Patricia Leavy and Keri E. Iyall Smith, eds., *Hybrid Identities.* Boston: Brill Publishers.

Whittle, Stephen. 2002. *Respect and Equality: Transsexual and Transgender Rights.* London: Cavendish Publishing.

Wickman, Jan. 2001. *Transgender Politics: The Construction and Deconstruction of Binary Gender in the Finnish Transgender Community.* Åbo, Finland: Åbo Akademi University Press.

Woolf, Virginia. [1928] 1956. *Orlando: A Biography.* New York: Harcourt Brace.

13

Third-Wave Feminism

SOURCES OF GENDER INEQUALITY

- Neglect of girls' and young women's agency
- Loss of the heritage of strong Black women
- Constraining ideas about women's sexuality

POLITICS

- Supporting movements for procreative rights, gay rights, economic equality, the environment, and peace
- Reviving the heritage of Black foremothers
- Empowering girls and "girlie" culture
- Creating "grrrls" rock music and art

CRITIQUE

- Split between Black feminists who valorize their "mother's garden" legacy and White feminists who want to forge their own movement
- Emphasis on creating distinctive individual identities rather than political groups
- Feminism is subsumed in a human rights perspective

CONTRIBUTIONS

- Including men and diverse multicultural groups in feminism
- Expansion of feminist politics to movements for peace, environment, and economic equality
- Loosening the constraints of heteronormativity by flaunting sexual diversity
- Creating a girls' culture

Third-wave feminism is both a continuation of and a break with second-wave feminisms. It emerged in the 1990s and built on multiracial/multiethnic feminism, feminist studies of men, and postmodern feminism. (Some feminist histories consider them all part of third-wave feminism.) It is inclusive of multiple cultures and feminist men, and plays with sex, sexuality, and gender. There is an ambivalence about motherhood. Like radical feminism, third-wave feminism valorizes women's agency and female sexuality as forms of power, but it rejects the politics of women as oppressed victims of patriarchy.

Third-wave feminist daughters and granddaughters of feminism (often literally, as several are daughters of famous feminists) don't see themselves simply as "women" but as "sexy girls," "strongblackwomen," and "queer dykes." They want to choose how they look, and some flaunt their femininity with short skirts and stiletto heels. They do not see heteronormativity as a threat to their autonomy, because they experiment with bisexuality and gender queering. Instead of a feminist sisterhood, they form fluid groups of "riot grrrls" and "guerrilla grrrls"—women's hip-hop bands and art producers. The "grrr" is a playful parody of a confrontational snarl.

No one claims to speak for a like-minded group. In activist politics, third-wave feminists are as apt to make a stand with men as with other women. Lesbians are no longer separatists, but join with gay men in fighting homophobia and AIDS. Black "brothas" join their fight against racism, even as third-wave sisters, daughters, and partners fight with them about sexism.

Third-Wave Feminism's Brief History

In 1991, in the Anita Hill–Clarence Thomas Supreme Court appointment hearings, a Black woman and man were pitted against each other in a bitter and very public fight over sexual harassment. In 1992, in what Astrid Henry argues was a response to this event, Rebecca Walker, Alice Walker's daughter, wrote a piece for *Ms.* magazine entitled "Becoming the Third Wave." Black women's third wave is a call to claim feminism in the name of their African American foremothers, both those who publicly identified and wrote as feminists and those who struggled against racial oppression and raised children on their own but did not call themselves feminists.

Subsequently, young White feminists declared their separation from second-wave feminism. They argued that they did not have to choose feminism as a special identity. They grew up with feminist parents and the visibility of women's public accomplishments. They are familiar with feminist theory and research from women's studies courses. Feminism is there for the taking, if they want it, but they do not want their mothers' feminism.

White third-wave feminists feel they have to forge separate identities from their feminist mothers and foremothers and find their own political goals. Some of the identities they choose are for fun—"girlie" culture—and some of their appearances seem calculated to shock their feminist mothers—punk clothes, piercings, tattoos, bizarrely cut and dyed hair. Heteronormativity is not a threat; they have bisexual relationships and friends; they have sex in nonexclusive relationships. Lesbians often identify as queer and find companions in the gay as well as young lesbian community. "Girlie culture" revels in outrageous sexual openness.

White and Black third-wavers shrug off the remnants of sexism, sexual harassment, and patriarchal privilege. Their battles are against restrictions on procreative choice, AIDS, racism, homophobia, and economic inequalities. They are outspoken against misogynistic popular culture, especially hip-hop and rock music lyrics, and create their own to express their rebellious identities.

Revolt of the Daughters

To third-wave feminism's White daughters, second-wave feminism is a dowdy, outmoded, puritanical mother. Much of their third-wave opposition to second-wave feminism's "vanilla" sexuality and rejection of heterosexuality exaggerates these stances to provide a foil for third-wave opposition. Yet the thrust for independence from critical mothers who created modern feminism is a way of creating a feminism of their own. Without the space to make a new mark, third-wave feminists feel they can only be lesser imitations of feminist icons they grew up with.

In the following excerpt from *Not My Mother's Sister*, Astrid Henry, a young feminist scholar, lays out the daughters' perspectives. She ends with a wry comment on how quickly the younger generation becomes in turn the older one.

Sisters vs. Daughters

Astrid Henry

St. Mary's College, Indiana

Handed to us at birth, feminism no longer requires the active identification that it once did.[a] We often don't need to get to feminism through some means—whether consciousness-raising, activism, or reevaluating our personal relationships—because feminism is already there for us.[b] As Barbara Findlen writes in *Listen Up*, "My feminism wasn't shaped by antiwar or civil rights activism; I was not a victim of the problem that had no name."[c] We don't need to create feminism, it already exists. We don't need to become feminists, we already are. Because women of my generation often do not experience feminism as a process—that is, as something we actively choose or help to create—we have a much more ambivalent identification with it. Even for those of us who see ourselves as aligned with second-wave feminism, our sense of owning feminism can still feel tenuous. We own feminism in the sense that it is our birthright, yet in other ways it is not ours. It belongs to another generation, another group of women: second-wave feminists. They were the ones who went through the heady experience of *creating* feminism; we just get to reap the benefits.

In order to get a sense of how different feminism felt for second-wave feminists, one need only look at Gloria Steinem's introduction to Walker's anthology, *To Be Real*. In it, she writes, "Because I entered when feminism had to be chosen and even reinvented, I experienced almost everything about it as an unmitigated and joyful freedom—and I still do."[d] When one compares Steinem's "unmitigated and joyful freedom" with the depressing sense of confinement and curbed independence found in some third-wave texts, it is clear that there has been a definite generational shift in the way that women experience feminism. Perhaps the third-wave complaint that feminism feels constricting—as opposed to feeling like "unmitigated freedom"—should be read as a lament for what we missed out on: entering feminism when it had to be chosen and reinvented.[e]

The tendency within much third-wave writing toward making a clean break with the past, rather than maintaining a sense of connection, may be inevitable given the language used to describe the third wave's relationship to feminism. Conceiving of feminism as a birthright passed from mother to daughter undoubtedly influences the third wave's understanding of and relationship to feminism. It may be that something inherited from one's mother is likely to be rejected, no matter what it is. It may be that a birthright, bound up as it is with one's mother, is unable to produce individuality. Defining what she terms "matrophobia," Adrienne Rich writes of "the womanly splitting of the self, in the desire to become purged once and for all of our mother's bondage, to become individuated and free."[f] Given this matrophobia, identifying with one's mother and with her feminism may ultimately incite rebellion, a desire "to move away," as Denfeld calls for.[g]

In fact, I would argue that the excessive focus on individualism by many third-wavers reveals more than just a preference for liberal feminism. In their descriptions of what this individuality is set in opposition to, one gets the sense that individuality provides a means of resisting the group identity implied by the terms "feminists" and "women." Beyond simply disidentifying with these two identity categories, this resistance might also suggest a desire to break away from their mothers, both real and figurative. In *Fire with Fire*, for example, Wolf describes power feminism, the feminism she advocates, as that which "[e]ncourages a woman to claim her individual voice rather than merging her voice in a collective identity."[h]

Wolf gives us a clue about what individuality represents for many third-wave feminists: it is the antithesis of "merging her voice in a collective identity." What is to be resisted is staying (sub)merged in collectivity. Wolf's description suggests that in order to retain—or even to gain—one's identity and autonomy, one must unmerge, move away, break free....

In the third wave's relationship to the second wave, I believe we see signs of the difficulty that individuation poses for women, particularly in the face of a powerful mother figure: in this case, feminism. As one third-wave writer notes, "A daughter fears that she will somehow be co-opted by her mother's desires, drives, and idiosyncrasies and will become the mother at the expense of the self."[i] In both their retaining of the identity "feminist" and in the rare moments when they champion second-wave feminism, third-wavers maintain a connection to their mothers' generation—and often to their real mothers. Like the shared gender identity between mother and daughter, they are not easily able to extricate themselves from the shared identity of feminist. In their frequent attempts to radically break free from the feminism of the past, however, their desire for autonomy and their own individual identity is revealed. They want a shared connection through feminism, but they want their freedom and individuality too.[j]

In her introduction to *To Be Real*, Walker describes a new generation of feminists that seeks to challenge many of the second wave's perceived orthodoxies; she argues for a feminism that includes contradictions and an ability to go beyond political correctness. As she describes the feminism of the previous generation: "For many of us it seems that to be a feminist in the way that we have seen or understood feminism is to conform to an identity and way of living that doesn't allow for individuality, complexity, or less than perfect personal histories."[k] Challenging the perceived dogmatism of second-wave feminism, third-wavers have steered clear of prescribing a particular feminist agenda and instead have chosen to stress individuality and individual definitions of feminism.[l] As Heywood and Drake note, "[T]he ideology of individualism is still a major motivating force in many third wave lives."[m] Individualism as a shared ideology makes for a political paradox, of course, since historically women's liberation movements, like other civil rights movements, have required some sense of collectivity to pursue political goals. Yet this collectivity—or what a previous generation may have termed "sisterhood"—no longer seems available or even desirable. "The same rights and freedoms feminists won for us have allowed us to develop into a very diverse generation of women, and we value our individuality," writes Denfeld. "While linked through common concerns, notions of sisterhood seldom appeal to women of my generation."[n]

Third-wave feminists' preference for defining feminism in their own terms—that is, for each individual feminist to define feminism *for herself individually*—can be seen in the original declaration of the third wave, Rebecca Walker's 1992 statement *"I am the Third Wave."* In calling for a new wave, Walker does not speak in a collective voice. There is no "we" in this statement, just an "I."[o] An early expression of what was to become a common theme within third-wave discourse, Walker's essay does not attempt to speak in the name of other women. Rather, she writes about her own, individual desire to devote her life to feminism.[p]

The third wave's "ideology of individualism" has found its perfect form in the autobiographical essay, the preferred writing genre of third-wavers and one that shares little with the group manifestos of a previous generation. The majority of third-wave anthologies published since the mid-1990s have been structured around such personal essays and, correspondingly, personal definitions of feminism. Such essays can be seen as the first step in the consciousness-raising process developed from the earlier women's liberation movement. That is, they provide a means by which to express individual experiences and to analyze those experiences in larger social and political terms. Where the third wave has often appeared stuck, however, is in moving from this beginning consciousness-raising stage of self-expression to developing a larger analysis of the relationship between individual and collective experience, culminating in theory and political action.[q]

The third wave's individualistic form of feminism also has an interesting relationship to another second-wave concept: identity politics. As it was conceived by second-wave feminists, as well as other groups from the period, identity politics posits a relationship between one's gender, racial, and class experience and one's political interests. While these identity categories are also routinely stressed in third-wave texts, there is little sense that they can provide a coalescing structure to bring people together, nor are claims in the name of any one group, such as "women," likely to be found in these texts....

In its attention to speaking from an embodied and particular position, one that is always inflected by race, class, sexuality, religion, and educational status, this litany of identity categories reveals the influence of second-wave feminism. Yet unlike the second wave, the third wave does not move beyond these individual assertions of identity to a larger, collective political identity. The Asian bisexual can only speak for herself, not for other Asians nor other bisexuals. For the third wave, identity politics is limited to the expression of individual identity.

Within this "ideology of individualism," feminism has frequently been reduced to one issue: choice. In its most watered-down version, this form of third-wave feminism is appealing to many since it rarely represents political and social issues in ways that suggest the need for collective action or change other than on the individual level. As Elspeth Probyn has noted, it is a "choice freed of the necessity of thinking about the political and social ramifications of the act of choosing."[r]

Feminism thus becomes an ideology of individual empowerment to make choices, no matter what those choices are....[5]

Generations

One of the great ironies of writing about generations—particularly when the topic is so contemporary—is that one inevitably finds one's own generation being replaced. In the years it has taken me to finish this project, I have watched the "new" generation of which I am a part become eclipsed by something even more current: the next generation of American youth, variably called Generation Y or the Millennial Generation.[t] Within feminism, a similar replacement may soon be occurring. As one of my students recently reported back from the Feminist Majority's "Feminist Expo," there is now talk of a "fourth wave" of feminism among women in their late teens and early twenties. While admittedly isolated, pronouncements of a feminist "fourth wave" make me recall Rosi Braidotti's comment that "[i]t's strange how quickly one ages within feminism." As she continues, "[H]ere I am: barely 40, still sexually active but having to represent the 'older generation'—how did this happen?"[u]

The inevitability of such generational replacement should be a caution. The mother-daughter trope is an impoverished model of generational relations, one that allows for only two possible points of identification: mother or daughter. Within the familial structure used to describe feminist generations, it is inevitable, then, that those who are now feminism's daughters will, over time, become its mothers—and given the negative image associated with such mothers, who would want such a fate?

While feminism's familial language is, in fact, figurative, the metaphors we use to describe feminism have real effects in the world and in the ways that feminists develop intergenerational relationships and participate in intergenerational dialogue. What does it mean, for example, for "younger" feminists to view "older" feminists—whether they are their friends, lovers, teachers, colleagues, or adversaries—as mothers? When we remain stuck in feminism's imagined family, we lose sight of the myriad relations feminists have with one another as well as the possibility of cross-generational identification and similarities. As Susan Fraiman argues, there "is a difference less between seventies and nineties feminists than between seventies and nineties *feminisms*—a difference that finds mothers and daughters alike more apt in the nineties to boot up than sit in and that calls for ideological rather than oedipal diagnosis."[v] The focus on generational differences has also limited our ability to recognize the various ideological and political differences among and between feminists and feminisms, reducing such differences to the singular difference of age and generation. "Attributing our differences to generation rather than to politics," writes Lisa Marie

Hogeland, "sets us firmly into psychologized thinking, and into versions of mother/daughter relations—somehow, we are never sisters who might have things to teach each other across our differences and despite our rivalries."[w]

In arguing against the dominant matrophor used to describe "the persistent nature of maternal metaphors in feminism," some feminists have maintained that we should return to the language of sisterhood as "an alternative to the divisive mother-daughter model."[x] While itself quite reductive, the sororal metaphor at least allows for a language of collectivity, something not seen in much of the "daughter" discourse examined here. Yet while I sympathize with the desire to break out of the mother-daughter dyad, I am not so optimistic that a return to sisterhood will solve the problem. This trope has its own troubled history, the least of which is its inability to recognize differences among women. While the mother-daughter dyad seems hopelessly fixated on the notion of difference—"I'm not like you"—the sisterhood trope seems to offer us the opposite problem—"We're the same."

As feminism has been made into a mother, the qualities that have been attributed to this maternal figure are disturbing, to say the least. While "younger" feminists may wish to depict feminists of the past as "dated and dowdy" in order to represent themselves as new and cutting-edge, such representations of "mother feminism" invariably conform to a conservative image of motherhood: one where mothers are moralistic, asexual prudes. For younger feminists who may not be mothers themselves, representing the maternal in these terms may seem an effective way to make feminism the repository of all that is to be rebelled against.[y] Ultimately, however, this representation only serves to maintain a conservative and ideologically suspect view of motherhood, one we should resist.

Finally, and potentially most troubling, the ubiquitous focus in recent feminist discourse on generational differences between women has ensured that much energy has gone into internal conflicts within feminism rather than external battles against sexism, racism, and homophobia, among other pressing concerns. As such, the focus on feminism's mother-daughter duo has meant that the father, as it were, has dropped out of the picture altogether.[z] As Judith Roof writes:

Seeing relationships among feminists as generational means adopting the metaphor of the patriarchal family in the throes of its illusory battle against mortality. Our enticement by this model with its chimera of order and all-too-real Oedipal drama focuses blame, energies, and even the dilemma of women's relationships in the wrong place: among women themselves.[aa]

Conflict within feminism, even when posited as generational, should not be avoided. Some of feminism's current struggles may very well be among women themselves and thus vitally necessary for feminists to examine in more detail. Unlike Roof, then, I do not think the solution to our current generational impasse is to sidestep the problem of generations in order to move on. Rather, we must continue to examine our generational differences and alliances in order to understand their psychological power for feminists.[bb] Where I am in agreement with Roof, however, is that the attention on generational differences has dramatically shifted feminism's focus from external enemies to internal ones. If feminism is indeed like a family, it would be wise of us not to forget its absent father.

Notes

a. As Rose Glickman has noted, "To be a feminist is one among many options for [women in their twenties and early thirties], because they do not recognize it as a process, as a perspective that informs other choices. They interpret the word as an end in itself." Glickman, *Daughters of Feminists* (New York: St. Martin's Press, 1993), 5.

b. On the generational difference regarding consciousness-raising, Denfeld writes: "While CR might have been helpful for women raised in eras where women didn't talk about their experiences with sexism—let alone talk about sex—my generation often finds it redundant. Unlike our mothers, we grew up in a world where issues such as sex discrimination, sexual harassment, abortion, birth control, homosexuality, and relationships are openly discussed. My friends and I have the kind of explicit talk about our sex lives and personal experiences that would give Jerry Falwell a heart attack.... Yet my mother tells me such a thing would have been unthinkable in her day." Denfeld, *The New Victorians*, 204–205.[*]

c. Findlen, "Introduction," xii. See also Laurie Ouellette, who writes, "I am a member of the first generation of women to benefit from the gains of the 1970s' women's movement without having participated in its struggles." Ouellette, "Building the Third Wave," *On the Issues* 14 (Fall 1992).

d. Steinem, "Foreward," in *To Be Real*, xxvi.[*]

e. For more on this process of reinvention, see Orr, "Charting the Current of the Third Wave," *Hypatia* 12 (Summer 1997): 32–33.

f. Adrienne Rich, *Of Woman Born: Motherhood as Experience and Institution* (New York: W. W. Norton, 1976), 236.

g. Rene Denfeld, "Feminism 2000: What Does It Really Mean (to You)?" *Sassy* 9 (May 1996): 60.

h. Wolf, *Fire With Fire*, 137.[*]

i. Madelyn Detloff, "Mean Spirits: The Politics of Contempt Between Feminist Generations," *Hypatia* 12 (Summer 1997): 92.

j. While the writers who are my focus here clearly see feminism as limiting their individuality—feminism as Big Sister or, more accurately, Big Mother—other third-wave writers offer a different understanding of what feminism has meant to them. For these writers, such as several featured in *Listen Up* and *To Be Real*, feminism is described as something which enables them to *acquire* individuality. In other words, feminism is depicted as an empowering force in their lives, allowing them to question society's rules about how they should be in the world. I would argue that this identification with feminism is much more like the descriptions offered by early second-wave writers who describe the process of becoming feminists in positive terms, emphasizing, in Steinem's words, "the joyful freedom" found in coming into feminism. It is interesting, however, that even this more positive third-wave understanding of what feminism has to offer seems inextricably linked to the mother-daughter relationship. See, for example, Sharon Lennon's essay in *Listen Up*: "My mother, who had allowed and encouraged me to be who I was through most of my youth, viewed [my interest in feminism] as a major point of contention between us....In my quest for individuality through feminism, there were a lot of screaming matches between my mother and me." Lennon, "What Is Mine," in Findlen, ed., *Listen Up*, 127.*

k. Walker, "To Be Real," xxxiii.*

l. Adds Paula Kamen, "The vast majority of people of my generation have little patience for anything that seems too ideological, dogmatic, or revolutionary. It smacks of extremist, shortsighted rhetoric from the late sixties. We mistrust such either-or, black-or-white thinking that renders us inflexible to changing conditions." Kamen, "My 'Bourgeois' Brand of Feminism," in *Next: Young American Writers on the New Generation*, ed. Eric Liu (New York: W. W. Norton, 1994), 87.

m. Heywood and Drake, "Introduction," 11.*

n. Denfeld, *The New Victorians*, 263.* Karen Lehrman adds, "the idea of a rigid political sisterhood—of a 'women's movement' with a distinct ideological agenda—has become not only anachronistic but counterproductive." Lehrman, *The Lipstick Proviso: Women, Sex and Power in the Real World* (New York: Anchor Books, 1997), 179.

o. Representing third-wave feminism as something individual feminists can define individually for themselves is also a key theme in and guiding structure of the documentary *Gloria Steinem, the Spice Girls, and Me: Defining the Third Wave of Feminism*, dir. Krista Longtin, 2002.

p. Walker, "Becoming the Third Wave," *Ms.* (Jan-Feb 1992): 39–41.

q. An exception can be found in *Catching a Wave*, where editors Dicker and Piepmeier explicitly describe their anthology's format as following the second-wave principle of consciousness-raising in order to move the reader from personal experience to theory and action. See Dicker and Piepmeier, "Introduction."*

r. Elspeth Probyn, "New Traditionalism and Post-Feminism: TV Does the Home," *Screen* 31 (Summer 1990): 156.

s. In this regard, I find it interesting that the next books published by Denfeld, Roiphe, and Wolf moved away from policy or academic issues to more personal topics. Denfeld's *Kill the Body, the Head Will Fall: A Closer Look at Women and Aggression* (New York: Warner Books, 1997) addresses her experience training as a boxer; Roiphe's *Last Night in Paradise: Sex and Morals at the Century's End* (Boston: Little, Brown, 1997) addresses HIV, AIDS, and sexual morality from a personal rather than policy perspective; and Wolf's *Promiscuities: The Secret Struggle for Womanhood* (New York: Random House, 1997) addresses the sexual-coming-of-age stories of Wolf and friends. For reviews of these books, see Michiko Kakutani, "Feminism Lite: She Is Woman, Hear Her Mate," *New York Times*, June 10, 1997, B6 (review of *Promiscuities*); and Courtney Weaver, "Growing Up Sexual," *New York*

Times Book Review, June 8, 1997, 12 (review of *Promiscuities* and *Last Night in Paradise*). See also Naomi Wolf, *Misconceptions: Truth, Lies, and the Unexpected Journey to Motherhood* (New York: Doubleday, 2001).

t. It's worth noting that the Millennial Generation, or Generation Y, is a substantially bigger demographic group than Generation X and is thus more like the Baby Boom generation in its population size.

u. Rosi Braidotti, "Generations of Feminists, or, Is There Life after Post-Modernism?" *Found Object* 16 (1995): 55. This point is echoed by Jacquelyn Zita in her introduction to the *Hypatia* special issue on third-wave feminisms, where she writes, "Strangely, I have become an 'old timer' as I look back now on more than a quarter century of feminist theory and politics." Zita, "Third Wave Feminisms: An Introduction," *Hypatia*, 12 (Summer 1997): 1.

v. Susan Fraiman, "Feminism Today: Mothers, Daughters, Emerging Sisters," *American Literary History* 11 (Fall 1999): 532, emphasis in original.

w. Lisa Marie Hogeland, "Against Generational Thinking, or, Some Things that 'Third Wave' Feminism Isn't," *Women's Studies in Communication* 24 (Spring 2001): 118.

x. Rebecca Dakin Quinn, "An Open Letter to Institutional Mothers," in *Generations: Academic Feminists in Dialogue*, ed. Devoney Looser and Ann Kaplan (Minneapolis: University of Minnesota Press, 1997), 179; Louise D'Arcens, "Mothers, Daughters, Sisters," in *Talking Up: Young Women's Take on Feminism*, ed. Rosamund Else-Mitchell and Naomi Flutter (North Melbourne, AU: Spinifex, 1998), 114. Susan Fraiman makes a similar call to return to sisterhood in her praise of *Third Wave Agenda* for "usefully direct[ing] our attention away from mother-daughter tensions and back to sisterly ties. Fraiman, "Feminism Today," 543.*

y. For more positive images of motherhood, see recent texts by third-wave mothers, such as Spike Gillespie's "Sex and the Single Mom," in *Sex and Single Girls: Straight and Queer Women on Sexuality*, ed. Lee Damsky (Seattle: Seal Press, 2000), 357–367. See also editors Ariel Gore and Bee Lavender's anthology, *Breeder: Real-Life Stories from the New Generation of Mothers* (Seattle: Seal Press, 2001).

z. For more on the "father" within feminist familial discourse, see Helena Michie, "Not One of the Family: The Repression of the Other Woman in Feminist Theory," in *Discontented Discourses: Feminism, Textual Intervention, Psychoanalysis*, ed. Marleen S. Barr and Richard Feldstein (Urbana: University of Illinois Press, 1989), 15–28.

aa. Judith Roof, "Generational Difficulties; or, the Fear of a Barren History," in Looser and Kaplan, eds., *Generations*, 85.*

bb. Here I am echoing Devoney Looser's point in *Generations: Academic Feminists in Dialogue*, where she writes, "we should continue to examine what are already quite entrenched and *perceived* feminist generational differences and alliances. These deserve to be further theorized now, even if they are ultimately cast out of our critical vocabulary." Looser, "Introduction 2," in Looser and Kaplan, eds., *Generations*, 33, emphasis in original.*

* See Suggested Readings.

Strong Black Women

African American women were an intrinsic part of third-wave feminism from its inception. But rather than rejecting their feminist foremothers, most African American third-wave feminists want to be like them—strong, active, political, and confrontational. Second-wave Black feminism was critical of sexist, domineering, heterosexual men, but tended not to reject them, so a return to heterosexuality is not a major part of Black third-wave feminism. More important is to claim an independent political and cultural space.

In the following excerpt, Kimberly Springer, professor of American studies and writer, editor, and independent radio producer, explores the politics of Black third-wave feminism.

Third Wave Black Feminism?

Kimberly Springer

King's College, London

The term *third wave feminism* as we now know it signals a new generation of feminists. It came to public consciousness, or at least leftist consciousness, in the form of Rebecca Walker's founding of the Third Wave Foundation in 1992, which initially conducted a Freedom Summer-styled voter registration campaign that same year.[a] This generation of third wave feminism credits previous generations for women-centered social and political advances. This acknowledgment, however, took the form of seeming ungratefulness and historical amnesia in Walker's anthology, *To Be Real* (Steinem 1995; Walker 1995). Some contributors voiced a sense of feeling stifled by the previous generation's organizing style and seemed to reduce the third wave's argument to a gripe about feminism as lifestyle dogma. Yet, more recent writings about third wave feminism—particularly Jennifer Baumgardner and Amy Richards's recent book *Manifesta: Young Women, Feminism, and the Future* (2000)—attempt to define third wave politics and mend the generational rift that arose between some older and younger white feminists. Moreover, *Manifesta* at least gives lip service to the role of women of color, lesbians, and, to a lesser degree, poor women in the third wave women's movement.[b]

The wave model perpetuates the exclusion of women of color from women's movement history and feminist theorizing. Still, as it is so deeply embedded in how we examine the history and future of the women's movement, it remains useful for internal critique. As it is used

Reprinted from "Third Wave Black Feminism?" 2002, *Signs* 27: 1063–1064, 1068, 1072–1074, 1077–1079. Copyright © 2002 by the University of Chicago. Reprinted by permission.

historically and today, it is too static. To serve a wide range of women's needs, it is imperative that the wave model includes women of color's resistance to gender violence.

What To Do With Our Mothers' Gardens?

If we proceed with this idea of third wave feminism in its most obvious form, that of denoting generations of feminism, what is the relationship between Black feminists of differing generations? Does a generational rift exist between them? One aspect of the generational tensions between feminists in general is the frustration that older feminists feel at watching younger women reinvent the wheels of social change. Michele Wallace, in retrospect, recognized the irritation of her mother and other women of her mother's generation. In her essay "To Hell and Back," Wallace writes of the late 1960s: "My thesis had been that I and my generation were reinventing youth, danger, sex, love, blackness, and fun. But there had always been just beneath the surface a persistent countermelody,... what I might also call my mother's line, a deep suspicion that I was reinventing nothing, but rather making a fool of myself in precisely the manner that untold generations of young women before me had done" (1997, 11). Other than this autobiographical insight by Wallace, few sources speak of conflicts or distinctions between Black feminists of different generations....

As young white feminists are seeking to step outside of what they consider rigid lifestyle instructions of their feminist foremothers (e.g., stylistic and political), young Black women are attempting to stretch beyond the awe-inspiring legendary work of women like Fannie Lou Hamer, Coretta Scott King, Ruby Doris Smith Robinson, Barbara Smith, bell hooks, and Angela Davis. Their work cannot be matched. When Jones poses the question, "Do you know who speaks through you?" (1994, 26), she poses a rhetorical question that recognizes the significance of history in giving current struggles meaning....

Another aspect of Black women's relationships is how Black women relate to one another. Young Black women writers both highlight the support they feel from other Black women and bear witness to the misguided power that Black women, sharing similar experiences around racism and sexism, exert over one another to wound in unfathomable ways. Competition, vying for status, and degraded self-worth can be Black women's worst interpersonal enemies. Morgan, Chambers, and Jones heed Audre Lorde's call in her essay "Eye to Eye" (1984) for Black women to face how we treat one another and what that says about how we feel about ourselves.

Chambers recalls encounters with other Black girls that, while not unusual, emphasize the ways that African-American women try to hold one another back, from calling Chambers a "sellout" to accusing her of "talking white" because she takes her education seriously. Morgan, in her chapter entitled "Chickenhead Envy," cogently calls out the behavior of said Chickenheads (Morgan 1999, 185–186).[c] To her credit, she is also self-reflective, exploring what so-called Chickenheads reflect back to Black women who are independent and ambitious. Morgan is initiating much-needed dialogue about Black women's culpability in our own oppression and how we oppress one another, especially in the areas of class, color, and sexual orientation. Morgan and Chambers, in fact, disrupt the notion that there is a unified Black sisterhood. While that may be the ideal, these authors point out how Black sisterhood is sometimes far from the reality of our relationships.

For all the emphasis on truth telling and exploring the totality of Black women's lives, the writers explored here are noticeably silent on issues of heterosexism, homophobia in the Black community, and Black women's sexuality in general. Jones and Morgan cogently delve into the history of stereotyping Black women as hypersexual and animalistic, yet there is no discussion of what a positive Black female sexuality would look like. Instead, Black women's (hetero)sexuality is alluded to in their musing on "fine brothers" and dating mores. Black women's sexuality is something to be repressed, except on a surface level of relationships with Black men.

Chambers's only mention of her own sexuality, for example, discusses her fear of an unwanted pregnancy derailing her educational and career goals. This deprioritizing of teen sexuality sheds light on her mother's understated reaction to Veronica's first menstrual cycle. Rather than celebrating her step into young womanhood, her mother makes sure Veronica knows how not to get pregnant. In her later potentially sexual encounters with young men, Chambers can only call on the experiences of friends raised by single mothers, as she was, and friends who were single mothers. Of flirting and potential intimate involvements, Chambers says, "No guy ever said a word to me that didn't sound like a lie. The answer [to sex] was always no" (Chambers 1996, 70–71). While access to her sexuality is by no means dependent on engaging in sexual relations with anyone, blanket denials of her sexual self vis-à-vis young men also deny Chambers access to her own sexual agency. Even an avocation of abstinence would be an exertion of sexual agency.

Given the abundance of writing by African-American lesbians and their influence on Black feminist theory, the lack of attention to heterosexism is a step backward in moving a Black feminist agenda forward. In her chapter on "The F-Word," Morgan declares her allegiance to feminism because she feels feminism claimed her. The most she says about lesbians or heterosexism is a toned-down rebuttal to a man who said she must just need the right man, "as if I'd consider being mistaken for a lesbian an insult instead of an inaccuracy" (Morgan 1999, 42). Yet, in the context of these three texts, examining heterosexuality as a construct is ignored. Instead, within the texts it is a given that they are "straight girls."

The absence of frank discussions about sexuality is an odd repression that barely even acknowledges the authors' own sexuality, much less the variability of human sexuality. This is a noticeable elision given their attentive focus on the complexity of Black women's identities. This omission, or tentative dance, around Black women's sexuality leaves one to conclude that sexual stereotypes have been so debilitating that refuting them only results in the negation of a fuller spectrum for Black female sexual expression. When Black women, for example Alice Walker, Michele Wallace, and Rebecca Walker, frankly discuss their own and Black women's sexuality—be they heterosexual, lesbian, bisexual, or transgender—they run a constant threat of censure inside and outside the Black community through the deployment of degrading, historically rooted stereotypes of licentious Black female sexuality....

In "Toward a Genealogy of Black Female Sexuality," Evelynn Hammonds makes critical note of Black feminist theorizing on Black women's sexuality. In particular, she observes that "historically, Black women have reacted to the repressive force of the hegemonic discourse on race and sex and this image [Black women as empty space] with silence, secrecy, and a partially self-chosen invisibility" (Hammonds 1997, 171). Hammonds later calls not only for intervention that disrupts negative stereotypes about Black women's sexuality but also for critical engagement between Black heterosexual women and Black lesbians to develop a fuller Black feminist praxis around sexuality.

In light of the historical, strategic use of silence around Black women's sexuality by nineteenth-century reformers and the contemporary maligning of Black women such as Anita Hill and Lani Guinier, it is not surprising that Morgan, Jones, and Chambers skirt the issue of Black women's sexuality. The challenge that comes from analyzing their work is, as Hammonds (1997) suggests, the disruption of stereotypes but also the frank discussion of Black women's relationship to their sexual lives through consciousness-raising at all age levels....

Keepin' It Real: Old School Analysis and New School Music

There is no guarantee that the work of Chambers, Morgan, or Jones will reach those young people who need it the most—young people who will not be exposed to Black feminist theory and thought in college classrooms. Though their writing appears in free publications in major cities, what guarantees that a young Black woman on her way to work or school in Manhattan will stop and pick up the *Village Voice* and find Black feminism within its pages? Moreover, these writers' regional focus—they all live and work in New York City—also raises questions about the reach of young Black feminist theorizing geographically.

Ideally, by even daring to write about gender and the Black community, these writers give organizers and educators a springboard.

Certain modes of resistance have lost their power; for example, Washington, D.C., marches have become more of a C-SPAN spectacle than the powerful form of radical agitation that the March on Washington was in 1963. Moreover, as we see with some protests against globalization, the state apparatus has become quite adept at shutting down direct action before it even starts. One reason that young people focus on writing and music as forms of protest—not that these are new—is because we need fresh modes for developing collective consciousness.

It is up to those of us with resources and commitment to take these writings and synthesize them into programs that appeal to the next generation, which needs them the most. I propose a project fusing music and intellectualism in much the same way that Public Enemy and Boogie Down Productions did with the resurgence of Black cultural nationalism in the early 1990s. Music is one of the most accessible educational tools left untapped.

How might educators and those who work closely with young people use a compact disc containing hip-hop, R&B, and rap songs along with an educator's guide to readings and discussion questions about gender and African Americans? How many more people would Black feminism reach if, instead of defending against what Black feminism is not, we offered Black feminist visions for the future?...

Young Black feminists are not uniform in political thought, so it would be dishonest to assert that Black women still feel the need to apologize for engaging feminist politics. Yet, in linking with the work of feminist foremothers, contemporary, young Black feminist writers continue to explain feminism's relevance to Black communities. Far from reinventing the feminist wheel, young Black feminists are building on the legacy left by nineteenth-century abolitionists, antilynching crusaders, club women, Civil Rights organizers, Black Nationalist revolutionaries, and 1970s Black feminists. They are not inserting themselves into the third wave paradigm as much as they are continuing the work of a history of Black race women concerned with gender issues....

Notes

a. Today, the Third Wave Foundation focuses on inspiring and cultivating feminist activism among women ages fifteen to thirty, who are considered within the demographic of the third wave. Defining the waves of feminism according to generation also raises the question of where women who are older than thirty, but were children during the height of second-wave activism, fall in this generational schemata.

b. Disability as an issue for women is wholly absent from this text, as well as the texts by young Black feminists examined here.

c. A "chickenhead" is a woman who is a materialist, dresses in barely there outfits ("skankwear"), and, according to Morgan, is adept at stroking the male ego (185). She is also calculating, cunning, and savvy when it comes to getting what she wants—all acceptable traits for men in white, capitalist patriarchy but wholly unacceptable for Black women.

References

Baumgardner, Jennifer, and Amy Richards. 2000. "Thou Shalt Not Become Thy Mother." In their *Manifesta: Young Women, Feminism and the Future*, 219–234.*

Chambers, Veronica. 1996. *Mama's Girl.*

Davis, Angela. (1971) 1995. "Reflections on the Black Woman's Role in the Community of Slaves." In Beverly Guy-Sheftall, ed., *Words of Fire: An Anthology of African-American Feminist Thought*. New York: New Press.

Hammonds, Evelynn. 1997. "Toward a Genealogy of Black Female Sexuality: The Problematic of Silence." In M. Jacqui Alexander and Chandra Talpade Mohanty, eds., *Feminist Genealogies, Colonial Legacies, Democratic Futures*. New York: Routledge.

Jones, Lisa. 1994. *Bulletproof Diva.*

Lorde, Audre. 1984. "Eye to Eye: Black Women, Hatred and Anger." In her *Sister Outsider*. Trumansburg, NY: Crossing Press.

Morgan, Joan. 1999. *When Chickenheads Come Home to Roost.*

Steinem, Gloria. 1995. "Foreword." In Walker 1995, xiii–xxviii.

Walker, Rebecca. 1995. *To Be Real.*

Wallace, Michele. 1997. *To Hell and Back: On the Road With Black Feminism*. Pamphlet. Brooklyn, NY: Olympia X.

* See Suggested Readings.

Critique

In a special issue of *Hypatia* on third-wave feminism, Rita Alfonso of the University of Memphis and Jo Trigilio from the University of Oregon recorded their email dialogue, "Surfing the Third Wave: A Dialogue Between Two Third-Wave Feminists." Their interchange showed considerable disagreement over what third-wave feminism is or could be. Trigilio argued that "one must be a postmodernist to be a third waver." Alfonso countered that "the two positions—postmodernism and third-wave feminism—are not equitable." On politics, Trigilio said, "No large, distinctive activist feminist movement seems to be occurring out of which a third wave of feminism is rising." Alfonso felt that the critiques of women of color in the United States and also grassroots AIDS activism were examples of third-wave politics.

They both agreed on the disruptiveness of third-wave "sexy sexuality." Trigilio said,

> I went to a dyke punk show the other night....Their antics most likely would have seemed offensive and male-identified to feminists twenty years ago. Two members of the band were hard-core butches, one is a sexy femme complete with low-cut shirt, and the lead singer performed bare-breasted and with a big black dildo hanging out of her pants zipper. She cut it off with a giant knife and flung it into the audience during the second to last song. (Alfonso and Trigilio, 1997, 12)

But she also noted that there aren't coherent political strategies to evaluate the production of new sexualities.

Alfonso discussed groups like the Riot Grrrls, who go back to the early 1990s. She says they were similar to the Redstockings, radical feminists of the 1970s who disrupted beauty pageants. The Redstockings had much more of a political impact in their critique of heterosexuality, femininity, and stereotypical beauty. They wanted a new view of beauty and femininity valorizing diverse looks and women's intellectual accomplishments. The Riot Grrrls, in contrast, parodied the glorification of "girlishness" revealing it to be a form of "sluttiness." Alfonso says,

> Unlike the Redstockings, who protested by throwing items used in the oppression of women into the "freedom trashcan" at the 1968 Miss America Beauty Pageant, the Riot Grrrls donned and reclaimed, in a perverse manner, the accoutrements of femininity. They made a display of the power that these accoutrements brought to them, and simultaneously mocked this power through parody. (Alfonso and Trigilio, 1997, 13)

Is this political? Yes, as a direct confrontation of heteronormativity. But does it have an effect beyond youth culture?

Summary

Third-wave feminism is a young feminists' movement that began in the early 1990s. For Black feminists, who began the movement, it is a search to shape a feminism beyond "our mother's gardens." Black third-wave feminists want to take feminism out of the academy and away from an ideology of women as victims and men as oppressors. While not ignoring Black men's sexism, Black third-wave feminism brings them along in the fight against racism, AIDS, and poverty. It continues the tradition of the strong and resistant foremothers, who were embodiments of women's struggles to survive and raise children in conditions of economic and racial ethnic disadvantage. These foremothers did not call themselves feminists, but to their real and spiritual daughters, they were the true feminists. Young Black women claim these foremothers and name their own continuing battles for economic, racial ethnic, and gender equality. Moving forward, they adapt Black hip-hop and rock culture for girls as a way of engaging them in feminism.

White third-wave feminism positions itself against and beyond second-wave feminism. Many young White feminists are critical of their actual feminist mothers and foremothers, claiming they are puritanical about sexuality, reject heterosexual relationships, and are reluctant to give up portraying women as victims of men and patriarchy. They grew up with feminism "in the air" and know the canonical feminist texts from women's studies courses. Their own brand of feminism is sexually assertive, bisexual, and transgendered in identities and relationships. They are more likely to call themselves queer than postmodern. Like Black third-wave feminism, White third-wave feminism embraces confrontational popular culture, making it into "girlie culture." Music, art, dress, and cosmetics are all turned into elements of "girl power."

The lifestyles and political views of Black and White third-wave feminists are complexities of racial ethnic, sexual, and gender identities. They are rebels with in-your-face body displays and sexuality, but their feminism does not engage directly with the gendered social order. They seem to shrug aside feminist claims that the revolution has not come and that gender inequality still exists.

Third-wave feminists can be found on peace marches, at procreative rights protests (although there is not a uniform political stance), in gay pride parades, and with electoral campaigns, joining men and women with diverse views on feminism. They have expanded feminism to encompass all kinds of political battles, ironically harking back to the liberal feminist claim that "human rights are women's rights." Humanity once again absorbs womanhood, and gender is still the taken-for-granted ground of social life.

SUGGESTED READINGS IN THIRD-WAVE FEMINISM

Alfonso, Rita, and Jo Trigilio. 1997. "Surfing the Third Wave: A Dialogue Between Two Third-Wave Feminists." *Hypatia* 12: 7–16.

Bailey, Cathryn. 2002. "Unpacking the Mother/Daughter Baggage: Reassessing Second- and Third-Wave Tensions." *Women's Studies Quarterly* 30: 136–154.

Baumgardner, Jennifer, and Amy Richards. 2000. *Manifesta: Young Women, Feminism, and the Future.* New York: Farrar, Straus, and Giroux.

Berger, Melody, ed. 2006. *We Don't Need Another Wave: Dispatches from the Next Generation of Feminists.* Emeryville, CA: Seal Press.

Bhavnani, Kum-Kum, Kathryn R. Kent, and France Winddance Twine, eds. 1998. Special Issue, Feminisms and Youth Cultures. *Signs* 23: Spring.

Bondoc, Anna, and Meg Daly, eds. 1999. *Letters of Intent: Women Cross the Generations to Talk about Family, Work, Sex, Love and the Future of Feminism.* New York: Simon and Schuster.

Braidotti, Rosi. 1995. "Generations of Feminists, or, Is There Life After Postmodernism?" *Found Object* 16: 55–62.

Carlip, Hillary. 1995. *Girlpower: Young Women Speak Out!* New York: Warner Books.

Chambers, Veronica. 1996. *Mama's Girl.* New York: Riverhead.

Corral, Jill, and Lisa Miya-Jervis, eds. 2001. *Young Wives' Tales: New Adventures in Love and Partnership.* Seattle, WA: Seal Press.

Denfield, Rene. 1995. *The New Victorians: A Young Woman's Challenge to the Old Feminist Order.* New York: Warner Books.

Dicker, Rory, and Alison Piepmeier, eds. 2003. *Catching a Wave: Reclaiming Feminism for the 21st Century.* Boston: Northeastern University Press.

Edut, Ophira, ed. 1998. *Adiós Barbie: Young Women Write About Image and Sexuality.* Seattle, WA: Seal Press.

Else-Mitchell, Rosalind, and Flutter, Naomi, eds. 1998. *Talking Up: Young Women's Take on Feminism.* Melbourne, AU: Spinifex.

Findlen, Barbara, ed. 2001. *Listen Up: Voices From the Next Feminist Generation,* 2nd ed. Seattle, WA: Seal Press.

Fraiman, Susan. 1999. "Feminism Today: Mothers, Daughters, Emerging Sisters." *American Literary History* 11: 525–544.

Garrison, Ednie Kaeh. 2000. "U.S. Feminism-Grrrl Style! Young (Sub)Cultures and the Technologies of the Third Wave." *Feminist Studies* 26: 141–170.

Gillis, Stacy, and Rebecca Munford, eds. 2003. Special Issue, Harvesting Our Strengths, Third Wave Feminism and Women's Studies, *Journal of International Women's Studies* 4: April.

Gillis, Stacy, Gillian Howie, and Rebecca Munford, eds. 2007. *Third Wave Feminism: A Critical Exploration.* Expanded 2nd ed, Houndmills, UK: Palgrave Macmillan.

Glickman, Rose L. 1993. *Daughters of Feminists.* New York: St. Martin's Press.

Henry, Astrid. 2004. *Not My Mother's Sister: Generational Conflict and Third-Wave Feminism.* Bloomington: Indiana University Press.

Hernández, Daisy, and Bushra Rehman. 2002. *Colonize This! Young Women of Color on Today's Feminism.* Seattle, WA: Seal Press.

Heywood, Leslie, ed. 2006a. *The Women's Movement Today: An Encyclopedia of Third-Wave Feminism, vol. 1, A–Z.* Westport, CT: Greenwood.

———. 2006b. *The Women's Movement Today: An Encyclopedia of Third-Wave Feminism, vol. 2, Primary Documents.* Westport, CT: Greenwood.

Heywood, Leslie, and Jennifer Drake, eds. 1997. *Third Wave Agenda: Being Feminist, Doing Feminism.* Minneapolis: University of Minnesota Press.

Johnson, Merri Lisa, ed. 2002. *Jane Sexes It Up: True Confessions of Feminist Desire.* New York: Four Walls Eight Windows.

Jones, Lisa. 1994. *Bulletproof Diva: Tales of Race, Sex, and Hair.* New York: Doubleday.

Kamen, Paula. 1991. *Feminist Fatale: Voices from the "Twentysomething" Generation Explore the Future of the "Women's Movement."* New York: Donald I. Fine.

———. 2000. *Her Way: Young Women Remake the Sexual Revolution.* New York: New York University Press.

Karp, Marcelle, and Debbie Stoller, eds. 1999. *The BUST Guide to the New Girl Order.* New York: Penguin.

Kittay, Eva, Anita Silvers, and Susan Wendell, eds. 1997. Special Issue, Third-Wave Feminisms. *Hypatia* 12: Summer.

Kitwana, Bakari. 2002. *The Hip Hop Generation: Young Blacks and the Crisis in African-American Culture.* New York: Basic Civitas Books.

Lay, Mary M., Janice Monk, and Deborah S. Rosenfelt, eds. 2002. *Encompassing Gender: Integrating International Studies and Women's Studies.* New York: Feminist Press.

Lehrman, Karen. 1997. *The Lipstick Proviso: Women, Sex and Power in the Real World.* New York: Anchor Books.

Looser, Devoney, and Ann Kaplan, eds. 1997. *Generations: Academic Feminists in Dialogue.* Minneapolis: University of Minnesota Press.

Maglin, Nan Bauer, and Donna Perry, eds. 1996. *"Bad Girls"/"Good Girls": Women, Sex, and Power in the Nineties.* New Brunswick, NJ: Rutgers University Press.

Minnich, Elizabeth Kamarch. 1998. "Feminist Attacks on Feminisms: Patriarchy's Prodigal Daughters." *Feminist Studies* 24: 159–175.

Mitchell, Allyson, Lisa Bryn Rundle, and Lara Karaian, eds. 2001. *Turbo Chicks: Talking Young Feminisms.* Toronto: Sumach Press.

Morgan, Joan. 1999. *When Chickenheads Come Home to Roost: My Life as a Hip-Hop Feminist.* New York: Simon & Schuster.

O'Barr, Jean, and Mary Wyer, eds. 1992. *Engaging Feminisms: Students Speak Up and Speak Out.* Charlottesville: University Press of Virginia.

O'Reilly, Andrea, and Sharon Abbey, eds. 2000. *Mothers and Daughters: Connection, Empowerment, and Transformation*. Lanham: MD: Rowman and Littlefield.

Purvis, Jennifer. 2004. "Grrls and Women Together in the Third Wave: Embracing the Challenges of Intergenerational Feminism(s)." *NWSA Journal* 16: 93–123.

Rasmusson, Sarah L. 2003. "Third Wave Feminism: History of a Social Movement." In Immanuel Ness, ed., *Encyclopedia of American Social Movements*. Armonk, NY: M.E. Sharpe.

Reger, Jo, ed. 2005. *Different Wavelengths: Studies of the Contemporary Women's Movement*. New York: Routledge.

Roiphe, Katie. 1993. *The Morning After: Sex, Fear, and Feminism on Campus*. Boston: Little, Brown.

———. 1997. *Last Night in Paradise: Sex and Morals at the Century's End*. Boston: Little, Brown.

Rosenberg, Jessica, and Gitana Garofalo. 1998. "Riot Grrrl: Revolutions From Within." *Signs* 23: 809–841.

Siegel, Deborah. 2007. *Sisterhood, Interrupted: From Radical Women to Grrls Gone Wild*. Hampshire, UK: Palgrave Macmillan.

Snyder, R. Claire, 2008. "What Is Third-Wave Feminism? A New Directions Essay." *Signs* 34: 175–196.

Taormino, Tristan, and Karen Green, eds. 1997. *A Girl's Guide to Taking Over the World: Writings From the Girl Zine Revolution*. New York: St. Martin's Press.

Trioli, Virginia. 1996. *Generation f: Sex, Power, and the Young Feminist*. Melbourne, AU: Minerva.

Walker, Rebecca. 1992. "Becoming the Third Wave." *Ms.*, January–February, 39–41.

———. 2007. *Baby Love: Choosing Motherhood after a Lifetime of Ambivalence*. New York: Riverhead.

———, ed. 1995. *To Be Real: Telling the Truth and Changing the Face of Feminism*. New York: Anchor.

Walter, Natasha. 1998. *The New Feminism*. Boston: Little, Brown.

———, ed. 1999. *On the Move: Feminism for a New Generation*. London: Virago.

Weir, Sara, and Constance Faulkner. 2004. *Voices of a New Generation: A Feminist Anthology*. Boston: Allyn & Bacon.

Wolf, Naomi. 1993. *Fire With Fire: The New Female Power and How It Will Change the 21st Century*. New York: Random House.

———. 1997. *Promiscuities: The Secret Struggle for Womanhood*. New York: Random House.

———. 2001. *Misconceptions: Truth, Lies, and the Unexpected Journey to Motherhood*. New York: Doubleday.

DO WE HAVE A NEW FEMINISM?

F eminism has been proclaimed dead, irrelevant, a movement whose goal of equality for women has been achieved, a Western middle-class movement that doesn't address the needs of poor women and women in developing countries, and a movement that should address all the ills of the modern world. In my view, feminism is alive and percolating in many political activities, even when it is not named. As Mary Hawkesworth said in her criticism of the "burial" of feminism:

> Within the official institutions of state in Africa, Asia, Australia, Europe, Latin America, and North America, feminist projects are ongoing through gender mainstreaming and the creation of "national machinery" for women, such as ministries for women, women's bureaus, and gender equality commissions. The feminist arm of the United Nations, the United Nations Development Fund for Women (UNIFEM), is working with indigenous women's organizations on all continents to safeguard women's lives and livelihoods and to secure their economic, political, and civil rights. Several states, such as Sweden and the Netherlands, have included gender equity efforts among their major foreign policy initiatives. Femocrats work within public agencies in all but one or two nations to structure policy initiatives that address women's needs, concerns, and interests, however contested these concepts may be (Eisenstein 1991). In the aftermath of four UN-sponsored world conferences on women, 162 nations have ratified the Convention to Eliminate All Forms of Discrimination against Women (CEDAW), and women's rights activists in all those nations are working to pressure their governments to change constitutions, laws, and customary practices in accordance with CEDAW provisions. A near universal consensus among nations supports the Beijing Platform for Action, and feminist activists work locally as well as through the UN monitoring processes to press for implementation of the Beijing Platform.
>
> Feminist NGOs have proliferated, creating a vibrant feminist civil society....The substantive scope of such feminist work includes subsistence struggles; the politics of food, fuel, and firewood; women's health and reproductive freedom; education for women and girls; employment opportunity, equal pay, safe working conditions, and protection against sexual harassment;

rape and domestic violence; sexual trafficking; women's rights as human rights; militarization; peace making; environmentalism; sustainable development; democratization; welfare rights; AIDS; parity in public office; women's e-news; feminist journals and presses; and curriculum revision, feminist pedagogy, and feminist scholarship. (2004, 961–962)

Feminist theories are still being debated and refined. They have changed as the limitations of one set of ideas were critiqued and addressed by what was felt to be a better explanation about why women and men were so unequal in status and power. It has not been a clear progression by any means, because many of the debates went on simultaneously, and are still going on. All of the feminisms have insight into the problems of gender inequality, and all have come up with good strategies for remedying these problems, so their politics are still very much with us.

As there have been from the beginning of the second wave of feminism, there are continuities and convergences, as well as sharp debates, among the different feminisms on how to conceptualize the focus of research and politics. Feminists want a social order in which men are not privileged and do not have power over women. As with feminists of the past, feminists today are faced with the dilemma of opting for gender-neutral *equality* or gender-marked *equity*. Feminists who argue for gender equality claim that women and men are more alike than different in their capabilities, so they should be treated the same. Feminists who take the perspective of gender equity focus on the physiological and psychological differences between women and men and look for ways to make them socially equivalent. These two perspectives have produced a debate over whether to talk about *gender* or *women*.

Gender Feminism and Woman's Feminism

At the beginning of the second wave of feminism, the use of *gender* in place of sex by English speakers was a deliberate strategy to counter prevailing ideas about the universality and immutability of sex differences. What we now call gender was originally conceptualized as *sex roles*—the social and cultural overlay that exaggerates and builds on the biological differences between males and females, with procreative functions the most obvious and universal. Sex roles are the appropriate behavior and attitudes boys and girls learn in growing up that are then applied to adult work and family situations.

As the concept of gender has developed in the social sciences, it has moved from an attribute of individuals that produces effects in the phenomenon under study (e.g., women and men have different crime rates, voting patterns, labor force participation) to a major building block in the social order and an integral element in every aspect of social life (e.g., how crime is conceptualized and categorized is gendered, political processes are gendered, the economy and the labor force are gender-segregated and gender-stratified).

As a concept, gender includes men as well as women. Gendering describes the practices and processes that shape the way organizations are run and people interact with each other. Gender status is one's place in a complex hierarchy of power and privilege. Gender intersects with other major statuses—racial ethnic group, social class, religion, nationality, education, occupation, sexual orientation, age, and physical ability—to produce the social advantages and disadvantages in people's lives. The increasing use of the concept of gender in place of women by feminists has been contested by those who feel it erodes feminist politics focused on the oppression of women (Foster 1999).

Gender feminism contends that sex, sexuality, and gender are constructed in everyday interaction within the constraints of social norms. The intertwining of sex, sexuality, and gender with each other and with other socially produced categories, such as social class, racial groups, and ethnicity, results in statuses within a social order. These statuses give people the privileges or disadvantages that help or hinder them throughout life. Gender feminists in addition contend that the social order itself is gendered—work organizations slot women and men into different jobs; men's jobs pay better and are valued more; women have much less political power and cultural clout.

Woman's feminism argues that the experience of female bodies and sexuality produces a common and stable identity—woman. In this perspective, women's procreative potential enhances their nurturing capacities; their emotional openness makes them good mothers and bonds them to other women. Their sexuality, however, makes them vulnerable to violence and exploitation. Conversely, the social encouragement of male aggression and their patriarchal entitlement encourages the violent potentialities of men's control of women's bodies, sexuality, and emotions.

Gender reform and *gender rebellion feminisms* use the concept of gender as a social status that is produced and maintained through social processes. *Gender resistance feminisms* are uneasy with the concept of gender because it downplays the distinctive qualities of women—their relationship to their bodies and sexuality, their emotional and nurturing capabilities, their special viewpoint in male-dominated societies and cultures. They also claim that a focus on gender erases the category "woman" on which so much of feminist theory, research, and politics are based. However, non-White, non-European feminists have already critiqued the global conceptualization of "woman" and insisted on recognition of racial, ethnic, and cultural diversity among women in feminist theory and research.

NEW DIRECTIONS IN FEMINIST RESEARCH

Feminist research now looks at men and women of many different social groups, not just women. It is sensitive to multiracial/multiethnic perspectives and tries not to impose Western values on data analysis. Feminist researchers have developed an awareness of the conflict between analysis and activism. They maintain a critical distance while doing research, although what is studied and the way questions are framed, as in any other form of research, are influenced by a gender politics whose goal is equality for all.

By recognizing the multiplicity of genders, sexes, and sexualities, and by dissecting the intersected strands of gender, social class, and racial ethnic status, feminist research is able to go beyond the conventional binaries. The problem is that we need categories for comparison, even while we are critically deconstructing them. We know that the content and dividing lines for genders, sexes, and sexualities are intertwined with and cross-cut by other major social statuses. How, then, do we do research without reifying the conventional categories?

What we consider inevitable opposing categories are actually variable cultural and temporal constructions of "opposites." Michael Kimmel (2002) told the following anecdote that illustrates the problem of "opposites" very well. When his son was three years old, they played a game where he would tell Zachary a word and Zachary would tell him its opposite. Once, when Zachary's grandmother was visiting, she played the game with him. She asked, "Zachary, what's the opposite of boy?" Zachary took a few seconds to think. Much to his father's relief, he did not invoke the gender divide. "Man," he said.

What Are the "Opposites" in Feminist Research?

In the past, most feminist research designs assumed that each person has one sex, one sexuality, and one gender, which are congruent with each other and fixed for life. Research variables were "sex," polarized as "females" and "males;" "sexuality," polarized as "homosexuals" and "heterosexuals;" and "gender," polarized as "women" and "men." But these vary, and for accurate data, we need the variations. How do we include intersexual and transgendered people and their partners in sexual relationships? How do we categorize masculine women, feminine men, bisexual women and men? We also need to compare women and men across different racial ethnic groups, social classes, religions, nationalities, residencies, occupations. In some research, we need to compare the women and men within these groups.

The main questions are, Who is being compared to whom? Why? What do we want to find out? The goal of our research design needs to be clear before we can decide on our comparison categories. The choice of categories is a feminist political issue because using the conventional categories without question implies that the "normal" (e.g., heterosexuality, boys' masculinity) does not have to be explained as the result of processes of socialization and social control, but is a "natural" phenomenon.

Deconstructing sex, sexuality, and gender reveals many possible categories embedded in social experiences and social practices, as does the deconstruction of "race." Multiple categories disturb the neat polarity of familiar opposites that assume one dominant and one subordinate group, one normal and one deviant identity, one hegemonic status and one "other."

As Barrie Thorne comments in her work on children,

> The literature moves in a circle, carting in cultural assumptions about the nature of masculinity (bonded, hierarchical, competitive, "tough"), then highlighting behavior that fits those parameters and obscuring the varied styles and range of interactions among boys as a whole. (1993, 100)

Multiplying the Conventional Categories

Multiplying research categories uses several strategies. One strategy is to recognize that sexual and gender statuses combined with other major statuses produce many identities in one individual. Another is to acknowledge that individuals belong to many groups. Therefore, it is extremely important to figure out what you want to know before choosing the variables and subjects for comparison. Samples have to be heterogeneous enough to allow for multiple categories of comparison.

The common practice of comparing women and men frequently produces data that is so mixed that it takes another level of analysis to sort out meaningful categories for comparison. It would be better to start with categories derived from data analysis of all subjects and see the extent to which they attach to the conventional global categories of sex, sexuality, and gender, or better yet, to one or more of the components of these categories (attributes, behavior, relationships, for example). However, in order to do this second level of analysis, the sample groups have to be heterogeneous in the first place.

The differentiating variables are likely to break up and recombine the familiar categories in new ways that go beyond the conventional dichotomies. As Linda Nicholson says in "Interpreting *Gender*,"

> Thus I am advocating that we think about the meaning of *woman* as illustrating a map of intersecting similarities and differences. Within such a map the body does not disappear but rather becomes a historically specific variable whose meaning and import are recognized as potentially different in different historical contexts. Such a suggestion…[assumes] that meaning is found rather than presupposed. (1994, 101–102)

There are revolutionary possibilities inherent in rethinking the categories of gender, sexuality, and physiological sex. Feminist data that challenges conventional knowledge by reframing the questions could provide legitimacy for new ways of thinking. When one term or category is defined only by its opposite, resistance reaffirms the polarity. The margin and the center, the insider and the outsider, the conformist and the deviant are two sides of the same concept. Introducing even one more term, such as bisexuality, forces a rethinking of the oppositeness of heterosexuality and homosexuality. "A critical sexual politics, in other words, struggles to move beyond the confines of an inside/outside model" (Namaste 1994, 230).

Problems of Perspective

Standpoint theory argues for presenting the woman's point of view; intersectionality argues for a multidimensional approach. How are we to do both? With an insider point of view? How many insides can we have? With a *verstehen* point of view—putting yourself in the shoes of the subject? That's a lot of different shoes!

In much activist research, the researcher engages in social interaction with the people being studied with a dual goal: to provide data that accurately reflects their lives and information for political action to benefit them. Such research is often conducted by participant observation, where the researcher becomes a member of the group being researched, or by in-depth interviewing, which sometimes involves a sharing of experiences. The advantages are well-known—insightful understanding of the perspectives and experiences of others, and a basis for action that will make a difference in their lives. The problems are perhaps less well known.

First, there is the problem of the *insider* and the *outsider*. If you are a member of the group, you don't have to study it—just relate your own experiences. And for some feminists, that is what feminist research should be.

But what group are you a member of? Everyone knows that people differ by social class (past and present), where you live, where you were born, what language you speak, what culture you are comfortable with, what religion and politics you practice, what your sexual orientation and sexual experiences have been, and how your body functions, so your membership in any one group is affected by your simultaneous membership in other groups. Reliance on insider knowledge can get severely shaken if it is assumed that women understand other women because they are all women.

If you are not a member of the group, but an outsider, there is the problem of trust and betrayal. Even if you were honest and above board about your role as a researcher, and you are careful to preserve anonymity, people may be hurt when you publish your findings—especially if you are critical. In asking whether one can be a reflexive participant observer and a true feminist, Judith Stacey honestly appraised the advantages and disadvantages of ethnography and her own use and response to intensive interviewing and involvement with her respondents' lives. She discussed the "delusion of alliance" and the "delusion of separateness." She says:

> [E]thnographic method appears to (and often does) place the researcher and her informants in a collaborative, reciprocal quest for understanding, but the research product is ultimately that of the researcher, however modified or influenced by informants. With very rare exceptions, it is the researcher who narrates, who "authors" the ethnography. In the last instance an ethnography is a written document structured primarily by a researcher's purposes, offering a researcher's interpretations, registered in a researcher's voice. (1988, 23)

I think it would be an unfortunate irony if feminists, in an attempt to counter the role of the male-oriented Other, felt comfortable researching only women like themselves, and only with methods that put them in their subject's shoes. To do any kind of research—sociology or anthropology or history or literary or art criticism—the scholar has to maintain some distance, has to closely examine the contradictions in data because they are likely to be crucially informative, and has to be able to challenge respondents' voices with voices from other worlds (Sprague 2005). Sometimes you have to be able to look at the familiar world as if you came from another planet. As Dorothy Smith says, we cannot take the everyday world for granted but must see it "as problematic, where the everyday world is taken to be various and differentiated matrices of experience—the place from which the consciousness of the knower begins" (1990, 173).

When researchers construct the patterns of social reality from everyday experiences of subjects, they do it from the standpoint of their own social realities. Even if the researcher and the subject are the same gender, they are not likely to come from the same social location. And even if they did, the social researcher still needs a bifurcated consciousness which can bring to bear a somewhat abstracted larger social reality (the social relations of capitalism, for instance) on the patterns and experiences of the everyday world (Smith 2005).

FEMINIST POLITICS AND MULTIPLE IDENTITIES[1]

The problem of standpoint in feminist research is mirrored by the problem of standpoint in feminist politics. Feminism has been a movement that is by, for, and about women, but the unity of this identity—*woman*—has been challenged by recent feminist theory, research, and politics. Theories aside, the lived reality of people's experiences is that they belong to many different groups and have multiple identities. Being a woman may be a major social identity, but it may not be a rallying point for everyone for political activity. Iris Marion Young (1994) argues that gender, racial category, and class are *series*—comparatively passive collectives grouped by their similar social conditioning. These locations in social structures may or may not become significant sources of self-identification or political action.

The shift in focus from woman to women creates a tension between *gender visibility*—attention to the ways in which societies, cultures, groups, and individuals are gendered and how this process comes about and is maintained through the practices of institutions, cultures, groups, and individuals— and *gender diversity*—attention to the ways in which women and men, boys and girls are not homogeneous groups but intersected by cultures, religions, ethnicities, social class, sexualities, bodies, and so on.

The effect of focusing on gender visibility is to foreground women's experiences, as standpoint feminism has urged. The effect of focusing on gender diversity is to incorporate diverse women's experiences, as multiracial/multiethnic feminism has urged. Diverse and intersecting perspectives can be both a source of knowledge and a source of political activism.

Can we recognize gender diversity and also continue to rally around the flag of womanhood? Judith Butler says, "Surely, it must be possible both to use the term, to use it tactically...and also to subject the term to a critique which interrogates the exclusionary operations and differential power-relations that construct and delimit feminist invocations of 'women'" (1993, 29). Is it possible to conceptualize woman as a stable category and to use the experiences of women with other important identities at the same time? There may be a common core to women's experiences, but feminist politics cannot ignore the input from social statuses that may be as important as gender. Therefore, it is not enough to take political action using only a woman's point of view; feminist politics has to include the experiences of women of different social classes; educational levels; racial, ethnic, and religious groups; marital and parental statuses; sexual orientations; ages; and degrees of able-bodiedness. These intersecting group memberships and multiple identities are not a weakness in the feminist movement, but a strength. If they become a basis for national and international coalitions, cross-cutting group memberships and multiple statuses can be a powerful feminist weapon (Bystydzienski and Schacht, 2001).

Feminist multidimensional political action goes beyond the sources of oppression that are specific to women. Without giving up the fight against sexual exploitation and violence against women, feminists have had to search for ways to open access to economic resources, educational opportunities, and political power. We have focused on gender when it is necessary, but we have also had to recognize that women of different classes may not be interested in political action because their statuses are superior, or because they feel they have too much lose from changes in the status quo. In some situations, it may be necessary to reach out to subordinated men who are similarly oppressed and who want similar changes in the redistribution of resources and recognition of distinct cultures.

Politics of Identification

Rather than identity politics, where membership in a particular social category is the basis for activism, Susan Hekman argues for a "politics of identification" (2000, 304–305). She advocates identification with political causes and activism for political goals without regard to personal status. But this kind of inclusion requires not only that "outsiders" see others' causes as important to fight for, but that the "insiders" accept them as legitimate political actors. Sylvia Walby says,

> Politics across difference demands...the acceptance of greater difference within the organization, collegiality rather than friendship, respect rather than empathy, voting rather than consensus. That is, a politics based on appeal to principles rather than to identity. It is this which facilitates transformation, rather than an embrace of existing identity. (2000, 199)

This thought was stated more bluntly by Dale Bauer and Priscilla Wald in the millennial issue of *Signs*:

> Coalition politics does not offer a united front of feminism.... The differences are always in view and always potentially disruptive.... So when we coalesce—come together—we have to give up any secure sense of self. We merge, and we change. And we cannot count on a supportive environment. A coalition comes together to get some work done, not to nurture. (2000, 1300)

What kind of coalitions can diverse groups of feminists form and what are the goals of their politics?

The Structure of Feminist Politics

There is a structure to feminist politics that takes us from identity politics at the grass roots level to coalitions of people of diverse identities in nongovernmental organizations. NGOs have the potential to work with feminists coming from different political groups who enter state, national, and international governments and bureaucracies.

At the grassroots level, political action centering in primary identities makes particular injustices visible and also forms a basis for organizing around those identities. Thus, poor women mobilize around their traditional roles as wives and mothers to fight for better living and working conditions and improved health care for their families. As Christine Bose and Edna Acosta-Belén note, in Latin America and the Caribbean, women organize

> collective meals, health cooperatives, mothers' clubs, neighborhood water-rights groups, or their own textile and craft collectives.... Thus, rather than *privatizing* their survival problems, these women *collectivize* them and form social-change groups based on social reproduction concerns. In these new terms, the political discourse and arena of struggle is...moral persuasion to place demands on the state for rights related to family survival. (1995, 28)

In the process, they define their needs not as family or gender issues, but as citizenship claims on states.

At this level, identities are primary, problems and solutions are localized. But since social problems of subsistence, shelter, and work opportunities in the face of economic restructuring are global, the collective solutions can become the basis for transcommunity and transnational organizing, and for a global redefinition of what it means to be a citizen.

At the next level, NGOs are formed to sustain the grassroots collective political action and problem-solving tactics, to bring in people with varied skills, and to raise money. The central identities of gender or racial ethnic group or class may blur as middle-class administrators and credentialed professionals join. The central focus shifts from identity politics to specific political issues, such as legal protections and rights or to specific social problems, such as battering, rape, or prostitution. A focus might be the needs of women in a particular area growing out of historic events, such as the Network of East West Women, a coalition of women in East European former Soviet republics and women in the United States. Within the geographic area, they have focused on legal issues, reproductive rights, and transnational prostitution.

Women Living Under Muslim Laws is an international informational and support network of women living in diverse Muslim communities. Through this network, women share knowledge of differing interpretations and applications of *shari'ah*, Islamic rules of conduct and personal status laws. The goals are exchange of knowledge and links to other women in similar situations in common projects as well as a base for political action (Shaheed 1994).

NGOs encourage data collection by feminist researchers and use feminist academics' theories and structural analyses. There is often reciprocal feedback between members of NGOs and feminist academics and researchers, with activism and the search for viable solutions to problems suggesting research designs and correcting theories and analyses.

At the next level, feminists start infiltrating governments and governmental agencies—local, state, national, and international—where they can showcase feminist issues and pressure for equal representation of women. A positive outcome of feminists within a government is South Africa's gender-egalitarian constitution (Seidman 1999).

When feminists work within established governments and bureaucracies, the thrust of their feminism will necessarily be diluted in the course of trying to gain allies to pass laws and promulgate policies. Any critique of the establishment has to be moderated, since they are now part of it. The searchlight on practices and problems that need changing floats as events reorder priorities, as happened after September 11, 2001 in the United States. Feminists within governments may not be as radical or critical as feminists at the grassroots or NGO levels, but they come in with a different perspective, and they can be reached by feminists on the outside (Eisenstein 1996).

In my view, the most productive international feminist work is done at the NGO level, where problem solving and political action can be focused, but not so narrowly as to preclude useful coalitions. Simultaneous memberships in groups can bring those groups together in what Nira Yuval-Davis (1997) calls *transversal politics*, where borders are crossed and boundaries are redrawn to create coalitions and bridge divides. Members of NGOs can work with members of grassroots collectives and government organizations as bridges to each and between them.

Some of the most powerful NGOs have been what Valentine Moghadam calls *transnational feminist networks*—"organizations linking women in developing and developed regions and addressing social, economic, and foreign policy issues in supra-national terms" (2000, 59). They are, she says, "a new organizational and a new form of collective action in an era of globalization" (58). Some of the networks she discusses are Development Alternatives with

Women for a New Era (DAWN), which has branches in the Caribbean, Latin America, and South America; Women in Development in Europe (WIDE), based in Brussels; and Women Living Under Muslim Laws (WLUML), whose members live in Muslim countries or practice Islam in non-Muslim countries (2005).

It is here that multiple identities become so valuable. Multiple identities encourage cross-fertilization of ideas and tactics. Multiple standpoints recognize differences but work with commonalities.

In short, what seems like fragmentation becomes, with the pressure of coalition politics, a multivoiced, multibranched, intertwined, and dense feminist political movement growing in force. We live with diversity and still do feminist political action by reaching out to people who are similarly oppressed and who want similar changes, by enlisting subordinated and sympathetic men in feminist political action, and by attacking the whole matrix of domination, not just women's part of it.

A NEW FEMINISM

Do we have a new feminism for the twenty-first century? It is clear from the trends of the last 20 years that new dimensions of feminist theory and research have emerged out of the diverse perspectives of situated knowledges. The multiplicities of sex, sexuality, and gender intersected with social class and racial ethnic and other statuses provide us with new research categories. Shifting identities and global coalitions give us new politics.

The future strength of the feminist movement lies in the variety and density of multiple identities—not just women. The primary identity of feminists may be gender, racial ethnic group, religion, social class, or sexual orientation in some combination. The focus of feminist work may be peace, sexual violence, political parity, economic opportunity, or one of many proliferating causes. The beneficiaries may be one specific oppressed group or many. Feminist identity may be way down the list, implicit, or even masked, but as long as the perspective is critical and the goal is political, economic, and cultural equality for all, then it is feminism.

NOTE

1. Adapted from Lorber 2005.

REFERENCES

Bauer, Dale M., and Priscilla Wald. 2000. "Complaining, Conversing, Coalescing." *Signs* 25: 1299–1303.
Bose, Christine E., and Edna Acosta-Belén. 1995. "Colonialism, Structural Subordination, and Empowerment: Women in the Development Process in Latin

America and the Caribbean." In *Women in the Latin American Development Process*. Philadelphia: Temple University Press.

Butler, Judith. 1993. *Bodies That Matter: On the Discursive Limits of "Sex."* New York: Routledge.

Bystydzienski, Jill M., and Steven P. Schacht, eds. 2001. *Forging Radical Alliances across Differences: Coalition Politics for the New Millennium*. Lanham, MD: Rowman & Littlefield.

Eisenstein, Hester. 1991. *Gender Shock: Practicing Feminism on Two Continents*. Boston: Beacon.

———. 1996. *Inside Agitators: Australian Femocrats and the State*. Philadelphia: Temple University Press.

Foster, Johanna. 1999. "An Invitation to Dialogue: Clarifying the Position of Feminist Gender Theory in Relation to Sexual Difference Theory." *Gender & Society* 13: 431–456.

Hawkesworth, Mary. 2004. "The Semiotics of Premature Burial: Feminism in a Postfeminist Age." *Signs* 29: 961–985.

Hekman, Susan. 2000. "Beyond Identity: Feminism, Identity and Identity Politics." *Feminist Theory* 1: 289–308.

Kimmel, Michael. 2002. Personal communication, Sept. 10.

Lorber, Judith. 2005. *Breaking the Bowls: Degendering and Feminist Change*. New York: W. W. Norton.

Moghadam, Valentine M. 2000. "Transnational Feminist Networks: Collective Action in an Era of Globalization." *International Sociology* 15: 57–85.

———. 2005. *Globalizing Women: Transnational Feminist Networks*. Baltimore: Johns Hopkins University Press.

Namaste, Ki. 1994. "The Politics of Inside/Out: Queer Theory, Poststructuralism, and a Sociological Approach to Sexuality." *Sociological Theory* 12: 220–231.

Nicholson, Linda J. 1994. "Interpreting *Gender.*" *Signs* 20: 79–105.

Seidman, Gay W. 1999. "Gendered Citizenship: South Africa's Democratic Transition and the Construction of a Gendered State." *Gender & Society* 13: 287–307.

Shaheed, Farida. 1994. "Controlled or Autonomous: Identity and the Experience of the Network, Women Living Under Muslim Laws." *Signs* 19: 997–1019.

Smith, Dorothy E. 1990. *Texts, Facts, and Femininity: Exploring the Relations of Ruling*. New York: Routledge.

———. 2005. *Institutional Ethnography: A Sociology for People*. Lanham, MD: AltaMira Press.

Sprague, Joey. 2005. *Feminist Methodologies for Critical Researchers: Bridging Differences*. Lanham, MD: AltaMira Press.

Stacey, Judith. 1988. "Can There Be a Feminist Ethnography?" *Women's Studies International Forum* 11: 21–27.

Thorne, Barrie. 1993. *Gender Play: Boys and Girls in School*. New Brunswick, NJ: Rutgers University Press.

Walby, Sylvia. 2000. "Beyond the Politics of Location: The Power of Argument in a Global Era." *Feminist Theory* 1: 189–206.

Young, Iris Marion. 1994. "Gender as Seriality: Thinking About Women as a Social Collective." *Signs* 19: 713–738.

Yuval-Davis, Nira. 1997. *Gender & Nation*. Thousand Oaks, CA: Sage.

GLOSSARY

Affirmative action   bringing women into occupations and professions dominated by men and promoting them to positions of authority

Borderlands   perspectives and politics based on panethnic and cross-racial affiliations and coalitions

Complex inequality   the interplay of social class, gender, and racial ethnic status in producing economic and social disadvantages

Consciousness-raising groups   small-group meetings where the topics of intense discussion come out of the commonalities of women's lives

Cultural feminism   development of a woman's world perspective in the creation of women's knowledge and culture

Deconstruction   making visible the gender and sexual symbolism in cultural productions that support beliefs about what is normal and natural

Degendering   not placing women and men in different categories, not doing gender

Discourse   cultural, social, and symbolic meanings embedded in texts and subtexts

Doing difference   constructing racial ethnic, social class, and gender differences

Doing gender   processes and practices that construct gendered identities and gendered social statuses

Dual systems theory   Marxist feminism's analysis of patriarchy and capitalism as twin systems of men's domination of women

Ecofeminism   linkage of the environmental exploitation of the earth and the exploitation of women

Flextime   workplace policy that offers employees a choice of what hours and what days of the week to work

Gender   a social status, a legal designation, and a personal identity

Gender balance   attaining equality or parity in numbers of women and men throughout society, in their domestic responsibilities, and in their access to work and business opportunities, positions of authority, political power, education, and health care

Gender diversity   attention to the ways that women and men, boys and girls are not homogenous groups but cross-cut by cultures, religions, racial ethnicities, social classes, sexualities, and other major statuses

Gender equality   treating women and men as legally and socially the same

Gender equity   treating women and men differently but as legally and socially equivalent

Gender feminism   takes the perspective that sex, sexuality, and gender are constructed in everyday interaction within the constraints of social norms

Gender ideology   the values and beliefs that justify the gendered social order

Gender mainstreaming   scrutiny of policies and laws to make sure that they do not have adverse effects on women but rather will be supportive of women's needs

Gender roles   behavior and attitudes appropriate to women and men that are learned in growing up and applied to adult work and family situations

Gender visibility   attention to the ways in which societies, cultures, groups, and individuals are gendered and how this process comes about and is maintained through the practices of organizations, cultures, groups, and individuals

Girlie culture   in third-wave feminism, using femininity and sexuality for empowerment

Glass ceiling   women's restricted entry into top positions, even where most of the workers are women

Glass escalator   rapid promotion of men in women-dominated occupations

Global economy   links countries whose economies focus on service, information, and finances with manufacturing sites and the sources of raw materials in other countries; workers and capital flow between them

Hegemony   dominance in values, knowledge, culture, and politics

Heteronormativity   the assumption that everyone is heterosexual and that only heterosexual relationships are normal

Intersectionality   the combined effects of race, class, gender, sexuality, religion, nationality and other major social statuses in producing systematic advantages and disadvantages

Job queues   the best jobs are kept for men of the dominant racial ethnic group; as jobs lose their prestige and income level, they open up for women and disadvantaged men

Jouissance   women's exultant joy in their sexual bodies

Kanter hypothesis   predicted that as workplaces became more gender-balanced, men would become more accepting of women colleagues

Male gaze   cultural creation of women as the objects of men's sexual fantasies

Marriage equality   the right of all people to legally marry the person they choose, without regard to gender identity, sex identity, or sexual orientation

Matrix of domination   the combined effects of discrimination by gender, race and ethnicity, social class, religion, nationality, and other disadvantaged statuses

Mentoring   coaching by a senior person about the norms and expectations of workplaces and professional organizations

Microinequities   denigration of women in face-to-face encounters at work, in school, in political and other organizations

Misogyny   verbal and visual depictions of women and girls as dangerous, destructive, and bitchy

Networking   making professional contacts and using them for job and promotion opportunities

Occupational gender segregation   division of jobs into women's work and men's work; men work with men and women work with women

Occupational gender stratification   men are more often in positions of authority than women are and dominate the best positions in organizational hierarchies

Outsider within   viewpoint of the disadvantaged in critiquing and changing hegemonic knowledge and culture

Patriarchal privilege   men's advantages over the women in their social group

Patriarchy   men's systematic and pervasive domination of women as built into the social order; men's control of economic resources, entitlement to sexual services, domination of political processes, and positions of authority

Performativity   gender does not exist without doing gender identity and gender display

Phallocentric   culturally male-centered, dominated by male symbolism

Queer theory   critiques and questions heteronormativity and gender and sexual binaries

Queering   subverting binary gender and sexual categories through deliberate mixtures of clothing, makeup, jewelry, hair styles, behavior, relationships, and use of language

Reserve army of labor married women who primarily work in the home but are hired when the economy needs workers and are fired when it does not

Second shift a woman's continued responsibility for the maintenance of the household and the needs of her husband and children even when she has a full-time job

Sex a complex interplay of genes, hormones, environment, and behavior, with loop-back effects between bodies and society

Sexuality lustful desire, emotional involvement, and fantasy, as enacted in a variety of long- and short-term intimate relationships

Social reproduction the work parents do in raising children to be future members of society

Standpoint the view of the world from where you are located physically, mentally, emotionally, and socially

Subtext hidden meaning in a text, sometimes emerging from what is not mentioned

Texts art, literature, the mass media, newspapers, political pronouncements, religious liturgy, and any other social or cultural production

Transgendering living in a gender that is different from that assigned at birth, with or without surgical and hormonal transformation of the body

Transnational feminist networks organizations that link women in developing and developed regions and address social, economic, and foreign policy issues in supranational terms

Transversal politics crossing national borders and redrawing political boundaries to create coalitions and bridge divides

Undoing gender reversing and counteracting the effects of gender discrimination

Womanist culture, theology, and ethics counters multiracial/multiethnic men's dominance with women's art, rituals, and nurturing and caring theology and ethics

Woman's feminism takes the perspective that the experience of female bodies and sexuality produces a common and stable identity among women

INDEX

Note: Page numbers followed by 'n' refer to notes.

Made in the USA
Lexington, KY
15 October 2011